German Agriculture in Transition

Also by Geoff A. Wilson

ENVIRONMENTAL MANAGEMENT: New Directions for the Twenty-First Century

German Agriculture in Transition

Society, Policies and Environment in a Changing Europe

Geoff A. Wilson
Lecturer in Geography
King's College
London

and

Olivia J. Wilson
Lecturer in Geography
De Montfort University
Bedford

palgrave

First published 2001 by
PALGRAVE
Houndmills, Basingstoke, Hampshire RG21 6XS and
175 Fifth Avenue, New York, N. Y. 10010
Companies and representatives throughout the world

PALGRAVE is the new global academic imprint of
St. Martin's Press LLC Scholarly and Reference Division and
Palgrave Publishers Ltd (formerly Macmillan Press Ltd).

ISBN 0–333–71795–3

This book is printed on paper suitable for recycling and made from fully managed and sustained forest sources.

A catalogue record for this book is available from the British Library.

Library of Congress Cataloging-in-Publication Data
Wilson, G. A. (Geoffrey Alan), 1961–
    German agriculture in transition : society, policies,
    and environment in a changing Europe / Geoff A. Wilson
    and Olivia J. Wilson.
        p. cm.
    Includes bibliographical references and index.
    ISBN 0–333–71795–3
    1. Agriculture and state—Germany. 2. Germany—Rural
    conditions. I. Wilson, Olivia J., 1964– II. Title.
    HD1957 .W55 2000
    338.1'0943—dc21
                                                        00–066576

10   9   8   7   6   5   4   3   2   1
10   09 08 07 06 05 04 03 02 01

Printed and bound in Great Britain by
Antony Rowe Ltd, Chippenham, Wiltshire

To Erik

Contents

List of Tables

List of Maps

List of Figures

xiv

List of Abbreviations

ABM	Arbeitsbeschaffungsmaßnahmen (Job creation schemes)
AEPs	Agri-environmental policies
AMS	Aggregate Measure of Support (GATT Uruguay Round)
BML	Bundesministerium für Ernährung, Landwirtschaft und Forsten (Ministry of Agriculture)
BSE	Bovine spongiform encephalopathy
BUND	Bund für Umwelt und Naturschutz (Organisation for Environmental and Nature Protection)
BVVG	Bodenverwertungs- und Verwaltungsgesellschaft (Company for Land Settlement and Administration)
CAM	Council of Agriculture Ministers
CAP	Common Agricultural Policy
CDU	Christlich Demokratische Union (Christian Democratic Party)
CEECs	Central and East European Countries
COPA	Committee of Professional Agricultural Organisations
CPs	Contracting parties (in the GATT)
CSU	Christlich Soziale Union (Christian Social Party)
DBD	Demokratische Bauernpartei Deutschlands (German Democratic Farmers' Party)
DBV	Deutscher Bauernverband (German Farmers' Union)
DM	Deutsche Mark (Deutschmark)
EAGGF	European Agricultural Guidance and Guarantee Fund
EC	European Community
ECU	European Currency Unit
EEC	European Economic Community
ELDCs	Economically less developed countries
ENGOs	Environmental non-governmental organisations
ERDF	European Regional Development Fund
ESAs	Environmentally Sensitive Areas
ESF	European Social Fund
EU	European Union
FDP	Freie Demokratische Partei (Free Democratic Party)
FRG	Federal Republic of Germany
GAK	Gemeinschaftsaufgabe Verbesserung der Agrarstruktur und des Küstenschutzes (Common Task for Improving Agricultural Structures and Coastal Protection)
GATT	General Agreement on Tariffs and Trade
GDP	Gross domestic product
GDR	German Democratic Republic

GmbH	Gesellschaft mit beschränkter Haftung (Limited company)
GMCs	Genetically modified crops
GRW	Gemeinschaftsaufgabe Verbesserung der regionalen Wirtschaftsstruktur (Common Task for Improving Regional Economic Structures)
ha	Hectare
HEKUL	Hessisches Kulturlandschaftsprogramm (Hessen)
KULAP	Kulturlandschaftsprogramm (Bayern)
LAGs	Local action groups (LEADER programme)
LFAs	Less Favoured Areas
LPGs	Landwirtschaftliche Produktionsgenossenschaften (Agricultural production cooperatives)
LU	Livestock unit
MCAs	Monetary compensation amounts
MEKA	Marktentlastungs- und Kulturlandschaftsausgleich (Baden-Württemberg)
MECU	Million ECU
N	Nitrogen
NPD	Nationalsozialistische Partei Deutschland (German Nationalist Party)
OECD	Organisation for Economic Cooperation and Development
PPG	Payments for public goods principle
PPP	Polluter pays principle
PSE	Producer subsidy equivalents
SED	Sozialistische Einheitspartei Deutschland (Socialist Unity Party)
SOZ	Soviet Occupied Zone
SPD	Sozialdemokratische Partei Deutschland (German Social Democratic Party)
THA	Treuhandanstalt (Agency for reprivatisation of industry in GDR)
UAA	Utilised agricultural area
URA	Uruguay Round Agreement
VEGs	Volkseigene Güter (Specialist state farms)
WTO	World Trade Organisation

Acknowledgements

This book could not have been written without the help of many people. We owe particular thanks to the staff at the Institut für Strukturforschung at the Forschungsanstalt für Landwirtschaft (FAL) in Braunschweig-Völkenrode for their hospitality and help during investigations for this book between January and April 1997. In particular, we wish to thank Professor E. Neander for allowing us to stay in the institute during that time, for his help and advice on the book, and particularly for his subsequent comments on drafts of the chapters. Special thanks also to B. Klages, R. Plankl, P. Mehl and all other staff at the Institut für Strukturforschung for useful information and help with some of the specific aspects of German agricultural politics. We are grateful for financial support provided by both the Nuffield Foundation and King's College London during our stay at the FAL.

We also wish to thank Professor W. von Urff (Lehrstuhl für Agrarpolitik, TU München at Freising-Weihenstephan) for productive comments on a draft of the book and specific advice on particular questions of German agricultural structures, politics and policies.

Many thanks also to Roma Beaumont and Carolyne Megan for the drawing of the figures, and to staff at Palgrave Publishers for help and advice on the production of the final manuscript. Finally, thanks to all our colleagues at King's College London and De Montfort University (Bedford Campus) for patiently allowing us to take 'time off' when we should have been in our offices dealing with more mundane academic and administrative matters.

1
Introduction

1.1 Aims of the book

The role of Germany as an economic and political force in Europe during
the twentieth century has attracted much international research interest,
not only because of Germany's geopolitical role in Europe during the two
world wars and its subsequent division into two states either side of the
'iron curtain', but also because of the Federal Republic of Germany's (FRG)
post-war economic miracle, which enabled it to emerge as Europe's economic powerhouse (see, for instance, Bulmer and Paterson, 1987, 1989;
Smyser, 1993; Larres and Panayi, 1996). The 1990 reunification of the two
Germanies has attracted further research interest (for instance, Heisenberg,
1991; Stares, 1992; Baring, 1994; Jones, 1994). German agriculture, however, has received less attention. Germany's reputation and position
within Europe and beyond have been mainly based on the power of its
manufacturing sector, and Germany's emergence as the most important
European political power has relied almost entirely on its strong post-war
economic performance based on the export of high-quality manufactured
products. German agriculture has always been seen as a marginal and
struggling economic sector operating in the shadow of manufacturing. It
comes as no surprise, therefore, that most researchers have been attracted
by the seemingly more challenging questions on Germany's role as an
industrial and political power, rather than by questions related to German
agriculture.

Most academic literature on German agricultural policy, and Germany's
role in European agricultural policy, relates to the FRG between 1957
(when the FRG became a founder member of the European Economic
Community, EEC) and 1989 (the eve of reunification). In the English language, Tangermann's (1979a, b, 1982) work is an important critique from
the perspective of a German agricultural economist of the German government's agricultural policies, and Neville-Rolfe's (1984) analysis of the politics of agriculture in the EEC also includes a good discussion of the

subtleties of German agricultural policy-making. Similarly, Tracy's (1989) analysis of government and agriculture in Western Europe includes a useful discussion of the FRG position on agriculture in Europe, as well as a good overview of agricultural structural developments in the FRG. The most comprehensive analysis of the FRG position towards the Common Agricultural Policy (CAP) in English has been provided by Hendriks (1991) who outlined the reasons for the often 'stubborn' stance taken by the FRG in CAP negotiations. Important German language texts include Priebe's (1985) seminal book on the FRG and the CAP as a 'subsidised absurdity' and Kluge's (1989a, b) exhaustive text on FRG agricultural politics. Less was written about agriculture in the German Democratic Republic (GDR) because of the restrictions on access to information that existed, especially for academics from the capitalist West. Most of the literature on the former GDR is by GDR and FRG academics (for example, Seidel *et al.*, 1962; Hohmann, 1984; Krambach, 1985; Thöne, 1993), with only limited reference to GDR agriculture in Anglo-American texts (for instance, Freeman, 1979; Dennis, 1988; Fulbrook, 1995).

The reunification of the FRG and GDR in 1990 was not foreseen in the late 1980s, and has added a new and potentially highly significant dimension to the agricultural policy environment in Germany. Both Kluge (1989a, b) and Hendriks (1991) were particularly unfortunate in that their books were published more or less at the same time as German reunification occurred. This meant that, although important, their analyses became immediately outdated and have to be seen as historical assessments of the situation in the former FRG rather than as analyses of the situation in the new Germany. Although much has been written about agricultural restructuring in the new *Länder*[1] of reunified Germany (for instance, Bergmann, 1992; Wilson O.J., 1996; Hagedorn *et al.*, 1997), the recency of reunification has meant that only little has been written about its impact on German agricultural policy-making as a whole, both on a domestic and European level.

In this book we aim to address these research gaps by examining the development of agricultural policy in divided and reunified Germany from 1945 to 2000, in the context of developments in the European Union (EU), the CAP, and wider international developments in agricultural trade. This involves four related areas of analysis. First, we will examine the development of domestic agricultural policy in the FRG and the GDR, with the aim of identifying key factors and processes that have characterised this development, including the role of actors and political and cultural ideologies. Linked to this is a consideration of whether reunification has changed the trajectory of agricultural policy development. Second, we will consider Germany's role in shaping the CAP, and the tensions between domestic and European concerns that have underlain this role. A key question in this analysis is whether it is possible to categorise Germany's role in European agricultural policy-making as leader, partner or obstructor, and whether Germany's role has changed since reunification. Third, we will examine the changing position of agriculture within the wider rural economy and society of Germany, and discuss the implications of these changes for agricultural and rural policy in Germany and the EU. Fourth, we will discuss external (international) and internal (European and German) challenges facing Europe's and Germany's agricultural sectors at the end of the twentieth century and the beginning of the twenty-first century, and their implications for the future of the CAP and German agricultural policy. Figure 1.1 outlines the historical patterns in Germany since 1945 that provide the framework for the analysis of 'German agriculture in transition' in this book.

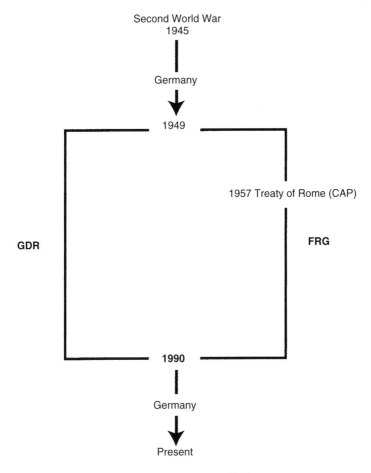

Figure 1.1 Historical patterns in Germany since 1945

There are five main reasons why we feel that this book is an important contribution to the literature on Germany and on the CAP. First, although the agricultural sector only contributes about 2 per cent to Germany's gross domestic product (GDP), Germany has a large food-processing industry and is a major player in world food trade (Ritson and Harvey, 1997). Second, the political importance of German agriculture far outweighs its economic importance, as illustrated by the fact that Germany's domestic and international agricultural policies often appear contrary to Germany's national interests. To understand this paradox, it is necessary to examine the nature of agriculture's political influence. Third, as highlighted above, little has been published on Germany's role in the CAP since Hendriks' (1991) analysis of the pre-reunification FRG period. In addition, since Hendriks' book was published the CAP has been reformed twice. This book, therefore, provides a much needed contemporary contribution to the literature on Germany and the CAP in a period of major transition at both the national and international scales. Fourth, in recent years there has been significant interest in the changing role of agriculture in the countryside of developed countries in the context of public reaction against productivist agriculture and growing environmental and amenity concerns (for instance, Cloke and Goodwin, 1992; Marsden *et al.*, 1993). Arguably, the environmental, social and amenity roles of contemporary agriculture are becoming as important as agriculture's economic role, a trend that has been termed 'post-productivist' (Ilbery and Bowler, 1998). As Hoggart *et al.* (1995) noted, much of this literature is based on research in Britain and the USA, and has, therefore, tended to emphasise the Anglo-American perspective. While this work has made a valuable contribution to the theory of agricultural change, there is a recognised need for other perspectives on rural change, and this book aims to provide a German viewpoint. Reunified Germany is especially interesting (and unique) in this respect as it embodies the experiences of both the Communist and the capitalist worlds. Finally, we believe that, as geographers, we can provide a fresh perspective on a subject that has been dominated by political scientists, historians and agricultural economists. A geographical perspective enables a holistic view of policy issues, taking into account political, economic, social, environmental and, last but not least, spatial factors. Further, our German and British backgrounds help to provide, we hope, a broad and balanced approach.

1.2   German agricultural policy within Europe: leader, partner or obstructor?

It is widely accepted that Germany and France have been the two key powers in the EU, but there is disagreement over whether Germany's influence in European policy-making is as *leader* (initiating policy changes), *partner* (working closely together with other member states to reach collective decisions) or *obstructor* (arguing against policy changes). It is obviously difficult to pick one of these three positions to characterise Germany's role in Europe, as Germany's position is likely to change according to the issue considered, and how Germany is classified may depend on the position of the commentator. The British have, for example, tended to view the French and Germans as obstructors because their views have often diverged from those of Britain, while other member states often view Britain as an obstructor. However, we believe that despite these caveats, these three policy positions provide a valuable conceptual approach to help achieve a better understanding of Germany's role in the CAP.

Many authors have considered both the FRG's and reunified Germany's political and economic role within the EU (Feld, 1981; Bulmer and Paterson, 1987; Guerrieri and Padoan, 1989; Borchardt, 1991; Tangermann, 1992; George, 1996). There is agreement that, of the major European economies, Germany has identified its national interest most closely with Europe, and has acted as a 'model European' (Bulmer and Paterson, 1987). This role is related to the aftermath of the political division of Germany following the Second World War, and Germany's desire to gain international acceptance. German politicians have shied away from voicing views that could be seen by other member states as 'nationalist' because of the lingering fear of German nationalism (Bertram, 1994). Thus, until reunification in 1990, Germany's position within Europe could best be described as 'partner'. The apparent subordination of German national to European interests is illustrated by Germany's 'chequebook diplomacy' (Smyser, 1993), Germany being the major net contributor to the EU budget. However, Germany's national interest has been well served by membership of the EU, as it has opened up opportunities for manufacturing exports and supported Germany's post-war economic prosperity.

Bulmer and Paterson (1987) also noted that, with some exceptions, Germany's approach towards EU policies has tended to be reactive rather than proactive. This is partly due to the constitutional structure of government that does not give high priority to collective ministerial decision-making and allows a high level of ministerial autonomy, even over European policy-making, and partly to the voting system of proportional representation which leads to coalition governments. In contrast to the British confrontational style of politics, the German model is more consensual (Wallace, 1988). The prevailing political consensus on the EU has been one of partnership, so that party politics have largely been kept out of European policy issues. However, because of the high degree of ministerial autonomy German policy on Europe has at times appeared uncoordinated or even contradictory, particularly in the case of agricultural policy where the agriculture minister has often adopted a position apparently contrary to Germany's national interest.

Since reunification, commentators have argued that Germany's role in Europe has changed (Bertram, 1994; Geiss, 1996). Reunification has increased Germany's political and economic dominance within the EU, while the breakdown of Communism in Central and Eastern Europe has raised Germany's geopolitical importance. Geiss (1996, p. 161) argued that these events have forced the Germans to re-evaluate their position in Europe, and have raised difficult questions:

> How can they and will they square the circle between their quantitative and qualitative weight, which inexorably throws on them the terrible burden of leadership or even hegemonic status on many accounts, on the one hand, and the aversion built into the European system against any such leader or would-be overlord, on the other?

In a similar context, Schwarz (1994) interpreted Germany's support for the Maastricht Treaty and its commitment to monetary union as a trade-off for reunification. By pushing for further political and economic integration, Germany would be surrendering some of its sovereignty. It is significant to note that, since reunification, Article 23 of Germany's constitution has been amended to include a commitment to the development of the EU and 'the realisation of a united Europe' (Larres, 1996, p. 324). This analysis, therefore, casts Germany into the role of reluctant leader. Yet, there is also a view that Germany may increasingly take the role of obstructor in European affairs. This is linked to the perceived growth of nationalism within German politics since 1990 due to the economic pressures of reunification. Germany's growing assertiveness over its contribution to the EU budget, for instance, can be linked to Germany's internal economic strains (Traynor, 1997). Moreover, the growth of nationalism within Europe as a whole in the post-cold war era may mean that Germany will have to take a more explicitly nationalist stance in European policy-making, as politicians will no longer be able to hide behind 'collective' interests (Bertram, 1994).

To what extent do these views apply to Germany's role in EU agricultural policy? Of all areas of federal government responsibility, agriculture shows the most direct influence of the European Commission in the form of the CAP (Bulmer and Paterson, 1987). Research suggests that Germany's role has often diverged from that of partner towards a more obstructive role because of agriculture's special position within the German economy (Kluge, 1989a; Hendriks, 1991), a view that will be reassessed in this book. A key question is whether Germany's role in European agricultural policy has changed since reunification. Is there evidence of greater leadership or greater obstructive tendencies, and how does this link to domestic politics?

1.3   The actor-oriented approach

The conceptual approach adopted in this book can best be termed an actor-oriented approach within a modified political economy framework. This approach seeks to situate national political structures and policies within the context of global economic trends, and recognises the role of actors within national and international policy-making and development. This broad approach (which has been adopted by many researchers, albeit with different levels of theorisation and theoretical emphases, for instance: Marsden, 1992; Marsden *et al.*, 1992; Ward and Munton, 1992; Long and van der Ploeg, 1994; Halfacree, 1997) has arisen out of criticisms of structuralist approaches on the one hand, which overemphasise the international scale, and criticisms of behavioural approaches on the other, which overemphasise the role of individual actors. Recent work on agricultural and rural change has tended to ignore or play down the role of the nation state, however, emphasising either the global or the local scales, but, as Hoggart *et al.* (1995, p. 7) noted, 'it is at the national level that institutional and ideological capacities are more capable of imposing a distinctive character on global trends' and 'there has been a tendency [in studies of rural development] to miss out the causal imprint of the national scale' (Hoggart *et al.*, 1995, p. 10). This book focuses on the level of the German nation state, and, thus, the majority of analysis relates to this level. However, we recognise the influence of international (both European and global) political and economic forces on the German state, and we also recognise the differential impact of international and national developments on regions, localities and actors within Germany.

There is a danger in analyses of national policy developments of adopting a top-down approach, whereby local actors are seen as merely reacting to external change, and traditional political economy accounts of agricultural change have been criticised for paying little attention to the role of actors or to the contingent and locally differentiated nature of rural change (Long and van der Ploeg, 1994; Ilbery and Bowler, 1998; Morris and Evans, 1999). We believe that the attitudes, perceptions and actions of actors represent one of the most important dimensions of rural change, and, thus, our analysis will pay particular attention to the role of key actors in the policy-making process within Germany. It is important, therefore, to introduce the key actors in agricultural policy-making, and to outline the different roles that they play. For the former FRG and reunified Germany seven different groups of actors can be identified: the government (federal and *Länder*); political parties; the farmers' union; environmental non-governmental organisations (ENGOs); consumers; the industrial lobby and agricultural scientists.

The key actor in agricultural policy-making is the government. As Germany is a federal republic, government is divided between the federal and regional (*Länder*) levels. Germany comprises 16 *Länder*: 11 'old' *Länder* (including West Berlin which is now unified with East Berlin) and five 'new' *Länder* (Map 1.1). The German constitution sets out the division of powers between the federal and *Länder* governments, yet, as Ardagh (1991, p. 86) has rightly pointed out, 'the share-out of responsibilities between [the federal government and the *Länder*] is a complex business'. The federal government has competence in the areas of foreign affairs, defence, currency, post/telecommunications, railways, motorways and nuclear power stations. The *Länder*, in turn, have almost exclusive responsibility for cultural affairs, education, radio and television, police, most environmental matters and local government and planning (Jones, 1994).

Agricultural policy is primarily a federal responsibility, but agricultural structural policy is a 'joint task' shared between the federal and *Länder* governments (see Chapters 2, 4 and 7). The *Länder* also have limited powers to formulate their own agricultural structural policies independently of the federal government, provided these remain within federal and European guidelines. This point is important, as it highlights that key decisions regarding Germany's agricultural policy are made at the federal (and European) levels, but the specific mix of policies may vary from one *Land*[2] to another. Although we recognise the geographically differentiated nature of rural change (see above), time and space prevent us from fully analysing variations between the *Länder*. The main focus in this book will, therefore, address the national (federal) decision-making level (see Chapters 2–5), while only in some cases will we refer to *Länder*-specific policies (particularly in Chapters 6 and 7). Although the *Länder* agriculture ministers are not key actors in federal agricultural decision-making, their views are heard by the federal government through the agriculture committee of the upper house (Bundesrat) on which they all sit (Bulmer and Paterson, 1987).

The most important arm of government for agricultural policy-making in Germany is the Federal Ministry of Food, Agriculture and Forestry (Bundesministerium für Ernährung, Landwirtschaft und Forsten [BML]) established in 1949 (Kluge, 1989a). The BML has four main stated aims: to improve the living conditions of farmers, fishers and foresters; to ensure the supply of high-quality food products to consumers at reasonable prices; to improve agricultural trade relations and the world food situation; and to protect and manage the environment and biological diversity, and to ensure wildlife protection (*Agrarbericht*, 1994). The BML is responsible for implementing and administering the CAP in Germany, and the federal minister of agriculture, as a member of the Council of Agriculture Ministers (CAM), is the key German actor in policy-making at EU level (Bulmer and Paterson, 1987). Table 1.1 outlines the eight agriculture ministers who have held office since 1949. As will be shown throughout this book, each

Map 1.1 The German *Länder*

Table 1.1   Agriculture ministers in the FRG and reunified Germany

Minister	Party[a]	Term of office
Niklas	CSU	1949–53
Lübke	CDU	1953–59
Schwarz	CDU	1959–65
Höcherl	CSU	1965–69
Ertl	FDP	1969–83
Kiechle[b]	CSU	1983–93
Borchert	CDU	1993–98
Funke	SPD	Since 1998

Notes
[a]For full names of political parties see explanation in the text.
[b]Since 1990 for reunified Germany.
Source: authors.

agriculture minister has exerted his own personality and political beliefs on German domestic policy and European policy. Ertl (the longest serving agriculture minister so far), for example, was described by Tangermann (1979b, p. 398) as 'a strong personality with some decisive conceptions about agricultural policy which have had a major impact on developments in Germany'. In the following chapters, we will investigate in detail the specific roles that these agriculture ministers have played in policy-making decisions.

The main political parties are also powerful players in agricultural policy, both at the federal and regional levels. Germany has an electoral system of proportional representation, which means that the percentage of votes a party obtains during national elections (usually every four to five years) determines the number of seats for that party in the parliament (Bundestag). A party has to achieve at least 5 per cent of the vote to be eligible for representation in the Bundestag – a factor which proved crucial in the FRG during the political turmoil of the late 1960s (see Chapter 3) but also in later elections (Neville-Rolfe, 1984). The Christlich Demokratische Union (CDU) is one of the two main parties in Germany and represents the centre-right. Since 1949, it has worked in close collaboration with the Bavarian Christlich Soziale Union (CSU) that has provided an important lobbying role for Bavarian interests at the federal level (including agricultural interests). The Sozialdemokratische Partei (SPD) is the other large party and has represented the political left (with a shift towards the centre in recent years). The Freie Demokratische Partei (FDP), meanwhile, representing liberal interests, has traditionally been a vital partner in coalition governments for both the CDU and SPD and, as Table 1.2 shows, has changed allegiance twice during the past decades.[3] The position of the FDP has been challenged, however, by the emergence of the Green Party

Table 1.2   Government coalitions in the FRG and reunified Germany

Government coalition	Period of government
CDU/CSU with FDP[a]	1949–57
CDU/CSU	1957–61
CDU/CSU with FDP	1961–66
CDU/CSU with SPD (Grand Coalition)	1966–69
SPD with FDP	1969–82
CDU/CSU with FDP[b]	1982–98
SPD with Die Grünen	Since 1998

Notes
[a]The 'Deutsche Partei' (dissolved in 1960) was also part of this coalition government.
[b]After 1990 in reunified Germany.
Source: Authors.

(Die Grünen), established in 1980 and elected to the Bundestag for the first time in 1983 (Geiss, 1996). Die Grünen have since occupied the role of 'second coalition partner', initially in *Länder* governments, but for the first time at the government level in coalition with the SPD after the 1998 elections (Table 1.2). As Chapter 6 will discuss, the emergence of Die Grünen as a political force has been closely linked to the development of German agri-environmental policies (AEPs).

The key political influence on the BML is the powerful farmers' union (Deutscher Bauernverband [DBV]), which acts as an umbrella organisation for the 16 individual farmers' unions in the *Länder*, and represents these organisations in national and international policy lobbying. The DBV represents about 90 per cent of all FRG farmers and 99 per cent of all full-time farmers (Ackermann, 1970; Hendriks, 1991). The DBV and the BML work in close cooperation (similar to the 'corporate' relationship between the National Farmers' Union and the Ministry of Agriculture in Britain; cf. Marsden *et al.*, 1993; Winter, 1996). The DBV has effectively managed to exclude other important interest groups from agricultural policy-making, namely the consumer lobby and agri-business lobby. In addition, the DBV is a member of the Committee of Professional Agricultural Organisations (COPA) which is the main farmers' lobby group in Brussels (Bulmer and Paterson, 1989). The DBV has generally shown conservative tendencies in its policy priorities and has tended to support the CDU/CSU parties, although for tactical reasons the DBV has also changed its political allegiances at certain times (Ackermann, 1970).

The agri-business lobby (comprising, among others, farm input manufacturers, food processors, wholesalers and exporters), is represented by the Federal Union of German Industry, but has little direct input into BML policy-making. Von Cramon-Taubadel (1993) noted that the Union has traditionally supported farmers, but that this tacit alliance has begun to break down in the late 1980s and 1990s due to diverging interests between the two groups over trade policy. The influence of the agri-business lobby is surprisingly limited given the economic importance of food processing to the German economy. One reason for this is that the agri-business lobby is too diversified in its interests, with food processors generally identifying closely with farmers' interests, while exporters have been more in favour of market liberalisation (Marsh, 1991).

As Chapter 6 will discuss, farmers have often clashed with the powerful German environmental lobby. The role of this lobby in agricultural politics is interesting and differs from that in many other European countries (for example, Lowe and Goyder, 1983, for Britain), in that the German environmental lobby has become incorporated into mainstream politics with the emergence of Die Grünen as a fully fledged political party in the early 1980s (see above), and environmental concerns are now well established on the political agenda. However, there is still scope for environmental activism at the local level. For example, ENGOs such as the Bund für Umwelt und Naturschutz (BUND) have played an important role in challenging productivist farming ideologies. Most environmental activism in Germany has either been channelled through the official political line of Die Grünen (often addressing broader issues such as nuclear power or genetically modified crops), or through grassroots campaigns at the local level (largely addressing local issues on habitat preservation or water protection).

German consumers as a lobby group have a weak political influence and have had little direct impact on the trajectories of German agricultural policies (see Chapter 3). This is linked to the broad spectrum of consumer interests and, therefore, the lack of a strong unified voice. Hendriks (1991) highlighted that consumers are highly heterogeneous, and that the main consumer organisation (Arbeitsgemeinschaft der Verbraucherverbände e.V.) comprises nearly 40 different groups. As a result, the BML has often been accused of focusing on producers (the farmers) rather than consumers (Bulmer and Paterson, 1987) – a situation not dissimilar to that in Britain. The influence of the consumer lobby has been greatest over questions of food safety, such as the recent bovine spongiform encephalopathy (BSE) crisis and the consumer (and government) boycott of British beef (see Chapter 6), while little consumer concern has been expressed over food prices.

A further group of agricultural actors are the loosely defined group of agricultural scientists who often act in an advisory role to the government. For instance, the Bundesforschungsanstalt für Landwirtschaft near Braunschweig in Niedersachsen employs about 1000 agricultural researchers to develop new agricultural technologies, monitor farming trends and to analyse policies. In particular, the Scientific Committee of the BML (Wissenschaftlicher Beirat), established in 1950, has played a key role in analysing policy trends and providing regular scientific assessments of the situation of German farming (for instance, WBBELF, 1975). Yet, German agricultural scientists and economists are a highly heterogeneous group of actors with widely diverging opinions, from free marketeers to protectionists. The group of agricultural economists at the University of Göttingen (often referred to as the Göttinger Schule), for example, have often conflicted with the BML because of their free-market liberal criticisms of government policy towards the CAP (see Chapters 2 and 3). The relative importance of this group (and other groups) of academics should not be underestimated, as often agriculture ministers have relied on expert advice and recommendations about specific agricultural policy trajectories (see Tangermann, 1979b, 1982, 1992; Köster, 1981; Priebe, 1985; Henrichsmeyer, 1986).

The discussion so far has focused on agricultural policy actors in the FRG and reunified Germany. Although the main part of this book considers these two political units, some mention of the situation in the former GDR is important. In comparison to the FRG, the influence of lobby groups on policy was tightly controlled. The GDR was effectively a one-party state and operated on the principle of democratic centralism, meaning that policy-making was 'top-down' (Dennis, 1988). The ideological nature of the GDR, with its adherence to Marxist–Leninist socialism, prevented open political discussion. Changes in policy were often due to external pressures (particularly from the Soviet Union) rather than to internal dissent. This continuity of policy was reinforced by the continuity of political leadership (Ulbricht from 1949 to 1973 and Honecker from 1973 to 1989[4]).

Although several small political parties existed in addition to the Sozialistische Einheitspartei Deutschlands (SED), and members of the GDR parliament were elected, in practice all candidates were vetted by the SED, and the electorate's role was to rubberstamp the SED's choices (Dennis, 1988). Farmers were, however, given political representation in the parliament through their own party, the Demokratische Bauernpartei Deutschlands (DBD), and in 1986 the main farmers' union, the Vereinigung der gegenseitigen Bauernhilfe, was also given representation in parliament (Dennis, 1988). The DBD was founded by the Communists during the Soviet occupation of 1945–49 to propagate socialist ideology among the farming community (Fulbrook, 1995). Dissent to SED policy was, therefore, unlikely. Agricultural policies were mainly formulated by the Politbüro, the SED's policy-making body, and implemented by the State Planning Commission in five-year plans. The parliament's role was, therefore, mainly advisory. The lack of democratic pluralism within the GDR, and the dissolution of all political structures following reunification, left a policy vacuum in the new *Länder*. As a result, the former GDR has adopted the FRG's policy-making structures (some commentators, for instance Geiss, 1996, argue that these structures were 'imposed' on the former GDR), and FRG lobby groups have quickly gained powerful positions. For instance, the DBV has established itself as the main farmers' union in the new Germany (see Chapter 4). However, the GDR period has left a political, social and economic legacy, which is likely to show itself as policy-making in the new *Länder* matures.

1.4 Structure of the book

The book is structured both chronologically and thematically. Chapters 2, 3 and 4 are concerned with agricultural policy developments from 1945 to 1989. Chapter 2 focuses on the development of agricultural structures and policies in the former FRG between 1945 and 1990, while Chapter 3 analyses the role of the FRG in CAP policy discussions. Although we are aware that this 'artificial' separation between the analysis of FRG agricultural structures in one chapter, and the discussion of the FRG influence in Brussels in another chapter, may be problematic, we nonetheless feel that the reader can only understand Germany's complex position towards the CAP once the specific situation of FRG farming and structural policies has been explained. Following from this, Chapter 4 examines agricultural structures and policies in the former GDR, discusses the restructuring of agriculture in the new *Länder* since reunification, and considers the nature of agricultural structures, actors and politics in reunified Germany.

Chapters 5, 6 and 7 are mainly concerned with policy developments in reunified Germany, but of necessity include some consideration of pre-reunification events and policies. Chapter 5 focuses on the international level, and examines the influence of agricultural trade policies on the development of the CAP in the 1990s, and looks at Germany's position on trade disputes. This chapter also includes an analysis of the 1992 CAP reforms and the 1994 Uruguay Round Global Agreements on Tariffs and Trade (GATT) agreement on agriculture from a German perspective. Chapter 6 examines the development of AEPs in Germany and the CAP, with a specific emphasis on Germany's role in the development of EU agri-environmental regulations, the geography of AEP within Germany and the role of green thinking for the implementation of policies for the protection of the countryside. Chapter 7 analyses rural change in the FRG and GDR, and the development of rural policy in Germany and Europe in the context of a changing countryside. Finally, challenges for German agriculture and rural society in the twenty-first century are discussed in the concluding Chapter 8, which also places specific emphasis on contemporary pressures on the CAP and Germany's role in the Agenda 2000 talks. Throughout the book, we relate the discussion to the main aims of the book, namely: how can we understand the German approach to agricultural policy-making? Has Germany acted as leader, partner or obstructor in respect to European agricultural policy? What role have different actors played in agricultural policy-making? Finally, what are the implications of reunification for domestic agricultural policy, Germany's role in Europe, and for actors in policy-making?

Inevitably we have had to strike a balance between detail and generality, and we recognise that certain subjects are covered in more depth than others. For instance, as mentioned above, we often concentrate on the federal rather than on the *Länder* level. We also assume a basic knowledge of the CAP and the EU. We have also had to make decisions concerning terminology: Figure 1.1 (above) highlights that we will use the term Germany for the period before the Second World War, between 1945 and 1949 (when Germany was divided into three western Allied zones and an eastern Soviet occupied zone) and again after reunification in 1990, while we will refer to divided Germany between 1949 and 1990 as the FRG and the GDR. Further, we will refer to the European Economic Community (EEC) for the period between the Treaty of Rome in 1957 and the implementation of the Single European Act in 1987 (referring to EEC6, EEC9 and EEC10 where appropriate), to the European Community (EC12) for the period between 1987 and the Maastricht Treaty in 1992, and to the European Union (EU) since 1992 (EU15 since 1995) (see also Pinder, 1995; George, 1996; Williams, 1996).

2
FRG Agricultural Structures and Policies, 1945–90

2.1 Introduction

Many studies have attempted to classify the development of agricultural policies in the FRG between 1945 and 1990. While all authors agree that the immediate post-war years until the establishment of the FRG (1945–49) form a distinctive phase of their own, there is less agreement over how the development of agricultural policy between 1949 and 1990 can best be conceptualised. Ehlers' (1988) analysis, for example, divides this period into three distinct phases: consolidation and agricultural modernisation between 1949 and 1960, agricultural integration into the EEC between 1960 and 1972, and a phase of permanent pressure for agricultural adjustment in the FRG within the framework of the CAP between 1972 and 1990. This framework was adopted by Jones (1994) in his analysis of the 'new' Germany, and also adopted in a modified form by Hendriks (1991) in her study of the FRG and European integration. Kluge (1989a, b), on the other hand, used the changing political structure in the FRG as a basis for a classification based on the terms of office of different agricultural ministers (see also Henrichsmeyer and Witzke, 1994).

We recognise the value of both these approaches to the analysis of FRG agricultural policy development between 1949 and 1990. While we recognise that membership of the EEC (and the CAP) remains a major turning point in the FRG agricultural policy-making framework, we have decided to analyse Germany's domestic policy development separately from its role in the CAP. In this chapter, therefore, we examine the evolution of domestic agricultural policy, broadly adopting Kluge's political classification, while in Chapter 3 we will focus on the CAP and Germany's role in CAP decision-making. A key aim of this chapter is to discuss the cultural significance of farming in the FRG, and the influence this has had on agricultural politics in the post-war period. We also want to analyse the role of actors within the policy-making process, and to consider the influence of individual personalities within the BML and DBV.

This chapter includes a brief discussion of the historical legacy of farming and agricultural policy which the FRG inherited in 1949 (Section 2.2), a brief section on the founding of the FRG and the evolution of state and regional powers (Section 2.3), an in-depth analysis of the nature and causes of agricultural structural deficiencies[1] in the FRG (Section 2.4), and a detailed discussion of the policy responses to these deficiencies by FRG governments between 1949 and 1990 (Section 2.5). This stepwise analysis will highlight the structural problems of FRG agriculture, as a basis for understanding both the national policy-making framework and the FRG position within European agricultural policy decisions discussed in Chapter 3. Furthermore, we argue that the policies established in the newly created FRG in the 1950s established the policy framework which has guided Germany's agricultural policy ever since, even in reunified Germany (see Chapters 4–8).

2.2 The legacy of the past: historical influences on FRG agricultural policy

There are three key historical legacies that the newly formed FRG inherited in 1949, that have had an important influence on subsequent policy development: a small family farm structure, a strong cultural commitment to family farming, and a tradition of economic protectionism. Some commentators have argued that FRG agricultural policy has been a continuation of a trajectory already apparent in the first half of the twentieth century, which aimed to make German family farming more efficient and competitive (Cecil, 1979; Tracy, 1989). Hendriks (1991, p. 26) also argued that FRG agricultural policies were 'largely predetermined by policy decisions taken in earlier times. The economic structure of the old Reich, the characteristics of its society, the social significance of peasant virtues, and the strategic importance of self-sufficiency in food, formulated agricultural policy.'

In 1949, the FRG had almost 1.7 million farms (excluding holdings under 1 ha), of which one-third were smaller than 2 ha (see Table 2.1). This small farm structure is almost entirely related to historical and cultural factors. Thus, the liberation of peasants in the early nineteenth century created a system dominated by a vast number of small family farms (Tracy, 1989; Fulbrook, 1990). In some parts of the FRG, these historical patterns were further exacerbated by the prevailing system of land inheritance. The north and east were characterised by undivided inheritance (*Anerbenrecht*), which generally enabled the oldest son to inherit the farm (as in Britain) (Map 2.1). This system encouraged the maintenance of holdings passed on through the generations at more or less the same size. Inheritance laws in the south-west and west, in contrast, were characterised by partible inheritance (*Realteilung*) which led to the farm being divided among all the children, leading to increasing fragmentation of farms with the characteristic

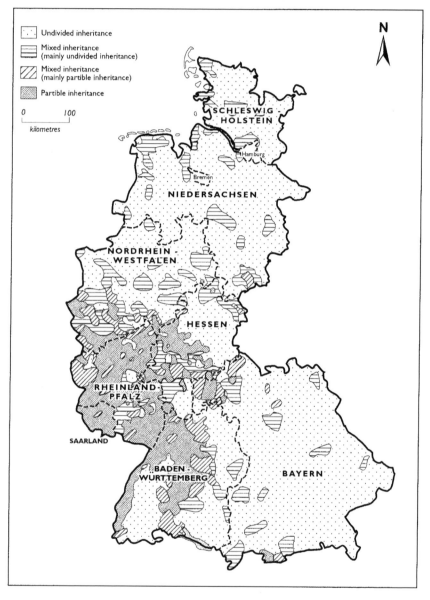

Map 2.1   Land inheritance customs in the FRG (*Source*: after Henkel, 1993)

development of narrow strips (*Streifenflur*). Fields belonging to one holding could be scattered among plots owned by other farmers (*Gemengelage*) (see Map 2.7a), which made it difficult and time-consuming for farmers to manage their land.

According to Hendriks (1991), the origins of the FRG's small farm structure went as far back as the medieval open field system, and subsequently to the Napoleonic Code which stipulated the equal distribution of land among heirs.[2] These farms became increasingly unmanageable as they were further subdivided between heirs over the years. The practice of partible inheritance more or less ended by the end of the nineteenth century, and further parcellisation rarely occurred during the twentieth century (Schmitt, 1996), but their legacy has lived on. Map 2.2 shows that as late as 1970 there was a correlation between regions in the FRG with partible inheritance and a predominance of farms comprised of more than ten plots of land. Particularly in the south-west of the FRG, over half of the farms were comprised of ten or more individual plots.

Tracy (1989) noted that the need to improve farm structures was felt as early as 1800 when the situation of small peasant holdings in Germany was described as 'barbaric' compared with the situation in Britain, where the enclosure movement was creating an efficient agricultural structure. Yet, attempts at improving structures in the first half of the twentieth century were thwarted by the two world wars, the depression of the late 1920s and the Nazi regime. Although the latter attempted to improve the efficiency of German farms (Cecil, 1979), structural policies were never implemented due to the onset of the Second World War.

Linked to West Germany's small farm structure was a strong cultural commitment to family farming. According to Hendriks (1991), farmers have been perceived as one of the basic pillars of society. This 'family farm model' (also referred to by Hoggart *et al.*, 1995 as the 'agrarian tradition') is embedded in age-old German notions of the virtues of peasant culture (*bäuerliche Kultur*) which has always placed great emphasis on the farm family as the carrier of peasant tradition and virtue – notions also widely expressed in German romantic literature and art (Pfeffer, 1989b), and exaggerated under the Nazi regime under the slogan 'Blut und Boden' (blood and soil; Tracy, 1989).

A further legacy was a long tradition of economic protectionism through price support and import controls, dating back to Bismarck in the 1870s in order to protect German farmers, and later to increase self-sufficiency in food for national security reasons following food shortages experienced during and after the First World War (Tracy, 1989). Hendriks (1991) argued that a political consensus developed between industrialists and farmers (especially the landlords) to protect agriculture in return for feeding the growing urban population and providing a reserve army of labour for industry.

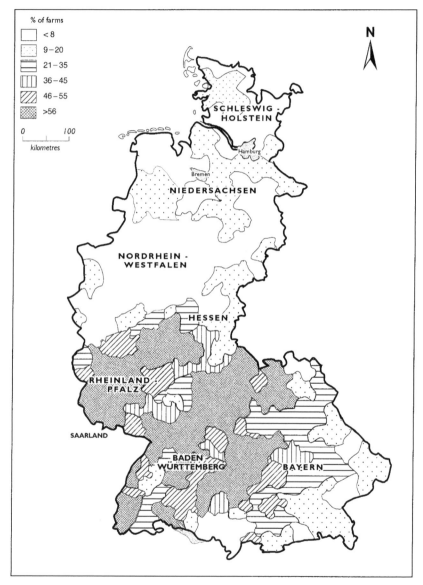

Map 2.2   Farms comprised of more than ten separate blocks of land in the FRG, 1970 (*Source*: after Kluge, 1989a)

Post-war FRG agricultural policy also has to be understood in the context of the devastation caused by the Second World War. Towns were in ruin, the infrastructure had collapsed, and industrial production was almost at a standstill. This meant that agriculture formed the economic and social mainstay of the country for the early post-war years (Ehlers, 1988; Henrichsmeyer and Witzke, 1994). People in the cities were starving and had to be fed as quickly as possible. This caused immense problems for German agriculture which had to supply the population as quickly as possible, as farming was also in disarray following the war, with shortages of inputs, poor marketing systems and a lack of agricultural workers. The severe food shortage was exacerbated by poor harvests in 1946 and 1947 (Cecil, 1979; Tangermann, 1982) and by the massive influx of refugees from former German territories in the East (over 12 million Germans fled from east to west immediately after the war).

The most serious problems were caused by the division of Germany into a western zone occupied by the USA, the British and the French (West Germany) and an eastern Soviet Occupied Zone (SOZ). Before the Second World War, arable production was concentrated in eastern parts of Germany which had more favourable soils and topography. Map 2.3 shows how most of the high-quality agricultural land between Hannover, Magdeburg, Erfurt and Leipzig (including the fertile loess-covered *Magdeburger Börde*) became part of the SOZ. Farming in West Germany was dominated by livestock farming and root crop cultivation, with dairy farming in upland, mountainous and coastal areas (such as the Alpine foothills, the central uplands and the northern coastal strip), a pattern that has not changed substantially in the post-war period (Map 2.4). The division of Germany also meant the loss of most large holdings (50–100 ha), as these were concentrated in the SOZ and other former German territories in the east. West Germany also inherited an unfavourable ratio of population to available agricultural area, with a higher population density in the west than in the SOZ (Franklin, 1969; Cecil, 1979). Further, political division interrupted vital commodity trade flows from the SOZ to West Germany. From its very beginnings, the iron curtain became a barrier to agricultural trade flows from east to west, leading to a virtual standstill of commodity flows across the border with the SOZ. Four years after the war, for example, only 3 per cent of agricultural imports to West Germany came from Eastern Bloc countries (including the SOZ). Thus, the division of Germany not only led to the loss of its agricultural heartland, but also to major dislocations of former patterns of agricultural trade. New trade relations had to be established with Western European countries and other parts of the capitalist world.

For West Germany, the period immediately after the war was critical for the re-establishment of actors who traditionally had held a stake in the agricultural policy process (see also Chapter 1). In 1948, the DBV was

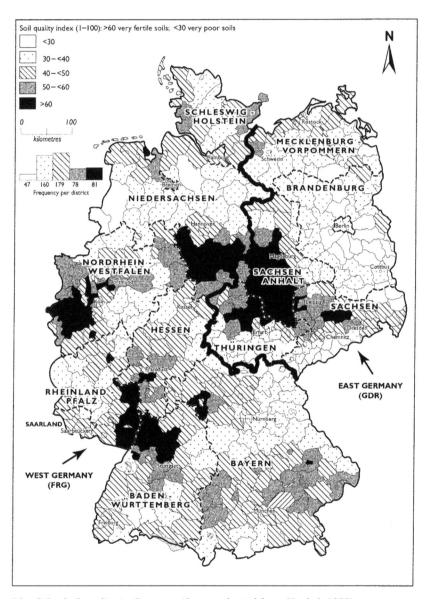

Map 2.3   Soil quality in Germany (*Source*: adapted from Henkel, 1993)

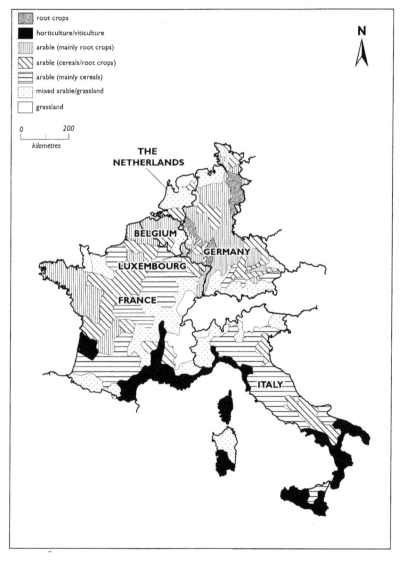

Map 2.4 Predominant land uses in the EEC6 (*Sources*: *Agrarbericht,* various years; Kluge, 1989a; Hoggart *et al.*, 1995)

reconstituted (after having been dissolved during the Nazi regime), and by 1951 the DBV had officially become the centralised and exclusive representative of farming interests in the FRG.[3] Indeed, it became one of the most powerful interest groups in the FRG (and later in reunified Germany). The DBV was established as an umbrella association with a federalist organisational structure with independent legal existence, whereby regular members were not individuals but farmers' associations of the *Länder* (a unique structure among interest groups in Western Europe). With the establishment of one farmers' organisation for the FRG, the traditional fragmentation of farmers' organisations, characteristic of many other European countries (for instance, France), could be successfully avoided. The DBV has since represented about 80–90 per cent of all FRG farmers, which gave it considerable lobbying power in FRG agricultural policy-making (Ackermann, 1970; Andrlik, 1981). The rapid reconstitution of the DBV highlights that the strength of the farm lobby survived despite drastic breaks in the FRG's political history (Hendriks, 1991; Heinze and Voelzkow, 1993). The development of the DBV coincided with the re-establishment of medium and short-term credit facilities for farmers in 1948 through the Raiffeisen bank, which actively supported the DBV through its 24 000 local organisations (Andrlik, 1981). Further, the introduction of the new Deutschmark (DM) in 1948 also gave the farm community confidence to increase production and exchange commodities in a more controlled way than in the 'bartering society' that had existed immediately after the war. With the introduction of a stable currency, prices for the most important agricultural commodities could be fixed until the formal establishment of the FRG in 1949.

The period between 1945 and 1949 was also characterised by discussions relating to more fundamental changes in the structure of West German agriculture. First, as in the SOZ (see Chapter 4), the question of land reform was considered. The principle of land reform was supported by the Allies and by the emerging West German political parties (the SPD and CDU in particular) as a way to reduce the power of the larger estates, to distribute the land more equitably, and to provide farmland for refugees and expellees. However, it was not a political priority, partly because there were fewer large estates in West Germany than in the SOZ, and partly because the problem of feeding a starving population took priority over the restructuring of property (Cecil, 1979). As a result, tangible action was delayed until the establishment of the FRG, and after 1949 more pressing problems relating to agricultural policies and structures had to be dealt with by the new FRG government (see below). In hindsight, the fact that larger units were never broken up in West Germany became a blessing, as a new generation of smallholders on former estate land would have further exacerbated agricultural structural deficiencies that have characterised FRG agriculture since 1949.

Second, the period between 1945 and 1949 also saw the establishment of the 'social market economy' – an economic philosophy which characterised the special approach of the FRG towards capitalist development, at least until the 1980s[4] (Smyser, 1993). What is important from an agricultural viewpoint is that agriculture was more or less exempted from participating in the social market economy (WBBELF, 1975; von Urff, 1999). In other words, FRG agriculture enjoyed higher levels of state protection than any other economic sector. As will be discussed in detail in subsequent chapters, this decision was to crucially influence the viability of German agriculture and the course of agricultural politics for decades to come, effectively relegating agriculture to an economic sector increasingly reliant on state subsidies for survival.

Despite immense problems relating to the ravages of the war, agriculture recovered quickly. Although statistical evidence is scarce for the early postwar years (*Grüner Bericht*, 1956), a variety of authors have suggested that the agricultural sector was one of the fastest growing sectors of the economy (for instance, Tangermann, 1982; Ehlers, 1988; Kluge, 1989a). This formed a crucial basis for the political stability that followed with the establishment of the FRG in 1949.

The FRG differed considerably from the former German Reich. It covered only 248 000 km^2 compared to the previous 471 000 km^2, which meant a loss of 7.1 million ha of agricultural land (about a quarter of the former agricultural area). The constitution, laid down in 1949, provided the nation and the *Länder* with powers to share in legislation all matters concerning the promotion of agricultural production, transfer of land, tenure, and tenancy (Woodruffe, 1989; Jones, 1994). From 1962, this also included the CAP (see Chapter 3). As a result, FRG agriculture has always been subject to the planning and policy influence of both the federal and the *Länder* governments (Jones, 1994). This has placed great powers into the hands of the agriculture minister, but has also enabled a degree of flexibility for the *Länder* to respond to federal government, and later also European, policies (Höll and von Meyer, 1996).

Before analysing the main trajectories of FRG agricultural structural policies, it is important to outline in more detail the nature and extent of structural deficiencies in FRG agriculture. Only by looking at the problems that policy-makers have faced during the period 1949–1990, is it possible to understand why specific policy-related issues have remained high on the political agenda, both at national and European levels.

2.3   Agricultural structural deficiencies in the FRG

Three problems have dominated FRG agriculture in the period 1949–1990 (see Table 2.1). First, as already discussed, the FRG inherited a legacy of small family farms. Second, since 1949 pronounced agricultural structural

Table 2.1 Farm holdings in the FRG by size classes, 1949–98 (number of holdings over 1 ha in 1000s)

Year	1–9 ha	10–19 ha	20–29 ha	30–49 ha	50–100 ha	>100 ha	Total	Average size (ha)	Annual reduction in number of farms (%)
1949[a]	1262	256	72	40	13	2.9	1647	8.1	—
1953	1172	258	113		13	2.9	1559	8.3	—
1955	1135	263	114		13	2.8	1528	8.6	—
1957	1090	270	116		13	2.8	1492	8.8	—
1958	1063	274	118		13	2.8	1471	8.9	-1.4
1959	1039	278	119		13	2.8	1452	9.0	-1.3
1960[b]	961	287	122		14	2.6	1385	9.3	-4.6
1961	944	290	124		14	2.7	1375	9.4	-0.7
1962	914	293	125		13	2.7	1348	9.6	-2.0
1963	880	297	126		14	2.6	1320	9.8	-2.1
1964	851	296	130		14	2.6	1294	10.0	-1.9
1965	808	292	135		14	2.7	1252	10.2	-3.2
1966[c]	781	291	138		15	2.8	1228	10.4	-1.9
1967[d]	760	289	94	47	15	2.8	1206	10.6	-1.8
1968	738	286	96	48	15	2.8	1186	10.7	-1.7
1969	709	281	100	50	15	2.8	1157	11.0	-2.4
1970	639	268	104	53	16	3.0	1083	11.7	-6.4
1971	599	253	106	57	17	3.2	1035	11.7	-4.4
1972	561	243	109	61	19	3.4	997	12.2	-3.7
1973	539	231	109	65	20	3.6	968	12.7	-2.9
1974	508	219	108	68	22	3.8	928	13.0	-4.1
1975	491	212	107	70	22	3.9	905	13.5	-2.5

26

Table 2.1 Farm holdings in the FRG by size classes, 1949–98 (number of holdings over 1 ha in 1000s) (continued)

Year	1–9 ha	10–19 ha	20–29 ha	30–49 ha	50–100 ha	>100 ha	Total	Average size (ha)	Annual reduction in number of farms (%)
1976	479	206	107	71	23	4.0	889	14.0	-1.8
1977	456	200	106	72	24	4.2	862	14.4	-3.0
1978	442	194	105	73	25	4.2	844	14.6	-2.1
1979	419	187	104	74	26	4.3	815	15.1	-3.4
1980	407	181	103	75	27	4.3	797	15.3	-2.2
1981	395	177	100	76	28	4.6	780	15.5	-2.1
1982	384	172	99	76	29	4.7	764	15.8	-2.1
1983	369	167	97	76	30	4.9	744	16.1	-2.6
1984	362	163	95	76	31	5.0	733	16.3	-1.5
1985	354	159	94	76	32	5.2	721	16.6	-1.6
1986	345	155	92	77	33	5.4	707	16.8	-1.9
1987	325	149	89	77	35	5.6	681	17.4	-3.7
1988	317	143	86	77	37	6.0	665	17.7	-2.3
1989	307	137	84	77	39	6.5	649	18.2	-2.4
1990e	296	129	80	76	41	7.1	630	18.7	-2.9
1991	273	121	76	75	43	7.8	595	19.6	-5.6
1992	268	115	72	73	45	9.0	582	20.2	-2.2
1993	260	110	69	71	47	9.8	567	20.7	-2.6
1994	251	104	66	70	49	11	550	21.4	-3.0
1995	236	97	62	67	50	12	524	22.3	-4.7

Table 2.1 Farm holdings in the FRG by size classes, 1949–98 (number of holdings over 1 ha in 1000s) *(continued)*

Year	1–9 ha	10–19 ha	20–29 ha	30–49 ha	50–100 ha	>100 ha	Total	Average size (ha)	Annual reduction in number of farms (%)
1996	228	93	60	66	50	13	509	22.9	–2.9
1997	221	88	57	63	51	14	494	23.6	–2.9
1998	216	85	55	63	51	15	484	24.1	–2.0

Notes
[a]No data for 1950–52, 1954 and 1956.
[b]Figures before 1960 exclude the Saarland.
[c]Until 1966 only aggregated data are available for holding sizes between 20 and 49 ha.
[d]Before 1967 the smallest statistical category of farms comprised farms of 0.5–2 ha. Figures for the 1–10 ha category are, therefore, approximations only and exclude the expected proportion of farms of 0.5–1 ha.
[e]Figures for 1990–98 only include farms in the territory of the former FRG (see Chapter 4 for the whole of Germany after 1990).
Sources: Grüner Bericht (1956–70); *Agrarbericht* (1971–97).

change has occurred, with a dramatic reduction in the number of farms and a concurrent increase in the average size of holdings. Third, these farm structures have led to low average farm incomes compared to many other European countries (Neville-Rolfe, 1984). In the following discussion, each of these three issues will be discussed in detail.

2.3.1 Smallholder family farming in the FRG: causes and consequences

The bulk of farms remained in the 1–10 ha size category between 1949 and 1990 (Table 2.1 and Map 2.5), despite rapid structural changes (see below), and the average size of holdings remained small compared to many other European countries. FRG farms are substantially smaller than farms in France, Denmark, Luxembourg and Britain, similar to Belgium and the Netherlands but larger than farms in Italy (Table 2.2). Even more revealing is the percentage of farms below 5 ha and above 100 ha. In 1980, for example, the FRG, with about a third of farms in the category below 5 ha farm size, was only surpassed by Belgium (42 per cent) and Italy (74 per cent). For farms above 100 ha (0.5 per cent in the FRG) only the Netherlands had a smaller proportion (0.2 per cent). In contrast, in Britain almost 14 per cent of holdings were 100 ha or larger in that year (Thiede, 1991).

The small-scale nature of farms has been an important explanation for high levels of off-farm employment characteristic of FRG farming,[5] especially in areas affected by partible inheritance. Part-time farming has been so important in the FRG that the German farm classification not only distinguished between full-time (over 90 per cent of household income from the farm) and part-time (under 50 per cent), but also included a separate category for those whose income derived 'mainly' from farming (50–90 per cent) but where, because of the insufficient size of the farm, additional income had to be sought by the farm couple (side-line farms).[6] Although full-time holdings managed most of the agricultural land (78 per cent of the utilised agricultural area [UAA] in 1984) and also owned most of the livestock (for example, 83 per cent of all dairy cows in 1984), Table 2.3 shows that less than 50 per cent of FRG farms have been farmed as full-time concerns over the last decades (albeit with a rising tendency), while about 40 per cent of farms have been part-time farms (Zurek, 1986). Even today, the former territory of the FRG has the highest proportion of part-time farmers in the EU, a fact stressed by Hendriks (1991, p. 36) who argued that 'the existence of worker-peasants became a substantial and integral part of Germany's post-war socio-economic life'. In 1975, for example, 55 per cent of FRG farmers were either part-time or side-line farmers, while the equivalent figures for Italy and France were only 29 and 20 per cent respectively (Neander, 1982). Map 2.6 shows that areas where full-time farming has predominated coincide with regions where larger

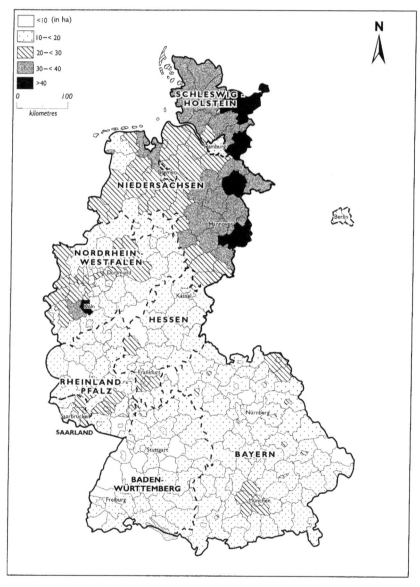

Map 2.5   Average farm sizes in the FRG in 1989 for holdings >1 ha (*Source*: adapted from BMBau, 1991)

Table 2.2 Comparison of European farm structures (average farm size in hectares, selected countries and years)

Year	FRG	B	Dk	F	I	Lux	NL	UK
1955–61	9.0	8.2	15.6	15.2	9.0	13.4	9.9	40.0
1980	15.3	12.3	23.8	23.7	6.4	25.1	13.7	62.5
1989	17.7	15.3	32.2	28.6	5.6	31.8	17.2	64.4
% of farms <5 ha (1980)	35	42	14	26	74	27	33	17
% of farms >100 ha (1980)	0.5	0.5	1.7	2.8	0.5	0.8	0.2	13.9

Sources: *Grüner Bericht* (1956–63); *Agrarbericht* (1981–90).

Table 2.3 Full-time and part-time farms in the FRG (over 1 ha)

Year	Full-time farms (%)	Side-line farms (%)	Part-time farms (%)
1965	41	26	33
1970	43	22	35
1975	45	15	40
1980	50	11	39
1985	50	10	40
1990[a]	49	9	42
1995	49	8	43

Note
[a]After 1990 for the territory of the FRG.
Sources: *Grüner Bericht* (1970); *Agrarbericht* (1975–97).

farms are the norm and where undivided inheritance exists. As a result, full-time holdings have tended to be concentrated in the north and the south-east.

2.3.2 Agricultural structural change 1949–90: causes and consequences

As Table 2.1 illustrates, the FRG experienced substantial agricultural structural change between 1949 and 1990. This has partly been a reason for, but also a consequence of, government policies. Both structural change and government incentives to accelerate that change went hand in hand (Ehlers, 1988). During the FRG economic miracle of the 1950s and 1960s, with good employment opportunities in industry, many farmers left their farms to work in non-agricultural employment. This trend was further helped by improved infrastructural links between rural areas and cities, making it easier for farmers to commute to work while still maintaining

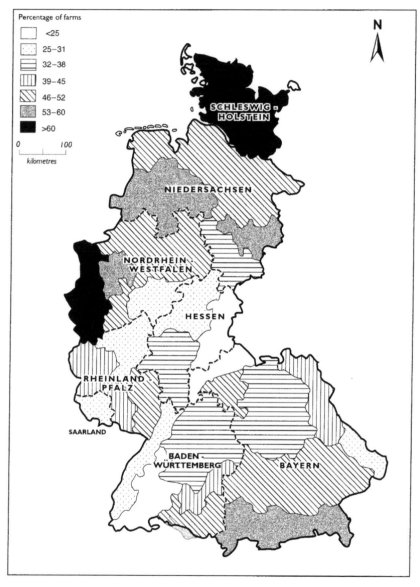

Map 2.6   Percentage of full-time farms in the FRG, 1971 (*Source*: adapted from Kluge, 1989b)

their farms on a part-time basis (Neander, 1982; Thieme, 1983). During this economic boom, many part-time farmers sold or leased their farms, and many full-time farmers changed to part-time farming. Yet, many part-time holdings were too large and were neglected through lack of time, while many full-time holdings were struggling to survive economically unless they had the financial means to expand rapidly (Kluge, 1989a). Table 2.1 shows that the number of holdings decreased from almost 1.7 million in 1949 to about 0.63 million in 1990, and to about 0.48 million in 1998 (on the territory of the former FRG). Thus, less than a third of the original farms that existed in 1949 have survived. This trend has been accompanied by an increase in average farm sizes from 8.1 ha in 1949 to 18.7 ha in 1990 (24.1 ha in 1998), and growing polarisation of farm size. While in 1949 only 3.4 per cent of all farms were 30 ha or larger, by 1990 about a fifth of all farms were in that size category.

Table 2.1 also shows that the pace of change (the percentage annual reduction in the number of farms) was greatest in the early 1960s, throughout the 1970s and between 1987 and 1997. In 1970 alone, for example, 74 000 farms were given up (6.4 per cent of all farms), equivalent to one farm family giving up every seven minutes! Yet, it is important to highlight that there have been considerable regional disparities in the pace of change, and that not all areas of the FRG have been affected in the same way. Areas with small, fragmented farms on poor soils next to rapidly growing industrial areas have lost more farmers than fertile areas with large and economically buoyant farms (Franklin, 1969; Neander, 1983). Changes in upland grassland farming areas have been slower than in the lowlands, because of the reduced off-farm employment opportunities in areas lacking industry and major urban centres (see also Chapter 7). However, agricultural structural change has also been pronounced in the more intensively farmed lowlands and northern parts of the FRG where intensification went hand in hand with farm amalgamation and rapid increases in farm sizes, while small family farms have remained the main farm type in less intensively farmed agricultural regions (*Agra-Europe Bonn*, 31.7.1995a, 9.12.1996b). Geographical differences on the nature and pace of structural change have been further exacerbated by different cultural traditions, particularly the different types of land inheritance outlined above (Mayhew, 1973; Born, 1974). As Table 2.1 shows, agricultural structural change decelerated during the mid-1970s and the early 1980s due to a lack of alternative employment in industry following the aftermath of the 1973 oil crisis and the economic depression of the early 1980s – and also partly due to policies introduced by the governments of the time (see below).

Structural change has been accompanied by intensification and regional specialisation. Livestock farming, in particular, became more intensive, especially during the 1970s and early 1980s, reflected in an average increase from 14 to 21 livestock units (LU) on livestock farms for the period between 1971 and 1983 (Kluge, 1989a), while mixed farming enterprises declined (for instance, the number of farms without any livestock increased from 11 per cent in 1971 to 18 per cent in 1984). There has also been a polarisation of farms, with a growth in full-time farms on the one hand, and the increasing marginalisation of part-time farmers on the other. Sideline farmers have been 'squeezed', forced either into full-time farming, part-time farming, or out of farming altogether (see Table 2.3). While 294 000 part-time farms still managed about 22 per cent of the UAA in 1985, by 1995 the remaining 228 000 part-time farmers managed less than 15 per cent. This is a further reflection of the implications of agricultural structural change for the viability – economic and political – of small part-time holdings, an issue considered in detail in Section 2.5.

Concurrent with the reduction in the number of farms and farmers, there has also been a substantial decrease in the farm workforce since 1949 (Table 2.4). While there had already been a substantial decrease in the agricultural working population for the whole German Reich before the Second World War (from 10.5 million in 1882 to 8.9 million in 1939), 5.3 million people (27 per cent of the workforce) were still working in agriculture in the FRG in 1949. By 1994, this figure had declined to only 0.69 million people (2.4 per cent of workforce), a decrease of almost 5 million people since 1949. This trend has also had major repercussions for rural communities – a crucial point that warrants discussion in a separate chapter (see Chapter 7).

Similar trends occurred in other European countries (Table 2.5). Between the 1950s and 1980s, all EEC countries lost agricultural workers, with a concurrent reduction in full-time workers. Table 2.5, however, also empha-

Table 2.4   People working in FRG agriculture (excluding fisheries and forestry)

Year	Number (millions)	Workforce (%)
1949	5.3	27.1
1950	5.1	23.2
1955	4.3	20.0
1960	3.4	13.8
1965	2.9	10.9
1970[a]	2.1	7.8
1975	1.7	6.7
1980	1.3	4.7
1985	1.1	4.0
1990	0.83	2.9
1994	0.69	2.4

Note
[a]Data before 1969 include farm workers and farm family workers, while after 1970 only farm family workers are listed.
Sources: Grüner Bericht (1956–70); *Agrarbericht* (1971–97).

Table 2.5   FRG agricultural employment in a European context (full-time workers per 100 ha UAA)

	FRG	B	Dk	F	I	Lux	NL	UK
1959	27.0	15.5	8.9	13.5	30.9	22.4	19.6	5.8
1980	8.6	8.7	5.9	5.6	11.5	6.9	11.9	3.3
1989	7.2	7.8	4.0	5.3	13.7	5.8	10.1	3.1

Sources: Grüner Bericht (1963); Agrarbericht (1990).

sises the economic disparities between countries. In 1989, for example, 13.7 full-time workers/100 ha UAA were still employed in Italy (mainly due to the intensive and specialised nature of many of its holdings), compared with 7.2/100 ha in the FRG and 3.1/100 ha in Britain (due to both the extensive nature of many of its upland farms and to the high degree of mechanisation on intensive holdings). Figure 2.1 shows that in the context of the EEC the net economic productivity per labour unit in FRG agriculture remained low during the 1970s and 1980s, despite high levels of mechanisation and increased applications of artificial inputs.

2.3.3   FRG farm incomes in a European context

Despite the amalgamation of holdings into larger and more efficient units, the relative economic importance of FRG agriculture vis-à-vis other sectors of the national economy has increasingly lagged behind. On the one hand, this can be explained by structural deficiencies in FRG agriculture, as low farm incomes have been linked to low productivity arising from small and fragmented farm structures. On the other hand, this has also been because other parts of the FRG economy – manufacturing in particular – experienced such dramatic growth (especially between 1955 and 1973) that the agricultural sector increasingly fell behind. The FRG economic miracle (*Wirtschaftswunder*) of the post-war years was based entirely on the rapid growth of manufacturing output, while the agricultural sector experienced only average growth (Neville-Rolfe, 1984; Smyser, 1993). Between 1950 and 1956 alone, the contribution of the agricultural sector to GDP decreased from 11.2 to 8.6 per cent, while in 1989 it only accounted for 1.5 per cent (Pfeffer, 1989b; Kluge, 1989a).

Table 2.6 shows that between 1976 and 1994 real average farm income in the FRG remained stable at between 109 and 144 per cent of the EC9/12 average, while farm incomes in many other European countries increased relative to the European average.[7] Most notable are France, with an increase from 102 to 152 (a 50 per cent real increase) between 1976 and 1994, and Italy where farmers had almost reached average EU farm incomes by 1994. It is also important to note that by 1994 farmers in countries such as Denmark, Belgium, Britain and the Netherlands earned almost twice as

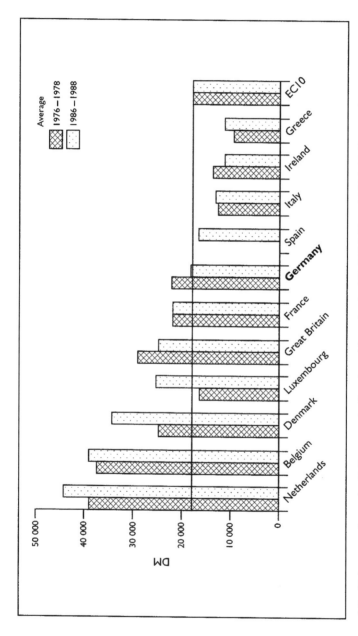

Figure 2.1 Net economic productivity per agricultural workforce in the EC, 1976–78 and 1986–88 (*Source*: after Kluge, 1989b)

Table 2.6 Real average[a] income for full-time farmers in the EC, 1976–94 (EC9/12 = 100)

Year	FRG	B	DK	GR	E	F	IR	I	LUX	NL	P	UK	EC9/12[b]
1976	109	187	209			102	80	65	141	223		162	100
1978	131	190	264			105	85	52	150	232		135	100
1980	132	220	199			118	63	53	143	249		107	100
1982	127	248	213			115	73	44	130	309		140	100
1984	144	242	201			114	63	42	153	283		131	100
1986	119	212	239	57	82	132	98	82	153	251	33	161	100
1988	109	199	200	55	76	150	112	86	162	267	24	202	100
1990[c]	142	260	281	54	55	165	108	74	197	333	23	200	100
1992	130	222	237	61	60	165	103	79	165	249	18	200	100
1994[d]	109	192	200	42	81	152	115	93	158	217	10	205	100

Notes

[a]Figures are inflation adjusted in relation to the GDP index on the basis of commodity prices.

[b]The average for the EC9/12 is based on all farm incomes (including part-time farmers).

[c]After 1990 for former FRG territory only.

[d]No separate data are available for the former territory of the FRG after 1994.

Source: Agrarbericht (1977–97); Ehlers (1988).

much as FRG farmers – an important factor to consider in the discussion about the continuous demand of FRG farmers for higher commodity prices in the CAP outlined in detail in Chapter 3.

Low farm incomes, a predominance of smallholder family farming and substantial agricultural structural change have all posed severe challenges for FRG policy-makers. The following section will analyse both how policy-makers have attempted to address agricultural structural deficiencies and what role the government, the DBV and other actors have played in shaping the policy-making process. Although, as stated above, Germany's role in European agricultural policy will be analysed in Chapter 3, Germany's agricultural policy-making has been increasingly influenced by Europe since the establishment of the CAP in the 1960s.

2.4   Policy responses to agricultural structural deficiencies

From the formation of the FRG in 1949, farmers were given special treatment by the government. In the following analysis, the policy trajectories of the five different periods of FRG government are analysed in an attempt to outline similarities and differences in the national agricultural policy priorities of the FRG between 1949 and 1990. This will form the basis for understanding the FRG position on EEC agricultural policy outlined in Chapter 3.

2.4.1   The Adenauer era: the family farm model under a conservative government

The family farm model

The first government in the newly established FRG was formed by a centre–right coalition between the CDU and the FDP (and the Deutsche Partei until 1960) which lasted from 1949 to 1963 under Chancellor Adenauer. This period in FRG history was characterised by a dramatic shift from starvation in the late 1940s to economic well-being in the early 1960s (Ardagh, 1991; Larres and Panayi, 1996). From the beginning, Chancellor Adenauer stressed the importance of increasing farm production, while at the same time maintaining a 'healthy peasantry'. A policy model was established which stressed the importance of maintaining family farms as a basis for the survival of rural communities, and to ensure adequate production of agricultural commodities (Sauer, 1990; Kallfass, 1991; Henrichsmeyer and Witzke, 1994).

There are a variety of reasons for the emphasis on maintaining family farming in the FRG after the Second World War. First, and similar to most other European countries (cf. Scott, 1942 for Britain), the aim of maintaining the farming population on the land was motivated by the need to safeguard adequate food supplies in a country still traumatised by the threat of widespread starvation in the immediate post-war years. Second, maintaining a substantial and productive agriculture was also crucial for social stability because of high unemployment (1.7 million in 1949; mainly expellees from former German territories in the east). Third, the need to balance external payments was initially based on increased food production (Cecil, 1979), although rapid industrial growth during the 1950s gradually removed all threats to the balance of payments. Fourth, the FRG was less self-sufficient in food (only 70 per cent in 1949) than the German Reich had been due to the loss of important agricultural areas to the SOZ (see Map 2.3) with a reduction by about one-quarter of its original commodity production (Kluge, 1989a).

Possibly most importantly, the Adenauer government quickly realised the political importance of the 1.7 million farmers and their families in 1949. This factor has continued to form a major incentive for all subsequent FRG governments to maintain a stable agricultural population (Hrbek and Wessels, 1984; Henrichsmeyer and Witzke, 1994). Hendriks (1991, p. 37) argued that 'Adenauer's policies toward Germany's post-war farmers were not only motivated by his sense of social justice, but also by his instinctive desire to exploit a voting potential. An artificially large peasantry . . . supported conservative governments.' Especially after the collapse of the Third Reich, the FRG government was keen to retain the political allegiance of farmers to prevent the re-emergence of right-wing attitudes in poor rural areas which had provided substantial backing for the Nazi regime during the 1930s (Larres and Panayi, 1996). FRG farmers have generally backed the CDU (and particularly its important Bavarian right wing the CSU), and the innate conservatism and suspicion of land reform, especially in the context of the geographical and cultural proximity to the GDR, have often alienated FRG farmers against the SPD. Thus, CDU-led governments were less interested in establishing a more efficient farming sector based on fewer and larger farms than in the preservation of farmers as a reliable 'voting reservoir'.

The 'Adenauer model', emphasising the importance of the family farm, had far-reaching socio-economic and policy-related repercussions for present-day reunified Germany. It was reflected, for example, in the Agricultural Act 1955 (see below), the FRG position on the CAP (see Chapter 3), and, more recently, in the fierce debates over agricultural policy reform in the world trade talks under the GATT (see Chapter 5) (Ehlers, 1988; Henrichsmeyer and Witzke, 1994). As Jones (1994, p. 60) reiterated, 'it has been the family farm which has served as the guiding image for West German agricultural policy since 1949'. In particular, the family farm model contradicted the need to establish policies aimed at increasing the efficiency of FRG farming through the establishment of larger farm units (Kluge, 1989a, b; Kallfass, 1991). This meant that agriculture was exempt from the principles of the social market economy (Cecil, 1979; Jones, 1994). Consequently, farm incomes increasingly diverged from incomes in other employment sectors. In 1950, farm incomes had already begun to lag behind, and by 1952, the average incomes from industry were already 36 per cent higher than in agriculture (Kluge, 1989a). This can be linked to the rapid structural change that occurred at this time, as outlined in Section 2.3.2 (Brandkamp, 1982; Neander, 1983). In response, the government introduced guaranteed prices for the main agricultural commodities. This protected farmers from price fluctuations, but increased food prices for consumers (Schöneweiß, 1984; Kluge, 1989a). Nonetheless, even a highly subsidised agriculture failed to keep FRG farmers abreast of economic improvements in other economic sectors. It soon became evident that the political objective of securing the participation of the farmers in the general economic and social development of the country could not be achieved (Ehlers, 1988).

The need for a competitive FRG agriculture

Despite the aim of protecting the family farm, there were growing pressures to make FRG agriculture more competitive in Western European and world markets. By 1951, most of the restrictions imposed by the Allies were withdrawn and normal trading relations with other countries could be established (Cecil, 1979). The degree to which agriculture and the food industry could be subjected to the free forces of the market was intensely debated from the beginning (Tangermann, 1982). The most favoured scenario was tight control of agricultural markets, continuing a pattern that had been established in the late nineteenth century (see Section 2.2). Kluge (1989a) describes the FRG position as a 'double strategy'. On the one hand, moderate protection of markets through a high price policy was advocated, while on the other hand a strategy of trade liberalisation was suggested to strengthen the FRG position in international politics and to appease its agricultural trading partners. In the early 1950s, however, the policy of protectionism was seen as the only solution to prevent widespread rural depopulation.

It comes as no surprise, therefore, that throughout the 1950s FRG farmers were seizing the opportunities provided by the protected market, resulting in rapidly rising output – developments also welcomed by the USA which encouraged the emergence of a strong and independent FRG as a crucial political buffer to Eastern Bloc countries (Guerrieri and Padoan, 1989; Geiss, 1996). By 1956, FRG farmers for the first time produced more (in most commodities) than during the peak period in the 1930s (Cecil, 1979). The rapid reconstruction and establishment of new trade links is described by many commentators as an impressive achievement in a short time-span (Hendriks, 1987; Haase, 1991). Yet, although improved links with Western European agricultural markets helped with the integration of the FRG into Western Europe, the re-emergence of old trade ties with the West also implied a long-winded and often painful adaptation process of FRG agriculture to some of the most efficient agricultural systems in the world (Kluge, 1989a; see Chapter 5).

The role of the DBV

During these formative years of the FRG the DBV was supportive of the minister of agriculture, Lübke (see Table 1.1). The DBV felt that Lübke would be vital in establishing policies that would help FRG farmers, and that he could extract an adequate price for agricultural commodities in return for political support from the DBV (Cecil, 1979). The policies enacted in the 1950s were, therefore, partly an outcome of mutual support between the government and the DBV. This was greatly helped by the fact that in the 1950s and 1960s more than half of the members of parliament from the CDU or CSU in the Bundestag had some connections with the agricultural sector (Hendriks, 1991).

To strengthen its case for government support of high commodity prices, the DBV published figures in the early 1950s showing the increasing income disparities between farmers and other sections of the workforce (Ackermann, 1970). They highlighted that the gap was rapidly increasing despite increasing productivity in the farming sector (the latter mainly due to reduced numbers of farm workers). Early on it became obvious that the DBV – more than any other non-state actor – could exert considerable pressure on the government over agricultural policy. In negotiations with the DBV, the government offered two policy responses to the income problems in farming. The first included the 'parity approach' where deficiency payments would make up for losses incurred by farmers – an approach already partly in place in the early 1950s through the price support system. The second approach involved tackling the structural deficiencies through the creation of viable holdings of adequate size. One proposal was to achieve this through farm consolidation and the complete abolition of subdivision. Not unexpectedly, the DBV was sceptical of the second proposal and demanded that the income issue be tackled at the same time as the restructuring of holdings (Cecil, 1979). There was also some opposition from the industry lobby (Deutscher Industrie- und Handelstag) who maintained that the basic need was to make agriculture more competitive internationally – not to give it a position of permanent privilege. Although the latter criticism was echoed many times by various opponents of government policy since 1949, opposition was limited. Lübke was, therefore, able to implement the first major set of structural policies without much criticism from other actors.

The Lübke Plan and the Land Consolidation Act 1953

The Lübke Plan in 1953 was a clear commitment towards improved support for farmers and provided an extensive bundle of measures aiming to increase farm size, consolidate farm holdings, rationalise and mechanise farms, and improve education levels. Further aims were the improvement of transport and communication in rural areas, the improvement of marketing structures, and village renewal schemes (for a discussion of the latter see Section 7.4.3).

The Land Consolidation Act 1953 (*Flurbereinigungsgesetz*) formed one of the centrepieces of the Lübke Plan. It warrants, therefore, closer investigation as it had repercussions for FRG agriculture until 1990 and beyond. *Flurbereinigung* was part of a series of structural reforms that aimed at discouraging farm fragmentation and at promoting the expansion of viable farms (Henrichsmeyer and Witzke, 1994).[8] It was estimated that on half of the UAA in the FRG (7 million ha) farm structures were so poor that they did not allow efficient farming, and it was argued that in these areas *Flurbereinigung* would be necessary (Kluge, 1989a). About 400 000 farms could not operate efficiently because of awkward field distribution and sizes, and because of infrastructural problems (such as lack of access to fields; fields too narrow for machinery; village roads unsuited for manoeuvring heavy farm machinery). However, there were large regional disparities in terms of the need for *Flurbereinigung*. The northern region of Schleswig-Holstein, for example, only required land consolidation on 13 per cent of its agricultural area due to the large holdings resulting from undivided land inheritance, while in Baden-Württemberg – characterised by partible inheritance – almost three-quarters of the land was in need of consolidation (see Maps 2.4 and 2.5). As a result, there were also large discrepancies in terms of total consolidated area between the *Länder*, with Bayern, Nordrhein-Westfalen and Baden-Württemberg together containing almost two-thirds of the consolidated land between 1953 and 1979 (Table 2.7). While the main aim of land consolidation in the north was to create new infrastructure and drainage, the main focus in the south was enlargement and amalgamation of holdings and the restructuring of villages.

Table 2.7   Land consolidation in different *Länder*, 1953–79

Region	Agricultural area consolidated (1000 ha)	Total consolidated area (%)
Bayern	2306	32
Nordrhein-Westfalen	1110	15
Baden-Württemberg	984	14
Rheinland-Pfalz	782	11
Hessen	763	10
Schleswig-Holstein	635	8.7
Niedersachsen	627	8.5
Saarland	60	0.8
Total 1953–79	7267	100

Sources: *Agrarbericht* (1981); Kluge (1989a).

Lübke argued that only farms over 50 ha offered most scope for adaptation to market fluctuations and local conditions, and one of the aims of his plan was to encourage the creation of as many larger farm units as possible. However, different *Länder* had different views as to what constituted an optimum farm size. For instance, 12 ha was suggested as optimal in Rheinland-Pfalz, characterised by small-scale mixed farming, while in Schleswig-Holstein, characterised by large-scale arable farming, it was 75 ha. In addition, and in line with changes in the global political economy of farming (Markovits, 1982; Guerrieri and Padoan, 1989), between 1949 and 1990 the suggested 'optimum' farm size in the FRG was continuously raised. As a result, areas that had been consolidated during the 1950s and 1960s, resulting in still relatively small farm sizes, often had to be reconsolidated in the 1970s and 1980s. For example, during land consolidation projects in the 1960s an average of only 1.5 ha was added per consolidated farm, an increase which soon proved too small (Schmitt, 1990). Yet, discussions about the optimum farm size have continued unabated to this day without resolution, and have been given renewed impetus since reunification because of the great discrepancies in average farm sizes between the former FRG and GDR (Balmann, 1994; Bernhardt, 1995; see also Chapter 4).

Land consolidation projects normally consisted of three distinctive phases including an initial phase (three to four years) that involved preliminary planning of road and drainage networks, evaluation of land quality and, since the late 1970s, also associated landscape conservation proposals. Land quality assessment was particularly important, as a main aim of the policy was to procure land of 'equal value' and 'equal soil conditions' to participating farmers after *Flurbereinigung*. The second phase (up to seven years) included the construction of community and public projects and the distribution of the newly consolidated land to landowners (including grants to encourage farmers to relocate their farms outside villages). The final phase (three to seven years) covered completion of other construction work, the finalising of legal agreements, the amending of land records and maps, and the solving of outstanding community-related problems (Ehlers, 1988; Henkel, 1993). Completed land consolidation projects peaked during the mid-1960s, although real term expenditure peaked later during the early 1980s due to continuously rising costs (Table 2.8). Between 1953 and 1990 over DM 26 billion (real costs based on 1990) were spent on *Flurbereinigung* (*Agrarbericht*, 1991). *Flurbereinigung* was seen as a long-term process with about 180 000 ha planned for completed consolidation per year. Between 1953 and 1964 alone, 6000 land consolidation projects had been started or completed, covering almost 3 million ha, with about 200 000 ha/year consolidated. For the 7 million ha in need of consolidation, a time period of about 40 years was envisaged. With the reconsolidation of some of the earlier consolidated areas, an additional 2 million ha had been

Table 2.8   Farm areas consolidated and real term expenditure, 1953–95

Year	Agricultural area consolidated (1000 ha)	Real term expenditure (million DM)
1953–55	537	203
1956–58	639	425
1959–61	833	1150
1962–64	862	1790
1965–67	877	2170
1968–70	857	2365
1971–73	799	2411
1974–76	692	2582
1977–79	623	2467
1980–82	554	2845
1983–85	508	2774
1986–88	387	2558
1989–91[a]	343	2518
1992–94	325	2359
1995	96	792

Note
[a]After 1990 for the whole of Germany.
Sources: *Grüner Bericht* (1956–70); *Agrarbericht* (1971–97); Kluge (1989a).

consolidated by 1995 (9 million ha total). Table 2.8 highlights that by the early 1990s *Flurbereinigung* was almost completed.

To illustrate how land consolidation has operated on the ground, Map 2.7 shows the example of *Flurbereinigung* in the village of Erdmannshausen (Baden-Württemberg). This area was characterised by partible inheritance with typical narrow and small fields (see Maps 2.3 and 2.5). Before consolidation in 1967, the average field size was only 0.14 ha, and farms were often comprised of 50 or more individual plots (see example of farm A in Map 2.7a). By the mid-1960s, the social and economic conditions of agriculture in the village had become so problematic that a reallocation of arable land and the reparcelling of individual plots became inevitable. As in many other districts characterised by narrow and highly dispersed fields, land consolidation in Erdmannshausen included the amalgamation of individual fields into larger blocks, the creation of a new road layout and new drainage systems based on the consolidated blocks, and, as in the case of farm A, relocation of farms outside the village (Map 2.7b). Simultaneously, parts of the old village centre were restructured to facilitate the movement of large machinery for farms remaining in the village, but also as part of a long-term strategy of village renewal aimed at improving the quality of village life (see Chapter 7). After 20 years of consolidation in Erdmannshausen, the end result in 1987 was a more efficient agriculture, fewer, larger and more compact farms with

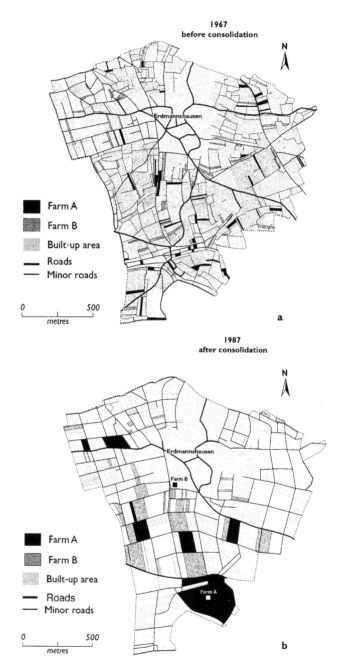

Map 2.7 Land consolidation in the village of Erdmannshausen (Baden-Württemberg) (*Source*: after Ehlers, 1988)

larger fields enabling more efficient use of machinery. The number of plots owned by farm A, for example, has been reduced from over 50 highly dispersed fields to seven larger ones.

For individual farms, *Flurbereinigung* was a long-term process that lasted up to 20 years until final completion. This meant major upheavals for rural communities over long time periods, and understandably farmers were initially sceptical.

Farmers were particularly anxious about the possibility of having new amalgamated blocks of land of inferior land quality, and officials in charge of planning the allocation of new blocks (which effectively meant swapping land between holdings) often had a difficult task matching previous land quality of a holding with the newly allocated blocks. Of crucial importance was the prevention of renewed subdivision of consolidated blocks of land. Although the practice of further subdividing fields had stopped in most regions by the end of the nineteenth century, in the early 1950s there were no legal means to prevent reparcellisation of consolidated holdings. Although legally the consolidated block could not be further subdivided, a farm comprised of several blocks (such as farm A in the above example) could still be subdivided among different heirs (Schmitt, 1996). It was attempted to prevent reparcellisation through educational programmes linked to the Land Consolidation Act, and in 1956 a comprehensive law was passed (*Grundstückverkehrsgesetz*) which gave authorities powers to promote transmission of property intact to single heirs to prevent undesirable subdivision (Cecil, 1979; Tissen, 1997). As small farms are no longer viable in economic terms, today's farmers with consolidated holdings have little interest in splitting the farm, and most consolidated holdings have been passed on intact to heirs or even enlarged in the general drive to further increase farm sizes.

As *Flurbereinigung* has continued over a period of more than 40 years, its main aims have been continuously adjusted, depending on the changing economic and political climate. Figure 2.2 highlights that between 1953 and the late 1960s the restructuring of holdings and the integration of refugees from the east into FRG agriculture were the main aims. From the late 1960s, rural community considerations became more important, highlighted by the amendment to the Land Consolidation Act in 1976 that placed more emphasis on village renewal and sustainable rural communities (see Chapter 7). From the mid-1980s, environmental considerations became increasingly important, while *Flurbereinigung* in the 1990s has been largely focused on countryside conservation issues, as structural adjustments are more or less completed (Henrichsmeyer and Witzke, 1994; Eichenauer and Joeris, 1994).

The 1955 Agriculture Act

The 1955 Agriculture Act was the second major piece of legislation initiated during the Adenauer era. Commentators have argued that the Act was 'the

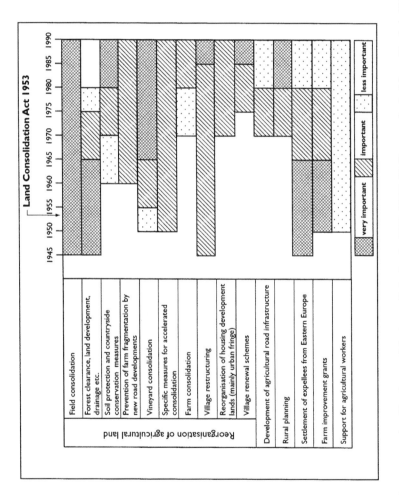

Figure 2.2 The changing goals of land consolidation policies in the FRG, 1945–90 (*Source:* adapted from Henkel, 1993)

most important single agricultural enactment of the post-war period' (Cecil, 1979, p. 50), providing the main policy framework for FRG agriculture for subsequent decades (von Urff, 1984; Born, 1995). Indeed, it still has major implications for agricultural policy-making in reunified Germany (see Chapters 4 and 6). Its main aims were: to increase agricultural productivity and efficiency; to guarantee a satisfactory standard of living for the rural population (parity principle for the farming sector); to stabilise agricultural markets; and to guarantee an adequate food supply to consumers at reasonable prices (Kluge, 1989a; Hendriks, 1991). The Act reinforced the traditional German notion of agriculture as a subsidised sector, and in the first decade after the Act about 50 per cent of all government agricultural expenditure went towards subsidising farmer incomes (Neville-Rolfe, 1984). The Act also established a framework for a comprehensive agricultural social policy which became one of the most important features of FRG agricultural policy over the next decades (see below). Another outcome of the Act was the publication of yearly agricultural reports (*Grüner Bericht*, 1956–70; *Agrarbericht* since 1971) to provide a sound statistical basis for policy evaluation and policy-making.

The implementation process of the Agriculture Act is interesting, as it stresses the relative consensus about agricultural matters between FRG political parties, and between the government and other actors involved in the policy-making process – a consensus that has shaped agricultural policy-making until 1990 and beyond. This has been reiterated by various researchers who have argued that in the FRG 'concern for the rural sector transcends party-political lines' (Hendriks, 1991, p. 139), and that during the passing of the Act, 'parliament showed, contrary to most other political decisions, political unanimity across the different parties' (Kluge, 1989a, p. 229). This was also echoed by the DBV who argued that no political party could circumvent the fact that structural problems of FRG agriculture had to be tackled head on. Although Andrlik (1981) argued that the Act could be seen as the DBV's first political success in trying to arrest the widening gap between agricultural and industrial incomes, the Agriculture Act only partly fulfilled DBV expectations. The farmers' union argued that the need to help farmers was not sufficiently rooted in law – a bone of contention that has characterised DBV–government relations ever since (Heinze and Voelzkow, 1993).

Commentators have argued that the Agriculture Act was also partly a response to increasing competition from European countries in agricultural markets, which meant that a solid policy framework was needed to support FRG agriculture. Indeed, the Act put in place mechanisms similar to those in other Western countries and was undoubtedly inspired by both the new agricultural plan for the USA and Britain's 1947 Agriculture Act (Neville-Rolfe, 1984). The protectionist nature of the FRG's Agriculture Act was a clear indication that Agriculture Minister Lübke put national interests before European interests. For instance, farm incomes were to be protected by price support, which in turn required protection from cheap imports for the FRG's main agricultural commodities, although commodities in which the FRG was less self-sufficient, such as vegetable oils, wheat and feed grains, were exempted from import controls. As Kluge (1989a, p. 238) argues, FRG agricultural policies in the 1950s were 'less interested in future European issues than in actual German interests'. Consequently, the Act set the general framework for subsequent FRG demands for high commodity prices within the CAP (Tangermann, 1982; see Chapter 3).

The agricultural budget was greatly increased, and between 1956 and 1968, for example, the yearly expenditure on agriculture increased fivefold. Massive subsidisation went into the mechanisation of farms to increase productivity. The Act also provided the basis for pension contributions by the state to farmers, which made it easier for older farmers to leave agriculture (especially during the economic boom period of the late 1950s and 1960s), and facilitated the expansion of farm units into economically more viable holdings. This paved the way for agricultural social policy in the FRG (established in 1957) – an important milestone in FRG agricultural policy-making, as social payments became the largest part of income support for FRG farmers after 1970 (see below).

The Act also enabled the allocation of government funds to lagging agricultural areas in the FRG (including parts of Bayern, Rheinland-Pfalz and Saarland, and many *Zonenrandgebiete* near the border to the GDR because of their peripheral location – see Section 7.4.2). Thus, between 1961 and 1967 about DM 700 million were provided for irrigation, drainage, new access roads or electrification of remote rural districts.[9] Most of the allocated funds went into structural programmes to keep part-time farmers on the land (Zurek, 1986), in close coordination with financial support for small industries in marginal areas which gave vital opportunities for off-farm employment. The latter was particularly important during the 1950s and 1960s when there were more part-time and side-line farmers than full-time farmers (see Table 2.3). The Agriculture Act saw a stable part-time farming culture as a key towards keeping rural communities alive (*Grüner Bericht*, 1958).

Although a main aim of the Act was to keep farmers on the land, it soon became obvious that agricultural structural change could not be controlled, let alone stopped. However, it had always been evident that increasing the efficiency of FRG agriculture could only be done by enlarging holdings, and by the late 1950s it was already evident that agricultural productivity had increased (*Grüner Bericht*, 1961). As Kluge (1989a) has argued, the main aim of the Act was to *control* the tide of people leaving agriculture, not to *prevent* it. Yet, the main opposition party (SPD) criticised the rapid structural change that was taking place, despite instruments put in place to stem depopulation of rural areas. This emphasises the policy dilemma that the government faced of, on the one hand, keeping farmers on the land to maintain rural communities, and, on the other hand, improving the efficiency of holdings through structural change which entailed many people leaving farming.

Policy impacts in a socio-political context

The wider impacts of both the 1953 Land Consolidation Act and the 1955 Agriculture Act can only be fully understood when other aspects of the FRG economy in the late 1950s and early 1960s are considered. Thus, policies under the Lübke Plan were greatly aided by wider changes in the FRG political economy (Haase, 1983; Neville-Rolfe, 1984). For example, by providing ample job opportunities for farmers wishing to leave the land (or wishing to continue with part-time farming) the economic miracle helped reduce farm numbers from 1.65 to 1.3 million between 1949 and 1963 – with the concurrent increase in average farm sizes from 8.1 to almost 10 ha during that period (see Table 2.1 above). As a result, 40 per cent of the people working in agriculture in 1949 had left the sector by 1963 (Röhm, 1964; Neander, 1983). Government policies expressed through the Agriculture Act were continued when Agriculture Minister Schwarz (1959–65) took over from Lübke. Schwarz had worked in the DBV and was 'a farmer at heart' (Hendriks, 1991, p. 96). Schwarz's appointment coincided with that of the new president of the DBV, Rehwinkel, who demanded the continuation of price support policies and more support for small farmers. Adenauer (re-elected in 1961), therefore, continued the same course on agricultural policies as before, emphasising the family farm as the model for FRG agriculture and advocating continued high prices for agricultural products to bolster agricultural incomes (Brandkamp, 1982).

However, the formation of the EEC in 1957 and the commitment to develop a common agricultural policy highlighted the agricultural structural and policy differences between the FRG and other EEC member states. The government was forced to acknowledge that if FRG farmers were to compete in the European market then structural change was inevitable. Agricultural structural change was now openly encouraged, had developed its own dynamics, and a certain threshold size for farms was suggested below which holdings were not seen to be viable (*Grenzbetriebe*). On these holdings, farmers were actively encouraged to either sell the farm or expand.

For some influential actors this incremental shift in policy thinking did not go far enough, and by the early 1960s criticisms of government structural policies increased among certain sectors of the policy-making community. In 1962, for example, a report by a group of university professors (*Professorengutachten*) openly criticised the half-hearted government measures at restructuring agriculture (Weinstock, 1987; Hendriks, 1991). They warned that FRG agriculture would never be competitive if current structures were not radically transformed. They demanded radical changes to existing social and structural policies to enable more farmers to leave agriculture and to allow remaining farmers to expand their holdings. Most controversially, they suggested that agricultural commodity prices had to come down in the long term if FRG agriculture was to compete on world markets. The strengthened SPD opposition party reiterated some of the arguments expressed in the *Professorengutachten* and particularly criticised the failure of price policy to raise farm incomes. Yet, any suggestion of price cuts was heavily criticised by the DBV, and 8000 farmers protested in Göttingen (the university town where the *Professorengutachten* had been published) against the report (Neville-Rolfe, 1984). Farmers were actively supported by Agriculture Minister Schwarz and the CDU government, and in the end the 'moderate' government line was pushed through. Yet, the *Professorengutachten* had a lasting impact, as it marked both the start of a general debate about the trajectories of FRG agricultural policy that was to intensify over the next years within the context of the CAP (see below and Chapter 3) and the beginning of tensions between one section of the academic community (particularly agricultural economists advocating free-market policies) and the government (Tangermann, 1997).

Against the background of these emerging tensions, the success of the agricultural structural policies put forward by the CDU/FDP coalition under Adenauer has been evaluated in different ways. While Kluge (1989a) put forward a pro-government argument that focused on the major achievements in a country still ravaged by the legacy of the Second World War, Tangermann (1982) described the general mood of the 1950s and early 1960s as inherently conservative. Tangermann argued that during the 1950s the difficulties of the farming sector were seen in a static context, despite the dynamic changes that took place. Although in the late 1950s the government began to question the primacy of the family farm model, the main philosophy embodied in the Agriculture Act still advocated that every farmer had a right to remain a farmer and to be supported by public policy, whatever the viability of the holding. Thus, neither politicians nor the DBV would acknowledge that only by politically 'sacrificing' the least economically viable section of the farming community could FRG agriculture become more competitive and efficient. These tensions increasingly characterised the policy debates in the following decades.

2.4.2   1963–69: agricultural structural policies under changing political conditions

In 1963, Chancellor Erhard took over the CDU/FDP coalition government from Adenauer. Erhard's approach to FRG agriculture did not differ substantially from his predecessor, and he continued Adenauer's agricultural policy of emphasising the importance of the family farm and aiming to keep as many people working in agriculture as possible. Yet, the coalition government under Erhard had to face new challenges. By 1963, agricultural structural change had generated its own dynamics, and the government had to acknowledge that agricultural policies could only *influence*, but not *control*, the course of change. Agricultural structural change was more affected by wider changes in the FRG economy than by government policies. By the mid-1960s, the FRG was experiencing its first economic crisis, and the recession slowed down the pace of agricultural change, irrespective of the policies associated with the Agriculture Act (see Table 2.1). The period between 1965 and 1969 was also marked by relative political instability compared to the stability of the previous Adenauer era. In 1965, Erhard was re-elected in a new CDU/FDP coalition (Erhard had taken over in 1963 before the end of Adenauer's official term), but was forced to resign in 1966, when the CDU agreed to a 'big coalition' government with the SPD under Kiesinger, which lasted until 1969 (Larres and Panayi, 1996; see Table 1.2). Moreover, the 1960s also saw the 'Europeanisation' of agricultural policy with the formation and implementation of the CAP (see Chapter 3), although structural policy remained a national concern.

Höcherl succeeded Schwarz as the minister for agriculture from 1965 to 1969. He was the first agriculture minister without any links to the DBV (Neander, 1999) and was, therefore, in a position to implement more 'radical' agricultural policies than his predecessors. Yet, challenging, or even continuing, established structural policies was made more difficult during the first recession between 1966 and 1968, as less money could be spent on structural adjustment (*Grüner Bericht*, 1969). Indeed, 'there were increasing signs that agriculture could no longer count on increased payments from the government' (Kluge, 1989b, p. 49). The emerging changes in policy direction sparked one of the most interesting periods of conflict in FRG agricultural policy history. For the first time, the DBV heavily criticised the government line and threatened political defection at a time when FRG politics were already in relative turmoil. The DBV, therefore, became a key actor in the policy-making process of the late 1960s. It is important to re-emphasise that from its inception in 1948, the DBV had traditionally been a strong backer of the CDU, and that the farmers' vote had been taken for granted by previous CDU governments (Ackermann, 1970; Heinze and Voelzkow, 1993). During the 1965 election most farmers voted for the CDU, but in the late 1960s they started supporting the SPD (which shared power with the CDU between 1966 and 1969) in the hope of obtaining renewed government backing of price support. The SPD exploited the potential defection of over 2 million agricultural voters in 1969 by tempting farmers with promises to provide more money for farmers wishing to retire or leave agriculture. By 1968, the SPD had launched a policy which made an effective appeal to farmers by emphasising the importance of maintaining agricultural structures (Haushofer, 1983). In 1969, a new SPD/FDP coalition won the election with the tightest of majorities, highlighting the power that the DBV had in influencing election outcomes at the time.

2.4.3 1969–82: the SPD/FDP coalition and the policy of selective subsidisation

Agricultural policies under the SPD/FDP coalition with chancellors Brandt (1969–74) and Schmidt (1974–82), and under Ertl as the new agriculture minister from the FDP (1969–83), were marked by major changes in policy thinking. Under Ertl it was openly acknowledged that FRG farming structures had to be drastically changed at the expense of many of its farmers. This change in rhetoric can be explained both by the more free-market economic philosophy of the FDP, but also by growing emphasis on farm structural improvement at the European level, following the publication of the Mansholt Plan in 1968 (see Section 3.4). The government initiated a new set of policies aimed at increasing the efficiency of FRG farming, including the Market Structure Act (*Marktstrukturgesetz*) that aimed at improving the cooperation of farms for the marketing of products. At the heart of this new policy were producer groups of at least seven farms which would receive government subsidies for improved cooperation (such as more efficient sharing of farm machinery), and for the joint marketing of specific products. As a result, by the 1980s, about one-fifth of all FRG farmers were part of a production organisation, a factor which has been hailed as one of the great successes of the Ertl administration (Kluge, 1989b).

Another key policy established under the new government was the 'common task for improving agricultural structures and coastal protection' (*Gemeinschaftsaufgabe Verbesserung der Agrarstruktur und des Küstenschutzes* or GAK), which provided not only an important framework for policy coordination and joint funding between the *Länder* and federal government, but also became increasingly important as a framework for countryside protection in the late 1980s and 1990s (Kluge, 1989b; Höll and von Meyer, 1996; see Chapters 6 and 7). Before implementation of the GAK, agricultural structural policy had been assigned to the *Länder* through the constitution of 1949, but it was increasingly felt that a common planning framework was needed to ensure an adequate financial contribution to structural policies from the federal level (Henrichsmeyer and Witzke, 1994). From 1973, the GAK became the main mechanism for implementing agricultural structural policy such as land consolidation, farm investment policies, the improvement of market structures, and later on for the implementation (at least in parts) of AEPs (see Chapter 6). In 1973, DM 2 billion of federal funding were already provided through the GAK, over 50 per cent of which went into land consolidation measures on the basis of the 1955 Land Consolidation Act (see Section 2.4.1). By 1980, federal expenditure through the GAK had reached DM 10 billion, half of which was spent on land consolidation, village renewal schemes and water management projects (all projects with 60 per cent federal contribution). The GAK also coordinated regional programmes that aimed at improving structures and lifestyles of rural communities in marginal agricultural areas such as the *Emslandprogramm* in the north-west (for drainage), and the *Alpenplan* in the south (encouragement of farming in upland areas).

The 1970 Ertl Plan

In 1970, Ertl announced the most radical reform to FRG agricultural policies since 1949 with the 'Ertl Plan' (*Einzelbetriebliches Förderungs- und Soziales Ergänzungsprogramm*). Following the political turmoil preceding the 1969 elections (see above), Ertl feared social erosion in rural areas if agriculture was not helped by the state to a greater extent (Ertl, 1985). Ertl was a farmer (again from Bayern like many other agriculture ministers) and had a diploma in agriculture and could, therefore, make ample use of his own farming experience in policy-making decisions. The SPD government placed greater emphasis on structural policy than previous CDU governments, and saw itself on a mission (influenced by socialist ideas) to improve the standard of living in rural areas (Hendriks, 1991). The SPD had also been forced to adopt a lenient line towards Ertl's FDP-backed proposals, as the FDP had made it clear during elections in 1969 that the SPD would have to make concessions if they wanted the backing of the FDP as a coalition partner. This view is also supported by Andrlik (1981, p. 108) who argued that the FDP was almost always able 'to place itself in a unique position from where it could influence [agricultural] policies to a much greater extent than a party of its size normally would have been able to do'. Through his plan, Ertl aimed to use structural policy to promote farm enlargement as well as modernisation. However, his plan also placed emphasis on social concerns, exemplified by the fact that the Ertl Plan put into place a set of policies aimed for the first time at improving the situation of farm women (Pfeffer, 1989a; Schmitt, 1994).

The Ertl Plan was based on the notion of 'more money for fewer farmers – fewer farmers, more food', and Ertl himself described his policy as a 'policy for rural areas' rather than just a 'policy for agriculture' (Ertl, 1980, 1985, 1988). It marked a policy shift away from high subsidies for many farmers, towards acknowledging that agriculture could only remain viable with fewer and larger farms. A new programme of investment aid for individual farms (*Einzelbetriebliches Förderungsprogramm*) restricted investment aids to farms that could compete successfully with other non-farm economic activities (Köster and Tangermann, 1977; Tangermann, 1982). Through the establishment of an eligibility threshold for subsidies, Ertl effectively singled out farms regarded as viable and capable of further development. Only farms capable of generating a yearly income within four years after the investment of at least DM 16000/labour unit (or DM 24000/farm) would be eligible for any investment subsidies. Farmers below this threshold would receive only interim help to tide them over until they either completely left agriculture or made their holdings more efficient (Cecil, 1979). As a result, about 50000 farms were supported through direct investment subsidies between 1971 and 1980, representing only about 10 per cent of all FRG farmers (*Agrarbericht*, 1981). To support farmers deciding to leave the land, new social measures were initiated, including improved education opportunities and subsidies for taking up new employment. Concessions were also made for agriculturally marginal areas, and during the 1970s some 100 000 farmers in mountainous areas received an average of DM 1300 per year in direct income aid – a crucial sum which helped many upland farmers to stay in farming. The Ertl Plan of selective subsidisation and income aid for farmers in marginal areas needs to be viewed in the context of discussions over structural policy at EEC level (see Section 3.4). Both measures were later incorporated into the CAP as structural measures, enabling some joint funding from the EAGGF. The latter policy was incorporated into the Less Favoured Area (LFA) scheme in 1975. In 1988, 19.9 per cent of all FRG farmers were in designated LFAs (Fennell, 1997).

The Ertl Plan marked a change from the policy trajectories of the 1960s. It moved away from Adenauer's and Erhard's broad-brush subsidisation of family farms towards a more targeted approach that blatantly excluded a large sector of the farming community from investment aid. Inevitably, such a radical policy shift caused a major uproar among the DBV and the wider farming community.

Ertl's agricultural policies and the DBV

Initially, the general philosophy behind the Ertl Plan had been supported by the DBV who acknowledged that FRG farming was increasingly lagging behind other Western European countries due to agricultural structural deficiencies. Similar to the debates on the introduction of the Lübke Plan in 1953 (see above), the DBV also agreed that the government had to put more effort into helping farms to become more efficient. However, initially the DBV strongly opposed selective subsidisation (Andrlik, 1981), criticised the rigid approach adopted by Ertl, and asked for more flexibility.[10]

At this point it is important to return to the role of the DBV in agricultural policy-making. One of the features of the DBV has been that it has managed throughout the FRG period (and beyond; see Chapter 4) to maintain a powerful political influence over agricultural policies, despite its declining membership base (Neville-Rolfe, 1984; Heinze and Voelzkow, 1993). Hendriks (1991, p. 148) argued that this situation is not uncommon in Western European countries, and the more farming becomes a minority occupation 'the more determined are the attempts by the rural population and its representatives to increase the ideological importance of the agricultural sector'. Continuing DBV power was linked to both the fact that it had the monopoly over the farm media (weekly agricultural journals and the monthly periodical *Deutsche Bauernkorrespondenz*; cf. McHenry, 1996) and that it continued to derive importance from the delicate balance between parties in a political system relying on coalition partners, although its support has always been based in the CDU and CSU parties. However, in the face of falling membership, the DBV has had to make concessions on policy issues, particularly during periods of SPD-led governments. Thus, although the DBV lobbied strongly during the 1970s against Ertl's selective subsidisation policy, it was hindered by the fact that the SPD was in power (Sontowski, 1990; Henrichsmeyer and Witzke, 1994). When Ertl officially challenged the traditional support for family farms, the DBV was not in a position to oppose him. Confronted with resistance to its costly protectionist agricultural policy, the DBV felt urged to modify both its strategy and discourse in the early 1970s (Tangermann, 1982; Heinze and Voelzkow, 1993).

Agricultural policy-making and changes in policy emphasis in the FRG have often been associated with changes in key actors. Indeed, one reason for the 'conservatism' of FRG agricultural policy could be the longevity of key agricultural policy actors (Hoggart *et al.*, 1995). Thus, the shift in the DBV's policy position in the early 1970s was partly linked to its new leadership. The new DBV president von Heereman (considered as moderate in policy circles) broke the taboo on structural change and, although not agreeing with the Ertl Plan of selective subsidisation, was willing to reconsider DBV policy priorities. Von Heereman remained leader of the DBV from 1970 to 1997 and was, therefore, an important long-term influence in agricultural policy-making in both the FRG and reunified Germany (Heinze and Voelzkow, 1993; Krause, 1997). The DBV has successfully managed to maintain its influential political position, but DBV power has largely depended on how much it has been able to influence agriculture ministers. The Ertl era (1969–83), in particular, was characterised by a powerful agriculture minister who allowed little interference by the DBV in policy decisions – a factor that may also explain why the radical Ertl Plan could be implemented at all (Neander, 1997; Klare, 1997). Ertl's political background was deeply rooted in the liberal FDP which has arguably been less farmer-friendly than the CDU/CSU and, therefore, less in tune with demands from the DBV (Ertl, 1985; Priebe, 1985). On the other hand, two of the subsequent three agriculture ministers, Kiechle (1983–93) and Borchert (1993–98), have come from the CDU/CSU and have, therefore, been more closely in line with the general DBV position (see Chapters 3 and 4).[11]

By 1970, it was clear to the DBV that it could not demand a return to the protectionist strategies of the 1950s and 1960s, particularly as market policy was now decided at European level through the CAP (Köster and Tangermann, 1977; see Chapter 3). The DBV was therefore caught in a dilemma not dissimilar to that faced by the government. On the one hand, it had to continue price policy demands to appease farmers but, on the other hand, it also had to respond to the challenge of accelerating structural change by accepting structural policy measures such as the Ertl Plan. The DBV, therefore, had to reluctantly accept a reduction in the number of farms and a decline in employment in agriculture, and consequently the erosion of its own membership base – issues that have influenced DBV agricultural policies throughout the 1970s and 1980s (Sontowski, 1990).

The Ertl Plan in a wider context

Although it marked a radical shift in policy priorities, the implementation of the Ertl Plan was marred by wider changes in the political economy of the FRG during the 1970s and early 1980s. Many commentators argued that the planned changes came too late, and FRG agriculture in the early 1970s was described by some as being at the 'brink of catastrophe' (for instance, Andrlik, 1981; Kluge, 1989a). In 1971, 50 000 farmers protested against policies that had failed to bridge income gaps between farming and other professions in one of the biggest demonstrations of post-war FRG. Ertl attempted to defuse the situation by arguing that compared to the situation in the GDR (see Chapter 4), farmers in the FRG were not that badly off – an indication that at times of crisis the comparison between the FRG and the GDR was often invoked to defend government policies. The main bone of contention continued to be Ertl's eligibility threshold for subsidies. The exact level of the threshold was continuously debated during the early 1970s, and due to pressure from the DBV (but also from among the ranks of the SPD/FDP coalition) Ertl changed the criteria in 1972 from one based on farm labour income to one based on net farm profit (which made more farms eligible). To be eligible for investment subsidies, farmers now had to prove that within four years they could generate more profit than before, with some leeway for farms in LFAs. For eligible farms, the investment subsidy amounted to DM 15500/labour unit/year and DM 23 250/farm/year (Kluge, 1989b). This was a considerable sum which could define the difference between farm survival and abandonment, especially for holdings near the eligibility threshold.

The Ertl Plan was implemented at a time of particularly rapid agricultural structural change. As Table 2.1 shows, the highest ever reduction in the number of farms occurred between 1969 and 1970 (–6.4 per cent), and the decline was highest in regions with the worst agricultural structural problems such as Baden-Württemberg. This was a reflection of both improved policies enabling farmers to leave their farms and good job opportunities for farmers outside agriculture. Policies, therefore, helped structural change, but wider economic changes also explain the accelerating or slowing of structural change at different times (Markovits, 1982; Guerrieri and Padoan, 1989). Yet, despite the rapid reduction in the number of farms and increasing average farm sizes (from 11.7 to 12.7 ha between 1970 and 1972), the Ertl Plan could not prevent farm incomes from further lagging behind other incomes – particularly for small farms with less than 20 ha where incomes were below 40 per cent of the national wage average[12] (*Agrarbericht*, 1973).

By 1972, the SPD/FDP coalition was at the verge of breakdown, and the political crisis led to early elections which, nonetheless, the SPD/FDP coalition won (Larres and Panayi, 1996). The DBV used the crisis to press for new medium-term policies to tackle agricultural and rural problems, and their manifesto became an important election issue – re-emphasising the continuing power of the DBV as a political force despite dwindling farm numbers. For political reasons, Ertl generally accepted the views of the DBV, a factor which some commentators have argued may have won the election for the SPD/FDP coalition (Kluge, 1989b; Hendriks, 1991). Although most farmers voted for the CDU (swinging back from the 1969 election to their 'traditional' party), the CDU lost many votes in rural areas, and the SPD became the largest party with 46 per cent of the vote (Kluge, 1989a; Larres and Panayi, 1996). The SPD saw the election result as a confirmation of their agricultural policies, and after re-election Ertl saw no reason for change.

Ertl was, however, faced with new challenges following the 1973 oil crisis. The rapidly rising oil price meant increases in costs for FRG agriculture which could not be sufficiently compensated by the government. In addition, the slow-down in the economy as a result of the oil price shock meant that opportunities for off-farm employment in industry were reduced, which substantially slowed the pace of agricultural structural change (particularly between 1973 and 1976; see Table 2.1). Yet, Ertl stuck to his policy course of selective subsidisation, although more financial support was now given to part-time farmers who, together with side-line farmers, comprised 55 per cent of all FRG farmers in 1975 (see Table 2.3). Yet, debates continued as to whether part-time farming should be seen as a permanent situation, and should therefore be subsidised, or whether it should be regarded as a transition towards either full-time farming on consolidated holdings or complete farm abandonment.

The year 1974 was marked by further political turmoil and the resignation of Brandt who was replaced by Schmidt in a continuation of the SPD/FDP coalition (until 1982). Ertl continued as the agriculture minister, indicating both that the government still backed the Ertl Plan and that Schmidt was as anxious as his predecessor to put policies in place that would accelerate agricultural structural change and increase the efficiency of FRG farming (Sauer, 1990; Henrichsmeyer and Witzke, 1994). At the same time, and due to the worsening economic recession, the SPD had to introduce agricultural budget cuts (*Agrarbericht*, 1975; Friedrich, 1975). As a result, the DBV became increasingly anxious about the agricultural policies of the SPD government, and von Heereman began to openly criticise the rigid government line. Partly as a result of the increasingly conflictual situation between the DBV and the government, the CDU benefited from electoral gains during regional parliamentary elections, and by 1975 most farmers had shifted back to supporting the CDU. The CDU saw this partly as a confirmation of its agricultural policies that continued to emphasise the importance of the family farm, and also as a challenge to the selective subsidisation policy. The CDU criticised the *Agrarbericht* of 1975 and called it a 'document epitomising the failure of the federal government' (Kluge, 1989b, p. 205). Indeed, Ertl had to concede that income disparities between farmers and other professions had still not been successfully tackled.[13] It also became obvious that Ertl's structural policy had not had satisfactory results, despite increases in the GAK budget. By 1975, GAK payments were in the order of DM 2.2 billion, with about a quarter spent on consolidation projects and DM 350 million spent on selective subsidisation. Most of the GAK payments went to the south of the FRG which had the poorest agricultural structures (particularly Bayern and Baden-Württemberg) (*Agrarbericht*, 1976).

Selective subsidisation for only a small fraction of farms was continuously criticised by the DBV, in particular as larger holdings in the north of the FRG (see Map 2.5) benefited disproportionately. The DBV also argued that too many medium-sized holdings were excluded from the subsidies, and it demanded more flexible threshold rules. As on many other occasions, the DBV referred to the principles outlined in the 1955 Agriculture Act and to the 'duty' of the FRG government to guarantee an adequate income to *all* farmers. Von Heereman argued that 'those in charge have politically dismantled the Agriculture Act and have betrayed its spirit' (Kluge, 1989b, p. 208). The CDU was even more outspoken in its criticism and demanded the dismantling of the subsidy threshold altogether. These criticisms forced Ertl to further modify his plan in 1976, conceding that farmers who did not make the threshold could now also receive investment subsidies, and that additional money would be made available through the GAK for farmers who wanted to modernise their farms (Ertl, 1980). As a result, 20 per cent of approved credits went to farms below the threshold. Ertl, therefore, saw the threshold increasingly as a *rough guideline* rather than a *strict selection criterion* for eligible farms.

The rising importance of agricultural social policy

These concessions also have to be seen as part of an attempt by the government to improve its image vis-à-vis the farmers. The SPD/FDP coalition, therefore, advocated further support of structural change to be accompanied by improvements to social policy. As a result, social security payments to farmers and their families were increased during the 1970s (for instance, from DM 0.8 billion to 3.7 billion between 1969 and 1981). Consequently, social payments, which included health and accident insurance and a farmers' pension scheme, became the single most expensive item of the agricultural budget, while GAK payments made up a fraction of the total budget[14] (Figure 2.3).

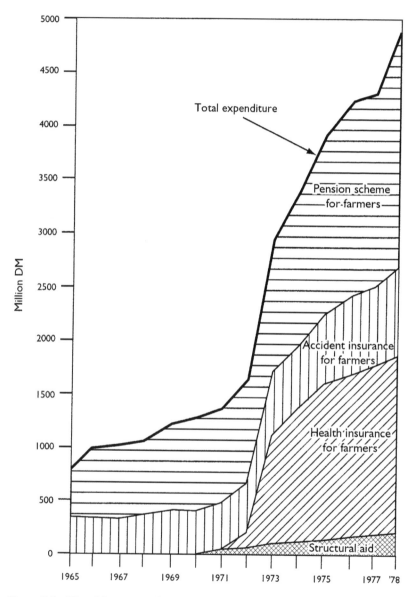

Figure 2.3   The rising cost of agricultural social policy in the FRG, 1965–1978 (*Source*: adapted from Kluge, 1989b)

Improved social payments to farmers also have to be seen as recognition by the government that agricultural policies had failed to address the problems associated with agricultural structural change (Weidner, 1979; Hagedorn, 1991). Like the DBV, the FRG government in the 1970s continued to be caught in a dilemma between the economic necessity of agricultural structural change on the one hand, and the social (and political) desire to maintain viable rural communities on the other. Improved social payments addressed both these issues. They 'lured' older farmers away from their farms by providing a safe income in old age, and through improved health and accident insurance they also provided an incentive for younger entrepreneurial farmers to stay on their farms (Ertl, 1980; Tenwinkel, 1987). By 1976, the pace of structural change was at its lowest since the first economic crisis in the late 1960s (see Table 2.1), partly due to wider economic factors leading to reduced off-farm employment opportunities, but also because more farmers were now willing to continue with farming due to improvements in social policies. This meant that structural change was now mainly occurring through older farmers retiring, rather than through younger farmers giving up agriculture and seeking employment elsewhere.[15]

Moves by the SPD/FDP government to increase the 'feel good factor' for farmers through improved social payments during the mid-1970s were politically motivated. Better social security for farmers was seen by the government as a way to appease farmers during the 1976 elections, and agricultural policy again became an electoral issue (Schöneweiß, 1984; Kluge, 1989b). The SPD was particularly aware that it had been weakened by recent regional elections where many farmers had switched back to the CDU. Yet, by 1976 Ertl could count on two positive points that had emerged from his policies. First, based on an international survey carried out at the time (cf. *Agrarbericht*, 1978), FRG farmers were considered as the most advanced in terms of mechanisation in the EEC and, secondly, FRG agricultural policies were also described as 'innovative', not only in the area of structural policy, but also concerning countryside conservation (see Chapter 6). Despite the DBV's criticisms of Ertl's selective subsidisation strategy, it agreed with the general policy trajectory adopted by Ertl. The DBV, therefore, decided to remain 'relatively quiet' during the elections. That the SPD/FDP coalition emerged as the winners (albeit by a slim majority of only four mandates) partly reflected the general support of Ertl's income policies by the farmers.

Policy cul-de-sac

Discussions on the 'ideal' economic unit continued unabated in the late 1970s. FRG agriculture was still characterised by many small farms (over 400 000 under 10 ha in 1979) and a few efficient and productive large farms (only 4300 farms over 100 ha), while Ertl's subsidy threshold was 'somewhere in the middle', having been substantially watered down. Although the government continued to encourage farmers below the subsidy threshold to leave their farms, the economy increasingly struggled to absorb people leaving agriculture. In the late 1970s, the unemployment rate stood at a record post-war high of 5 per cent (compared to only about 0.5 per cent during most of the 1960s), and it became increasingly apparent that the future of a structurally sound agriculture relied on the performance of other economic sectors. Agricultural structural change was, therefore, increasingly dependent on the performance of the FRG economy.

By 1980, after almost a decade of structural and social policies related to the Ertl Plan, the government had to face the reality that many of its initial promises – particularly that of raising farmers' incomes – had not been fulfilled (Henrichsmeyer, 1986; von Urff and von Meyer, 1987). In particular, the government was criticised by the DBV for the growing income differential between large and small farms. While in 1980 the top quarter of farms (average size 40 ha) earned DM 70 000/farm, the bottom quarter (less than 10 ha) earned only DM 12 000/farm (less than half the average FRG farm income of DM 25 000) (Kluge, 1989b). Ertl admitted that especially for the bottom quarter of farms (still about 200 000 holdings in 1980) structural policies, together with the protectionist high commodity price policy that had been in place since 1949, had failed to provide farmers with sufficient income (Neander, 1983). He also conceded that the exclusion of small farms from investment subsidies was morally wrong (Ertl, 1988) and suggested that social policy should be increasingly used as a way to grant farmers compensation for income losses (see Figure 2.3). Yet, he continued to argue that a satisfactory income could not be guaranteed for all holdings, and that the only solution was to focus on viable farms through selective subsidisation. He therefore argued that the government should continue to press for policies encouraging agricultural structural change, as long as this change occurred gradually and without social hardship.

Despite these debates, agricultural policy was not a major political issue for the SPD-led government (Hendriks, 1991). The early 1980s in particular were marked by wider geopolitical tensions between the FRG and the USA – especially over the issue of whether to allow the stationing of nuclear missiles on FRG territory which led to the eventual downfall of the Schmidt government – compared to which agricultural issues seemed largely irrelevant. The result was that during the 1980 general election campaign, the CDU tactically exploited the government's failure to raise farm incomes, although this issue assumed less importance in the election outcome (another victory for the SPD/FDP coalition) than other political issues not related to agriculture. In addition, not all farmers were unhappy with what Ertl had achieved. Large farms in the northern regions of Niedersachsen and Schleswig-Holstein (see Map 2.4), for example, continued to support the SPD/FDP coalition, as they had benefited disproportionately from Ertl's selective subsidisation (Kluge, 1989b). Further, and as Figure 2.3 has high-lighted, by 1980 most farmers had begun to benefit from generous social payments, a factor that contributed greatly to the fact that the DBV – as during the previous election – did not greatly challenge the government line on agricultural policies.

Yet, by the early 1980s Ertl was increasingly concerned about the slowing pace of agricultural structural change. Renewed oil price rises led to a further slowing of the economy, which led to further reductions in employment opportunities for farmers outside agriculture. Many farmers were in a precarious financial situation (*Agrarbericht*, 1983, 1984), and in 1981 farm incomes stagnated or declined. The situation for farmers was made worse by further cutbacks in the agricultural budget, including the GAK, and by fears that social payments might also be cut due to runaway costs (a fear that never materialised). By 1982, FRG agricultural policy was in a cul-de-sac. Policy-makers were increasingly caught in a web of deepening economic recession and disillusionment about the lack of progress in improving the structural and economic situation of FRG farms (Neander, 1983) – a difficult legacy that had to be tackled head on by the new government coalition.

2.4.4 The Kohl era: back to family farm values?

In 1982, tensions between the coalition partners of the SPD and FDP came to a head, and resulted in a vote of no confidence in Chancellor Schmidt (Larres and Panayi, 1996). Kohl was elected as the head of a new CDU/FDP government,[16] but differences over agricultural matters had played virtually no part in the eventual break-up of the coalition (Neville-Rolfe, 1984). As a result of the 'defection' of the FDP to the right, Ertl resigned his position a year later and was replaced by Kiechle (1983–93), who was also in charge of supervising the transition of agricultural policy in reunified Germany after 1990 (see Chapter 4).

New challenges for agricultural policies

Kohl continued the cautious approach to agricultural expenditure that had marked the final years of the SPD/FDP government, and by cutting the 1983 budget by 2.4 per cent he attempted to reduce the soaring social costs that by now made up most of the agricultural budget (see Figure 2.3). Kiechle had to face challenges which differed substantially from the situation Ertl had encountered (Kiechle, 1985). Many have argued, therefore, that, right from the start, Kiechle's position was difficult (for instance, Kluge, 1989b; Hendriks, 1991). Not only did he have to address the increasingly divergent income situation of farmers and tackle the burden of rising social policy payments, he was also constrained by a deepening economic recession which allowed less flexibility on structural change and budgetary adjustments. In 1982, unemployment stood at about 1.8 million people

(7 per cent of the workforce), rising to 2.3 million by 1989 (*Der Spiegel*, 1998), which meant a reduced absorptive capacity of the FRG economy for people wishing to leave agriculture. As a result, and in sharp contrast to the 1950s and 1960s, agricultural structural change was now almost entirely driven by succession, with few farms coming onto the market. The DBV expressed grave concern about the state of FRG agriculture, arguing that while farmers had doubled production per capita between 1969 and 1983, their income had remained static. Kiechle responded by promising changes in agricultural structural policy. He re-emphasised the importance of the family farm as expressed in the 1955 Agriculture Act, and openly criticised Ertl's selective subsidisation policy.

Yet, Ertl's policy was not abandoned altogether. An eligibility threshold was maintained, but Kiechle also introduced other eligibility criteria (for instance, 'financial viability of a holding' and intangible factors such as a 'farmer's willingness to work') which would also allow smaller farms to benefit from additional government subsidies (Kiechle, 1985). Kiechle did not want an investment subsidy policy geared almost entirely towards large economic units, which would exclude most small farms from additional income. He acknowledged that, as income opportunities outside agriculture were reduced, more emphasis had to be placed on family farms – reiterating the CDU policy line of the 1950s and 1960s. Kiechle was strongly in favour of continuing – and even expanding – subsidisation of farms in LFAs, as particularly in these areas additional subsidies had proven to be a success in terms of maintaining rural populations.

Kiechle's policies were strongly influenced by wider changes in West European agriculture during the 1980s, in particular the beginnings of a shift from a productivist (maximising commodity production) to a post-productivist (farming with a view towards improved management of the countryside) farming regime (Whitby and Lowe, 1994; Baldock and Lowe, 1996; Ilbery and Bowler, 1998). In contrast to Ertl, Kiechle saw the role of structural policies as contributing towards extensification of agricultural production (Kiechle, 1986). This, of course, was a dilemma, as existing structural policies were aimed at increasing the efficiency of farming. It was only after a lengthy transition phase – still not completed in many EU countries (cf. Whitby, 1996; Buller *et al.*, 2000) – that social and agri-environmental policies have begun to replace production-oriented policies (see Chapter 6).

The Kiechle Plan

Kiechle pushed through a plan to provide improved credit facilities to farmers. In 1983, the Agricultural Credit Programme (*Agrarkreditprogramm*) was established which provided low-interest loans of up to DM 100 000 for 6–15 years for all full-time farms with (joint) incomes below the 'prosperity threshold' of DM 65 000. From 1984, an agricultural credit programme was also put in place for part-time farmers (with a threshold of DM 65 000 minus a maximum of DM 35 000 for external incomes). It is evident that the Kiechle Plan, which targeted farms *below* a certain income, was an almost complete reversal of Ertl's selective subsidisation which had targeted farms *above* a specific income. In contrast to the Ertl Plan, the Kiechle Plan was aimed less at increasing productivity, and more at maintaining farm incomes. It consequently put more emphasis on family and part-time farms (Kiechle, 1986; *Agrarbericht*, 1987). The new aim was to guarantee an adequate income to all farmers, but without increasing commodity production – echoing a shift from productivist to post-productivist agricultural policy thinking that also gradually became apparent in other European countries (Whitby and Lowe, 1994).

Kiechle abolished Ertl's subsidy threshold in 1984, which meant that more farmers were now eligible for investment subsidies. Yet, farmers below the prosperity threshold did not automatically qualify for credits, but had to provide a plan which specified how they would use the money to prove investments on the farm would be useful. As 91 per cent of the subsidies through the Kiechle Plan went to full-time farms, it suggests that many part-time farmers could not, or had no interest in, drawing up a farm improvement plan (Henrichsmeyer and Witzke, 1994). Although the Kiechle Plan placed more emphasis on including part-time farms, it still failed to deliver additional subsidies for part-time farmers who were, yet again, slipping through the 'subsidy net'. It is also important to stress the geographical implications of this turnaround in policy emphasis. The three regions of Baden-Württemberg, Niedersachsen and Hessen benefited disproportionately from the Kiechle Plan (altogether 71 per cent of all eligible holdings), highlighting that the Agricultural Credit Programme particularly benefited regions characterised by both small to medium-sized farms and part-time farmers. The north–south tensions that had been reinforced by the Ertl Plan (larger eligible farms in the north) were, therefore, partly reversed (*Agrarbericht*, 1987).

Kiechle's first years in office were also marked by renewed conflict between the agriculture ministry and academics who rekindled arguments from the *Professorengutachten* of 1962 (see Section 4.2.1). In particular, eight agricultural economists (from the Göttinger Schule) challenged the agricultural policy of the CDU. Although their criticism from a free market liberal perspective was mainly aimed at the FRG position towards the CAP in the early 1980s (see Chapter 3), they also questioned the softening of the selective subsidisation policy and criticised the Agricultural Credit Programme envisaged by Kiechle to help small farms (see below). In their eyes, FRG agriculture could only become competitive on world markets through the culling of small inefficient farms. Although the Göttinger Schule sparked a useful debate on the future trajectories of FRG agricultural policy, their arguments were again criticised from many sides. It was argued that their view was short-sighted by placing too much emphasis on the economic consequences of agricultural policy (Priebe, 1985), and that they were neglecting the social implications of removing hundreds of thousands of farmers from the land (Henrichsmeyer and Witzke, 1994). Kiechle also heavily criticised the Göttinger Schule and highlighted that social consequences of agricultural policies were at least as important as economic considerations (Kiechle, 1985, 1986). He also argued that no change in government policy was possible at a time of reduced employment opportunities outside agriculture, which effectively restricted alternative policy options.

Accompanying the Kiechle Plan was a continuous increase in agricultural budgets between 1984 and 1989 (*Agrarbericht*, 1990). Yet, only by 1985 was the same budget level reached as in 1980, emphasising the substantial budget cuts that had taken place in the last years of the Ertl administration. Consequently, Kiechle strongly criticised the budgetary 'overspending' by Ertl between 1978 and 1982. In line with the Kiechle Plan, social policy expenditure rose steadily during the 1980s. In 1984, it already amounted to DM 3.5 billion, equivalent to 60 per cent of all expenses in the agricultural budget, while the GAK share for these payments amounted to 'only' DM 1.2 billion, leaving most of the costs of social policy to the *Länder* (*Agrarbericht*, 1986; Hagedorn, 1991). Social payments were by now about three times as high as structural payments – further emphasising the policy shift away from support for structural change towards supporting farm incomes through social payments.

It is important to consider the position of the DBV and the role it may have played in influencing the Kiechle Plan. As mentioned earlier, through the continued process of structural change the DBV was continuously losing members. The number of farms had been reduced from 1.15 million at the beginning of the Ertl era in 1969 to 750 000 farms in 1983 (when Kiechle took over), a reduction of 35 per cent in only 14 years. This number was further reduced to 630 000 farms by the time of German reunification in 1990 – about half the number of farms that existed in 1969! Thus, although the DBV had managed to secure its monopoly of representation and, therefore, successfully survived the period of massive structural change, by the 1980s the DBV was a dwindling political organisation whose political influence was diminishing correspondingly (Heinze and Voelzkow, 1993). However, this dwindling political power was amply made up by the increasing confidence of its leader, von Heereman (Kluge, 1989b). By the 1980s, von Heereman (in office since 1970) had built up a considerable power base and was well networked within national and EEC agricultural policy-making circles (Krause, 1997). While von Heereman may not have been able to greatly influence Ertl during the 1970s, many commentators have argued that Kiechle, who came from the ranks of the DBV himself, 'got on quite well' with von Heereman (Klare, 1997; Mehl, 1997).

There is no doubt, therefore, that von Heereman had a substantial influence on Kiechle's policies. Kluge (1989b) even suggested that through the introduction of the Agricultural Credit Programme, Kiechle had finally yielded to long-standing demands by the DBV for broad-based subsidisation of the farming sector. The credit programme was, therefore, more akin to the long-term DBV line than the Ertl Plan. Despite the diminishing political power of the DBV, farmers still played an important role during the 1980s, particularly before federal elections (1983 and 1987). Although during the mid- to late 1980s the danger of farmers shifting their votes away from the CDU/CSU was minimal (Tenwinkel, 1987; Heinze and Voelzkow, 1993), the DBV could still exert considerable influence by threatening to abstain from voting at elections altogether. Like his predecessors, Kiechle dreaded protest actions by farmers and opted for a strategy of conflict avoidance. Thus, the Kiechle Plan has to be partly seen as a policy response to appease FRG farmers.

Structural change and social policies in the late 1980s

Despite the structural measures put in place through the Kiechle Plan to help farmers' incomes, by 1985 profit per agricultural labour unit in the FRG had decreased by another 18 per cent compared to 1984. As this marked the strongest decrease in any of the EC10 countries since the mid-1970s (Brandkamp, 1982; Kluge, 1989b), there was unanimous agreement among all political parties to further support family farms, and the Kiechle Plan was greeted with relative enthusiasm – even by the SPD and the newly established Green Party.[17] The Agricultural Credit Programme, therefore, remained the main structural and farm income policy throughout the 1980s (and beyond reunification for farms in West Germany). To some extent, the Kiechle Plan led to a slowing down of agricultural structural change (Henrichsmeyer and Witzke, 1994). Indeed, the pace of change remained stable with 'only' about 20 000 farmers leaving agriculture every year (1985–90), and with a resultant increase in average farm size from 16.6 to 18.7 ha (see Table 2.1).

Yet, the late 1980s under Kiechle were characterised by growing criticism of the rising costs of social policies. Social measures that had been put in place during the Ertl era were further supplemented by improved support for farm women and older farmers (Pfeffer, 1989a). These included increased child benefit and special pension regulations for women in 1985 (a survey had shown that one-third of all farm work was conducted by farm women), and a new policy in 1986 which provided older farmers with additional subsidies (Schmitt, 1994). On the one hand, this was a concession to the DBV to provide further financial support to small and medium-sized farms, but, on the other hand, it was also seen as a means to reduce the escalating agricultural budget through better targeting of social policy. Yet, Kiechle could not prevent the social security budget from soaring from DM 3.5 billion to

5.1 billion between 1983 and 1989 – a development that led to heated debates immediately before reunification (Kluge, 1989b; *Agrarbericht*, 1991). However, almost all these problems paled into insignificance compared to the new challenges for structural policies faced by a reunified Germany (see Chapter 4).

2.5   Conclusions

This chapter has highlighted that FRG agriculture was characterised by severe agricultural structural deficiencies, including both a prevalence of small, often fragmented, family farms (especially in the south), many of which were economically marginal, and a large proportion of part-time and side-line farmers. These structural deficiencies have been a constant challenge to policy-makers to find a way to improve farm structures, make FRG farming more competitive, but at the same time to raise average farm incomes to acceptable levels compared to other professions, and to prevent rural depopulation. Between 1949 and 1990 FRG agriculture experienced massive agricultural structural change – mainly due to economic and social factors, but also due to government policies that aimed to control and influence the process of structural change. To some extent policies have been successful, but, at times, structural change developed its own dynamics. The pace of change varied considerably, and about 1 million farmers (out of 1.65 million in 1949) had left their farms by 1990.

Six key themes emerge from the discussion. First, and arguably most importantly, the FRG faced a constant dilemma between improving the competitiveness of agriculture and supporting the welfare of the farm population. Almost independent of which government was in power, agricultural policy-makers were caught between the various interest groups lobbying for farm support or improvement of farm structures. As a result, governments had to find compromises which, until 1990 (and beyond, as Chapter 4 will highlight) have failed to significantly improve farm structures or farm incomes. While CDU-led governments before 1966 benefited from a buoyant economy that readily absorbed farmers leaving agriculture, the SPD-led governments between 1969 and 1982 had to find other means (mainly through generous social policies) to help the survival of farm families at times of economic recession, cuts in agricultural budgets, and shrinking job opportunities outside agriculture. This situation worsened during the Kohl government of the 1980s. However, although the 'family farm model' guided agricultural policy throughout this period, the policy emphasis and political discourse had changed. During the Lübke era policies aimed to support all family farms, whereas under Ertl the policy emphasis was on supporting competitive family farms. During the Kiechle era a new 'post-productivist' rhetoric started to emerge, based on the view of farmers as guardians of the countryside and producers of high-quality food.

Second, none of the policy mechanisms put into place by various FRG governments were able to adequately solve the problem of income disparities between agricultural and non-agricultural occupations, and by the end of the 1980s FRG farmers (especially full-time farmers) were worse off than ever before in relative financial terms. Although many FRG farmers were part-timers and obtained a second income from other sources, most full-time farmers in the late 1980s were disillusioned about future farming prospects. This, compounded by the challenges of German reunification in 1990, has posed the most severe challenge to agricultural policy-makers in reunified Germany in the 1990s – issues discussed in detail in Chapters 4 and 8.

Third, the territory of the FRG has been characterised by great geographical variations in terms of soil fertility, steepness of terrain and agricultural structures, with each region having its specific agricultural policy priorities, but with a general north–south divide apparent, with northern *Länder* having more favourable agricultural structures, while the bulk of small, economically marginal family farms occur in southern *Länder* (mainly due to the legacy of land inheritance laws). Yet, many agriculture ministers (for instance, Ertl, Kiechle) have been southerners and, therefore, have often lobbied for the interests of small southern farmers. The federal structure of the FRG, with individual regions with substantial policy-making powers, often exacerbated the problems of regional disparities and, at the same time, also often hampered nation-wide and effective implementation of agricultural policies.

Fourth, agricultural policy-making in the FRG occurred in a climate of political consensus between the main actors, and the major political parties (CDU, SPD, FDP and the Greens) only rarely disagreed about what directions FRG agricultural policies should take. The BML and the DBV have built up and maintained a close understanding over policy-making, although there were subtle shifts in the lobbying power of the DBV depending on whether or not agriculture ministers came from their ranks. Arguably the most confrontational situation occurred during the period of the politically liberal (FDP) Agriculture Minister Ertl (1969–83), who adopted a relatively independent policy position.

Fifth, FRG agricultural policy can only be fully understood in the context of the FRG–GDR relationship. The situation in the former GDR will be explored in detail in Chapter 4, but this chapter has already highlighted that many structural problems in the FRG emanated from the loss of its most fertile agricultural areas to the GDR (which also had some of the largest and most efficient holdings). The division of Germany also created a substantial ideological rift which influenced FRG agricultural policies. The reluctance of FRG policy-makers to initiate radical programmes of structural change and to maintain its line on the family farm model was often attributed to the 'GDR problem' where massive government-enforced restructuring and industrial agriculture based on the Soviet Union (USSR) model had brought hardship and misery to many former farm families – developments which the FRG did not want to mirror. As Chapter 4 will discuss, reunification has not only created a need for policies that address the different farm structures in the two Germanies, but also for finding ways with which to 'absorb' 40 years of socialist agricultural ideologies and to combine these with the specific FRG way of agricultural thinking.

Finally, FRG structural policies can only be understood in the wider context of the EEC (EC after 1987) and the CAP. The discussion of FRG structural policies in this chapter presents a valuable context for understanding the FRG's position towards the CAP. Building on the discussion in this chapter, Chapter 3 will analyse in more detail the FRG position within European agricultural policy-making. More specifically, it will focus on both the FRG relationship to the CAP between 1957 and 1990 and whether the FRG acted as a leader, partner or obstructor in the European agricultural policy-making process.

3
The FRG and the CAP, 1957–90: Leader, Partner or Obstructor?

3.1 Introduction

The aim of this chapter is to focus on the FRG's position within European agricultural policy-making between the formation of the EEC in 1957 and the eve of reunification in 1990. The analysis in this chapter, therefore, sets the arguments presented in Chapter 2 in a European context, by discussing how the CAP has affected agricultural development in the FRG and agricultural policy. While the focus of Chapter 2 was on farm structures, the focus of this chapter will be on market policy. A key aim of the chapter is to consider whether the FRG's position on the CAP can be classified as leader, partner or obstructor. We noted in Chapter 1 that the FRG has identified its national interest more closely with European integration than other member states, but that its position on agricultural policy has often seemed contradictory to its national interest, and we will explore this paradox more fully in this chapter. Like Chapter 2, emphasis will be placed on the role of actors in policy-making, and links between policy developments at the domestic and European levels will be drawn. The analysis is divided into five periods related to stages in the development of the CAP: negotiations before the emergence of the CAP in 1957, the FRG position in the first years of CAP development, the Mansholt Plan of the late 1960s, the challenges faced by the first CAP crisis from the late 1960s to the late 1970s, and problems related to the second CAP crisis during the 1980s.

3.2 Agricultural negotiations before 1957 and the FRG 'dilemma'

The CAP is generally seen as a policy driven by the French, as France had by far the greatest interest in establishing a common policy (France produced 40 per cent of all agricultural commodities in the EEC6 in 1957). However, the development of a European agricultural policy was seen by

FRG policy-makers as part and parcel of European integration, and as early as 1949, FRG politicians advocated a 'Europeanisation of the agricultural economy' (Kluge, 1989a). Niklas, the minister for agriculture in 1949, argued that the FRG

> would have missed the opportunity offered by this period in time if [it] were not willing to wholeheartedly embark on this one and only path for the rescue of Europe. No country in Europe is as interested in this opportunity as the FRG. This is the only way for us to regain our full position within Europe, a position which has been destroyed by unreasonable politics and the loss of the war (Kluge, 1989a, p. 77).

FRG integration into Europe was launched with the establishment of the European Coal and Steel Community between Germany and France in 1950 (Tangermann, 1992; Rhenisch, 1995; Opelland, 1996), a move which institutionalised the principle of controlling FRG economic power from outside and which was welcomed by other Western European states. During the 1950s, the FRG's position as an independent nation state was reinforced by membership of the Organisation for European Economic Cooperation (after 1960 Organisation for Economic Cooperation and Development [OECD]) and membership of the GATT (see Chapter 5).[1] From the first years of its existence, therefore, the FRG was exposed to international pressure to liberalise trade. Although agriculture was treated as a special case in international trade talks, the success of the Coal and Steel Community led to the drafting of plans for an agricultural common market based on similar principles (Cecil, 1979; Williams, 1996; Rhenisch, 1999). In particular, the French argued that there could be no industrial Europe without an 'agro-Europe' (Schöneweiß, 1984).

Niklas' successor as agriculture minister, Lübke, cautiously supported the concept of a common agricultural policy. His view was closely related to the first phase of agricultural restructuring in the FRG through the Agriculture Act 1955 (see Chapter 2) and the reorientation of FRG agricultural markets from east to west (Haase, 1991; see Chapter 5), which both highlighted the need for closer economic links between the FRG and West European states. Academics, meanwhile, argued that while the FRG could expect to derive great benefits from an industrial customs union, it would have to make substantial concessions on agriculture. Early critics warned that if the highly protected FRG agriculture was to be exposed to competition, drastic steps would have to be taken to counteract potential income losses for FRG farmers.

Nonetheless, in 1951 the FRG government agreed with the French plan for a common agricultural market among six European countries (France, FRG, Italy and the Benelux countries), which would result in a lowering of border duties, a reduction in agricultural prices for FRG farmers, and thereby greater pressure on FRG agriculture to become more efficient and competitive. The decision to agree to the French plan was an early indication of the willingness of FRG policy-makers to sacrifice the interests of farmers for the sake of European integration. Inevitably, this move was heavily criticised by the newly re-established DBV, who argued that agriculture was an unpredictable economic sector difficult to control 'externally', and that the resulting massive structural adaptation of FRG farms would be catastrophic for its farmers (Ackermann, 1970).

Partly because of DBV criticism, the FRG adopted a hesitant position on the planned agricultural union during the European Conference on Agriculture in 1952 (Averyt, 1977). It was argued that the Coal and Steel Community should not be the model to be followed by an agricultural union, as the starting position in FRG agriculture was different from that of its rapidly expanding industrial sector. Contrary to the situation in the Coal and Steel Community, future collaboration in an agricultural union would strongly depend on the goodwill of FRG farmers who could not be forced to increase production and become more competitive in international markets. Discussions were also influenced by the fact that the question of whether political reunification of the FRG and GDR could be achieved was not resolved at the time. Understandably, the FRG delegation wanted a possible future agricultural union to consider the specific situation of a divided Germany.

By 1954, discussions on a common agricultural union had evolved sufficiently for Mansholt (the Dutch agriculture minister) to put forward concrete proposals for a common policy based on a European community of six member states (EEC6). FRG Agriculture Minister Lübke reacted quickly and asked for a long transition period for the FRG in order to implement a common agricultural policy. He argued that the FRG would not survive sudden changes and increased competition brought about through a common policy, and, under increasing pressure from the DBV, expressed his dislike of the planned union (Kluge, 1989a). Lübke was, therefore, caught in the FRG dilemma of, on the one hand, wanting to advocate European economic and political integration, while, on the other hand, having to appease an increasingly outspoken DBV – at the time representing almost 5 million people working in agriculture. Lübke's position was also influenced by the 1953 general elections in which voters from rural areas played a crucial role. Lübke was, however, not alone in his cautious approach. The problems of unifying six countries under a common agricultural policy were evident, as all countries had a 'dirigiste' approach to agricultural policy and were not used to external interference (Fearne, 1997). It was obvious, therefore, that a common policy would have to address the needs of individual countries and that a lengthy transition period would be necessary to adjust country-specific practices to an agricultural union.

While preliminary negotiations on agricultural policy were under way, the EEC6 were already experiencing a degree of cooperation on agricultural matters. For instance, the three Benelux countries already coordinated agricultural production and export policies, and in 1955 the FRG and France signed an agricultural trade agreement (which lasted until 1958). This agreement was important for the FRG dairy sector (opening up the French market for FRG dairy farmers after the loss of export opportunities in Eastern Europe), and helped to pave the way for the CAP (Schöneweiß, 1984). Although the FRG lost financially through the agreement with France, closer economic integration was welcomed as an important step towards further FRG integration into Western Europe.

Overall, the FRG position towards a European agricultural union in this early phase of European integration has been described as a cautiously supportive 'wait-and-see strategy' (Hendriks, 1989) and 'lukewarm at best' (Tangermann, 1992). It could see few economic advantages arising from closer agricultural union, and politicians foresaw considerable opposition from farmers. However, the economic advantages arising from closer European integration for the FRG's manufacturing sector were too great for politicians to let agriculture get in the way (Bulmer and Paterson, 1987). The need for political security was also a motivating factor, especially in the context of political instabilities such as the Soviet intervention in Hungary, the Suez crisis and the Algerian civil war. The leadership role was taken by France as the main driving force behind the establishment of the CAP, and by powerful personalities such as Mansholt from the Dutch agriculture ministry (Fearne, 1997). Consequently, it has been argued that the CAP was created as part of a 'package deal' between the FRG and the agricultural exporting countries, such as France and the Netherlands, who would have never accepted an EEC excluding agriculture (Fennell, 1987; Fearne, 1997). Further support for this viewpoint is given by Fearne (1997) who argued that the aims for agriculture were kept deliberately vague in the 1957 Treaty of Rome, in order that economic integration could be achieved before tackling the politically more difficult task of getting agreement on policy measures to be included in a common agricultural policy.

3.3   Early CAP policy-making: the FRG as a partner or obstructor?

3.3.1   Aims of the CAP

The aims, principles and policies of the CAP that were formulated between the Treaty of Rome in 1957 and the mid-1960s, have been discussed and analysed in detail by many authors (for instance, Bowler, 1985; Fennell, 1987, 1997). We will restrict ourselves here, therefore, to a very brief outline of the CAP framework. The aims for a common agricultural policy were laid down in Article 39 of the Treaty of Rome. The five aims were: to increase agricultural productivity by promoting technological progress and by ensuring the rational development of agricultural production and the optimum utilisation of the factors of production, in particular labour; to ensure a fair standard of living for the agricultural community; to stabilise markets; to assure the availability of supplies; and to ensure that supplies reach consumers at reasonable prices (Fennell, 1997). The policy framework which was worked out during the early 1960s was based on three principles: a single market in agricultural goods, community preference and common financing.

The key policy adopted was one of price support through guaranteed, target and intervention prices. From the start, different agricultural commodities were treated in different ways. The commodities with highest protection (with both protection from cheap imports and guaranteed prices) were beef, dairy products, grains and wine (Figure 3.1A). Another group of commodities, including pork, lamb and vegetables, had external protection, but no internal guaranteed price, while other commodities (for instance, oilseeds, flowers, fruit) had no protection and operated, therefore, under 'normal' market conditions. The target prices were negotiated annually by agriculture ministers in the CAM, with decisions based on a variety of political and economic factors (for instance, development of farm incomes in that year; world market prices, etc.). Community preference was achieved by a common customs policy for agricultural imports, using a system of variable levies (Figure 3.1B). This protected farmers in the EEC from cheap imports from 'third' countries. Finally, export subsidies were introduced to cover the gap between internal market prices and prices on the world market (Figure 3.1C). Internal market prices were to be maintained through intervention buying. The CAP was, therefore, established as a productivist policy, reflecting the priorities of the time of maximising food production and increasing levels of self-sufficiency in member states. It supported prices through market intervention as opposed to direct payments to farmers, a decision that reflected the policy approach in the FRG and to a lesser extent France, Italy and Belgium, but which has subsequently been strongly criticised by commentators (for instance, Fearne, 1997). In addition, however, there was a commitment to support farm incomes, although no clear policy mechanisms to achieve this aim were set out. There was no stated aim to improve farm structures, although this was implied in the first aim of the Treaty of Rome, and initial discussions on the CAP policy framework sidelined the question of structural policy (Fennell, 1997).

To finance these measures, an agricultural fund was established (the European Agricultural Guidance and Guarantee Fund [EAGGF]). The Guarantee section of EAGGF has always made up the bulk of the CAP budget (on average about 95 per cent) and has been used to pay for the price support measures outlined above, while the Guidance section has

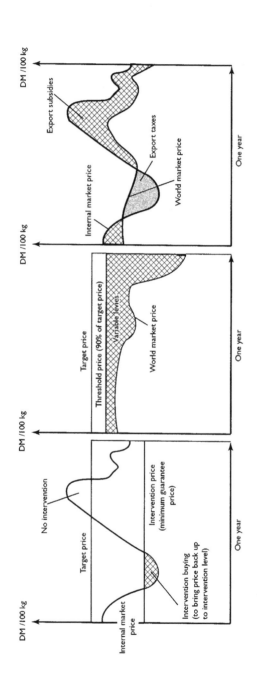

Figure 3.1   A model of the CAP pricing system (*Source:* Authors)

provided finances for structural policies (assuming greater importance after 1972). Initially, the EAGGF was funded by fixed national contributions, but from 1971 it was funded from the Community's 'own resources' (Fearne, 1997). National contributions were initially to be linked to each country's share of agricultural imports from 'third' countries, but following opposition from the FRG who was the largest importer, contributions were fixed (see Table 3.1). From 1971 onwards, funding was switched to a common mechanism based on income from customs duties and import levies plus a proportion of value added tax contributions (initially set at 1 per cent) (Pinder, 1995).

The structure of contributions to EAGGF has always favoured net exporting countries, as their farmers benefit from subsidised prices and the country earns foreign exchange from exports (which are often subsidised). Net importing countries on the other hand, such as the FRG, were disadvantaged as they had to pay for expensive food imports. The FRG was, from the start, the main net contributor to the EAGGF, a situation it accepted as a trade-off for access to the Community for industrial exports (Neville-Rolfe, 1984). This strategy paid off, as by 1990 over 50 per cent of all FRG manufacturing exports were to other EEC states, in contrast to less than 30 per cent in 1950 (Hendriks, 1991).

As the CAP formed a radical break from the national agricultural policy structures that existed before 1957, a transition period was agreed for adjustment. This was a concession to the FRG who pushed for a long transition period. Although Mansholt (the first agriculture commissioner) suggested a brief transition period of only six years, the Community agreed to a 12-year period until 1969 (Weinstock, 1987). During this transition phase, countries would be allowed to make up for any income losses arising from the new agreed prices through national subsidies. Initially the CAP, therefore, still left member states with considerable scope for preparing their agricultural sectors for full membership. The FRG was, thus, given a 'breathing space' during which it could continue its high price policy, but at the same time it had to adapt to a set of policies that did not fit easily with the FRG situation.

Table 3.1   EAGGF contributions, 1970

Member state	Contributions (%)
France	32.6
FRG	32.4
Italy	20.6
The Netherlands	7.3
Belgium	6.8
Luxembourg	0.7

Sources: *Agrarbericht* (1971); Kluge (1989b).

3.3.2   The early FRG position on the CAP: leader or partner?

Among the six founding members, the FRG was probably the most deeply committed to the ultimate objective of a European Union. This staunchly pro-European stance of the FRG also has to be understood in a wider context (Guerrieri and Padoan, 1989). By the time the CAP came into being, the FRG was already experiencing its 'economic miracle' which meant that, even if joining the CAP was to prove costly, the economic gains arising from new manufacturing export opportunities would more than cover the costs of the CAP (Ardagh, 1991; Smyser, 1993). Nonetheless, Tangermann (1982) argued that the particular difficulties which FRG agriculture was about to face in the EEC6 were not fully recognised at the time. As long as the FRG economy remained strong, the potential costs of the CAP were not an issue, but as soon as the economy slowed down (after the late 1960s and again during the 1980s), the problems of CAP costs having to be covered by industrial growth increasingly came to the fore (see below).

Despite the evident enthusiasm of most FRG politicians for European integration, the FRG could not exert much influence on agricultural issues in the first years of the CAP by virtue of its weak post-war political position (Feld, 1981; Geiss, 1996). In contrast, France quickly assumed the role of a leader in CAP negotiations, highlighted, for example, by blocking a British proposal to extend the free trade zone between the EEC6 countries and the rest of the OECD in the 1960s. Kluge (1989a) highlights how FRG support for the British idea of wider trade liberalisation was criticised by France which urged the FRG to adopt an anti-British stance (see also Weinstock, 1987). To appease its important EEC neighbour, the FRG backed down and France's argument won the day.

It would, nonetheless, be wrong to argue that the FRG exerted no influence at all in the first years of the CAP. It is important to remember that the FRG had to tackle serious agricultural structural deficiencies, and that policies had already been initiated nationally to address these problems (see Chapter 2). Indeed, it has been argued that the aims for agriculture laid down in the Treaty of Rome and the subsequent CAP policy framework were modelled on the FRG's agricultural policies. Fennell (1997, p. 14) noted the 'familiar ring' of Article 39 with the FRG's 1955 Agriculture Act, while Hendriks (1991, p. 38) contended that 'the inception of the Agriculture Act caused great interest in Europe. Two years later, the basic ideas and principles of the Act were incorporated in the Treaty of Rome.' The emphasis on supporting family farms expressed in the FRG Agriculture Act also coincided with the verdict of a meeting convened in 1958 by the European Commission (Stresa Meeting) which unanimously agreed to regard the family farm as the main farm policy model at EEC level for economic, social and political reasons (Cecil, 1979). There is, therefore, no doubt that some of the CAP policies were modelled on FRG policies, but the inherent scepticism of the FRG towards the notion of a common agricultural policy would suggest that EEC policy-makers reacted pragmatically by incorporating some of the innovative ideas of FRG agricultural policies, rather than being 'pushed' by the FRG to shape the CAP according to its legislation. The timing of the implementation of the Agriculture Act 1955 was also ideal to provide a basis for ideas expressed in Article 39 of the Treaty of Rome. On the other hand, the similarities between the 1955 Agriculture Act and Article 39 may have been coincidental, as all the EEC6 member states shared to a large extent similar agricultural structural problems (Table 3.2), and as noted above, the aims set out in Article 39 were deliberately vague and designed to be acceptable to all member states.

National attitudes towards the CAP framework varied, however, with a broad division between the agricultural 'exporters' (France, Italy and the Netherlands) and the 'importers' (the FRG, Belgium and Luxembourg). The exporters (dominated by France) argued most forcefully for community preference, and were generally in favour of guaranteed minimum prices, but at low levels (Fearne, 1997). The importers dominated by the FRG, on the other hand, were in favour of high minimum prices, but less in favour of community preference. While the exporters would clearly be winners from an expanded agricultural market, the benefits to importers were less clear. There were well-grounded fears that the structural deficiencies of FRG agriculture would be exposed in an expanded and more open agricultural market (Kluge, 1989a). Moreover, agricultural prices in the FRG were supported at higher levels than in any of the other member states (Table 3.3). Not surprisingly, therefore, political wrangling over 'appropriate' price levels formed the major hurdle to be overcome during early CAP negotiations, and has remained one of the most problematic issues ever since, particularly for the FRG. FRG farmers had the most to lose from any agreement.

3.3.3   The first price-fixing rows

In 1960, the Commission put forward proposals for common pricing for the most important commodities and community preference through variable levies on imports (Fennell, 1997). The then FRG agriculture minister,

Table 3.2   Agricultural structural indicators in the EEC6, 1961

Indicators	FRG	B	F	I	Lux	NL
Number of farms (1000)	1375	199	2110	2878	10	230
Average farm size (ha)	9.4	8.2	15.2	9.0	13.4	9.9
% farms <50 ha	1.2	1.1	4.5	1.7	1.8	0.9
Full-time workers/ year per 100 ha	27.0	15.5	13.5	30.9	22.4	19.6

Sources: *Agrarbericht* (1974); Tangermann (1981); Ehlers (1988).

Table 3.3   Cereal prices in EEC countries, 1958 (average = 100)

	FRG	NL	B	F	I
Wheat	114	85	104	75	121
Rye	126	92	94	74	113
Barley	123	93	103	75	107

Source: Kluge (1989a, p. 296).

Schwarz, used conciliatory rhetoric, arguing in 1961 that 'as we want the EEC for political reasons, and as we have to contribute to its development, others should not be able to argue that we delay or postpone it' (Kluge, 1989a, p. 318). From the start, however, Schwarz took a strong line on prices, and this led to the first serious agricultural policy conflict between Bonn and the Commission. In defence of high guaranteed prices, the FRG referred to Article 39 of the Treaty of Rome which stipulated that farmers should be given a fair standard of living (see above), which in the FRG could only be achieved by maintaining high agricultural prices. Schwarz even argued that, if need be, the FRG would make use of Article 226 of the Treaty of Rome which enabled member states to initiate measures which would safeguard a country's economy during emergency periods (Gaese, 1975; Feld, 1981; Rhenisch, 1995). The FRG position was strongly criticised by Mansholt, who described the FRG approach as 'very disappointing' (Kluge, 1989a, p. 326). Schwarz was also criticised by the FRG industrial lobby who wanted a quick agreement on the common market, and who opposed the stubborn FRG position on agricultural matters which put the FRG's wider interests at risk (Borchardt, 1991; Smyser, 1993). As a result, Schwarz had to retreat from his confrontational position. As Müller-Roschach (1980, p. 105) argued, 'in the interests of European unity and over-riding political objectives Germany was prepared to subjugate German sectoral interests to the utmost defensible limit'.

The most important commodity in the price negotiations was cereals. As Table 3.3 shows, cereal prices varied between the member states, with the FRG having the highest prices. Following intense pressure from the FRG, in December 1964 the CAM finally agreed to set the guaranteed cereal price 'towards the upper end of the price spectrum' (Fennell, 1997, p. 30). It was, nevertheless, below the FRG price, and represented a compromise between the French and the Germans (known as the 'Brussels compromise') (Andrlik, 1981; Hendriks, 1989). Farmers in the EEC6 were to be paid a guaranteed price of DM 425 per tonne of wheat, as opposed to DM 473 in the FRG (Cecil, 1979; Tangermann, 1979a, 1982). This meant that the FRG government had to subsidise each tonne of wheat by DM 48 to keep farmers' incomes at current levels. Hendriks (1989, p. 80) argued that the cereal price compromise was 'of historical importance for German attitudes to the

CAP. The psychological impact of the price reductions reinforced German attempts to counteract any real or imagined economic disadvantage which might result from lower national agricultural prices.' Schwarz and the FRG government were aware, however, that the Brussels compromise also opened the way for trade agreements with the USA, indicating that, once again, geopolitical considerations overshadowed the FRG urge to push for maximum agricultural prices (Geiss, 1996).

By agreeing to the Brussels compromise, the FRG had sacrificed agricultural interests for the sake of European integration, and the concessions which the FRG had made 'were partly a recognition of the importance of showing that the Germans were now good Europeans' (Neville-Rolfe, 1984, p. 70). However, it should be stressed that the FRG also gained from the agreed cereals price, as the EEC was now faced with a legacy of FRG agricultural protectionism based on a high agreed wheat price which had to be carried over into future price-fixing negotiations (Hendriks, 1991). Further, the cereal agreement only came into force in 1967 – a concession to the FRG for accepting the lower price. Continued compensation payments to FRG farmers were, therefore, authorised for another three years (1964–67).

Not surprisingly, the Brussels compromise did not please the DBV. Commentators such as Tangermann (1982, p. 20) have argued that 'the process of deciding on the common grain price level turned into a heated fight in which the DBV used all its power and shrunk back from no method in safeguarding what it supposed to be the interests of its members'. The DBV argued that farmers would lose about 2 billion DM through reduced grain prices, and their dissatisfaction was expressed during farmers' protests in many parts of the FRG. This view is not shared by Kluge (1989a) or Hendriks (1991) who argue that, although the DBV was dissatisfied, it also acknowledged that the government had managed to obtain substantial concessions from Brussels, particularly for being able to continue to pay subsidies to its farmers during the transition period (see also Gaese, 1975; Bulmer and Paterson, 1987). There is no doubt, however, that the DBV used the CAP price-fixing rows to increase their political platform during the 1963 national elections (Cecil, 1979). The DBV made it clear that its members would change political allegiance away from the CDU/CSU, if the government continued to seek agreement through compromises in Brussels. George (1996) argued that the DBV's anger with the government contributed to Adenauer's resignation in 1963.

The FRG's position in the formative years of the CAP was paradoxical. On the one hand, it objected to the level of contributions to the EAGGF, while on the other hand it demanded high prices (which added to the cost of the EAGGF). This position can be explained with reference to the FRG's protectionist agricultural policy position (see Chapter 2), the political influence of the DBV and the FRG's growing economic prosperity during the 1960s based on industrial expansion. This paradoxical position on agricultural policy led the FRG into the role of obstructor in CAP discussions (Kluge, 1989a; Tangermann, 1997). However, on both issues the FRG was prepared to compromise in order to reach agreement, as were the other EEC member states who were well aware that the FRG was a crucial player in CAP negotiations and a key figure in the move towards wider European integration (Smyser, 1993; Fearne, 1997).

CAP price agreements have to be seen as permanent compromises, where each country tried to gain the best possible price levels for their own farmers. Thus, FRG 'delaying tactics' at times also received backing by other EEC member states (for instance, France and Italy). The FRG was by no means the only, or the most influential, obstructor during the 1960s. In early price-fixing discussions (and in subsequent decades) the role of obstructor shifted between countries (in 1961 this role fell, for example, to Italy because it felt treated unfairly by CAP price discussions). It was France, however, which remained the main influence on the development of the CAP (and the EEC) throughout the 1960s, under the nationalist leadership of de Gaulle. Arguably, France took a more obstructive role than the FRG, for instance, by vetoing Britain's application for EEC membership in 1963 (the FRG supported Britain's bid as it saw Britain as an important ally over the question of CAP financing; Bowler, 1985). France also weakened the principle of majority voting on Community matters by walking out on discussions over Community financing in 1965. This crisis was only resolved by the introduction of what has been termed the 'Luxembourg compromise', whereby member states are allowed the right of veto over matters of important national interest (Fennell, 1997).

Although the FRG had about five transition years before national income subsidies were to be phased out, questions were asked about how FRG agriculture could survive in a common market after 1969. The FRG government was faced with a delicate balancing act, since too generous subsidy levels would hinder structural change, while too stringent price cuts would put the livelihood of too many farmers at risk. Through the implementation of a special act (*EWG Anpassungsgesetz*), the FRG government committed itself to spend DM 1 billion/year over and above regular spending for agriculture until the end of the transition period (Andrlik, 1981). This enabled the government to yield to EEC pressure for reduced support prices, while at the same time satisfying the DBV by granting full financial compensation for income losses. These debates again highlight the power of the DBV and the relative weakness of the FRG to negotiate its own terms with Brussels.

EEC price negotiations on other agricultural commodities after 1965 went more smoothly than the cereals negotiations. In 1966, for example, member states found it easy to agree on target prices for milk and dairy products (Hendriks, 1991). Although incomes of FRG dairy farmers were affected by the phasing out of subsidies on milk by the end of the CAP transition period, they gained new export opportunities. In 1967 the price agreements for cereals, pigmeat, eggs and poultry came into force – marking an important step towards 'real' implementation of the CAP. This meant a reduction of market prices for the FRG, Italy and Luxembourg, for which compensation was paid. Although it had been agreed initially that compensation would in part be paid from the EAGGF Guarantee section, the economic recession of 1966/67 meant that less was paid from Community resources than promised (Fennell, 1987). In the end, FRG consumers had to pay a larger part of the bill through increased food prices. However, the common market effectively only lasted between 1967 and 1969. After prices for most CAP products had been harmonised by 1968, price uniformity broke down in 1969 as a consequence of exchange rate disparities (see below).

3.3.4   The effects of the CAP on FRG farming

It is important to reflect briefly on the effects of the first decade of the CAP on FRG farmers, agricultural structures and land use. There is general agreement that price cuts, together with increased competition within the EEC6, affected FRG farmers – despite massive financial compensations through the *EWG Anpassungsgesetz* and payments through EAGGF (Cecil, 1979; Hendriks, 1991). However, where opinions differ is over the severity of this effect. Thus, while Tangermann (1979a, p. 248) argued that the FRG lost out in all agricultural sectors (with the exception of dairying) and that 'the establishment of the CAP was regarded by German farmers as well as by many officials in German agricultural policy as a national catastrophe',[2] commentators such as Baade and Fendt (1971), Kluge (1989a) or Hendriks (1991) are more cautious. They argued that, as long as farm incomes were not directly affected, FRG farmers and the DBV were neutral, if not even supportive, of the CAP. Many FRG farmers felt that the effects of the CAP had not been as bad as feared in the late 1950s, and public opinion was also favourable due to the economic success of the EEC. During the 1960s farm incomes steadily increased which would tend to corroborate the latter opinion. Overall, the transition to the CAP regime is seen as having been relatively 'smooth' – despite earlier fears to the contrary. FRG policy-makers, although sceptical about the CAP in the initial phase, were beginning to realise that the CAP could also offer benefits to FRG agriculture, and 'all in all the BML saw the CAP as a base for European agricultural policy that could be further developed' (Kluge, 1989a, p. 348).

There is less debate concerning the effects of the first decade of CAP policies on FRG agricultural structures. Despite the concerted effort of FRG policy-makers to protect the family farm (see Chapter 2), FRG integration into the CAP dramatically increased the pace of agricultural structural change (Neander, 1983; Tangermann, 1984). Ehlers (1988) refers to this as 'forced change', highlighting that the dynamics of structural change were reinforced by the increased international competition engendered by the CAP. In the 1960s, the FRG lost 300 000 farms, with a concurrent reduction in agricultural workforce from 3.4 to 2.1 million, while average farm size increased from 9.3 to 11.7 ha (see Tables 2.1 and 2.4). Thus, the relative satisfaction of FRG farmers with the CAP was only present among those who had survived the structural changes of the 1960s, and who had emerged with larger and more efficient farms, often better integrated into the European agricultural economy (Köster, 1981; Henrichsmeyer, 1982; Willgerodt, 1983). There is no doubt that the hundreds of thousands of farmers and agricultural workers who abandoned agriculture during the 1960s felt ambiguous and often bitter about the CAP (Neander, 1983). However, it is impossible to directly quantify the impact of the CAP on agricultural structural change, as FRG membership of the EEC occurred at a time of natural attrition of the agricultural sector due to broader changes in FRG economy and society and the introduction of domestic structural policies (see Chapter 2).

The same is true for possible changes in FRG land use engendered by the CAP, although there is little doubt that common European prices for specific agricultural commodities affected FRG land uses. Farmers quickly grasped the opportunities offered by the CAP regime and expanded production of cereals (especially wheat, barley and maize) at the expense of less supported products such as rye, oats and potatoes. At the same time, stock numbers increased dramatically, particularly dairy cows, pigs and poultry (Ehlers, 1988). Indeed, throughout the CAP regime, farmers quickly adapted to changing marketing conditions, and land uses were changed to maximise benefits from CAP support (Fennell, 1987; Kluge, 1989b).

3.4   The Mansholt Plan and the FRG position

In the early years of the CAP the question of structural policy was sidelined, but in 1968, Mansholt, the agriculture commissioner, formulated a radical plan (the 'Mansholt Plan') to tackle agricultural structural deficiencies in the EEC6 (CEC, 1968; Hendriks, 1991). The Mansholt Plan was a response to the worsening crisis of CAP funding, but also a reaction towards inherent structural problems in EEC agriculture that had not been properly addressed in the first decade of the CAP. Mansholt suggested that all EEC partners (and other states wishing to be part of the EEC) should substantially reduce their agricultural population (a proposed reduction in the European agricultural workforce of 5 million, or 30 per cent of the total workforce), and thereby increase farm efficiency and reduce the increasing income disparity between agriculture and other economic sectors (Fennell, 1997). This was to be done through a combination of a 'careful' pricing policy, which would guarantee higher incomes for farmers, and structural policies aimed at accelerating structural change towards fewer and larger farms, including an early retirement policy (at the time over half of the

EEC's farmers were older than 55, of which three-quarters did not have a successor; Potter, 1990). Mansholt recommended that special grants should be paid to marginal farmers wishing to find other employment, and that small farmers who remained should be encouraged to amalgamate to form more viable farm units (Hubbard and Ritson, 1997).

Inevitably, the Mansholt Plan was too radical for national politicians and was opposed by EEC member states. Yet, not all policy-makers rejected Mansholt's suggestions outright. While the Netherlands generally supported Mansholt (who had been their agriculture minister), France adopted a neutral position on the basis of its 'healthy' agricultural structures, while Italy strongly opposed the plan. It was the FRG, however, who most strongly opposed the plan, both in terms of its proposals and on principle as an infringement of national competence over structural policy matters (Fennell, 1997). Mansholt envisaged an 'ideal' farm size of 80–120 ha, with livestock farms containing four to five employees and 350–400 LUs (Cecil, 1979; Henrichsmeyer and Witzke, 1994). This was seen as very large by FRG agricultural policy-makers, considering that in 1968 the average FRG farm still had less than 11 ha. Although Höcherl (the then FRG agriculture minister) agreed with the plan's basic assumptions, he doubted whether it was possible to stipulate a standard farm size regardless of local conditions. He argued that it would be too risky to adopt a strategy which relied entirely on an untested theoretical model of ideal farm units. To try to impose a preconceived structure within a specific period would expose the farming community to undue pressure, and exacerbate income disparities between agriculture and industry. Mansholt was particularly criticised for not sufficiently acknowledging the special structural problems of FRG agriculture (Priebe, 1985).

The Mansholt Plan was, therefore, described in the FRG as 'naïve' in light of the reality of EEC agriculture (Kluge, 1989b), and was referred to as a brutal policy of technocrats (Tangermann, 1982). FRG politicians particularly disliked the modern rhetoric of the plan which referred to farms as 'agricultural enterprises' and 'production units' rather than family farms, as this represented a threat to accepted ideology of the FRG in the late 1960s (Kluge, 1989b; Sauer, 1990). In particular, the FRG criticised Mansholt for failing to consider the socio-political implications of his proposal – a criticism that gained strength as the FRG economic miracle began to fade (Smyser, 1993). Indeed, the slowing down of the economy meant that the capacity of FRG industry to absorb farmers leaving the land was more limited than during the 1950s and early 1960s, which was an important reason to encourage farmers to stay on the land. Further, Mansholt's focus on large full-time farms also neglected the specific FRG situation characterised by many part-time farmers (see Table 2.3).

The negative FRG position towards the Mansholt Plan was also motivated by political factors. The period before the 1969 general elections was characterised by the possible defection of many traditionally centre–right farming voters to the left. The DBV made clear its opposition to the Mansholt Plan. It particularly criticised Mansholt's notion of 'optimum farm size', and in the eyes of the DBV Mansholt was using structural policy as a replacement for price policy – an approach that went against all that the DBV had fought for since inception of the CAP. The political situation in the FRG before the 1969 elections was more complex than just the usual wrangling of the CDU-led government with the DBV (Opelland, 1996). A new extreme right-wing party (Nationalsozialistische Partei Deutschland [NPD]) had emerged in 1968 with a nationalist programme that condemned any form of international cooperation. In light of the traditionally right-wing tendencies of many FRG farmers (see Chapter 2), the FRG government feared that the DBV would show sympathy for the NPD, and there were indications that traditional CDU/CSU voters from farming circles had already shifted allegiance to the NPD in regional elections to 'punish' the government for its stance on the CAP (Neville-Rolfe, 1984; Hendriks, 1991). Both the CDU and SPD were anxious not to further alienate farmers before the elections by supporting Mansholt's ideas (Tangermann, 1982). Although the NPD failed to obtain seats in the general elections,[3] the government paid the price at EEC level by emerging as one of the key obstructors to the Mansholt Plan (Andrlik, 1981).

However, there was no need for the FRG to fight a lone rearguard action, as there was enough opposition from other member states to ensure that the Mansholt Plan was not implemented (Fearne, 1997; Hubbard and Ritson, 1997). The DBV also received the backing of most EEC farmers' unions (Ackermann, 1970; Averyt, 1977). Criticism was particularly directed at the disastrous and costly social consequences that would result. As a result, Mansholt issued a revised plan which took, for example, more account of part-time farming (a concession to FRG criticisms) and was less adamant about 'ideal' farm sizes. In the end, however, the Mansholt Plan was rejected by the Commission in 1969.

It has been widely argued that the Mansholt Plan came too early in terms of CAP evolution, as no structural policies had so far been formulated (Bowler, 1985; Fennell, 1997). Indeed, all CAP discussions of the 1960s, including the early price-fixing rows, had focused almost entirely on the Guarantee section of EAGGF, while structural policy had remained a domestic policy concern. Mansholt was also criticised because his plan suggested that structural policy could be a viable alternative to price policy – an untested assumption at the time. Yet it would be wrong to argue that Mansholt had no impact on the course of EEC agricultural policies (Neville-Rolfe, 1984; Potter, 1990). He sparked a heated discussion between member states and the Commission, usefully refocusing attention on the question of agricultural structures. The structural policies that were eventually agreed in 1972 were a much-watered-down version of the Mansholt

Plan (referred to as the 'mini-Mansholt' package) (Tangermann, 1982; Hubbard and Ritson, 1997). The package contained three directives: farm modernisation, early retirement and socio-economic guidance and training for farmers (Fennell, 1997).

In this context, it is interesting to analyse briefly the FRG response to Directive 159/72/EEC on 'farm modernisation'. The directive allowed considerable freedom to individual member states over implementation, and the response, therefore, varied considerably across the EEC6. Interestingly, the FRG was the only member state to comply 'by the book' and topped the list of implementers with 7600 agreed farm modernisation plans (Kluge, 1989b). Similarly, only in the FRG were holdings enlarged to any significant extent from land released through the early retirement directive (Neville-Rolfe, 1984; Fennell, 1997). This shows both that these directives were particularly suited to FRG farmers' structural needs (and were also acceptable to the DBV as they did not discriminate against certain types of holdings), and that the FRG was particularly eager to show goodwill to the Commission after initially obstructing the structural package proposed by Mansholt. The latter point stresses that if Mansholt had put forward his original proposals a few years later, during the more liberal SPD/FDP government (1969–82), the FRG position might have been more favourable towards the original plan. As it happened, Mansholt's radical ideas came too early (in FRG terms) and coincided with the end of a phase of CDU-led governments characterised by conservative and narrow-minded incrementalism.

3.5 The first CAP crisis and the FRG

The debates at EEC level over the Mansholt Plan coincided with the CAP's first major crisis. Problems included rapidly rising food surpluses linked to commodity subsidisation through the CAP (Fearne, 1997), the oil crisis of 1973 resulting in a slowing down of economic growth and the expansion of the EEC6 (also in 1973) by three additional members (Denmark, Britain and Ireland).

3.5.1 Problems with the EAGGF

By the late 1960s, surpluses were already beginning to accumulate as farmers responded to high prices by increasing production. As a result, EAGGF expenditure rose from DM 150 million in 1962 to DM 10 billion in 1969, resulting in a funding crisis (Ritson and Harvey, 1997). This first CAP crisis was welcomed by many FRG political actors as a clear sign that the CAP was 'unworkable' in an FRG context. It also lent credence to the scepticism of the staunchly conservative FRG farming lobby towards the CAP. The main FRG concern, however, related to the rapidly rising EAGGF costs, because of its position as net contributor. Although the financial contributions of all member states had increased dramatically in absolute terms since inception of the CAP, the discrepancy between money spent and money received was greatest for the FRG, and the FRG saw itself as subsidising food exports which mainly benefited countries such as France and the Netherlands (Cecil, 1979).

In addition to increasing dissatisfaction at government level with the CAP, discontent among FRG farmers was also high during the late 1960s, largely because of a fall in agricultural prices at a time when farm costs were rising and domestic agricultural budgets were cut (see Chapter 2). The notion that many of the problems that FRG farmers were facing were to blame on Brussels bureaucrats gained strength, and farmers continued to be critical of the fact that CAP prices were lower than FRG prices had been. While the government may have brushed aside farmers' grumbling about the CAP at other times, during the months before the crucial elections of 1969 (which the SPD/FDP coalition won) farmers' opinion was an important element in the government's response to the accelerating CAP crisis. Agriculture Minister Höcherl, therefore, voiced his concern in Brussels over the negative effects of the CAP on farm incomes.

3.5.2   The introduction of MCAs

Common prices had been agreed during a period of currency stability on international markets, linked to the Bretton Woods agreement of 1944 (George, 1996). Agricultural prices were, therefore, fixed in units of account equivalent to the gold value of the 1960 US$, on the premise that exchange rates between EEC member states would remain stable. Yet, from the late 1960s pressure on international financial markets led to hitherto stable European currencies beginning to diverge, both through the revaluation of 'strong' currencies and the devaluation of 'weak' currencies (Smyser, 1993).[4] By 1969, the FRG economy was the strongest in the EEC6, which led to the revaluation of the DM by the newly elected SPD–FDP coalition. Changes in currencies meant that the price-fixing agreements under the CAP were severely challenged, as the relative value of these commodities was no longer the same across member states. Thus, although the EEC6 was, in theory, ready to implement the CAP for the first time after the 12-year transition phase (until 1969), the emerging currency disparities prevented its 'true' implementation.

After revaluation of the DM, strict interpretation of the CAP would have meant that support prices for FRG farm products would have fallen by the extent of the revaluation (an estimated annual loss of farmers' incomes of about DM 1.7 billion). This scenario was politically unacceptable to the FRG. Agriculture Minister Ertl argued that FRG farmers had already borne the brunt of common market decisions during the 1960s (by agreeing to reduced CAP prices for grains, for example), and that prices for FRG farm products could not fall further (Kluge, 1989b). Ertl firmly believed that the

CAP could only work with the establishment of a currency union, otherwise currency fluctuations would continue to pose problems. The FRG was not the only country to suffer from exchange rate disparities. Also in 1969, France devalued the franc by 11 per cent (because of fears of rapidly rising inflation) thereby facing the opposite problem as its agricultural prices were suddenly too high[5] (Hendriks, 1989; Fearne, 1997).

In order to solve these currency pressures, a 'green currency' arrangement was introduced whereby prices were agreed according to a fixed exchange rate between units of account and national currencies (known as 'green rates'). This system protected farmers from sudden changes in national exchange rates, but introduced a new problem, whereby traders could exploit differences between the green and actual currency conversion rates by strategic buying and selling across national boundaries (George, 1996). To counteract this danger, in 1970, the Commission introduced monetary compensation amounts (MCAs), a system of border taxes and subsidies to iron out price differences caused by divergence between green and actual rates (Tangermann, 1982; Neville-Rolfe, 1984). Positive MCAs were applied to strong currency countries (such as the FRG) while negative MCAs were applied to weak currency countries (such as France). Thus, the green currency and MCAs allowed differing levels of support prices in member states (Fennell, 1987; Fearne, 1997). The introduction of MCAs, therefore, terminated the (newly established) common market, although still giving the illusion of a common system. With the turmoil in international currencies threatening to destroy the CAP, MCAs were seen as the only possible solution to prevent the CAP from complete disintegration (Ritson and Tangermann, 1979). Initially, MCAs were only envisaged as a short-term measure. Yet, the increasingly uncertain economic climate in Europe and abroad (exacerbated by the 1973 oil crisis) meant that MCAs became a quasi-permanent device for retaining a degree of price differentiation between member countries.[6]

After introduction of MCAs the FRG price level for agricultural goods stood 10–15 per cent higher than the now fictitious common price level – a level that the FRG tried to maintain for as long as possible in the following decades (see below). The FRG could now fix national support prices at higher levels, without having to persuade other member states to follow. As a result, by the late 1970s, there was up to 40 per cent difference in agricultural prices between the FRG and France – a greater difference than existed before the CAP was established! The immediate result was that FRG farmers were better off in 1973 than in 1969 (*Agrarbericht*, 1974). Although most countries used the system of negative or positive MCAs, none defended the system as vehemently as the FRG who benefited more than any other member state (Ritson and Tangermann, 1979; Rodemer, 1980). MCAs were, therefore, greatly welcomed in the FRG, and were seen as a vital mechanism by which the country could regain some control over price levels. In particular, MCAs enabled FRG agricultural policy-makers to respond to farmers' continuous criticisms of low incomes and 'unfair' treatment by Brussels technocrats. Neville-Rolfe (1984, p. 72) argued that the FRG 'doubly pursued its own interests' for the continuation of MCAs, as it gained from positive MCAs through higher incomes for its farmers, and by agreeing not to dismantle negative MCAs in other countries it benefited from savings to the EAGGF budget (which would have increased substantially through the abolition of negative MCAs).

The strong FRG support for MCAs can be interpreted as a key indicator for both its role as an obstructor in the CAP policy-making process and its increasing assertiveness in European matters. As Hendriks (1991, p. 57) argued, 'the 1970s witnessed a change in German attitudes to Community affairs. National interests were redefined and at times rigorously pursued.' MCAs have been interpreted as a further 'estrangement' of the CAP to suit FRG needs, as the country gained a level of agricultural protection which was higher than the Community average. This put the FRG into a privileged position which, at times, generated envy from its European partners (Tangermann, 1982; Folmer *et al.*, 1995). Is this an indication of the increasing power of the FRG to shape the CAP according to its own will, helped by its now dominant position in the EEC6 as the major economic and political force? In response to this, many authors (for instance, Kluge, 1989b; Hendriks, 1991) have highlighted that it would be wrong to overstate the importance of the FRG in establishing MCAs. Countries such as France and the Netherlands benefited as much from MCAs as a tool to protect their farmers from the vicissitudes of exchange rate turmoil – highlighting that in this particular case the interests of most member states coincided with FRG interests. Some authors (for instance, Hu, 1979; Kluge, 1989b) have argued that MCAs were closely linked to the FRG's spectacular rise to the world's fourth largest agricultural exporter in the 1970s and 1980s, because positive MCAs encouraged increases in commodity production. Hendriks (1989, p. 83) also argued that 'it is not surprising . . . that Germany's spectacular rise to being one of Europe's main agricultural exporters has been closely linked with MCAs'. Thus, the high levels of self-sufficiency (at least compared to the low levels in the 1950s) in most agricultural products in the FRG in subsequent decades were partly a result of MCAs that strongly encouraged increases in agricultural production.[7]

Arguably the most important outcome of the introduction of MCAs at EEC level was that the price-fixing debates, that had caused much tension in the CAP during the late 1960s, subsided (Manegold, 1984). FRG farmers and the DBV were now relatively satisfied with the CAP, a fact which guaranteed the political support of farmers for the SPD/FDP coalition until the beginning of the second major CAP crisis in the late 1970s. For this reason, Tangermann (1979a) refers to the introduction of MCAs as the 'golden age' of FRG agricultural policy within the EEC – an era marked by little discontent between FRG policy-makers and the Commission.

3.5.3   EEC enlargement and the 1973 oil crisis: the FRG viewpoint

The enlargement of the EEC6 in 1973 by Denmark, Ireland and Britain (EEC9) put further pressure on the CAP and FRG agriculture (Kluge, 1989b), although enlargement was smoothed by the introduction of MCAs which solved the problem of exchange rate fluctuations and divergent national prices. The new member states were also all given transition periods before becoming full members of the CAP. Contrary to the early 1960s, when on the insistence of France the FRG had reluctantly blocked Britain's bid to join the EEC (see above), in 1973 the FRG more actively supported enlargement of the Community. The FRG hoped to benefit from British membership, as Britain would be another net importer of foodstuffs with an expected high share of EAGGF payments (Denton, 1984). Expansion also enabled a renegotiation of financing arrangements, with contributions pegged at 22.6 per cent for the FRG, 21.5 per cent for Britain and 20.7 per cent for France (Kluge, 1989b). This reduced the FRG's concerns over the EAGGF, albeit only for a limited time as Britain successfully negotiated a reduction of its EAGGF contributions through the Fontainebleau Agreement in 1984 (Denton, 1984). Although the Commission pressed for an ending of MCAs, continuing currency instability during the 1970s prevented this option. As a result, the FRG (and other countries) were allowed to continue the system of MCAs (effectively until 1993).

Further pressure was added to the CAP through the international oil crisis in 1973, and the FRG was hit particularly hard because of its reliance on oil imports. On average, oil prices rose by more than 8 per cent in that year alone (the price for farm diesel, for example, even doubled). For FRG farmers, this meant additional production costs at a time of agricultural crisis. Yet, while in many other EEC member states discussions began to concentrate on the 'renationalisation' of policy powers away from the EEC and the CAP (Denton, 1984), no such debates emerged in the FRG because of the price protection enabled by MCAs. Despite protest by farmers and the DBV over rapidly rising costs and further dwindling incomes related to the aftermath of the oil crisis, the CAP and EEC price policy were defended by Agriculture Minister Ertl. Throughout the first CAP crisis, therefore, the FRG continued to be a committed advocate of European integration (Kluge, 1989b; Hendriks, 1991). Indeed, the FRG was one of the main driving forces in Europe at the time for ensuring the survival of the CAP through one of its most difficult periods.

3.5.4   The FRG as a mediator during the first CAP crisis?

The position of the SPD/FDP coalition (which came into power in 1969) towards the CAP did not differ substantially from that of the CDU-led governments of the 1960s. Generally speaking, the FRG attitude towards the CAP in the 1970s can be described as 'moderately supportive' (Cecil, 1979; Hendriks, 1991). Since the introduction of positive MCAs pressure had been removed from possible tensions in the FRG–Brussels relationship. Nonetheless, the FRG government under both Brandt (1969–74) and Schmidt (1974–82) remained sceptical of the CAP, partly because the SPD had no agro-political tradition (compared to the CDU/CSU), but also because the SPD saw isolated support for one economic sector as going against the grain of 'social solidarity'. Hendriks (1991, p. 116) argued that 'the most profound difference between the SPD and the CDU/CSU attitudes toward the agricultural sector lies in the former's total absence of an emotional relationship with the farmers and the land'. This reluctance of the SPD to fully support farmers has been referred to as a 'hostility toward farmers' (*Bauernfeindlichkeit*) by some commentators (for instance, Kluge, 1989b; Hendriks, 1991). That an FDP politician (Ertl) occupied the strategic role of minister for agriculture during the SPD-led government periods has to be seen as a move to both appease farmers and to partly neutralise SPD criticisms of the CAP. Indeed, Ertl remained a fervent supporter of the CAP during his entire term of office, leading Neville-Rolfe (1984, p. 88) to argue that Ertl 'was a dominant figure in the history of the CAP'. Ertl continued with the high price policy of the 1960s, but, in contrast to his predecessors, he was more supportive of structural policy (see Chapter 2), and even criticised the Commission for seeing price policy as a general solution to structural problems in European agriculture.

There is no doubt that the first CAP crisis, and the introduction of MCAs in particular, led to a retrenchment of many EEC member states away from the notion of centralised policy-making by the Commission (Fearne, 1997). Indeed, there was a general feeling during the 1970s that individual member states should have more freedom to regulate their own agricultural prices and implement policies suited more to national needs (Fennell, 1987). In the FRG, for example, there were continuous debates with the Commission as to whether the Ertl Plan was in accordance with CAP structural policy regulations, or whether it was purely a national measure geared towards addressing the needs of FRG farmers that should, therefore, not receive co-financing through the CAP (the Commission, nonetheless, agreed to contribute 25 per cent of the budget necessary for Ertl's selective subsidisation). As a result of the growing tension during the first CAP crisis, the Commission increasingly worried that member states were introducing measures without prior consultation, and warned against bilateral agreements that bypassed the Commission and, therefore, went against the principles established in the Treaty of Rome (Hendriks, 1991; Fearne, 1997). Although the FRG was satisfied that their decision-making powers vis-à-vis Brussels had increased, the disintegration of discipline in the EEC9 was strongly criticised by Ertl. Once again it became evident that under no circumstance would the FRG allow further dismantling of the CAP – a system still seen by *all* FRG politicians as a vital stepping stone for further European integration (Larres and Panayi, 1996).

By the mid 1970s, it became evident that MCAs would remain an established means of maintaining farm incomes. The fear of further currency fluctuations led the FRG to defend its MCA policy, and Ertl saw the differential currency trajectories of member states as an increasing problem that would require drastic measures in the long term if the CAP was to survive. This highlights that the FRG began to assume the role of a mediator in CAP policy-making. Ertl wanted a constructive policy from Brussels, not destructive national protests, and argued that member states had to recognise that European agricultural policy was at a crossroads (Ertl, 1980, 1985). Yet, it is difficult to gauge what the FRG's real role was in guaranteeing the continuation of the CAP during its first major crisis. There is generally a strong bias in the literature towards national interests, with authors from each member state attempting to highlight the importance of their country in safeguarding the continuation of the CAP during its first major crisis (cf. Feld, 1981; Manegold, 1984; Fennell, 1987). Although authors such as Kluge (1989b) overstate the role of the FRG in the process, more 'neutral' observers such as Hendriks (1991) also stress the important role that the FRG played in supporting the CAP through this crisis. Further, the relative power of member states to set their own agendas during the 1970s also has to be seen in the light of a weak European Commission, often described as *reactive* rather than *proactive* at times of crisis (Fearne, 1997). What emerges from the debate on the FRG position is the importance of the optimism towards the CAP expressed by FRG Agriculture Minister Ertl. Had the CAP crisis occurred earlier during the phase of CDU-led governments before 1969, the situation might have been different.

3.5.5 The Schmidt government and the CAP

'Ostpolitik' and deteriorating relationships with Brussels

The period of government of Chancellor Schmidt (1974–82) was characterised by increasing tensions between the various actors involved in FRG agricultural policy-making. Neville-Rolfe (1984, p. 91) argued that 'the division of opinion within the German cabinet now no longer ran along purely economic lines but along party ones' (especially with increasing tensions between the FDP and the SPD). Schmidt was generally more critical of the CAP than his predecessor, Brandt, and advocated a general re-evaluation of the CAP (Neville-Rolfe, 1984; Hendriks, 1991). This criticism should particularly be seen in light of the wider geopolitical context of the SPD-led government at the time. Both Brandt and Schmidt were strong advocates of closer ties with Eastern Bloc countries (*Ostpolitik*) and were less pro-Western than their CDU predecessors (Hrbek and Wessels, 1984). The CAP was, therefore, seen as a policy that pushed the FRG too far into the Western 'camp'. In particular, Schmidt began to question the utility of MCAs in light of increasing surpluses at EEC level. The Commission was in general agreement with Schmidt's position and continued to criticise the FRG's high MCA policy, arguing that MCAs led to distortions in intra-EEC trade and to the shifting of trade flows away from countries with positive MCAs towards countries with negative ones. FRG agricultural policy analysts retaliated by arguing that MCAs had no effect on trade patterns, and that there was no evidence of shifts in trade flows (for instance, Haase, 1983, 1991; Hendriks, 1994). The CDU parliamentary opposition even asked for higher MCAs for FRG farmers, hoping to win back farming votes lost in the last two national elections.

The ambiguous FRG policy position at the time encouraged the Commission to persuade the FRG to reduce MCAs in the mid-1970s (Kluge, 1989b). Pressure was also placed on the FRG by Britain, who threatened to leave the EEC because of its high net contribution to the EAGGF, and by the French who saw MCAs as a distortion of the common market in favour of FRG farmers and against French farmers. This conflict culminated in 1979 when France unexpectedly vetoed the inauguration of a European Monetary System, arguing that monetary union would not be possible without the dismantling of MCAs (Neville-Rolfe, 1984; Simonian, 1985).[8] Ertl, therefore, agreed to reduce MCAs – a move heavily criticised by FRG farmers and the CDU, but welcomed by the Commission as the start of price convergence. The Schmidt government tried to justify its decision to the FRG public by arguing that this was the only solution for CAP survival (Tangermann, 1979b). In return, and in a move to appease farmers in member states with high MCAs, concessions were made by the Commission through so-called 'gentleman's agreements' (1975 and 1979). For FRG farmers, for example, these agreements guaranteed that they would not suffer income losses because of changes in currency policies. It also gave the FRG more freedom to adjust MCA levels at times when farmers' incomes were severely at risk through currency fluctuations – a practice which the FRG government made ample use of in the years to come.

The question of MCAs was not the only source of tension between the FRG and the Commission. Schmidt criticised national efforts to maximise benefits for farmers in individual countries, rather than attempting to develop policies with a European-wide vision – an ironic position, given that the FRG was one of the worst culprits in this respect. Schmidt was particularly concerned about rapidly rising milk surpluses – a particular problem for the FRG as one of the main milk producers in the EEC – and suggested increased participation of producers in paying for surplus storage. Although 'Europe' became an issue during the 1976 national elections in the FRG, the CAP crisis never featured prominently during the electoral debate. Ertl could still count on the support of farmers because of the continuation of positive MCAs. Consequently, farmers played an important role in re-electing the SPD–FDP coalition to government. Yet, further currency discrepancies by 1976 highlighted that the CAP crisis was far from over. The FRG and the Benelux countries were again forced to revalue their currencies, further increasing the rift between countries with strong currencies (such as the FRG and the Netherlands) and those with weak currencies (such as France and Italy).

Continuing demands for high agricultural prices

By 1976 the FRG had emerged as a key actor in CAP discussions (Kluge, 1989b; Hendriks, 1991; Fearne, 1997), and FRG lobbying to maintain high commodity prices became increasingly effective (Tangermann, 1982). This highlights the increasing power of the FRG in Europe due to both the economic power of the FRG, and the increasing acceptance of the FRG as a fully fledged nation state in an expanding EEC (Smyser, 1993; Larres and Panayi, 1996). This increased influence was associated with a shift from partner to increasingly vocal obstructor. Although the FRG appeared to be the main obstructor on MCAs and prices, however, there were few occasions where the FRG was isolated during price negotiations. Since the inception of the CAP, individual member states had continually pressed for high prices for specific products, often higher than the FRG demands. Indeed, many have argued that, until the end of the 1970s, the FRG's international political power was so limited that it could not have managed to push CAP prices up 'on its own' (Tangermann, 1979b; Neville-Rolfe, 1984).

The centre–left coalition government under Schmidt continued to be influenced by the DBV's demand for high prices (Heinze and Voelzkow, 1993). While in the 1960s farmers had to be convinced that they needed to make sacrifices to keep the process of European integration on track, the 1970s (and 1980s) were characterised by increasing demands on consumers and taxpayers to bear the extra costs of the CAP to strengthen the EEC (Tangermann, 1979a). Chancellor Schmidt, therefore, continued to advocate that there could be no EEC without a fully functioning CAP – which, in turn, relied on the satisfaction of FRG farmers through high agricultural prices.

The role of FRG consumers in CAP discussions

At this point, we should briefly pause and discuss the role of another potentially important actor in the agricultural policy context: the consumer lobby. Questions have to be asked about why the consumer lobby did not protest about high food prices resulting from positive MCAs (Tangermann, 1979b; Ziegler, 1980). Although in the late 1970s the public became more critical of the growing cost of the CAP at a time of deepening economic recession, there was little concern over food prices (von Urff, 1984). Unlike countries such as Britain, for example, the level of food prices was never an issue in the FRG, partly because the general cost of living was rising more rapidly than food prices. In 1982, for example, expenditure on food in the FRG rose by only 3.3 per cent (with DM 500 spent per month by an average

household), compared to 5.4 per cent inflation (Kluge, 1989b). That the relatively wealthy average FRG family household could easily absorb rising
food prices should not be underestimated (Tangermann, 1982). Indeed, the
proportion of expenditure for food for the average FRG household even
decreased over the years (1949: 48 per cent; 1960: 38 per cent; 1970: 20 per
cent; 1980: 15 per cent; 1990: 13 per cent).

German customers have also historically been accustomed to high farm
product prices after 100 years of agricultural protectionism (Cecil, 1979). A
wealthy country such as the FRG could afford a high level of protectionism,
as long as it did not interfere with the objective of European integration.
This has been reiterated by Neville-Rolfe (1984, p. 76) who argued that 'the
consumer interest in agricultural matters has made itself little felt either in
parliament, or through the trade union organisations, or through consumer groups'. Indeed, farmers' privileges on tax concessions earned them
far greater unpopularity than high food prices.[9] Bulmer and Paterson
(1987) suggested that public support for FRG farmers might be linked to
the legacy of post-war memories of food shortages, loss of agricultural land
through political division and the important role that farmers played in
post-war reconstruction. It might also be linked to the ideological threat of
the neighbouring GDR where farmers were dispossessed of their lands (see
Chapter 4). FRG consumers, thus, are a special case within the Community,
and political parties have been more anxious to keep farmers' votes rather
than to satisfy the politically heterogeneous consumer groups (Hendriks,
1991).

Agricultural economists such as Tangermann (1982) go even a step
further and argue that because of the general 'apathy' of FRG consumers,
there has always been a lack of interest about agricultural policy in German
society. Indeed, 'high non-farm incomes and a relatively small share of
agriculture in total labour force allows the German non-agricultural population to be generous to farmers' (Tangermann, 1979b, p. 397). In addition,
FRG consumer groups have lacked political power as they have rarely been
able to threaten government policies through strikes or by withholding
purchases, leading Hendriks (1991, p. 162) to suggest for the 1980s that 'a
radicalisation of consumers is extremely unlikely'.[10] For these reasons, the
level of information of the FRG public on agricultural issues has traditionally been low, and the FRG media were reluctant to engage in wider debates
on agricultural policies in general. Agricultural policy was made an 'object
of amusement rather than of criticism' (Tangermann, 1982, p. 39). The FRG
position was, therefore, opposite to that of Britain, where the CAP burden
was continually used as an argument *against* the EEC, while in the FRG the
need *for* European integration continued to be pleaded as an excuse *for* the
high costs of the CAP (Tangermann, 1982; Hendriks, 1991).

The role of consumers also has to be understood in the wider political
framework of the FRG. At least until 1983, when Die Grünen gained their

first seats in the Bundestag, there was a lack of an effective opposition group that would take an anti-farmer stance. Indeed, as highlighted in Chapter 2, throughout FRG history there has been political consensus over agricultural policies. Even the emergence of the Green Party did not break the political consensus over high agricultural prices, although the debate tended to shift more towards environmental issues related to agriculture (see Chapter 6). Indeed, the Green Party has continued to advocate high food prices within the CAP, as low commodity prices might mean a need for intensification on farms, which, in turn, would have negative environmental side effects. Rather than challenge the notion of protectionism and provide a possible political ally to some of the more vociferous consumer groups, the Green Party has tended to reinforce pre-existing protectionist policy tendencies – albeit for completely different reasons. However, as a result of Green Party lobbying consumers have become more aware of food-quality issues (Baumgartner, 1988). Indeed, a variety of commentators have highlighted how FRG consumer groups in the 1980s became increasingly critical of chemical residues of pollutants in food (Hendriks, 1991). FRG consumers, therefore, were willing to continue to pay high prices for food, but only for top-quality products produced in an environmentally friendly way (see also Chapter 6).

3.6 The FRG and the second CAP crisis

The combined effect of increasing social security payments for FRG farmers (see Chapter 2) and the continuation of high MCA payments meant that, by the late 1970s, both the FRG government and its farmers felt that agriculture had fared better from the CAP than had been anticipated (reminiscent of feelings at the end of the 1960s noted in Section 3.3.4). Tangermann (1992) noted that from the late 1970s onwards the value of domestic and CAP subsidies exceeded the value of FRG agricultural production, indicating that farmers and policy-makers felt a false sense of security. This positive mood dominated the agricultural debate in the late 1970s, although the CAP had not contributed greatly to the solution of the three most pressing problems facing FRG agriculture: deficient agricultural structures, high-cost production and increasing income disparities with other economic sectors (Cecil, 1979; FAO, 1988). By the late 1970s, the MCA system was, therefore, still strongly supported by Ertl and the DBV, as it allowed the FRG to peg prices for agricultural commodities at more than 10 per cent above 'real' EEC prices.

By the early 1980s, however, deepening problems associated with the CAP overshadowed all discussions on the FRG's high MCA policy. The debate within Europe was dominated by the problem of surpluses and the associated budget crisis (Winter, 1996). By 1980, the EEC9 was producing significant levels of surpluses, particularly of wine, butter, wheat, barley and sugar (Winter, 1996). As Table 3.4 highlights, production had increased by about 2.6 per cent/year between 1973 and 1983, while consumption had only risen by 0.8 per cent over the same period, leading to an increasing discrepancy between food production and consumption. Problems were exacerbated by special import deals with 'third' (non-EEC) countries which added to surpluses (such as sugar). The costs of storing and disposing of agricultural surpluses continued to rise and began to swallow most of the CAP budget. The contradiction between the financing of surpluses, while still paying production subsidies to farmers, led many policymakers to increasingly question the aims of the CAP (Fearne, 1997).

3.6.1 CAP budget debates

The most pressing problem was the budget, as the cost of the Guarantee section of the EAGGF had sky-rocketed from ECU 4.5 billion in 1975 to ECU 11.3 billion in 1980[11] (*Agrarbericht*, 1981; Kluge, 1989b). Although national contributions had been readjusted several times since inception of the CAP, and particularly after expansion of the EEC in 1973 (see above), the FRG remained the largest net contributor to the EEC budget (Kluge, 1989b; Fearne, 1997). FRG politicians argued that this discrepancy must be solved, and Ertl argued that all member states needed to make 'financial sacrifices' if the CAP was to survive (Ertl, 1980, 1985). However, in this debate the FRG was able to hide behind the much more vocal demands for budget reform coming from Britain (Winter, 1996). Although both member states shared a common interest in reducing the cost of the CAP, however, they differed in the means to achieve this. Britain argued for a 'free market' option (price cuts) while the FRG supported a more managed solution.

In 1980, the Commission published a discussion document on the future of the CAP (CEC, 1980), in which it proposed the introduction of producer co-responsibility in the main commodity sectors (Fennell, 1997). The proposal was supported by the FRG as a preferable option to control surpluses than price cuts, and Ertl asked the other member states 'to show willingness for co-responsibility so that the established system

Table 3.4 Surpluses in the EEC, 1973 and 1983

	1973 (EEC9)	1983 (EEC10)	Average annual increase (%)
Production (million cereal units)	281	364	2.6
Consumption (million cereal units)	298	323	0.8
Self-sufficiency (%)	94	113	1.9

Source: Kluge (1989b).

that orders agricultural markets does not collapse because of a lack of funds' (Kluge, 1989b, p. 229). Ertl, therefore, continued to play the role of mediator – a role which he had already assumed at certain times during the 1970s (see above). The FRG's negotiating position was weakened, however, by domestic pressures. Talk of co-responsibility levies angered the DBV, who feared that, once again, the government would sacrifice farmers' interests for the interests of European integration. Tensions came to a head in 1981 when 200 000 FRG farmers protested across the country about their increasingly disadvantaged position in Europe – the largest farm protest in the history of the FRG (Hendriks, 1991). The DBV argued that Chancellor Schmidt was more interested in obtaining the right economic climate for industry than for agriculture, emphasising the conflict between FRG agricultural interests and the national interest. With an upcoming national election, FRG politicians were reluctant to antagonise the farm lobby. Discussions between member states over reforms were also marred by renewed currency turmoil, which put severe devaluation pressure on the French, Italian and British currencies. Despite the establishment of the European Monetary System in 1979, economic divergence between EEC countries increased and agricultural markets in various member states became more and more inflexible (Buckwell, 1997; Ritson and Harvey, 1997).

The increasing instability of the EEC milk market put further pressure on the CAP during the early 1980s. Already by 1976, rapidly rising milk surpluses at EEC level became a problem, and FRG farmers were some of the main culprits (Fearne, 1997). These problems were exacerbated by large milk surpluses in the USA and, therefore, low world market prices. A co-responsibility levy for milk introduced in 1977 for two years had been ineffective in curbing production (Fennell, 1997). The milk crisis and the CAP budgetary crisis were tightly linked, as by 1980 payments for dairy farmers swallowed a third of the entire Guarantee budget (Harris and Swinbank, 1997). Thus, politicians focused on reform of the milk regime as a way to solve the CAP's financial crisis. Countries particularly affected were France and the FRG, which together produced more than half of all dairy products in the EEC9.

To reduce the rapidly rising surpluses in the milk sector (50 per cent more milk was produced in the EEC in the early 1980s than was consumed), the Commission suggested a variety of mechanisms through which overproduction of milk could be regulated. Some scenarios envisaged a dramatic reduction of the number of dairy cows, a lowering of the milk target price, or tiered payments per cow (depending on the size of herd and holding). In 1982, co-responsibility levies for milk, cereals and rapeseed were introduced (which would kick in if production thresholds were exceeded), but the levy was set at too low a level to be an effective deterrent to producers (Fennell, 1997). More radical reform was needed.

3.6.2   The FRG and the call for CAP reform

The literature has been strongly divided about the specific role that the FRG played in calls for a more radical reform of the CAP in the early 1980s. While academic writers such as Tangermann (1979b, 1982) – a free-market proponent of the Göttinger Schule (see Chapter 2) – argued that the FRG squandered an opportunity to take a leadership role and push for major reform, more conservative writers such as Kluge (1989b) and Hendriks (1991) argue that the FRG had to steer a more cautious course as a mediator or partner, because it could not reshape the CAP on its own. Changes to the CAP could only be achieved through coalitions of various member states, and, as Winter (1996, p. 140) noted, 'the majority of member states had no pressing reason to support radical reform measures', being net beneficiaries.

The different demands placed on Agriculture Minister Ertl in the early 1980s meant that he repeatedly clashed with the Commission about fundamental questions concerning the CAP. Ertl felt increasingly frustrated about the inertia of the Commission and, according to Kluge (1989b, p. 232), he 'did not hide his at times strong disinclination toward the Brussels bureaucracy'. He complained that, despite good intentions, the will for change in Brussels was missing (Ertl, 1985). Ertl continued to argue that structural development was the key to solving the problems of the CAP and, although he was facing increasing criticisms from within the FRG about his policy of selective subsidisation, he persisted in attempting to persuade Brussels and other member states of the advantages of the Ertl Plan for structural improvement (see Chapter 2). The Commission retaliated by accusing Ertl of being a 'pawn' of the DBV – highlighting that the Commission was well aware of the powerful role of the DBV in influencing FRG agricultural policy-making decisions.

Negotiations between member states were further complicated by the accession of Greece in 1981, and preparations for the accession of Spain and Portugal (who eventually joined in 1986). Like the first phase of EEC enlargement in 1973 (see above), most FRG politicians supported further expansion. Yet, faced with the escalating second CAP crisis, Agriculture Minister Ertl (and his successor Kiechle after 1983) adopted a more cautious stance vis-à-vis EEC expansion. They feared that financial pressures on the CAP – which would inevitably increase with membership by the three southern European countries – would again have to be borne by the FRG. Possibly even more important, they feared that EEC expansion would renew pressures for price cuts detrimental to FRG farmers. However, other member states also feared that enlargement would add further to already escalating surpluses, particularly as production capacities in all three aspiring member states were above their national consumption levels (Fearne, 1997). The applicant states were all characterised by poor agricultural structures and large agricultural workforces, and were all likely to be net beneficiaries of the EAGGF (Hoggart *et al.*, 1995). However, the lure of 50 million new consumers for EEC agricultural products provided an important counter-argument which, in the end, won the day (Fearne, 1997).

3.6.3 Kiechle and the CAP: back to the family farm model

By 1983, when Agriculture Minister Kiechle took over from Ertl,[12] the budgetary problems of the CAP were at crisis point. Continuing currency discrepancies, the use of MCAs to avoid 'common' agricultural prices and the high costs of storing food surpluses, meant that solutions had to be found rapidly if the CAP was to survive. The FRG, Britain and the Netherlands insisted on balancing CAP income and expenditure, and Kiechle pleaded for reduced surpluses and better income stabilisation for farmers. He particularly urged a rapid solution to the milk surplus crisis, and highlighted that the system of co-responsibility had failed to reduce milk production (between 1982 and 1983, for example, FRG milk production had further increased by 4.5 per cent). Kiechle even threatened to stall negotiations on Spain and Portugal's accession to the EEC if no solution to the milk market crisis could be found.

Opinions in the FRG over how best to solve the milk crisis were divided. In 1980, the DBV conceded that a reduction in milk production was necessary, and argued that milk quotas represented the 'least worst' option (Neville-Rolfe, 1984). Indeed, as early as 1976 the DBV had been one of the first groups in the EEC to suggest milk quotas. As many commentators have argued, this reaction can partly be explained by the fact that the DBV saw quotas as the least damaging option. The DBV wanted to prevent at all costs the continuation of a system based on co-responsibility as this heavily penalised FRG dairy farmers (Tangermann, 1982; Heinze and Voelzkow, 1993). The DBV, therefore, hoped that even small family farms could generate sufficient income through a quota system to survive. However, Ertl was unable to push through the milk quota option in the early 1980s because of lack of support from the Commission and other member states, a factor that arguably contributed to Ertl's dwindling popularity among FRG farmers (Kluge, 1989b).

Ertl's replacement as agriculture minister in 1983, Kiechle, came from Bavaria where dairy production was important, and had an intimate knowledge of the milk sector. His appointment coincided with Germany's presidency of the Council of Ministers, and it was during the German presidency that the Commission issued a new set of CAP reform proposals (Fennell, 1997). These proposals included a set of drastic measures, including price cuts, maximum production guarantees together with co-responsibility levies, controls on intervention spending, and milk quotas. The FRG, possibly because of its role as president of the Council of Ministers, generally supported these proposals, although it continued to criticise the Commission's 'policy of price pressure' as a solution to surplus management. However, any discussion of MCA cuts was 'completely unacceptable' to the FRG (Kluge, 1989b, p. 301), showing that, yet again, the FRG was willing to accept CAP reform as long as it could make up for farm income losses through adjustments of MCAs. By arguing that without MCAs FRG farm incomes would be reduced by about 15 per cent, Kiechle referred to the previous gentleman's agreements of 1975 and 1979, which allowed the FRG to raise (or at least maintain) MCAs if farmers' incomes were at risk. The DBV, however, was particularly incensed by the Commission's proposals, and predicted increasing frustration among FRG farmers if the reforms were implemented. For the first time the DBV used 'environmental blackmail', as they warned that farmers would need to intensify to make up for income losses, with potentially devastating implications for the environment. In a confrontational situation, Kiechle warned FRG farmers not to intensify (particularly not to further increase milk production), and he promised that the government would try to do the utmost to safeguard FRG farmers' livelihoods.

In 1984, agreement was reached between the EEC10 member states to introduce milk quotas. FRG's acceptance of milk quotas, despite concern within the DBV, has been interpreted in a number of ways. While Kluge (1989b) argues that many factors within the EEC10 provided favourable ground for the introduction of quotas (not least the failure of co-responsibility and the threat of drastic price cuts), Lechi (1987) suggests that Kiechle was a key factor in their implementation. Hendriks (1991) meanwhile, sees the acceptance of the principle of milk quotas by Kiechle as mere damage limitation in the absence of any other viable solution that would help maintain FRG farmers' incomes. Given that Kiechle was newly appointed, and 'new to the game', it is unlikely that he could have exerted strong influence within the CAM. It is more likely that Chancellor Kohl was the driving force behind milk quotas, as he was a much stauncher 'Euro-enthusiast' than his predecessor Schmidt, and therefore gave European integration a high priority. He was also newly elected and, therefore, could afford to anger farmers early on in his four-year term of office.

Milk quotas were calculated for each country based on 1981 production levels (plus 1 per cent). A maximum quota level of 100 million tonnes of milk was agreed, of which the FRG share was about one-quarter – a reduction by about 7 per cent compared to output in 1983. On the basis of this national quota, individual quotas could be allocated to dairy farms. Because quotas were calculated according to 1981 production levels, young farmers who were in the process of expanding their dairy herds were particularly penalised (Henrichsmeyer, 1986; Kluge, 1989b). Although the milk quota system did not immediately solve milk market problems (for instance, butter production continued to rise until 1986), it was successful enough to remain in place as a supply control mechanism to this day (Winter, 1996). In the FRG, the milk quota system showed rapid results, with a reduction in dairy farms by over 10 per cent and dairy cow numbers by about 5 per cent.

The introduction of milk quotas was used by the DBV as a further argument to call for adequate agricultural prices for FRG farmers, and Kiechle responded by continuing the high price policy line that had characterised the FRG position since inception of the CAP. Kiechle defended high MCAs in the FRG (which in 1984 were still the highest in the EEC10), and argued that they should not be seen as *substitutes* for income subsidies but as *part of* a vital farm survival policy. Both Kiechle and the DBV were against the dismantling of MCAs, and saw pressure from other EEC partners as unjustified intervention in FRG income policy. Kiechle's rhetoric, therefore, differed from Ertl's in that he increasingly tried to justify MCAs as a permanent arrangement to protect farm incomes rather than a temporary mechanism to overcome exchange rate disparities (Kluge, 1989b). He argued that the FRG had already gradually reduced MCAs (with the two gentleman's agreements of 1975 and 1979; see above) and that in real terms they should be at 27 rather than 13 per cent.

Kiechle also adopted a different rhetoric to Ertl concerning the family farm, returning to the traditional conservative discourse of protecting the small family farm that had dominated FRG policy in the 1950s and 1960s (see Chapter 2). This change of ideology was evident at the 1983 European Council meeting in Stuttgart where Kiechle attempted to influence EEC structural policy guidelines with a view to supporting family farms. Kiechle indicated that he intended to move away from the earlier Ertl/Mansholt ideas of selective subsidisation. The CDU-led government, therefore, strongly advocated a more conservative and 'voter-friendly' approach akin to the Adenauer era of the 1950s, which included promoting the virtues of policies that would help the survival of family farms.

3.7 The mid- to late 1980s: the FRG as a CAP policy shaper and obstructor

3.7.1 Increasing domestic pressure

By the mid-1980s Kiechle had emerged as an outspoken obstructor in European agricultural policy negotiations. This was due to his increasing political assertiveness, enabled by the political strength of the CDU-led government under Kohl, but also to the good relationship that developed between the DBV (and its leader von Heereman) and Kiechle, in contrast to the more distant relationship between von Heereman and Ertl. Although the importance of the Kiechle–von Heereman relationship should not be overestimated (Hendriks, 1987; Kluge, 1989b), it provides an additional explanation for the conflictual course that Kiechle began to adopt vis-à-vis the Commission over price policy and MCAs. However, there was dissent within the FRG over the protectionist policy line pursued by Kiechle and the DBV, particularly from the Göttinger Schule who criticised milk quotas as distorting the internal market. The Göttinger Schule, therefore, re-emphasised their dislike of state control of agricultural markets and urged the government to adopt policies in line with EEC Commission suggestions – in particular the lowering of agricultural prices (Hendriks, 1991). They argued that only by readjusting prices to 'normal' levels could a market balance be regained.

The main cause of conflict between the FRG and the Commission and other member states at this time was, however, over MCAs. The MCA issue flared up again during a European summit meeting in Athens in 1983, when France strongly criticised the MCA system, and President Mitterrand referred to it as a system that subsidised agriculture in one country (referring to the FRG) on the back of other member states (referring to France). As a result, no agreement on the refinancing of the CAP could be reached in that year. Despite growing pressure from Europe, Kiechle was unable to agree to any cuts because of well-founded fears that a reduction in MCAs would result in the bankruptcy of many farms. Pressure was exerted on Kiechle not to give in to the Commission by the DBV. It pointed out that FRG agricultural incomes (at least those of full-time farmers) had further fallen short of comparative industrial wages – particularly between 1980 and 1985 (Ehlers, 1988; von Urff, 1990). Net economic productivity per worker in FRG agriculture remained low in comparison to other EEC10 states (see Figure 2.7), and especially during the late 1970s and early 1980s the CAP had aggravated the income gap between smaller and larger farms. By the mid-1980s, for example, 10 per cent of FRG farmers controlled almost one-third of the total farming income, while the lower 40 per cent accounted for less than one-fifth (Jones, 1994). Faced with increasing costs and reduced support, many farmers gave up farming altogether (in 1987, for example, there were 3.7 per cent less farms than in 1986; see Table 2.1), or sought non-agricultural sources of income (see Table 2.3). In his first two years of office, therefore, Kiechle had to repeatedly defend himself against criticisms from farmers that he was 'not doing enough' to safeguard FRG farmers' incomes (von Urff and von Meyer, 1987). Indeed, Kiechle was often seen by farmers and the DBV as the culprit for unpopular EEC decisions. Another complaint often voiced by the DBV was that FRG farmers faced higher production costs than farmers in other parts of Europe because of stricter FRG environmental and planning legislation (Tangermann, 1992).

As a result of irreconcilable domestic and European pressures, a complicated compromise agreement was reached in 1984, whereby the FRG appeared to agree to a 5 per cent cut in positive MCAs. This meant that, for the first time since their inception, FRG MCAs were below 10 per cent (for instance, milk 7.9 per cent, beef 6.8 per cent, cereals 7.4 per cent), sparking another spate of farmer demonstrations during which Kiechle was branded as a 'traitor' and 'criminal' (Hendriks, 1991). However, at the same time a 'switchover mechanism' was introduced which altered the way in which guaranteed prices and MCAs were calculated, effectively pegging prices to the level of the DM (Tangermann, 1992). This meant that, in effect, prices were allowed to rise, despite the fact that price cuts were agreed! The switchover mechanism continued until MCAs were finally dismantled in 1993 (see Chapter 5).

How could the DBV continue to exert such power over Kiechle? Chapter 2 outlined in detail reasons why the DBV had remained a powerful agricultural actor throughout the period of the FRG, despite rapidly dwindling numbers of people working in agriculture (see Table 2.4). The percentage of members of the Bundestag from the ranks of the DBV (mainly CDU/CSU and FDP) had also dwindled from 12 per cent in 1957 to about 6 per cent in the late 1980s (Henrichsmeyer and Witzke, 1994). Yet, Andrlik (1981, p. 104) has argued that 'the DBV has been able to control West German agricultural policies both domestically and within the EEC'. This view was reiterated by Heinze and Voelzkow (1993, p. 32) who suggested that 'the DBV has been able to preserve its *de facto* power of veto, preventing a radical reform of the costly protectionist agricultural policy'.

In addition to the good personal relations between Kiechle and von Heereman, there are a number of other explanations for the DBV's strong voice in FRG agricultural politics in the mid-1980s. First, some have argued that the dwindling membership of the DBV was largely made up by the growing importance of the European farmers' pressure group (COPA), which in cases of common policy demands may have increased the lobbying power of national farmers' unions[13] (Hendriks, 1991; Heinze and Voelzkow, 1993). Second, von Heereman's emergence as a charismatic and outspoken (and internationally well respected) figurehead of the DBV possibly made up for the reduction in members (Kluge, 1989b). Third, internal political factors in the 1980s also continued to play an important role. Although the CDU/FDP government had gained power with a respectable majority in 1983, it struggled to maintain its lead in the 1987 elections, and relied yet again on winning votes in rural areas. Increasingly conscious of being a minority lobby group in a highly developed industrial country, the DBV retrenched into a defensive attitude towards FRG policies and the CAP. As a result, it strongly urged Kiechle to take a confrontational stance on the Commission's suggested price cuts.

3.7.2 The 'historic' Kiechle veto

Tensions came to a head in 1985 when the Commission proposed a reduction in the cereals intervention price of 3.6 per cent because of surplus production the previous year (Fennell, 1997). This reduction was in line with the co-responsibility policy that had been introduced in 1982, whereby if production thresholds were exceeded, support prices in the following year would be automatically reduced in relation to the surplus produced (Swinbank, 1989; Tangermann, 1992). In addition, price cuts were proposed for beef (–1 per cent) and for rape (–3 per cent). These proposed cuts would have a serious effect on FRG farm incomes (Weinstock, 1987). The value of rape produced in the FRG in the mid-1980s, for example, amounted to DM 1 billion/year, and the large cuts suggested by Brussels threatened to put several thousand farmers specialising in rape production out of business (Kluge, 1989b).

As a result, Kiechle vetoed the price package. This 'historic veto of 1985' (Mehl, 1997) which was of 'exceptional gravity' (Bulmer and Paterson, 1987; Hendriks, 1989, 1991) was the first time since FRG membership of the EEC that the country openly challenged CAP price proposals, and only the second time that it vetoed a proposal by the Commission.[14] For the first time, the FRG stood alone as obstructor, and Kiechle argued that agreeing to lower prices for cereals at this point in time would set a whole price reduction avalanche into motion, with catastrophic results for FRG farming (Kiechle, 1986).

There is no doubt that the Kiechle veto was partly influenced by the electoral defeat of the ruling coalition in regional elections in Nordrhein-Westfalen (CDU/CSU 36 per cent; SPD 52 per cent!) and fears of losing farmers' votes in the upcoming 1987 national elections. The press was also adopting an increasingly sceptical discourse about the CAP at the time (especially leading national newspapers such as *Die Zeit* and the *Frankfurter Allgemeine Zeitung* and critical weekly magazines such as *Der Spiegel*) which put increasing pressure on Kiechle to 'act tough'. Kiechle argued that by agreeing to the introduction of milk quotas, the country had already accepted an unfavourable deal. This meant that if price cuts were to go ahead, other mechanisms had to be put into place to help farmers' incomes. The FRG, therefore, openly acted as a policy obstructor. The veto was particularly directed at the proposed cereal price reductions, but was also meant as a signal that the FRG was increasingly unhappy with the general direction of price policy debates in Brussels. Hendriks (1991) argues that Kiechle knew exactly that his veto would be strongly opposed by the Commission and other member states, and that it would lead to increasing isolation of the FRG in the EEC12. She, therefore, sees the Kiechle veto as a sign of increasing assertiveness of the FRG in CAP policy-making, epitomising the shift from a policy partner to one of policy leader/obstructor in which the FRG, perhaps for the first time, put national agricultural interests before the interests of European integration. Bulmer and Paterson (1987) argue, however, that Kiechle acted without the full support of the federal government. They noted that at the same time that Kiechle was using the veto, the Foreign Office was promoting European integration in discussions over completion of the single market. Thus, Kiechle directly contravened the FRG's wider European policy position.

Pressures were mounting for CAP reform, however. These pressures came from three sources (Fennell, 1997). First, the Single European Act of 1985 laid down a commitment to complete the single market by the end of 1992. This highlighted the absurdity of MCAs within the CAP, and increased pressure for their removal (Tangermann, 1992). Second, it was also evident that agriculture would be on the agenda in the next round of GATT talks (see Chapter 5), and this could lead to external pressure for CAP reform. Third, internal pressure for reform came from the ever-worsening budgetary situation, and particularly the cost of intervention storage.

3.7.3   The aftermath of the Kiechle veto

The Kiechle veto became crucial in shaping EEC price negotiations for the remainder of the 1980s. The impact of the veto was felt not only in the 1985/86 price negotiations, but it also put the FRG into a new bargaining position that was to disrupt future CAP discussions. Hendriks (1991, p. 108) argued that the veto led to a substantial boost in FRG government self-confidence, with newly emerging government rhetoric about the FRG 'as a great and powerful member state'. The veto may have also delayed the complete dismantling of positive MCAs until 1993, instead of the more rapid planned abolition by the late 1980s (Kluge, 1989b; Henrichsmeyer and Witzke, 1994).

Although Kiechle was dissatisfied with the price agreements reached in 1986 (for instance, the cereal price was lowered by 1.8 per cent), he abstained from another veto as this would have led to the introduction of emergency measures, placing the CAP under further strain. Hendriks (1991, p. 70) argued that at the time 'Bonn appeared to modify its principles in relation to the crucial question of agricultural support prices. Germany's decision was dominated by the bitter wisdom learned from previous years and influenced by the budgetary situation: it did not indicate a change of heart.' In addition, it was vital that an agreement on prices was reached in 1986 as a basis for the start of the 1986–93 GATT Uruguay Round (see Chapter 5). However, the CAP continued to be under extreme pressure throughout the remainder of the 1980s.

In 1987, facing another serious budget crisis, the Commission proposed a number of CAP reform measures to both curb production and contain spending, including the continuation of co-responsibility, but with new rules to make it more effective (Fennell, 1997). In the FRG, these proposals sent shock waves through the farming community, and larger producers of grain, livestock and milk felt particularly threatened (Swinbank, 1989; Jones, 1994). Rather than take a purely obstructive policy line again, however, the FRG lobbied hard for the introduction of measures to encourage farmers to extensify production in return for payments, as an alternative strategy to price constraints[15] (Jones, 1990, 1991). This time the FRG was successful in getting this proposal accepted as part of a compromise package in return for FRG agreement on modest price increases. In 1988, the extensification regulation was replaced by a new regulation (1094/88) which retained extensification for beef and wine, but introduced set-aside for cereals (Winter, 1996). Initially, these measures were introduced on a voluntary basis.

Kiechle argued that the price negotiations of 1987 had been the most difficult so far, and although he reluctantly agreed to the modest price increases suggested for most commodities, he hoped that his position made it increasingly clear to the EC that the FRG refused to use price policy as a way of addressing EC surplus problems. Kiechle re-emphasised the importance of the two gentleman's agreements from 1975 and 1979 (see above), whereby it was guaranteed that FRG farmers should not be disadvantaged by EC price policies.

The FRG proposals for extensification and set-aside indicate its increasing assertiveness within European agricultural policy-making. It could be argued, therefore, that the FRG adopted a role as policy leader (cf. Kluge, 1989b; Hendriks, 1991). According to Hendriks (1991, p. 73) 'the agreement ... was in line with German demands'. It is important to stress that the idea of paying farmers to extensify beef and wine production, and to set-aside arable land formed a logical continuation of the persistent FRG demands for mechanisms to safeguard FRG farm incomes (following on from FRG support for milk quotas in the early 1980s), and the FRG was also in a position to afford this expensive policy option (see below). The FRG was, therefore, the main advocate of production controls as an alternative to price control as a way to regulate agricultural markets (von Urff, 1987, 1988; Henrichsmeyer and Witzke, 1994). Set-aside would tackle the problem of surpluses, while still guaranteeing incomes for FRG farmers.[16] The FRG was also the main advocate of introducing an early retirement scheme for farmers, as it would support domestic agricultural structural policy (see Chapter 2).

As a result of the input that the FRG had during the formulation of set-aside policies, the set-aside scheme in the FRG was one of the most successful in the EC12 (HMLFN, 1990; Ilbery, 1998). As member states were free to set their own levels of set-aside payments for their farmers, countries such as France or Spain (least enthusiastic about the policy) offered small sums (resulting in low farmer participation), while the FRG offered generous subsidy levels (Jones *et al.*, 1993). The result was an enthusiastic participation of FRG farmers, with over a quarter of all set-aside land in the Community located in the FRG. The disappointing figure for the rest of the Community (only about 2.8 per cent of the EC's arable land was set aside by 1990) re-emphasised that the FRG had lobbied for a policy which suited its farmers and was, arguably, less suited to the situation in other member states.

Yet, the increased influence of the FRG on CAP policies in the mid- to late 1980s was not solely linked to Kiechle's assertiveness. Wider changes in the EC12 political economy meant that some of the CAP measures in the late 1980s, that turned out to be highly favourable for the FRG, were also in the interest of the Community as a whole (von Urff, 1987, 1988). In addition, by the late 1980s the Kohl government had established itself as the most dominant political driving force for European integration among the EC12 (Larres and Panayi, 1996) – epitomised by the FRG's position as the third largest global economic power (Smyser, 1993). Kiechle's rising influence, therefore, also has to be understood in the context of the FRG's growing political and economic influence that simultaneously increased its bargaining power in the EC[17] (Fearne, 1997). Nonetheless, there is no doubt that 1985 marked a turning point in FRG–Brussels relationships. The FRG had moved from an early CAP policy partner to an increasingly assertive policy leader (and at times policy obstructor).

3.8   Conclusions

Building on the discussion of agricultural structures and national policies in the FRG outlined in Chapter 2, this chapter has discussed the changing policy position of the FRG towards the CAP between 1957 and 1990. The underlying question was whether the FRG acted as a leader, partner or obstructor within the EEC agricultural policy-making framework. The discussion has highlighted that the FRG's role has been highly complex and that it has shifted considerably, depending on internal and external factors, both in terms of how the FRG has influenced developments of agricultural policy in the EEC and how, in turn, the CAP has affected domestic problems in the FRG. Whether the FRG is seen as policy leader or obstructor also depends on the perspective of the analyst, and different commentators have taken different views (for instance, Neville-Rolfe, 1984; Fennell, 1987; Hendriks, 1991; Henrichsmeyer and Witzke, 1994).

We have shown that the FRG has, at different times, acted as leader, partner and obstructor in the CAP, as summarised in Table 3.5. While in the early years of the CAP the FRG's position could best be characterised as partner, in the 1980s it increasingly adopted the role of obstructor and leader. Throughout the CAP's history, however, the FRG has shown 'obstructing tendencies' in its demands for high prices and the continuation of MCAs. There is general consensus that, from the beginning of the CAP, the FRG was largely responsible for the protectionist character of CAP market regimes and for high commodity prices. These obstructing tendencies were often exacerbated by the politically powerful DBV, which was able to exert considerable pressure on the FRG government to maintain a high price policy, particularly during election periods. Only once, however, with the Kiechle veto of 1987, has the FRG adopted an outright position as isolated policy obstructor, and this event is dwarfed by the much more vocal and frequent obstructive behaviour of other member states (notably France and Britain).

Table 3.5   The FRG as a leader, partner or obstructor in CAP decision-making

Obstructing tendencies	• The FRG's high price policy to protect farm incomes • Use of positive MCAs to maintain artificially high prices • Opposition to the Mansholt Plan • The Kiechle veto • Criticisms over FRG contributions to the EAGGF
Partnership tendencies	• Support for the CAP despite its negative impact on FRG farmers • Acceptance of high EAGGF contributions • Willingness to seek compromises in CAP reform negotiations • Support for EEC enlargement and continued integration
Leadership tendencies	• Influence over the form that the CAP took • Support for structural policies • Support for milk quotas • Support for extensification and set-aside

Source: Authors.

Arguably, the role that best describes the FRG's role in the CAP is partner, as the FRG has continually 'lost out' from the CAP but has accepted it in return for European integration and industrial growth. The government has also been prepared to buy farmer support for the CAP by accepting high budget contributions. As a result, agricultural interests have been 'sacrificed' on a number of occasions for the wider national interest. The predominant role of partner is also due to the FRG's desire to be a 'good European' – strongly linked to the guilt-shedding process in the post-war FRG, and the need to subordinate its national identity to a European identity. Indeed, 'to question the idea of European integration is a political taboo ... and, since the CAP has always been regarded as the necessary prerequisite for the European take-off, critics of the CAP tend to be treated as critics of Europe' (Hendriks, 1991, p. 203). As a result, Neville-Rolfe (1984) argued that the FRG has tended to be *reactive* rather than *proactive*, and the FRG has tried repeatedly to hide behind other countries in negotiations over CAP reform measures. The mismatch between the FRG's agricultural and national interests has at times led to clashes between the government and the DBV, and indeed between the government and the BML, but on only one occasion (the Kiechle veto) has the FRG put the interest of FRG farmers before the national interest (and in this case we have argued that the BML was acting alone without the support of the government). However, the FRG has on many occasions been an influential partner, in that in return for agreement on fundamental decisions it has been able to extract important concessions. In this way, many aspects of the CAP (for instance, price support and structural policy) are modelled on FRG policy priorities. Indeed, given the structural and ideological differences between the FRG and other EEC member states, it is a tribute to the FRG's powers of compromise and negotiation that the FRG successfully managed to manipulate the CAP to maintain its agricultural policy goals, namely the maintenance of the family farm and the managed adjustment of farm structures.

Leadership tendencies only began to emerge as the FRG assumed an increasingly assertive position within Europe, linked to its growing economic and political strength. Leadership tendencies became particularly apparent during the 1970s and 1980s when the FRG began to introduce policy measures subsequently adopted at EEC level, associated with what some have termed 'the rebirth of Germany's self-confidence' (Smyser, 1993; Larres and Panayi, 1996). Due to its increasing economic and political power in the EEC in the 1980s, the FRG influenced the CAP agenda to a degree that would have been inconceivable in previous decades. Arguably, the FRG was a key player in solving the CAP crises of the 1980s through the introduction of production controls such as milk quotas, extensification and set-aside. Given the FRG's particular agricultural policy priorities, however, of protecting farm incomes at all costs, it is debatable whether FRG leadership (or influence exerted through partnership) in the agricultural field has been positive or detrimental to the overall development of the CAP. Tangermann (1992), for instance, is an outspoken critic of FRG policy, arguing that the FRG has obstructed the development of a single market in agriculture through its demands for MCAs. He also points out that the FRG has managed to maintain high domestic subsidies for agriculture outside the CAP (mainly social security payments), thereby disregarding one of the key principles of a single market. It is indisputable, however, that the FRG's commitment to European integration was a key factor in the survival and expansion of the EC, and in this respect the FRG has played a fundamental leadership role.

The fact that the CAP survived all the crises of its first three decades is seen as a tribute to the political commitment of all member states to European integration, which is why it has been described as a 'symbol of cooperation' (Hill, 1984, cited in Hoggart *et al.*, 1995, p. 110). However, by the late 1980s the fundamental problems of the CAP had still not been tackled, and pressures for more radical reforms were mounting. At the same time, a new 'agri-environmental' discourse was beginning to emerge (see Chapter 6) in the FRG and other member states, which was to have an important influence on future CAP development. Thus, German reunification occurred at a time when the CAP was under immense pressure, and when questions were beginning to be raised about the role of farmers and food production in society. These issues will be the focus of discussion in the remainder of this book.

4
The Challenge of German Reunification

4.1 Introduction

Chapters 2 and 3 have analysed in detail the development of agricultural structures and policies in the former FRG from 1945 to 1990, and have examined the former FRG's role in the development of the CAP. The aims of this chapter are twofold: to outline the development of agriculture in the former GDR from 1945 to 1990, and to analyse the restructuring of agriculture since reunification of the two Germanies in 1990. The first part of this chapter will focus on the former GDR and the contrasting path that agriculture took here to that in the West. This first section of the chapter is divided into two subsections: the first considers changes in landownership, land rights and farm structures, while the second focuses on the development of agricultural production.

The restructuring of agriculture in the former GDR following reunification occupies the main part of this chapter. The socialist agricultural sector of the GDR has been incorporated into the market economy of the FRG and into the CAP, with associated fundamental upheavals to the economy and society of rural areas of the new *Länder*. Never before in Europe's history has such an agricultural policy challenge been faced in such a short time-span, and, not surprisingly, the restructuring of agriculture in the new *Länder* was a significant agricultural policy issue in Germany in the early 1990s (although it coincided with important agricultural policy debates at European and international levels which will be explored in Chapter 5). On one level restructuring can be seen as a technical problem, but it touches more deep-seated legal, economic and social problems which have made it a highly politicised issue. Thus, while this chapter focuses on restructuring within the new *Länder*, it also considers the impact that reunification has had on agricultural structures and politics in Germany as a whole.

4.2 Agricultural structures, production and trade in the GDR, 1945–90

4.2.1 Land reform and collectivisation

The end of the Second World War saw the division of Germany among the four Allied powers (see Chapter 2). The Soviet military authorities occupied the eastern sector of Germany that was soon to become the GDR (so-called Soviet Occupation Zone or SOZ). The four-year occupation by the Soviets initiated fundamental changes in the structure of agriculture which have had lasting effects on the region. All four Allied powers were concerned about the survival of large landed estates in Germany with their negative associations with the old political order (Fulbrook, 1990), but the geographical concentration of landed estates in the SOZ, together with the Soviet commitment to Communist principles, made landownership a particularly pressing issue for the Soviet authorities. Twenty-eight per cent of the agricultural area in the SOZ was owned by estates of 100 ha or more (Table 4.1), with even higher concentrations in the northern part of the SOZ (present-day Mecklenburg-Vorpommern). A comparison with Table 2.1 (showing holding sizes in the FRG) highlights the differences between the eastern and western zones. The Soviet authorities advocated a sweeping land reform. Agreement was reached among the Allies for a land reform to be carried out throughout Germany, but in practice it was only carried out with any effect in the SOZ (McInnis *et al.*, 1960; Fischer, 1994).

The so-called 'democratic land reform' of 1945–49 led to the confiscation of 13 699 holdings covering 3.3 million ha of agricultural and forested land out of the total SOZ agricultural and forested land area of 9.5 million ha (Ehrenforth, 1991). All estates of over 100 ha were confiscated without financial compensation, as were many smaller estates whose owners were accused of being Nazis and war criminals (Sinclair, 1979; Hohmann, 1984). The expropriated land was placed in a land fund (*Bodenfond*). Many

Table 4.1 Structure of agriculture in the SOZ, 1939

Farm size groups (ha)	Per cent of farms	Per cent of agricultural area
<5	57.7	9.2
5–20	31.7	31.8
20–50	8.2	22.4
50–100	1.4	8.4
<100	1.0	28.2

Source: Thöne (1993, p. 8).

expropriated owners fled to the west, where they later received partial compensation from the FRG government. Of these expropriated lands, about 2.1 million ha were redistributed in small plots (average size 8 ha) to landless farm labourers and non-farm workers, refugees from former German territories to the east, and small farmers (Reichelt, 1992). These land reform beneficiaries were known as new farmers or land recipients (*Neubauern* or *Bodenempfänger*).

The land reform resulted in a more equitable distribution of landownership and a significant increase in the number of farms from 570 000 in 1939 to over 800000 (Hohmann, 1984). However, it did nothing to improve productivity. Despite a subsidised building programme to provide farm houses and sheds for the *Neubauern*, most of the newly created holdings were far too small to be economically viable, and production was also hampered by shortages of farm inputs and by the absence of any effective marketing and distribution system (Löwenthal, 1950; Hohmann, 1984). Many land reform holdings were later abandoned and the land returned to the land fund (BMIB, 1985). In 1953, agricultural output was still below pre-war levels (McInnis *et al.*, 1960).

The expansion of private landownership proved short-lived following the creation of the GDR in October 1949, as the second SED conference in 1952 introduced a farm collectivisation policy (Bergmann, 1992). This was in line with Soviet-imposed policies in other Eastern Bloc countries. Collectivisation was seen as a way to socialise the countryside by turning farmers into 'workers' and farming into an 'industry'. Although inspired by Marxist ideology, there were also economic reasons for collectivisation, such as the economies of scale that could be achieved through large-scale farming. In 1952, food rationing was still in force and there was an urgent need to increase food supplies. Further, the agricultural workforce was a reserve army of labour for the growing industrial sector, and collectivisation would free up agricultural workers (Berentsen, 1981).

Collectivisation was officially a voluntary process, but was accompanied by strong political pressures. Farmers, including *Neubauern*, were offered financial incentives, such as tax reductions and debt write-offs, as well as lower production targets and better access to farm input supplies, to enter their farms into so-called agricultural production cooperatives (*Landwirtschaftliche Produktionsgenossenschaften* or LPGs), while farmers wishing to remain independent were penalised by higher production targets (Reichelt, 1992). The collectivisation process continued throughout the 1950s, with penalties for farmers remaining outside the LPGs becoming increasingly harsh, until 1960 when LPGs covered about 87 per cent of the agricultural land area (Thöne, 1993). The state also took ownership of the 1.1 million ha of expropriated agricultural and forested lands which had not been redistributed, of which approximately 450 000 ha of agricultural land went to form specialised state farms (*Volkseigene Güter* or VEGs).[1] The amount of state-owned land increased by 700 000 ha during the 1950s due to the further expropriation of land from farmers accused of political crimes (such as failure to meet production targets) and due to the appropriation of lands abandoned by farmers who fled to the west (BMIB, 1985). Between 1953 and 1960, 11 per cent of refugees to the FRG were farmers (Ehrenforth, 1991), and their lands were largely entrusted to LPGs to manage.

Given that collectivisation proceeded so rapidly on the heels of land reform, the purpose of that reform has been subsequently questioned (Hagedorn, 1992; Reichelt, 1992). By creating a new class of property owners, it could even be seen as counter-productive to the Communist cause. It is thought that Stalin did not want to risk angering the other three Allies following the end of the war by introducing collectivisation immediately. Hagedorn (1992) speculated that the land reform was intended to pave the way for collectivisation by creating inefficiency and instability in the farm sector, so that farmers would be more willing to join collectives at a later date.

The LPGs, with control of 87 per cent of the agricultural land area, played a crucial role in agricultural production in the GDR. There were initially three types of LPG. In type 1 LPGs, members handed over control of their arable land to the cooperative, but retained control of their livestock, pasture land, buildings and machinery. Members, therefore, retained a large degree of independence. In type 2 LPGs, livestock and machinery were collectivised as well as arable land (control was taken over by the cooperative). In type 3 LPGs, pasture land and farm buildings were additionally collectivised (Vogeler, 1996). The type 3 LPG was, therefore, cooperative in name only; in practice it was a collective farm and was the type preferred by the SED. Although, in theory, members retained ownership of land, in practice ownership was meaningless as all rights to use, manage and profit from the land were taken over by the cooperative (in contrast to cooperatives in Western democracies). Land could not be bought or sold, as under Marxist ideology land is the means of production but has no market value in itself (Hagedorn, 1992). The type 3 LPG farmers were paid in 'work units' according to the amount of work contributed and the profit of the LPG, but not according to the size of their land holding (*Agra-Europe Bonn*, 27.8.1990). Agricultural work on LPGs was highly specialised and regulated. There was strict division of labour according to work teams (for instance, tractor drivers, milkers, machine repairers), and workers had set working hours and paid holidays. The workforce was also highly qualified, with 91 per cent having a specialist training (Fink *et al.*, 1994). In line with the GDR's commitment to female employment, almost 40 per cent of the agricultural workforce was female. However, women tended to be concentrated in traditionally 'female' work (such as small livestock husbandry, catering, cleaning and welfare) (Fink *et al.*, 1994).

By 1973, 94 per cent of LPGs were type 3 (Hohmann, 1984). Thus, the concept of private ownership of land gradually lost significance (Hagedorn, 1992), and in 1977 the state announced that LPG workers had the same rights and duties as LPG landowning members (BMIB, 1985). Since landownership no longer conferred any special benefits, many landowners left the LPGs, while non-landowning members joined, and so over time the proportion of LPG members with ownership rights declined (Hagedorn, 1992). By 1989, over two-thirds of LPG members were non-landowners (Panzig, 1995). Boundary markers between individual farm properties were lost as fields were enlarged, and the distinction between state-owned and privately owned land became blurred as parcels of state-owned land were scattered between privately owned plots (*Der Spiegel*, 1991a; Hagedorn, 1992). Further, new farm buildings were erected without reference to landownership (Hagedorn *et al.*, 1997).

However, some agricultural land remained in private ownership through-out the GDR period. This consisted of specialised horticultural and viticul-tural smallholdings, and church estates that were never expropriated. Although the number of private farms declined during the GDR period, in 1989 there were still about 3500 private holdings farming 5.4 per cent of the agricultural land area (Neander, 1992) (Table 4.2). In addition to these full-time farms, private allotments played an important economic and social role. Members of LPGs were entitled to own and manage small allot-ments (up to 0.5 ha per family) for their own consumption, but were also allowed to sell surplus produce for profit. LPG allotments made up 5 per cent of the LPG land area (*Agrarbericht*, 1991). Many non-agricultural

Table 4.2   Development of farm holdings in the GDR, 1960–89 (number of holdings)

Farm holding type	1960	1970	1980	1989	UAA (1989) (%)
State farms:	669	511	469	464	7.5
arable	–	–	66	152	6.8
livestock	–	–	319	312	0.7
LPGs:	19 313	9009	3946	4015	86.8
arable	–	–	1047	1164	80.8
livestock	–	–	2899	2851	1.2
household plots	–	–	–	–	4.8
GPGs[a]	298	346	213	199	0.2
Private and church	28 238	n.d.	5000	3558	5.4

Note
[a]*Gärtnerische Produktionsgenossenschaften* (specialist market garden cooperatives).
Sources: Zentralverwaltung für Statistik (1989, p. 181); Brezinski (1990); *Agrarbericht* (1991, p. 141).

workers were also allowed private allotments (Brezinski, 1990; Neander, 1992). Although occupying only a small share of the agricultural land area, the contribution of this privately owned/managed land to total production was significant for certain products, such as fruit (22 per cent), honey (98 per cent), eggs (34 per cent), chicken and rabbit meat (both 25 per cent), and wool (28 per cent) (*Agrarbericht*, 1991; Neander, 1992). The allotments provided an important additional source of income for village residents, as well as providing fresh, good-quality food for home consumption (Zierold, 1997). The productivity of private farms and allotments in the GDR compared to the inefficiency of the state and collective farms (see below) was a fact exploited by FRG politicians and the media to illustrate the failure of socialist agriculture.

4.2.2 Industrialisation of agriculture: the drive to increase food production

Despite (or because of) collectivisation, agricultural yields continued to fall further behind those in the FRG. While in the late 1930s yields in the east had been equal to, or higher than, those in the west, in the period 1966–70 cereal yields in the GDR were only 86 per cent, sugar beet only 70 per cent, potatoes only 66 per cent and milk yields only 81 per cent of those in the FRG (Hohmann, 1984). This situation was politically embarrassing to the SED party leadership and counter to the Marxist ideology of self-sufficiency in agricultural products. The state, therefore, introduced new policies throughout the 1960s and 1970s to raise agricultural output by promoting further specialisation, intensification and concentration of production, rather than by a relaxation of controls and a return to private enterprise (BMIB, 1985).

One policy was to increase the size of LPGs. Table 4.2 shows that between 1960 and 1970 the number of LPGs fell by more than 50 per cent through rationalisation and amalgamations (and at the same time types 1 and 2 LPGs were converted into type 3 LPGs). In the 1970s, the state took the questionable decision to reorganise LPGs and state farms into specialist arable or livestock enterprises, and at the same time to increase their size, thus further reducing the number of LPGs (Bergmann, 1992). By 1989, there were only just over 4000 LPGs. The average size of arable LPGs was 4600 ha, while the average livestock LPG had little land but over 1600 LU, and often considerably more than this (*Agrarbericht*, 1991). For instance, dairy LPGs kept up to 10 000 cows, and poultry LPGs up to several hundred thousand hens (Vogeler, 1996).

Although the agricultural area declined by 5.5 per cent between 1950 and 1989, the ratio of agricultural area to population of 0.37 ha per capita was almost twice as high as in the FRG (Hohmann, 1984; see also Chapter 2). The percentage of arable and pasture land remained constant over the whole GDR period, with the majority (about 80 per cent) of the agricultural area under arable production, but the number of livestock expanded dramatically (Table 4.3). This expansion was enabled by the development of intensive livestock farming methods, whereby livestock could be kept indoors and fed on fodder crops. Thus, much arable land was given over to fodder crop production.

Higher arable yields were encouraged by increases in farm inputs such as fertilisers and tractors (Table 4.4) which were, in turn, manufactured and distributed by state-owned companies. By 1988, fertiliser applications were higher than in the FRG (for instance, in the FRG levels of nitrate and phosphate fertiliser applications in 1988 were 125 and 49 kg/ha respectively) (Hagedorn, 1992; see also Chapter 6). The state also invested in irrigation schemes (Schubert, 1990).

These intensification policies achieved partial success. Although cereal and milk yields almost doubled between 1960 and 1989, potato and sugar beet yields remained relatively static (Table 4.5). A comparison with Table 6.2 shows that yields in the GDR still lagged far behind those in the FRG. Nevertheless, the GDR's self-sufficiency in food increased from 86.8 per cent in 1971 to 92.9 per cent in 1989 (CEC, 1991). By 1989, the GDR was more than self-sufficient in potatoes, beef, veal, pork, chicken, milk, butter and eggs, and about 80 per cent self-sufficient in cereals and sugar

Table 4.3   Development of livestock numbers in the GDR, 1950–89 (millions)

Year	Cattle (beef and dairy)	Pigs	Sheep	Poultry
1950	3.6	5.7	1.0	22.7
1960	4.6	8.3	2.0	39.9
1970	5.2	9.7	1.6	43.0
1980	5.7	12.8	2.0	51.6
1989	5.7	12.0	2.6	49.2

Sources: Zentralverwaltung für Statistik (1989, p. 202); *Agrarbericht* (1991, p. 154).

Table 4.4   Intensification of agriculture in the GDR, 1960–88

Year	Application of fertilisers (kg/ha)				Number of tractors
	Nitrates	Phosphates	Potash	Lime	
1950	28.7	15.4	59.7	84.5	n.d.
1960	36.7	34.0	77.4	121.0	70 566
1970	81.3	65.2	97.7	186.8	148 865
1980	119.9	62.0	79.2	197.8	144 502
1988	141.3	56.4	94.4	272.7	167 529

Source: Zentralverwaltung für Statistik (1989, pp. 187, 191).

Table 4.5 Agricultural productivity in the GDR: selected commodities, 1960–89 (t/ha)

Commodity	1960	1970	1980	1989
Cereals	2.75	2.82	3.81	4.40
Potatoes	19.24	19.57	17.97	21.25
Sugar beet	28.78	32.01	28.10	28.60
Milk yield (kg/cow)	2315	2900	3433	4120

Sources: Zentralverwaltung für Statistik (1989, pp. 196–7); Agrarbericht (1991, p. 154).

(*Agrarbericht*, 1991). Per capita annual meat consumption was higher in the GDR than the FRG (114 kg compared to 103 kg) as was dairy product consumption (mainly milk, cream and butter) (388 kg compared to 346 kg in the FRG) (*Agra-Europe Bonn*, 23.7.1990). However, higher output was obtained at a high cost, both economically and environmentally (see also Section 6.2.2), and many problems can be identified in retrospect.

First, the political desire for self-sufficiency in agricultural production meant that patterns of production were dictated more by political than agricultural or economic considerations. Not only did the state seek national autarky but also regional autarky (*Der Spiegel*, 1990; *Agrarbericht*, 1991; Schultz, 1994), with the result that all *Bezirke* (see Chapter 7) had at least 60 per cent of agricultural land in arable production. Much marginal land was, therefore, put into arable production, even in regions with poor soil quality as illustrated in Map 2.2 (parts of present-day Brandenburg, southern Mecklenburg-Vorpommern and southern Thüringen) (*Agrarbericht*, 1991). Nevertheless, some regional specialisation of production was apparent. For instance, the percentage of arable land was highest in the most fertile *Bezirke* (Magdeburg, Halle and Leipzig) and yields were also highest here, while livestock production was most dominant in the southern *Bezirke* (Hohmann, 1984).

Second, increasing the size of LPGs did not lead to increased efficiencies but to diseconomies of scale due to, for instance, greater administrative costs and loss of time and energy spent in travelling to outlying fields (Bergmann, 1992). By 1980, GDR agriculture was more energy intensive than agriculture in the FRG, which meant higher production costs following the oil price rises of the 1970s (Hohmann, 1984). The centrally planned agricultural industry was also inefficient due to top-down and inflexible decision-making structures, resulting in lack of coordination and cooperation between the state, LPG managers and other actors in the food industry. LPGs and state farms were set annual production targets based on political rather than market considerations, which meant that targets were often unrealistic and encouraged LPG managers to falsify records

(Dirscherl, 1991). Both arable and livestock LPGs were dependent on external supplies of all farm inputs, including fertilisers, fodder and seeds, making them vulnerable to shortages and delays. By the 1980s, agricultural production was frequently hindered by shortages of farm input supplies due to the deteriorating economic situation (Panzig, 1995). Many LPGs were forced continuously to repair farm machinery and, in 1989, 50 per cent of tractors were more than 15 years old (*Agrarbericht*, 1991).

Third, productivity was hampered by environmental degradation. The disposal of slurry waste from livestock LPGs caused localised but severe soil and groundwater pollution (see Section 6.2.2). Heavy, outdated farm machinery caused soil compaction, while soil erosion was also a problem due to deterioration in soil quality and large exposed fields without hedges or trees to act as shelter belts (Hohmann, 1984; *Der Spiegel*, 1991b). Finally, inefficiency was also caused by lack of incentives among the workers to improve productivity (Dirscherl, 1991). However, it would be wrong to say that all LPGs were inefficient, as some were well managed and profitable. Soil quality obviously had an influence on success, but also social relations among LPG members. LPGs whose members had a strong tradition of family farming were more cohesive and successful than those whose members had weaker farming traditions and less solidarity (for instance, LPGs where many members were *Neubauern*; Gerbaud, 1994).

Inefficiency was not just confined to agricultural production but was found throughout the agricultural sector. The food-processing industry was organised along product lines in state-owned *Kombinate*, although for some more specialised products such as bread, cakes, sausage and beer, private production remained important (BMIB, 1985). By the 1980s, the productivity of state-owned food-processing factories lagged far behind the FRG due to outdated machinery and lack of investment. As a result, there was much wastage and food products were often of poor quality (*Agra-Europe Bonn*, 23.7.1990; *Agrarbericht*, 1991).

By the mid-1980s, in the face of rising agricultural support costs and a deteriorating economic situation, the SED leadership finally started to relax its hard-line ideological position on agriculture, and many reforms were introduced. In 1984, an agricultural price reform was carried out to bring prices more in line with market forces and introduce more competition into the farm sector (Schubert, 1990). Despite the 1984 price reform, however, agriculture remained a high cost sector, and in 1988 agricultural commodity prices were on average 2.4 times higher than in the FRG (*Agra-Europe Bonn*, 26.11.1990). Prices were so high that the state had to additionally subsidise the price of food to consumers (Landwirtschaftliche Rentenbank, 1990). Even so, food purchases represented 39 per cent of household expenditure in 1989 (*Agrarbericht*, 1991), compared to only 12 per cent in the FRG (see Chapter 2).

Another reform measure was to introduce formal cooperation between arable and livestock LPGs, and between LPGs and state farms, to try to overcome the inefficiencies caused by excessive specialisation. Cooperative associations (*Kooperative Einrichtungen*) were set up which mostly consisted of one arable and two or three livestock LPGs or state farms (Gerbaud, 1994). Formal cooperation between LPGs and state farms for farm machinery repairs and maintenance, farm building work and land improvement work was also encouraged (Landwirtschaftliche Rentenbank, 1990). In recognition of the higher productivity of private farming the party relaxed its opposition, and in 1986 the SED leadership even pronounced that private production constituted 'an integral part of agricultural production' (Brezinski, 1990, p. 536). At the same time, the state continued to promote new agricultural technologies, such as biotechnology and the use of computers in farm management (Schubert, 1990).

As in the FRG, the agricultural workforce declined with increasing mechanisation, but at a slower rate than in the FRG (see Table 2.2). However, in the early 1980s there was concern that the workforce was declining too quickly and that agriculture was suffering from a labour shortage (Krambach, 1985). In 1949, 38.3 per cent of the workforce was employed in agriculture, while by 1988 this had dropped to 10.8 per cent (about 800 000 workers) compared to 3.2 per cent (880 000 workers) in the FRG. In addition to the agricultural workforce, 164 500 were employed in farm input industries and 275157 in food-processing (Schultz, 1994). This high figure for agricultural employment is misleading, however, as it included all LPG and state farm employees, many of whom were employed in non-agricultural activities. Hohmann (1984) estimated that about 20 per cent of the 'agricultural' workforce was employed in administrative and service jobs (such as cooking, cleaning, child care), 10 per cent in repair work and about 35 per cent in transport and distribution, leaving only 35 per cent employed in agricultural work (about 280 000). This makes it difficult to compare labour productivity in the FRG and GDR.

Although agriculture's share in economic production declined over time, in 1988 it was still the third largest industrial sector in the GDR (after machinery/vehicles and chemicals) with 8 per cent of the GDP (Zentralverwaltung für Statistik, 1989). Given the political aim of the SED leadership to achieve autarchy in food production, trade in agricultural products in the GDR was of minor importance. The share of agricultural products in GDR trade declined over time: in 1987 they contributed only 2.3 per cent of all exports and only 8 per cent of all imports (Teller, 1990). Agricultural exports had to be so heavily subsidised that benefits to national income were questionable, although they were a source of foreign exchange, and the value of agricultural imports always exceeded the value of exports. Despite the GDR's large arable area, it still could not produce enough fodder crops to supply the expanding livestock sector and hence had to import additional supplies (Hohmann, 1984). Other imports were mainly products that could not be grown in the GDR, or high-quality processed foods. The main traded agricultural commodities and trading partners are shown in Table 4.6. It can be seen that the majority of trade in agricultural commodities was with Eastern Bloc countries, although trade with the FRG was important economically for the GDR. Under an agreement between the two states, GDR agricultural and food exports to the FRG were not subject to CAP tariffs, but could not be re-exported from the FRG to other EC member states (Haase, 1991). In 1988, agricultural exports from the GDR to the FRG totalled DM 659 million (9.7 per cent of GDR exports to the FRG) while imports into the GDR totalled DM 607 million (8.4 per cent of imports from the FRG) (*Agrarbericht*, 1990, p. 115). For the FRG, this trade was mainly important for political reasons to maintain diplomatic relations (Jones, 1994).

4.2.3   Reflections on agricultural development in the GDR and FRG

The previous discussion highlights that contrasts outweigh any similarities between agricultural development in the FRG and GDR in the 44-year period from 1945 to 1989. Agriculture in the SOZ and subsequent GDR underwent two major reforms (land reform and collectivisation) and several minor reforms (reorganisation and enlargement of LPGs). Agricultural change in the GDR was *revolutionary* in comparison to the FRG where agricultural structural change was essentially *evolutionary*. In the GDR private ownership of land and family farming were effectively abolished, while in the FRG they were carefully protected (see Chapter 2). Agricultural production in the GDR was guided by the state according to the Marxist goal of autarky, while in the FRG social market principles prevailed (albeit within the CAP framework).

In hindsight, the collectivisation and industrialisation of agriculture in the GDR and other Eastern Bloc countries can be seen as an unsuccessful

Table 4.6   GDR agricultural trade patterns

Main import commodities	Livestock feed, cereals, oilseeds, sugar, cotton, soft drinks, wine, beer, fruit, vegetables, coffee, tobacco
Main sources of imports[a]	USSR, Cuba, Hungary, FRG, Switzerland
Main export commodities	Live animals, meat and meat products, barley, butter, eggs, sugar, beer and spirits
Main export destinations[a]	FRG, USSR, Switzerland, Hungary, Britain

Note
[a]In decreasing order of importance.
Source: Teller (1990).

experiment. This is shown by lower yield levels than in the FRG and the unsustainably high financial burden on the state. There is, however, a danger of painting the policies of the GDR and FRG in black and white (Fulbrook, 1995). It is easy in retrospect to criticise the GDR, but it is important to remember that in 1945 the Allies were in agreement over the need for land reform, particularly in the SOZ where the large estates were concentrated. In the 1950s, collectivisation was an attempt to industrialise and modernise the farm sector, which could be seen as much more forward-looking than the FRG's policies which aimed to protect family farms. Collectivisation might have been more effective if the LPGs had been given more autonomy, but it was unfortunate for the collectivisation experiment that the oil crisis occurred in the early 1970s, as rising fuel costs added to diseconomies of scale. Given this situation, it was perhaps misguided of the SED leadership to continue to advocate farm amalgamation and specialisation during the 1970s. Nevertheless, the GDR achieved the highest productivity levels in Central and Eastern Europe, as well as outperforming many West European countries (Dawson, 1986). The partial reforms of the 1980s were too late to achieve any substantial improvements. However, although collectivisation failed in the GDR, the FRG's family farm model also was suboptimal in terms of efficiency and cost (see Chapter 2). Perhaps farming in both the GDR and FRG suffered from the ideological battle fought between politicians in the two states, in that it possibly increased the determination of the GDR to pursue collectivisation on the one hand, and the determination of the FRG to protect the family farm on the other.

Table 4.7 summarises some of the differences in agricultural structures and production between the FRG and GDR on the eve of reunification in 1989. These figures give some indication of the scale of problems facing farmers and policy-makers in trying to integrate the two farm sectors following reunification, but do not show the depth of legal, social and political issues raised by reunification. Restructuring has not just required a reorientation of farming away from a centrally planned economy to a social market one, but has also necessitated a reassessment and 'undoing' of the past land reform and collectivisation policies. The next section will identify some of these deeper issues as well as analyse how policy-makers have approached the integration process.

4.3 Reunification and agricultural restructuring: problems, conflicts and policies

The wide range of actors with an interest in agricultural restructuring meant that it was an impossible task for the federal government to achieve consensus over what policies to adopt to guide the restructuring process. Actors included: LPG members (both landowners and non-landowners); land reform victims (and owners whose land was expropriated after 1950)

Table 4.7   Comparative agricultural indicators: GDR and FRG, 1989

Indicator	GDR	FRG
Agricultural area (million ha)	6.171	11.886
Arable (%)	81.2	62
Grassland (%)	18.8	38
Cattle (millions)	5.736	14.563
dairy cows	2.000	4.929
Pigs (millions)	12.039	22.165
Poultry (millions)	49.269	76.883
Cereal yields (t/ha)	4.40	5.54
Potato yields (t/ha)	21.25	37.26
Sugar beet yields (t/ha)	28.6	54.2
Milk yields (kg/cow)	4120	4853
Number of farms	8668	648 800
Average farm size (ha)	4107	18.2
Agricultural workforce	800 000	880 000
Number of tractors	171 000	1 398 000

Source: *Agrarbericht* (1991, p. 154; 1997, p. 9).

and the *Neubauern*; private farmers in East Germany; FRG farmers; farmer lobby groups (particularly the DBV); the new *Länder* governments; and financial institutions. Both FRG farmers and the DBV were concerned that their 'family farm' interests might be threatened by reunification, as the farm sector in the new *Länder* had the potential to become highly competitive. Because of the important social, legal and political issues involved, restructuring could not be left to the free market and required regulation. Restructuring was also not merely a domestic issue but a European one, and the federal government was, therefore, constrained by the rules of the CAP. The German government's challenge was to find a way to regulate restructuring that was acceptable to the main parties, and that achieved a satisfactory outcome in terms of an economically, socially and environmentally viable farm structure.

In the months leading up to reunification there was general agreement that full private property rights should be restored to their owners, but there was much discussion as to how this should be done and what new agricultural structures should be aimed for. Should the LPGs be reformed or abolished? Should family farming be encouraged? What should happen to state-owned land? A panel of FRG agricultural experts advised the government to ensure a 'level playing field' and not to give one farm business type preference over any other, but to allow the farmers and the market to decide (*Agra-Europe Bonn*, 2.7.1990). The DBV, however, argued strongly for a policy to promote family farming (*Agra-Europe Bonn*, 8.10.1990).

Four goals for agricultural policy in the new *Länder* were set out by the federal government in 1990:

(a) to support the development of a variously structured, viable, agricultural, forestry and food sector that would be competitive within the European single market;
(b) to support workers in agriculture and forestry in the development of income and living standards and the adjustment of rural society to the requirements of the social market;
(c) to reorient the agricultural production structure to a market responsive and high-quality oriented one;
(d) to halt environmental damage caused by agriculture and to support an environmentally friendly and sustainable agriculture (*Agrarbericht*, 1991).

These goals were suitably broad to please all parties, and the first goal suggests that the government was committed to maintaining a level playing field for all business types in the restructuring process. The early rhetoric of the BML, however, indicated support for the (re)establishment of family farming in the new *Länder* as illustrated in the following quote: 'the government believes that a variously structured '*bäuerliche*' agriculture consisting of competitive full and part-time farms best meets the various expectations of the public from farming' (BML, 1991a, p. 1, own emphasis added). However, the reference to family farming is ambiguous as the term *bäuerlich* can be translated as 'rural' or 'rustic', and therefore refers to traditional rural ways of life rather than family farming per se. The BML went on to define *bäuerliche* agriculture as an agricultural structure characterised by independent management of owned or rented land by family farmers, with close links between land and livestock production, and with production based on environmental and sustainable as well as market principles. According to the BML, this definition could include a variety of legal and business forms. This implies that the BML was prepared to take a typically pragmatic approach to agricultural restructuring, aiming to please the DBV and farmers in the old *Länder* by stating its commitment to family farming without ignoring the interests of farmers in the new *Länder* – an approach that had also characterised BML–DBV relations in the FRG (see Chapter 2).

The following sections of this chapter will examine whether and to what extent policies have favoured family farming over other forms, and what impact they have had on farm structures. This examination can best be done by separating restructuring into three areas: (a) landownership and farm business structures (further subdivided into collectivised and expropriated lands); (b) agricultural production; (c) the agricultural workforce.

4.3.1 Landownership and farm business structures

Collectivised land

In June 1990, before political unification, the Agricultural Adjustment Act (*Landwirtschaftsanpassungsgesetz*) was passed by the GDR government which set out a framework for the restructuring of LPGs. This act set out three goals: (a) to re-establish private ownership of land; (b) to create a viable and varied agricultural structure; (c) to treat all farm business forms fairly and equally. Guidelines were set out for the dissolution or restructuring of LPGs, return of full landownership rights to their owners (whether or not they were still LPG members), and repayment of capital (such as livestock or machinery) originally brought into the LPG. Landowners could choose whether to remain in a restructured LPG successor business (a registered cooperative or a limited company), to rent or sell their lands, or to withdraw them and farm on their own as returning occupiers (*Wiedereinrichter*).

In July 1991, the Agricultural Adjustment Act was revised as it was realised that the 1990 Act did not give LPG members sufficient legal protection (*Agrarbericht*, 1991). This revised act tightened up regulations over return of land and property to members, and set a deadline of 31 December 1991 for the restructuring or dissolution of LPGs, after which date the LPG as a legal entity would cease to exist (*Agra-Europe Bonn*, 28.3.1994). In order for an LPG to be restructured into a new legal form, two-thirds of the members had to agree, including a majority of landowners (*Agrarbericht*, 1992). The Act also included measures for voluntary land exchange or formal land consolidation schemes needed to ensure viable holdings, as many land holdings were fragmented (*Agra-Europe Bonn*, 28.3.1994). In addition, property rights had to be clarified where the LPG had erected buildings on members' land without legal agreement.

As a precondition for the restructuring of LPGs, a comprehensive list of all landowners was required (estimated at 800 000) (DBV, 1995), as was a valuation of the LPGs' assets (Fischer, 1994). In most LPGs, this required a lengthy process of tracing owners who had often moved away, and establishing the value of property (livestock, buildings and equipment) each farmer had originally brought into the cooperative as individual property (*Inventarbeiträge*), as well as establishing what was 'common' property (items built or purchased after collectivisation). The valuation of the latter property was particularly difficult, as there was a large difference between value on paper and market value. For instance, prices for livestock had plummeted because of over-supply and low demand so that the market value was well below the book value (DBV, 1995).

The financial situation of the LPGs varied considerably. Some LPGs had accumulated considerable wealth because of the difficulty of making new investments in the GDR in the 1980s due to lack of building materials and machinery (*Der Spiegel*, 1990; *Agrarbericht*, 1991). Other LPGs that had borrowed capital at 1 per cent interest rates from the state-owned Bank for

Agriculture and Food were in a dire financial situation as they now faced higher interest rates (up to 10 per cent) and falling incomes. Many were not in a position to make full or even partial payments. Although the currency union, with the exchange rate for savings/debts set at 2 : 1, acted to reduce both savings and debt levels, it was not sufficient to solve the financial situation of many LPGs (*Der Spiegel*, 1992b; DBV, 1995).

LPG debts were estimated to amount to DM 7.6 billion (*Agra-Europe Bonn*, 28.3.1994). To prevent large-scale financial crisis, and to help new farming businesses to become established, the federal government introduced special policy measures. A debt relief scheme was introduced, administered by the Treuhandanstalt (THA), the state agency set up to oversee the privatisation of all the GDR's industrial assets (Wild and Jones, 1994). DM 1.4 billion was provided to write off so-called 'old debts' on condition that the LPG successor business also undertook an approved restructuring plan. This was mainly targeted at LPGs that had borrowed money to fund projects of communal benefit, such as village services or roads. Altogether, 1400 LPG successor businesses received partial debt write-offs under this scheme (BML, 1995a). In addition, a balance sheet discharge scheme was introduced to regulate repayment of old debts to ease financial pressure on heavily indebted LPG successor businesses (Scholz, 1992). This scheme stipulated that LPG successor businesses should not be obliged to make repayments unless they made a profit, and even then not more than 20 per cent of the profit should go towards debt repayment (Hagedorn *et al.*, 1997). It was also dependent on the production of a business rationalisation plan. This took care of a further DM 2.8 billion of debt, helping 1530 LPG successor businesses. No capital gains tax was charged on LPG successor businesses, and they were also exempted from industrial tax in 1992 and 1993 (BML, 1994a).

Critics of the government's policy on old debts have argued that they should be written off by the government, as the debts were incurred under completely different economic and political circumstances to those prevailing in reunified Germany (Nick, 1995). Further, the legality of the decisions taken by the THA and banks as to which LPG successor businesses were viable, and which were not, has been questioned. In 1997, a test case was brought to the German High Court by a former LPG in Sachsen-Anhalt which was indebted to the sum of DM 2.8 million. It challenged the requirement for repayment (*Süddeutsche Zeitung*, 1997a). The High Court decided against the former LPG and thereby ended the hopes of many others. The situation will be reviewed again in the year 2000, however, to monitor the rate at which debts are repaid (*Süddeutsche Zeitung*, 1997b).

Because of the debt burden facing many LPGs, the revised Agricultural Adjustment Act stipulated a priority list giving the order in which repayments to members were to be made: the *Inventarbeiträge* were to be repaid first to landowning members. *Wiedereinrichter* were entitled to repayment within a month of leaving the LPG, as their need for assets was urgent (they could be repaid in kind if necessary), while payments to other members could be stretched out over five years (to 1996). If money was left over, landowning members would be paid interest for use of land equivalent to at least DM 2/soil point per ha for every year of membership, and for use of other property at 3 per cent interest per year. Landowners who had left an LPG before 1990 were not entitled to this payment, although they were entitled to reclaim both their land and their *Inventarbeiträge* (Hagedorn, 1992). If at least 20 per cent of the LPG's capital remained after making the above payments, then 50 per cent of this amount should be paid to all members according to the length of time they had worked for the LPG (DBV, 1995). In 1996, a further revision of the Agricultural Adjustment Act extended the period over which repayments could be made for a further five years until 2000, to ease the financial burden on LPG successor businesses (*Agra-Europe Bonn*, 23.12.1996c).

About 40 per cent of LPGs were dissolved before the December 1991 deadline, either due to mutual agreement between members or because of financial insolvency (Hagedorn *et al.*, 1997). Most LPGs were restructured into registered agricultural cooperatives followed by *Gesellschaften mit beschränkter Haftung* (GmbHs – a corporate business form similar to Britain's limited companies). Often, arable and livestock LPGs that had worked together as cooperative associations joined to form one legal entity (Gerbaud, 1994). In all cases, the non-agricultural functions of LPGs were excluded from the new businesses, and often were closed down (*Agrarbericht*, 1991). However, the new cooperatives are a far cry from the LPGs. They are solely agricultural businesses employing a fraction of the former workforce (a cooperative must have at least seven members but may have many more; some of the newly established cooperatives had 100 members). The members contribute land and capital, but are paid rent for the land and are entitled to a share of profits. Moreover, all cooperative members have a democratic say in running the business. In corporate holdings the farmers are shareholders and, therefore, entitled to a share of profits and to a say in how the farm business is managed, their influence being dependent on the size of their shares. In addition, non-landowning investors can also purchase shares (Hagedorn *et al.*, 1997).

The number of family farms increased rapidly between 1992 and 1993 and has since risen steadily to 25 925 in 1998 (Table 4.8). Yet, this category includes a wide variety of farm sizes, with part-time farms averaging 14.6 ha and full-time farms averaging 126.7 ha, compared to 9.4 and 41.1 ha respectively in the old *Länder*. In 1997, over 70 per cent of holdings in the new *Länder* were classified as part-time (*Agrarbericht*, 1999). There are also a growing number of farm partnerships (consisting of at least two related or unrelated farmers), with an average size of 416.7 ha in 1998 (*Agrarbericht*, 1999).

Table 4.8   Development of farm businesses in the new *Länder*, 1992–98

Farm type (legal form)	Number of businesses				Average size (ha) 1998
	1992	*1994*	*1996*	*1998*	
Family farms	14 602	22 601	25 014	25 925	49.3
Farm partnerships	1 125	1 977	2 820	3 064	416.7
Total private	15 727	24 578	27 834	28 989	–
Cooperatives	1 432	1 333	1 293	1 218	1 432.3
GmbHs	1 180	1 388	1 432	1 560	773.5
Other corporate	423	588	284	164	525
Total corporate	3 035	3 309	3 009	2 942	–

Sources: *Agrarbericht* (1994, 1997, 1999); Kruse (1995); DBV (1997).

Private farm businesses may dominate the farm structure numerically, but corporate farms and cooperatives dominate the farm structure spatially, farming 54 per cent of the agricultural land area in 1998. They are particularly important for livestock farming. In 1994, 78 per cent of beef cattle, 75 per cent of dairy cows and 83 per cent of pigs were raised on corporate or cooperative farms (Kruse, 1995). Table 4.8 also shows that the number of cooperatives is declining, while the number of corporate farms is increasing. This is because many LPG successor cooperatives have been forced to restructure into corporate farms or to break up due to debt burdens. Despite special measures to alleviate debt, of the approximately 3000 LPG successor businesses in 1995 about half were still burdened by old debts, of which 1000 were in such a poor financial position that they were likely to be indebted for at least 30 years, with their members possibly not receiving any repayments (DBV, 1995). Moreover, banks were reluctant to give loans to these businesses because they were seen as a lending risk (König, 1994). Since cooperatives are most likely to be indebted, the number of cooperatives is likely to decline further, while the number of corporate farms, partnerships and family farms will increase (König, 1994; Hagedorn *et al.*, 1997).

There are also regional patterns of restructuring which reflect pre-GDR patterns of landownership (Hagedorn *et al.*, 1997). Proportionately more family farms, including part-time farms, have been (re)established in the southern *Länder* of Sachsen and Thüringen which both have a stronger tradition of family farming than the northern *Länder* which, in turn, have a greater concentration of cooperatives and corporate farms (AID, 1991; Steinmetz and Höll, 1993; Hagedorn *et al.*, 1997). Sachsen-Anhalt occupies an intermediate position with the north having a higher percentage of cooperative/corporate farms and the south a higher percentage of family farms and farm partnerships. A relationship between soil quality and farm structure can also be recognised, with family farms and farm partnerships more prevalent in the most fertile agricultural areas (König, 1994) (see Map 2.2). In addition, the majority (90 per cent) of farmland is rented, compared to only 47 per cent in the old *Länder* (*Agrarbericht*, 1997). This is partly because landowners not wishing to remain in farming themselves have decided to rent their land until the land market improves. As outlined in the next section, a major obstacle to the development of an active land market in the new *Länder*, however, is the expropriated state-owned land which represents almost a third of the agricultural area.

Expropriated land

The question of how to dispose of state-owned land has been tackled separately by the government because of the complexity and political sensitivity of this issue. The key question which the government has had to address is what rights the victims of land reform – so-called 'old owners' (*Alteigentümer*) – have in terms of compensation or restitution of land. The Unification Treaty of 1990 stated that expropriations carried out during the land reform of 1945–49 could not be reversed (Jones, 1994). Hence, victims of land reform (the former owners of large landed estates) were not eligible for restitution, and their lands, which had mainly been managed by LPGs during the GDR period, were to be sold. Estates formerly owned by public institutions, many of which became state farms, could be restituted, however, as could farms expropriated during the GDR period. Owners of these lands (mainly former small and medium sized farms) were, therefore, entitled to reclaim their lands, which, it is estimated, amount to about 500 000 ha of agricultural land (Hagedorn *et al.*, 1997). It should be noted that state-owned land to be sold off includes lands that were redistributed to *Neubauern* during the land reform, but were subsequently given up as the *Neubauern* or their heirs left the farming industry. Under GDR law, expropriated land could not be inherited unless the heirs remained in agriculture (Watzek, 1995).

The process by which state-owned land that could not be returned to its former owners was to be sold was contested from the start. It was decided to sell the state farms on the open market as whole estates, or in lots where the state farm was too indebted and rundown to be sold as a unit. The sale of the remaining approximately 900 000 ha of state land was more problematic. The *Alteigentümer* lobby felt that they had been unjustly treated by the Unification Treaty, and demanded recognition for past injustices from the government. The East German farm lobby, supported by the governments of the new *Länder*, opposed the immediate sale of these lands as they felt that they would be disadvantaged compared to Western investors due to lack of capital. However, they wanted the government to act swiftly because uncertainty over the future of these lands was delaying the agricultural restructuring process (*Agra-Europe Bonn*, 2.3.1992). Regions with a concentration of state-owned land, such as Mecklenburg-Vorpommern, were particularly disadvantaged by this uncertainty (Table 4.9). Under strong political pressure from both sides, the government decided not to sell these lands on the open market, but to seek a compromise agreement to regulate the privatisation process.

Responsibility for privatisation was initially handed to the THA, but as it was soon evident that the process would continue beyond the planned lifetime of the THA, responsibility was passed in 1992 to a newly formed public agency: the Land Settlement and Administration Company (Bodenverwertungs- und Verwaltungsgesellschaft or BVVG). In November 1992, a compromise agreement was finally reached (the so-called Bohl model after the chair of the government working party). This model set out a phased privatisation in three stages: lease, subsidised sale and sale on the open market. It also proposed that *Alteigentümer* should receive some compensation. The proposed time-scale and main policy measures of each stage are shown in Table 4.10.

Phase 1 was critical to the whole process, as the way leases were awarded affected the subsequent subsidised sale of land (because tenants were given first refusal on land purchase in Phase 2). Applicants for leases were judged on the strength of their farm business plan, rather than on the amount of rent offered. As shown in Table 4.10, where two equally valid applications were submitted, priority was given to returning occupiers (*Wiedereinrichter*) and locally resident *Neueinrichter*. *Alteigentümer* could also apply for land, although not for their own expropriated estates. Phase 1 was completed by the end of 1995, and Table 4.11 shows the distribution of rented land between different categories of tenants and the average size of lease (many tenants, however, leased more than one land parcel). The majority of state-owned land was rented to corporate farms and cooperatives, while the area rented to *Alteigentümer* (*Wiedereinrichter* without right of restitution) was

Table 4.9   Leasing of state-owned land by *Bundesland*, September 1996

Bundesland	Area of leased land (1000 ha)	Average size of lease (ha)	BVVG[a] land as % UAA
Mecklenburg-Vorpommern	398	132	30
Brandenburg	278	99	21
Sachsen-Anhalt	167	68	14
Sachsen	94	40	10
Thüringen	74	46	9
Total	1011	84	18

Note
[a]Bodenverwertungs- und Verwaltungsgesellschaft.
Source: Klages (1997).

Table 4.10   The Bohl model for privatisation of state-owned land in the new *Länder*

Phase 1: 1993–95 Lease land for 12-year terms	*Conditions* • Applicants must demonstrate that their farm is economically viable and that they will farm the land themselves • Where two equally valid applications are submitted for the same land parcel, then *Wiedereinrichter* and *Neueinrichter* who are resident locally will be given priority		
Phase 2: 1996–2003 Sell land at subsidised rates and compensate *Alteigentümer*	(a) Compensation scheme: partial and degressive; compensation to be paid to *Alteigentümer* (not to be paid out until 2004)	(b) Instead of compensation, *Alteigentümer* can apply to purchase land at subsidised rates worth up to half their compensation entitlement and not more than 3000 soil points in value *Conditions*: • Must respect existing leases and extend them from 12 to 18 years • Land may not be resold for 20 years and must be used for agricultural purposes	(c) Tenants of state land can purchase land with a value of up to 6000 points at subsidised rates *Conditions*: • Land may not be resold for 20 years and must be used for agricultural purposes • Not more than 50% of the farm, including the purchased land, may be owned
Phase 3: 2004–? Sell remaining land on open market			

Sources: After Hagedorn *et al.* (1997).

negligible. The average size of lease contracts also varied with the corporate farms and cooperatives having the largest average size. Thus, although over 6000 private farmers received land, the main beneficiaries were the corporate farms and cooperatives, of which about 90 per cent obtained a lease contract (Klages, 1997). They were, therefore, also likely to be the main beneficiaries of Phase 2 of the model.

To implement this Phase 2, a Compensation Act (*Entschädigungs- und Ausgleichsleistungsgesetz*) was passed in September 1994 (*Agra-Europe Bonn*,

Table 4.11   Leasing of state-owned land in the new *Länder* by tenant (December 1995)

Tenant	Number of tenants[a]	Number of leases	Area (ha)	% of total leased area	Average size of lease (ha)
Wiedereinrichter[b]					
Resident	3 970	5 159	200 336	19	39
With right of restitution	170	213	12 135	1	57
No right of restitution	450	608	61 049	6	100
Neueinrichter					
Resident	1 500	2 022	102 312	10	51
Newcomer	680	880	52 497	5	60
Corporate/cooperative	2 850	4 269	591 830	58	139
Other applicants	980	1 171	8 673	1	7
Total	10 600	14 322	1 028 834	100	72

Notes
[a]Data refer to February 1995.
[b]The *Wiedereinrichter* can be divided into three groups: resident (meaning landowning members of LPGs); with right of restitution (properties expropriated after 1950); and those without right of restitution (properties expropriated between 1945 and 1949).
Source: Klages (1997).

28.3.1994). The Act stated that *Alteigentümer* were entitled to receive partial compensation for land expropriated during the 1945–49 land reform, but that compensation payments would be calculated degressively; that is, former owners of large estates would receive proportionately less compensation than those of smaller estates (Hagedorn *et al.*, 1997). The subsidised sale of land would take place as follows. Tenants would be given first option to purchase land at subsidised rates up to a value of 6000 soil points (for example, this would be 120 ha for land with an average value of 50 soil points; see also Map 2.3). *Alteigentümer*, on the other hand, unless they had rented land from the BVVG, would only be entitled to purchase land worth up to half of their compensation entitlement at subsidised prices (and worth not more than 3000 soil points). Further, they would be required to respect existing tenancy agreements and, in addition, to increase the length of these tenancies from 12 to 18 years (this would mean that agreements signed in 1994 would be extended to 2012). The land sold under this subsidised scheme would be valued at three times the 1935 rateable value of the land (Hagedorn *et al.*, 1997).

Implementation of Phase 2 of the model has been highly controversial, and has sparked criticism over treatment of *Alteigentümer*, the level of subsidy offered, eligibility for subsidy, and the time-scale involved. First, the government has been accused of being too lenient towards the

Alteigentümer and of even trying to reverse the land reform (Panzig, 1995; Watzek, 1995). Attempts by some *Alteigentümer* to reclaim their old estates have caused social tensions in villages where their return is not welcomed (see, for example, *Der Spiegel*, 1993). This accusation has been challenged by Klages and Klare (1995) who pointed out that few *Alteigentümer* are likely to apply to purchase land because of the strict conditions of sale, in contrast to the corporate farms and cooperatives likely to be the main beneficiaries of the subsidised land sales. Second, the level of subsidy has been criticised by Klages and Klare (1995) for being unjustifiably high, as land would be sold for, on average, less than half the market price for agricultural land in the new *Länder* (with the difference greatest for fertile arable land). Even though there are conditions on resale, purchasers are likely to make large financial gains in the long term. Third, eligibility for the scheme has been questioned, as it is limited to tenants of state-owned land and will, therefore, take place in a 'closed shop'. Finally, despite the generous level of subsidy, it has been estimated that only about two-thirds of the state-owned land will be purchased under Phase 2 of the scheme, as some tenants may not be in a position to purchase all of their entitlement, while others renting land of marginal quality may not find even the subsidised price economically attractive (Doll and Klare, 1994). Thus, about 300 000 ha will be sold off at market prices in Phase 3 of Bohl's model after 2004. At the time of writing a question mark hangs over the subsidised sale of state-owned land due to the intervention of the European Commission on the grounds that the policy infringes EU competition laws. In response, the federal government has proposed that the subsidised sale price be based on the market value as of the end of 1998, minus 35 per cent (*Agra-Europe Bonn*, 21.6.1999c). If this revision is accepted by the European Commission it may mean that even less land is purchased before 2004.

4.3.2   Agricultural production

In addition to restructuring the farm structure of the new *Länder*, the government also had to address the problems of integrating the farm sector into the FRG economy and the CAP. In contrast to the highly politicised nature of the restructuring of farm business ownership and management, the restructuring of production has been treated more as a 'technical' problem (Tangermann, 1997). However, the two aspects of agricultural restructuring are closely interrelated, and have exerted a mutual influence on each other. From a European perspective, the accession of the new *Länder* to the CAP was not a difficult addition because of their small size (unlike the accession of Spain, for instance, which increased the number of EU holdings by 22 per cent) (Fearne, 1997). It was even seen as beneficial in that accession has added 16 million consumers to the EU's internal market and has thereby increased demand for food products, especially for Mediterranean products (*Agra-Europe Bonn*, 23.7.1990). However, the main agricultural products in the new *Länder* (dairy, beef, pork, cereals) were already in surplus within the Community and therefore accession would add to EU surpluses and place additional costs on the EAGGF (*Agra-Europe Bonn*, 26.11.1990).

All farm businesses in the new *Länder* faced immense financial difficulties, particularly in 1990 and 1991 immediately before and after reunification, and a drought in 1992 added to their problems, especially in Mecklenburg-Vorpommern and Brandenburg (Manegold, 1993). On 1 July 1990, the GDR government adopted a new agricultural policy framework that mirrored that of the CAP, and a month later the GDR entered a de facto customs union with the EC. Food prices in the GDR were brought into line with FRG prices. This was a harsh blow for GDR farmers, as markets for GDR produce disappeared almost overnight. Consumers demanded Western food products and shops in the new *Länder* were flooded with FRG and other EC produce (König and Isermeyer, 1993). In 1990, imports from the GDR into the FRG increased by 210 per cent, but exports from the FRG to the GDR increased by 1252 per cent (*Agrarbericht*, 1990). The sudden fall in consumer demand, together with a reduction in public support, led to a collapse of commodity prices. For instance, cereal prices fell by 40 per cent and milk prices by 60 per cent (Weinschenck, 1992). On the other hand, consumer food prices rose rapidly in the run-up to reunification as subsidies were removed (*Agrarbericht*, 1991).

Short-term supply control measures were used to counter the agricultural crisis following monetary union. Surpluses of cereals, butter and skimmed milk powder and meat were disposed of through exports to third countries, especially the former USSR and Central and East European countries (CEECs), while prices were supported through state intervention buying (*Agrarbericht*, 1991; Hagedorn *et al.*, 1997). However, longer-term market adjustment measures were also required. To meet the requirements of the CAP and to ensure economically competitive farm businesses, two main changes had to occur. First, livestock farming had to be 'de-intensified', meaning the balance between livestock and land had to be dramatically improved to meet EU requirements over stocking densities (*Agrarbericht*, 1991). Second, the area of arable land had to be decreased as marginal lands were no longer economically competitive for arable production. Thus, land of marginal quality had to be turned over to grassland or to alternative uses, such as forestry or recreation (Ahrens and Lippert, 1995). To accelerate the restructuring and integration of agriculture in the new *Länder*, the European Commission permitted the German government to offer special financial support policies to farmers for a limited period. Initially these were to last until the end of 1993, but were later extended until the end of 1996.

The dairy industry had to be rationalised to avoid adding to already existing EU milk surpluses, and to enable the dairy industry to compete in the CAP. Milk quotas were introduced in April 1991. The new *Länder* received a quota of 6.6 million tonnes, which was 20 per cent less than production in the base year of 1989. LPGs received quotas equal to on average 70 per cent of their 1989 production levels. Where LPGs were restructured, outgoing members wishing to (re)start a farm business were entitled to a proportion of the LPG quota, and 10 per cent of the milk quota was set aside in a reserve fund to help newly establishing farm businesses enter the dairy industry (BML, 1991a).

Special set-aside rules for the new *Länder* were introduced in 1990, funded from the federal budget as an income support as well as supply control measure. Land under potato cultivation, as well as cereals and oilseeds, was counted as eligible for set aside. Farmers had to set aside at least 20 per cent of their arable land, but not more than 50 per cent (to prevent whole farms being put into set-aside). Only land worth at least 18 soil points could be entered in order to exclude the most marginal land. The premium payments were linked to soil quality with better quality soils attracting higher payments up to a maximum amount (*Agrarbericht*, 1991). In addition, EU surplus products were eligible for extensification measures (reduction in yield/livestock numbers per hectare of at least 20 per cent). Eligible commodities were potatoes, cauliflowers, tomatoes, apples, beef and sheep.

In July 1990, special structural support measures were introduced to aid the restructuring of farm business structures and agricultural production. These mirrored the GAK (see Chapter 2), but contained additional special measures. The key aims were to aid the restructuring of LPGs; (re)establishment of family farms; improvement in production and marketing structures; introduction of energy-saving measures and alternative energy supplies; introduction of agri-environmental schemes; and to support improvements in rural living standards and minimisation of social hardship from reduction of employment. In addition, adjustment aid (*Anpassungshilfe*) was offered as partial compensation for loss of income during restructuring (*Agrarbericht*, 1990). Altogether, over DM 6 billion was allocated to these measures, of which 44 per cent was earmarked for adjustment aid (*Agrarbericht*, 1991). This was paid according to the calculated workforce requirements of each farm (all but very small part-time farms were eligible), but larger farms received lower payments per worker. The adjustment aid initially included a locational supplement (additional per hectare payments for poor quality land), which can be seen as a forerunner to the designation of LFAs in the new *Länder* in 1992. In addition, in December 1990 the European Commission agreed to allocate structural funds for regional development to the new *Länder* for the period 1991–93 (see Chapter 7), including funding from the EAGGF Guidance Fund. This increased the budget for agricultural structural policies considerably (Hagedorn *et al.*, 1997), with DM 1.2 billion earmarked for agriculture and rural development between 1991 and 1993 and a further DM 5.2 billion for the period 1994–99 (BML, 1994a).

Agricultural structural policy for the new *Länder* was brought into the GAK budget in 1991, but special programmes continued to be offered for the new *Länder* until 1996. As well as adjustment aid, three schemes were targeted to help the restructuring of farm businesses, a scheme to help (re)establishing family farm businesses, an agricultural credit programme for investment in farm machinery, livestock and housing for all farm business types and a scheme to help the restructuring of LPGs and LPG successor businesses (BML, 1991b; 1995b). This latter scheme required new businesses to meet EU environmental standards for livestock stocking densities of 2.5 LU/ha (as part of the extensification process), and to meet slurry disposal regulations (minimum of six months storage capacity). It also offered grants for energy-saving measures and for purchase of new machinery and equipment. A precondition for all schemes was the preparation of a farm business development plan. Table 4.12 shows the federal budget allocated to these measures between 1990 and 1996. It can be seen that the scheme to help the establishment and modernisation of family farms was allocated the second largest budget after adjustment aid, a fact which could lend support to critics who argue that the federal government has favoured family farming, although it could also be argued that there are many more family farms than corporate farms and that families (re)establishing farms have higher start-up costs.

At the end of 1996 special structural policy measures for the new *Länder* ceased, and since then structural policies have been applied uniformly across Germany. How successfully did farms in the new *Länder* adjust production during the period of special assistance? The arable and livestock sectors fared differently, with the former offering better prospects than the latter. By 1995, cereal yields had almost caught up with those in the old *Länder* at 6.01 tonnes/ha compared with 6.10, and may well soon overtake yields in the old *Länder* because of the productivity advantages of larger average farm sizes (DBV, 1996). Arable farms on the most fertile soils are

Table 4.12   Special structural policies for the new *Länder* in the GAK[a] (million DM)

Year	Adjustment aid	Restructuring of LPGs	Establishment and modernisation of family farms	Agricultural credit programme
1992	686	2.9	222.2	9.5
1993	385	22.9	253.5	12.0
1994	378	27.6	198.3	6.2
1995	128	43.6	215.4	6.1
1996	–	66.1	181.4	7.1

Note
[a]Federal funding only.
Source: *Agrarbericht* (1994, p. 113; 1997, p. 108).

particularly advantaged. However, the livestock sector remains in a depressed state, although milk yields have caught up with those of the old *Länder* (Forstner and Isermeyer, 1998). Between 1990 and 1993, beef and dairy cattle numbers fell by 50 per cent, pig numbers by 60 per cent, sheep by 65 per cent and poultry by 21 per cent (*Agra-Europe Bonn*, 4.9.1995). The decline of the livestock sector is due to the uncompetitiveness and poor environmental record of East German producers compared to other EU member states, and that both beef and dairy produce are in surplus and, therefore, subject to production and environmental controls (see above). Large amounts of investment are required in new buildings and equipment to bring conditions up to EU standards, which few farm businesses can afford. The beef and dairy industries have also been affected by the general downturn in the European beef market due to the BSE crisis (see Chapter 6).

While the financial situation of farm businesses as a whole has improved, there is considerable variation in their performance, and in the financial year 1994/95 only just over 50 per cent of all farm businesses made a profit. Key factors influencing business performance are legal form, type of production and location. The farm cooperatives have experienced the greatest difficulties due to the added burdens of inherited debts and repayments to outgoing members. Family farms and farm partnerships fared best, with the profits of the former rising by 22 per cent between 1994 and 1995, and those of the latter by 18 per cent over the same period (DBV, 1996). The arable sector has fared better than the livestock sector, particularly arable farms on the most fertile soils (*Agrarbericht*, 1997). Forstner and Isermeyer (1998) suggested that the large GmbHs and cooperative arable farms have been more competitive than expected by West German experts, with the economic advantages of economies of scale in the use of machinery, specialist technology and in marketing outweighing any extra labour costs. Levels of investment in farm businesses have been higher than in the old *Länder* because of the greater need and the special subsidies available, but by 1996 investment levels were slowing and lack of capital was still a concern. Prices paid to producers in the new *Länder* had almost caught up with those in the old *Länder* for milk and livestock produce, and had overtaken the old *Länder* for cereals (DBV, 1997).

Restructuring has also affected the farm input and food-processing industries. As state-owned enterprises they were entrusted to the THA to be privatised. Most were taken over by West German food-processing companies, such as the Schleswig-Holstein-based Hansa-Milch dairy company (which has now moved its headquarters to Mecklenburg-Vorpommern) (BML, 1995a), and have been subjected to rationalisation. For instance, in 1989 there were 246 dairies and 43 sugar refineries in the GDR, but by 1995, only 48 dairies and 5 sugar refineries remained. The surviving processing factories have experienced high levels of investment, helped by GAK subsidies for improvement of production and marketing structures, and have had state-of-the-art technology installed to increase productivity

(*Agra-Europe Bonn*, 4.9.1995). For instance, sugar-beet processing capacity has more than tripled since reunification, despite the dramatic decline in the number of factories (Schultz, 1994). In contrast to the decline in the number of food-processing factories, the number of small private butchers and bakers has increased in response to rising consumer demand (BML, 1995a).

4.3.3 Agricultural workforce

The agricultural sector of the former GDR has been proportionately more affected by job cuts than any other sector of the economy (Hagedorn *et al.*, 1997). This is because the restructuring of LPGs involved the rationalisation (and mostly closure) of all non-agricultural activities, with high job losses among agricultural workers. Because of the financial difficulties faced by LPGs and their successors in the immediate years after reunification, redundancies were an unavoidable survival strategy. The livestock sector suffered high job losses because of the cutbacks in livestock numbers, and this affected the female workforce in particular. Rapid rises in wage rates towards FRG levels put further pressure on jobs (Hagedorn *et al.*, 1997).

Massive job losses occurred within a few years: between 1989 and early 1992, the agricultural workforce fell by more than 50 per cent from 800 000 to 300 000 (*Agra-Europe Bonn*, 2.3.1992). By 1994, only 164 600 were employed in agriculture, a fall of 80 per cent since 1989, and in 1996 the number had fallen further to 159 500 (*Agrarbericht*, 1997). It is likely that the size of the agricultural workforce will continue to fall, especially in cooperatives and corporate farms (Forstner and Isermeyer, 1998). This is a severe blow to the rural economy of the new *Länder*, especially as the rural population had been used to full employment, although, as stated in Section 4.2.2, by 1989 only about 280 000 workers were directly employed in agricultural production, the rest being employed in ancillary activities. It is the latter workforce that has been most liable to redundancy. While the percentage of the working population employed in agriculture in the GDR had varied regionally from 20 per cent in Mecklenburg-Vorpommern to 7.4 per cent in Sachsen, in many rural districts 25 per cent or more of the population had been employed in agriculture (*Agra-Europe Bonn*, 18.2.1991). In addition, substantial job losses occurred in other sectors of the food chain. Employment in food-processing industries declined by 75 per cent between 1989 and 1994 from 275157 to 70838 (Schultz, 1994). Employment policy has, thus, been an important part of the federal government's strategy for restructuring the rural economy.

The government launched schemes to ease the transition of workers out of agriculture. These have focused on the older age groups who had little chance of re-employment, and the younger age groups who needed retraining to adjust to the new labour market. For the older age groups, the government agreed to contribute towards voluntary early retirement packages for agricultural workers as a short-term measure between July and October

1990 (before reunification). Following reunification, 'retirement transition money' was offered to workers over the age of 55 (later reduced to 50) who had been made redundant. It is estimated that about 135 000 agricultural workers took early retirement under these schemes (*Agrarbericht*, 1992). Agricultural workers over the age of 50, who had lost their job because of restructuring of agricultural businesses, could also claim a small monthly payment from the adjustment money budget.

For younger age groups, the government launched measures to help unemployed workers back into work. Retraining courses were subsidised to enable the workforce to gain new skills. This is important, as qualifications gained in the GDR were often not recognised by West German employers, and were often inappropriate for the new labour market (Fink *et al.*, 1994). Job creation schemes (*Arbeitsbeschaffungsmaßnahmen* or ABM) were also set up to give unemployed workers work experience. In 1991 and 1992 alone, over DM 70 billion was paid out for employment measures (BMBau, 1994). Job creation has concentrated on 'public good' measures, such as environmental and social projects or infrastructure schemes. It is a key policy in rural areas for maintaining social stability and preventing outmigration (see Chapter 7), as without ABM schemes unemployment in the new *Länder* would be more than twice as high (BMBau, 1994). However, Fink *et al.* (1994) noted that the manual nature of most ABM schemes means that more men than women are employed. As a result, and due to the changing labour market in which women find it harder to find new employment, more women than men are unemployed (BMBau, 1994). Although ABM schemes are seen as transitional, the continuing poor economic situation in the new *Länder* means that these measures are likely to continue for the foreseeable future (see, for example, MRLUSA, 1996). By 1995, it was estimated that only about 20 per cent of the original 800 000 agricultural workforce were still in agriculture, 17 per cent were unemployed, 21 per cent had taken (early) retirement, 10 per cent were in retraining schemes and 32 per cent had found alternative employment (including ABM workers) (Förderwerk Land- und Forstwirtschaft, 1995). It remains to be seen whether the 27 per cent who are unemployed, or on retraining schemes, will be able to find permanent work.

The second area of employment policy concerns social security for those still employed in agriculture. Following reunification, the FRG social security system was transferred to the new *Länder* (Mehl and Hagedorn, 1992), but the transfer to agriculture was problematic. As mentioned in Chapter 2, the FRG had developed a special social security system for its farmers (including pensions, health and accident insurance), which by the 1980s was seen as too costly and in need of reform (Hagedorn, 1991). As the FRG system was geared to self-employed family farmers, it was inappropriate for agricultural employees in the LPGs and their successor businesses. In addition, transfer of the existing system would have been exorbitantly expensive for the government. Thus, the agricultural pension scheme was not transferred to farmers in the new *Länder* (Mehl, 1997). The government decided instead to reform the whole agricultural social security system, and to develop a new system that would be applicable to farmers in the old and new *Länder*.

As a result, reforms were then introduced in January 1995 with the *Agrarsozialreformgesetz* (BML, 1994c). The new system provides more choice for farmers and links farm pensions more closely to the national pension scheme, although farmers still obtain a higher level of government subsidy. It also provides better pension protection for farm women. Agricultural employees, including farm managers, are covered by the national social security system, although special accident insurance applies to all agricultural workers (employed and self-employed) (Mehl, 1997). The 1995 reform also introduced the *Produktionsaufgaberente* into the new *Länder* (offered in the old *Länder* since 1989). Under this scheme, farmers who are at least 55 and transfer their farm to another farmer, or take it out of agricultural production, are entitled to an early pension (*Agrarbericht*, 1995). Although these reform measures were meant to curb expenditure on social policy, the proportion of the agricultural budget allocated to social policy was still 67 per cent in 1997. Over half of the social policy budget is allocated for old age pensions, and this is likely to remain high for the foreseeable future as Germany has an ageing farm workforce (33 per cent of farmers are aged 55 or over) (*Agrarbericht*, 1997).

4.3.4 Agricultural restructuring in the new *Länder*: success or failure?

The restructuring of agriculture in the new *Länder* can be seen as another 'revolution' following on from the earlier socialist revolutions of 1945 and the 1950s. At the time of writing, 10 years after the reunification of Germany, the worst of the restructuring seems to be over and the farm structure of the new *Länder* is stabilising. While the years 1990–93 can be described as a period of crisis and fundamental upheaval, the years since have been ones of adjustment and stabilisation, and the sale of state-owned land is the only major part of the restructuring process still taking place. Sachsen's agriculture minister even claimed recently that Sachsen's agricultural sector was fully restructured and in a competitive position (*Agra-Europe Bonn*, 19.7.1999a). It is now possible to start to evaluate how restructuring has taken place and the outcomes that it has achieved.

The outcome of the (re)privatisation of both collectivised and expropriated lands is now becoming apparent as the farm business structure begins to stabilise. It is dominated numerically by family farms, but economically by corporate farms and cooperatives which together control over half of the agricultural land area. While the number of cooperatives is likely to decrease further, many will be restructured into corporate farms or farm partnerships rather than family farms. These former two business forms are proving to be economically competitive due to the greater economies of scale that can be achieved in comparison to family farms. Thus, the number of family farms is unlikely to increase significantly. It could be said, therefore, that the BML's aim of achieving a 'variously structured' agricultural sector has been achieved.

To what extent is this outcome the result of government policies? Has the government provided a level playing field for all business types? The government would appear in many respects to have advantaged family farmers, particularly *Wiedereinrichter*, over corporate and cooperative farms. *Wiedereinrichter* have been prioritised for repayment of LPG capital, for access to BVVG leases, and have been given beneficial grants to help start-up costs. Small farms also enjoy preferential tax concessions and higher social security subsidies (BML, 1994a; Forstner and Isermeyer, 1998). LPG successor businesses, on the other hand, have been burdened with inherited debts. It could be argued, however, that family farms had to be given preferential treatment to achieve a level playing field, as the large corporate farms and cooperatives enjoyed initial advantages in terms of access to land, buildings, machinery and livestock, and they are also likely to be the main beneficiaries of the subsidised sale of state-owned land. Moreover, landowners suffered during the GDR period, when their property rights were sharply curtailed, and it could be argued that they deserve some special support.

Despite all the policy and rhetorical support given to re-establishing and newly establishing family farmers by the federal government and the DBV, farmers in the new *Länder* have been ambivalent in their attitudes towards family farming. Several reasons can be identified as to why not more family farms have been established. First, many land holdings are too small to form viable full-time farms without the owners renting additional land, and most owners lack necessary start-up capital (Kallfass, 1991). Second, after more than 30 years of collective farming, the tradition of family farming has been undermined and family ties to the land have loosened. Many landowners prefer to remain within a farm cooperative, or farm company, as they lack the necessary experience to farm alone, and prefer the security and social benefits of working in a large farm business (*Agra-Europe Bonn*, 23.7.1990; Bergmann, 1992). Third, it is important to remember that many parts of the new *Länder* (especially in the north) have no tradition of family farming. For farmers in these areas, the family farm is not the obvious model with which to replace collective farming. Finally, many East German farmers have rejected family farming on economic grounds as uncompetitive in the modern economy. It would be misguided for the federal government to try to impose an inefficient farm structure on the new *Länder*, when it had the opportunity to promote an economically efficient one.

The BML now appears to have accepted that the farm structure of the new *Länder* will differ from the old *Länder*, as the following statement spells out:

> The federal government holds the view that agricultural holdings managed individually on an ownership or leasehold basis as full-time or part-time farms will be best suited to fulfil the multifarious expectations that society has of agriculture as well as to meet the future challenges of the EC market. In view of the agricultural structures in Eastern Germany, of the historical conditions and of the wishes expressed by many farmers in the new *Länder*, the federal government is, however, also prepared to accept that forms of joint farm management will continue to play a role for some considerable time. Further, the size of farms will, in the long run, be larger in the new federal *Länder* than it is in the old federal states (BML, 1994b, p. 8).

The restructuring of agricultural production in the new *Länder* can be seen as a partial success, and productivity levels are nearing those in the old *Länder*. However, it will take some time until all East German farmers have taken on board the business know-how to compete in EU and global markets. One continuing area of concern is the low market share of East German produce in food sales. In 1994, East German produce constituted only 50 per cent of food sales in the new *Länder*, and a mere 2 per cent in the old *Länder* (*Agra-Europe Bonn*, 4.9.1995). The low market share in the new *Länder* is partly due to the establishment of West German-owned retail chains, which already have purchasing contracts with food processors in the old *Länder*. It is also due to a continuing 'image problem' for East German products, despite the rapid improvements in quality that have been achieved. East German food processors are finding it difficult to break into the West German market for the same reasons.

The rapid reduction in the farm workforce since 1990 (see above) has also caused concern. Bergmann (1992) commented that structural adjustment in the farm workforce took place over 40 years in the FRG, but has been telescoped into only a few years in the former GDR. The government has not tried to slow down the exodus of workers, but has tried to cushion the blow by offering early retirement, retraining, work experience and unemployment benefits. This reduction has been necessary to increase the competitiveness of farm businesses, but the concern now is that the sluggish economy is not creating sufficient jobs to soak up former agricultural workers. The issue of the wider rural economy will be considered further in Chapter 7.

So far in this chapter we have focused on changes in the new *Länder*, with little reference to the wider context in which these changes have taken place. In the final section of this chapter therefore, we, broaden the discussion to reflect on the significance of reunification for the agricultural structure of the former FRG, and the challenge that reunification presents for farmers and policy-makers in reunified Germany as a whole. First, we will comment on the agricultural structures of the old and new *Länder* and the agricultural structure of reunified Germany, and second, we will discuss whether reunification is likely to lead to any significant shift in agricultural policy-making at the domestic or European levels.

4.4　Implications of reunification for German agricultural policies

4.4.1　Agricultural structures in the new Germany

The following tables highlight the contrasts in farm structures that exist between the old and new *Länder* within reunified Germany. Table 4.13 shows that only 3.1 per cent of all farms in the old *Länder* are larger than 100 ha, whereas about 25 per cent of farms in the new *Länder* are above 100 ha. In all categories of farm production, farm sizes are on average larger in the new *Länder* than in the old (Table 4.14). The contrast in the structure of the dairy sector is particularly marked (Table 4.15), as over a third of dairy farms in the new *Länder* have herds of over 100 cattle compared to less than 0.5 per cent in the old *Länder*. The structure of the farm workforce is also contrasting (Table 4.16), with 88 per cent of the agricultural workforce of the old *Länder* classified as 'family workers', compared to only 30 per cent in the new *Länder*. However, in both parts of Germany most family farm workers are part-time farmers. In 1997, almost 60 per cent of all family farms in Germany were part-time farmers, with the proportion of part-time farms higher in the new *Länder* (70.8 per cent) than the old *Länder* (58.8 per cent) (*Agrarbericht*, 1999).

Table 4.13　Farm size distribution in the new and old *Länder*, 1992 and 1998

Farm size (ha)	Old Länder (1000s)		New Länder (1000s)		Germany (1000s)	
	1992	*1998*	*1992*	*1998*	*1992*	*1998*
1–9	268	216	7.7	13.8	275	230
10–19	115	85	2.2	3.7	117	89
20–29	72	55	1.1	1.7	73	57
30–49	73	63	1.1	1.9	74	64
50–100	45	51	1.4	2.4	47	54
>100	9	15	5.2	8.5	14	23
Total	582	484	19	32	601	516

Source: *Agrarbericht* (1994, 1997, 1999).

Table 4.14   Farm types in the old and new *Länder*, 1995 (number and size)

Farm type	Number of businesses (1000)		Average farm size (ha)	
	Old	New	Old	New
Cereals	143.5	11.8	25.4	253.7
Fodder crops	232.5	12.3	25.2	158.8
Livestock	40.9	1.1	20.5	57.4
Permanent cultivation	48.0	0.6	5.5	37.1
Mixed	26.8	1.7	25.8	263.7
Market gardening	15.3	2.6	4.3	5.2

Source: *Agrarbericht* (1997, p. 15).

Table 4.15   Structure of livestock farming in the old and new *Länder*, 1995

	Old	New
Dairy		
Number of cows (1000)	4 203.3	1 024.0
Number of farms:	196 111	7 585
farms with 100+ cows	699	2 609
Fattening pigs		
Number of pigs	13 515.5	2 180.4
Number of farms:	190 886	9 296
farms with 1000+ pigs	914	607
Broiler hens		
Number of hens (1000)	30 963.8	9 529.0
Number of farms:	162 228	13 217
farms with 5000+ hens	890	77

Source: *Agrarbericht* (1997, p. 20).

Table 4.16   Structure of farm workforce in old and new *Länder*, 1996 (1000 persons)

	Old	New
Family workers	1 049.7	48.5
Full-time	265.7	11.7
Part-time	784.0	36.8
Hired workers	70.0	103.6
Full-time	49.4	93.6
Part-time	20.6	10.0
Temporary	75.3	7.4
Total workforce	1 195.0	159.5

Source: *Agrarbericht* (1997, p. 9).

4.4.2   Agricultural politics in the new Germany

To evaluate the impact of reunification on agricultural structures and politics in the old *Länder* and in reunified Germany, three key issues need to be considered: the ideological challenge to the 'family farm model', the political influence of the different farm interest groups and the economic competitiveness of different farm business forms.

To what extent has reunification challenged the dominance of the family farm model in the old *Länder*? As Section 4.2.3 of this chapter suggested, the existence of the GDR may have strengthened the political commitment of the former FRG to family farming, even though it was recognised to be a suboptimal model in economic terms (Kallfass, 1991). The collapse of the GDR has removed an important ideological reason for supporting family farming, and may have exposed the farm sector of the old *Länder* to more critical examination by politicians, and paved the way for more rapid structural change (Weinschenck, 1992; Tangermann, 1997). This scenario is supported by the fact that family farming has not (re)established itself in the new *Länder* as strongly as was expected at the time of reunification (see Section 4.3.4). Structural change has continued throughout the 1990s in the old *Länder*, with a reduction of 23 per cent in the number of farms between 1990 and 1998 (from 630 000 to 484 000), while average farm size increased from 18.7 to 24.1 ha (see Table 2.1). The decline has been fastest for farms under 50 ha, while the number of farms over 50 ha has increased (*Agrarbericht*, 1999). Significantly, this structural change has taken place during a national economic recession, which would suggest that push factors out of farming are now strong enough to override the threat of unemployment (Tangermann, 1997). This trend could also reflect the unwillingness of the new generation to enter farming. It is likely that over the next decade the pace of structural change will be faster in the old *Länder* than in the new *Länder*, as it has been estimated that more than two-thirds of full-time farms in the former FRG are economically unviable, and could not survive without subsidies (Weinschenck, 1992).

It is difficult to identify to what extent structural change in agriculture in the old *Länder* in the 1990s can be attributed to ideological change, and whether it has been due to economic changes arising from changes in the CAP and changes in international trade (see Chapter 5), but ideology has certainly played a part, as shown in changing government rhetoric. This has been illustrated already in this chapter by the broad definition of *bäuerlich* used by the BML (see Section 4.3). As will be discussed in Chapters 5 and 6, a subtle change of emphasis in official rhetoric has occurred during the 1990s, with less emphasis on landownership relations, and more emphasis on environmental management and public responsibility. There is also more emphasis on the need for competitiveness, which again could be interpreted as a challenge to the small family farm. The shift in rhetoric can be associated with changes in key actors, in particular the replacement of Kiechle with Borchert as federal agriculture minister in 1993 and the retirement of von Heereman as DBV president in 1997 and his replacement by Sonnleitner, both of whom have been more prepared to use the 'new rhetoric' than their predecessors. Borchert's successor since 1998, Funke, has also continued with the new rhetoric (von Urff, 1999). The family farm model will not go without a struggle, however, and various old *Länder* governments have re-emphasised their commitment to the maintenance of family farming (*Agra-Europe Bonn*, 10.7.1995e, 24.2.1997). The (West) German public also retains a strong allegiance to family farming, as indicated by their acceptance of high food prices to subsidise the small family farm (see Chapter 3). Authors such as Weinschenck (1992) have argued that public opinion may place additional pressure on agriculture ministers to continue with the 'traditional' family farm-oriented policy line.

On an economic level, reunification has had a surprisingly small impact on Germany's agricultural sector as a whole. Although the difference in farm structures in the old and new *Länder* is striking (see Section 4.4.1), the agricultural area of the old *Länder* is almost twice the size of that in the new *Länder* and the number of farms is 20 times greater, so that the agricultural sector of the new *Länder* is dwarfed by its neighbour (*Agra-Europe Bonn*, 3.7.1995c, 9.12.1996a; *Agrarbericht*, 1999). Thus, reunification has made little difference to average farm size in reunified Germany. What impact has reunification had on Germany's position as an agricultural producer within the EU? Reunified Germany now has the third largest agricultural area in the EU after France and Spain (the FRG was in fifth position before 1990), and it is now the largest producer of oilseed rape (41 per cent of EU production), potatoes, milk and pork; and the second largest producer of sugar, beef, veal, cereals and eggs after France (Jones, 1994; Hoggart *et al.*, 1995; *Agrarbericht*, 1997). Despite this increased economic importance, Germany remains one of the structurally weaker members of the EU. Average farm size in Germany is still only 28.1 ha (behind Denmark, France, Luxembourg, Sweden and Britain), while the average size of dairy herds is only 23 cows (higher only than Greece, Italy, Austria, Spain, Portugal and Finland). However, Germany now has a more polarised farm structure than before, and has the largest farm businesses in the EU. Thus, its agricultural policy interests are also more polarised, which is likely to cause divisions within both Germany's domestic and European policy positions.

The extent to which farmers in the new *Länder* can influence German agricultural policy-making depends on their political as well as economic strength, and on both counts they have been, up to now, weak in relation to West German farmers. Within Germany's federal political system the five new *Länder* are in a minority numerically, and are also among the smallest of the federal *Länder* (both in terms of population and area), which further weakens their political influence. Possibly the most important reason why the East German farm lobby has not made more of a political impact is due to the process of reunification itself, whereby the West German political system, including its main political parties and its agricultural policy-making structures, was 'imposed' on the new *Länder* while the GDR system was destroyed (Geiss, 1996; Williams, 1996). This enabled powerful political actors from the former FRG (such as the DBV or large environmental organisations such as BUND) to become quickly established in the new *Länder* in the early 1990s.

It is worth briefly investigating the role that the DBV has played since 1990 due to the key lobbying position of this actor in German agricultural policy-making (see Chapters 2 and 3). It might be expected that its position would be undermined by the relative failure to re-establish family farming according to the West German model in the new *Länder*, and due to the divergent interests that now exist among German farmers. However, the DBV has managed to maintain its position as the key farm lobby group (*Agra-Europe Bonn*, 3.7.1995d, 27.1.1997). In 1991, the three main farmers' unions of the former GDR agreed to merge with the DBV as the formal representative of all farmers in Germany,[2] and today over 80 per cent of the former LPGs have joined the DBV, while about 50 per cent of family farmers have joined (Krüger, 1997). Opinions differ as to how much the DBV has changed its political position as a result of reunification to include the interests of large farm businesses. DBV spokespersons are keen to stress that the DBV is sympathetic towards the problems of farmers in the new *Länder* (for example, Krüger, 1997), and Sonnleitner, the new DBV president, won the support of the LPG successor businesses by standing up for their interests (*Agra-Europe Bonn*, 10.3.1997a; Raabe, 1997). One of the four current vice-presidents of the DBV is a farmer from Sachsen, suggesting a commitment by the DBV to represent the new farmers.

Outside commentators are more sceptical, however, arguing that the DBV only appears to be inclusive on the outside while closer scrutiny of policy discussions (cf. McHenry, 1996) highlights continued pro-West German discourses that often tend to sideline new *Länder* issues (Neander, 1997). It should be remembered that the DBV is an umbrella organisation consisting of *Länder* branch unions, and in the new *Länder* the regional farmers' unions have tended to give more support to LPG successor businesses than to family farmers, who feel politically bypassed (von Urff, 1999). This situation may explain the surprisingly low membership of the DBV by family farmers in the new *Länder*. The DBV's position also needs to be understood in the context of a dwindling national membership due to the reduction of farm numbers in the old *Länder* (see Chapter 2). It cannot afford to alienate farmers in the new *Länder*, because they offer a new lease of life for the DBV (Tangermann, 1997).

It is too simplistic to portray German agricultural politics as being divided only between the interests of the old and new *Länder*. As highlighted in Chapter 2 in relation to the Ertl Plan, for example, farmer interests in the old *Länder* can be divided into the large, mainly arable, commercial family farm sector (in the northern *Länder* of Niedersachsen, Schleswig-Holstein and Nordrhein-Westfalen) and the small, mainly dairy and livestock, 'traditional' family farm sector (in the southern *Länder* of Bayern and Baden–Württemberg), while farmers in the new *Länder* are divided between corporate/cooperative farmers and family farmers. Now that the worst of the restructuring in the new *Länder* is over, new farmer alliances may emerge, cutting across the old FRG–GDR border. In addition, and as will be discussed in Chapter 5, changes to the CAP are also likely to create new, or increase existing internal divisions within Germany.

4.5 Conclusions

In this chapter we have examined the development of agriculture in the GDR and analysed the restructuring of agriculture in the new *Länder* since reunification. We have also considered to what extent reunification has altered agricultural structures and the agricultural policy-making environment in the new Germany. The key conclusions to draw from this analysis are that agriculture in the GDR underwent two revolutionary changes with the land reform of 1945 and the collectivisation policy of the 1950s. The collective farms were subsequently enlarged and became highly specialised. By the 1980s the economic and environmental costs of these policies were becoming apparent, and the SED leadership began to soften its policy on private farming, but GDR farming still lagged behind the FRG in terms of yields and costs of production.

Agriculture in the new *Länder* has undergone another revolution since 1990, with its incorporation into the social market economy and the CAP. Agricultural restructuring has been highly regulated by the federal government, which has aimed to achieve a balance between economic efficiency and social justice. However, inevitably tensions have emerged between the government and different actors with a stake in the restructuring process. Concern has been expressed that the federal government has favoured family farming over corporate or cooperative farming, in line with the dominant family farm ideology of the FRG. However, the farm structure that has emerged in the new *Länder* is dominated by large corporate/cooperative farms, and the average size of family farms is larger than in the old *Länder*. Farming in the new *Länder* now has the potential to become more competitive than farming in the old *Länder*.

We have suggested, however, that the impact of reunification on agricultural policy in the new Germany has not been as great as might be expected. This can be attributed to the imbalance in political and economic power between the old and new *Länder*. The larger farm area and larger farm population of the old *Länder* means that the new *Länder* have had little impact on overall farm structures or agricultural production. The imposition of FRG policy-making structures on the new *Länder* has also hindered farm leaders and politicians in the new *Länder* from forging a distinctive agricultural policy. The main impact of reunification on agricultural policy in Germany has been ideological, in that the apparent competitiveness of corporate and cooperative farms is a challenge to the dominant family farm ideology of the old *Länder*, resulting in a new agricultural policy discourse. However, the economic and political importance of the farm sector in the new *Länder* is likely to increase in future, as productivity levels continue to improve and as farmers become more integrated into national policy-making networks.

Arguably, events outside Germany have had as big an influence on agricultural politics and policies during the 1990s as events within Germany, and this is likely to be the case in the future as well. German reunification has not only created a new economic and social geography within the country, but it has also changed the nature of Germany as an EU member state (Jones, 1994). Germany's role in the context of changing European and international policies will be the subject of the following chapters. Has reunification changed Germany's position as leader, partner or obstructor within the EU?

5
Germany, the CAP, the GATT and Agricultural Trade

5.1 Introduction

The restructuring of agriculture in the new *Länder* of reunified Germany in the 1990s outlined in Chapter 4 has taken place against a backdrop of changes in international agricultural trade rules, and changes in the CAP. In this chapter we broaden the discussion to examine these changes, their background, and to consider their implications for reunified Germany.

The period since the end of the Second World War has seen a rapid growth in world food production and trade, but also of protectionist trade policies, including the CAP. This has led to tensions and conflicts between trading nations, particularly between the USA and EU as the two major players in world agricultural trade. The period since 1986 has been particularly significant in that international rules have been agreed to liberalise world trade in agricultural products and to reduce domestic agricultural subsidies through the GATT. During the same period, the CAP has been reformed to bring EU prices more into line with world prices. These changes have significant implications for agricultural production and policies in reunified Germany, and are, therefore, important to analyse in some detail.

This chapter is structured into three sections. First, we will examine the nature and importance of agricultural trade to Germany and the EU as a whole, as this is important for understanding both Germany's and the EU's positions on the GATT and CAP in relation to trade policy. Second, we will discuss the political and economic background to the 1986 Uruguay Round talks before examining in more detail how the 1986 talks progressed, and the role that the Commission and Germany played in them. Third, we will consider the details of the Uruguay Round Agreement (URA), together with an analysis of the 1992 CAP reforms, and will assess the implications of CAP reform and the URA for agriculture in the EU and reunified Germany. While we shall generally refer to the former FRG when discussing events prior to 1990 and Germany for post-1990 issues, this distinction is not always practicable given that we cover the whole period from 1949 until 1999 in this chapter. By necessity, the discussion in much of this chapter concerning the GATT and CAP reform will be at a general level, as Germany has only been one of the negotiating partners in these events. However, in each section the role of Germany will be examined, as will the impact of these policy changes on agricultural production, structures and domestic agricultural policy in Germany. Following on from the discussion in Chapter 4, we will consider whether reunification has altered Germany's position in European and international policy negotiations.

5.2   Europe, Germany and world food trade

EU member states, together with the USA, dominate world trade in agricultural products. The EU15 collectively accounts for about 16 per cent of all agricultural imports (down from 21.6 per cent in 1977) and about 12 per cent of all exports (up from 7.3 per cent in 1977) (CEC, 1987a, 1989). While the USA has long been a major agricultural exporter, the EU has steadily increased its share of exports over the last 30 years. This growth is attributed to the CAP because of its encouragement to farmers to increase production (Hoggart *et al.*, 1995). Gardner (1996) noted that before 1972, the EEC6 together with Britain, Denmark and Ireland (who joined the EEC in 1973) were net importers of butter, milk powder, beef, feed and food grains. In the 1970s, however, the EEC9 switched from being a net importer to a net exporter of all these commodities. Between 1973 and 1984, the value of agricultural imports into the EEC rose by 51 per cent while the value of agricultural exports rose by 154 per cent (Tracy, 1989). In 1992, the EU12 had a trade surplus in all major temperate food products except oilseeds. The EU15 now dominates the world market in wine, cheese, and milk powder, and holds an important share of the market in wheat, sugar, butter, beef and veal, pigmeat, poultry meat and eggs (CEC, 1995a).

The EU's emergence as a major exporter of agricultural commodities has been of increasing concern to other agricultural exporting nations, in particular the USA. This is not only because the EU has captured market share from other exporters, but also because the EU distorts world market prices through export subsidies paid to bring increasingly expensive EU produced commodities down to world prices (see Figure 3.1), and because of the practice of 'dumping' surplus products on the world market below market prices (Gardner, 1996). It is thought that this has contributed to the growing instability of world market prices (Lingard and Hubbard, 1997).

The CAP has also had a major influence on agricultural trade patterns of EU member states, as most EU agricultural trade now takes place between EU member states within the Single European Market. Many 'third' (non-EU) states have lost market share as intra-European trade has increased (so-called 'trade diversion'), although since 1975 many African, Caribbean and

Pacific states, all former colonies of EU member states, have benefited from preferential access to the EU market for certain tropical commodities under the Lomé Convention (CEC, 1987a), and other economically less developed countries (ELDCs) also benefit from preferential trading agreements (Lingard and Hubbard, 1997).

As outlined in Section 3.3.1, member states can be divided into net agricultural exporters and net importers. In the EU15, the net exporters are: France, the Netherlands, Denmark and Ireland, while the net importers are Germany, Britain, Belgium, Luxembourg, Greece, Italy, Spain, Portugal, Finland, Sweden and Austria. The exporters have benefited most from the CAP and preferential access to member state markets, while the importers have suffered from having to pay more for food imports, due to high internal CAP prices and levies on imports from third countries to protect the internal market (Fearne, 1997).

Germany is the world's largest importer of agricultural products (DBV, 1997), and has the largest agricultural trade deficit of all 15 EU member states (Hoggart *et al.*, 1995). However, Germany has significantly increased its agricultural exports and in 1994 was the world's fourth largest agricultural exporter after the USA, France and the Netherlands, up from thirteenth position in 1969 (DBV, 1997). In the pre-war period most of Germany's trade was with CEECs, but after 1949 the FRG switched its trading focus to Western Europe (Kluge, 1989a; see Chapter 2). This trend was reinforced by the FRG's membership of the EEC in 1957. Since the fall of Communist regimes in Central and Eastern Europe in the early 1990s, however, new markets have opened up with CEECs, and in 1995 they accounted for 8 per cent of German food imports. This increase has been regulated by association agreements signed between the CEECs and the EU15 which include agreements over preferential access to the EU for certain agricultural commodities (Buckwell and Tangermann, 1997). However, the reunification of Germany has not led to any significant change in Germany's trade patterns because of the small volume of agricultural output in the new *Länder*. As noted in Chapter 4, the GDR was a small player in agricultural trade, and, like the FRG, had an agricultural trade deficit.

The impact of EEC membership on the FRG's agricultural trade is shown in Tables 5.1–5.3. The proportion of agricultural commodities imported from other EEC states rose from 42 per cent in 1967 to 64 per cent in 1988 (although part of this increase can be attributed to the expansion of the EU that has taken place over this period). The main EEC countries from which Germany imports agricultural commodities are (in decreasing order of importance by value): the Netherlands, France, Italy, Belgium/Luxembourg and Denmark. These imports consist principally of meat products, vegetables, cheese, wine, grain and fruit (Haase, 1991). Just over one-third of all imports from the EU15 in 1995 were processed goods (*Agrarbericht*, 1997).

Table 5.1   German agricultural imports[a] (billion DM[b])

	1967	1977	1988	1991	1993	1995	1997
EU[c]	7.1	14.6	34	45	38.8[d]	42.3	47.9
CEE	n/a	n/a	1.4	2.5	2.4	2.8	3.3
USA	n/a	n/a	n/a	n/a	2.7	2.6	3.0
ELDCs	4.3	10.0	10.2	12	10.6	12.3	17.5
Others	4.5	8.9	6.2	7.3	4.7	5.4	3.1
Total	16.9	38.5	52.2	68	59.3	65.4	74.8
EU% of total	42	47	64	67	66	65	64

Notes
[a]From 1991 onwards statistics refer to united Germany.
[b]Not inflation adjusted.
[c]1967 = EEC6; 1977 = EEC9; 1988–92 = EC12; from 1993 statistics are for EU15.
[d]In 1993 there was a change in the way intra-EU trade was recorded, which meant that small transactions were excluded.
Source: Agrarbericht (1994, 1997, 1999).

The main import commodities from third countries are oilseeds, coffee, tea, cocoa, tobacco, rice, vegetables and fruit (Haase, 1991). Many of these are raw materials for Germany's food-processing sector, but just over a third of imports in 1995 were of processed goods (*Agrarbericht*, 1997). Imports from third countries have declined relatively as the EU's share has increased. Imports from ELDCs constituted almost 19 per cent of total imports by value in 1995 (down from 25 per cent in 1967). The main ELDC import partners are Brazil, Argentina and Colombia (all outside the Lomé Convention). ELDCs have been negatively affected by Germany's membership of the EU, as trade diversion has occurred. For instance, the FRG was a major importer of grain from Argentina before the CAP was formed (Fearne, 1997), but once the CAP cereals regime had been established, Argentinian grain exports were subject to import levies to protect European producers. Interestingly, rather than purchasing European grain, German livestock farmers reacted to higher cereal prices by switching to cheaper imported US soya beans and cassava from Thailand as substitutes for cattle feed, because these commodities were allowed into the EEC6 without levies (see Section 5.3.1). One recent example of trade diversion concerns banana imports. Until 1993 there was no common market for bananas under the CAP, and member states could pursue their own import policies. The FRG imported bananas from Latin America without imposing import duties (due to a concession reached in the 1957 Treaty of Rome). Completion of the single market, however, meant finding a common banana regime to protect the small number of EU banana producers in the Canary Islands, Madeira and Crete. Latin American (and other) suppliers were given import quotas, with high tariffs for imports above this quota (Swinbank, 1996).

This move caused an outcry in Germany where consumers were used to cheap bananas and faced price rises of up to 60 per cent (*Der Spiegel*, 1994).

The value of FRG exports has risen rapidly since the 1960s (Table 5.2), largely due to an increase in the export of high value processed goods. Germany has the largest food processing sector by value in the EU (Harris and Swinbank, 1997). In 1995, 82 per cent of exports to EU15 member states and 81 per cent of exports to third countries were processed goods, including dairy, meat, oilseed, tobacco, coffee and cocoa products (*Agrarbericht*, 1997). The main market for German agricultural exports is the EU15, accounting for over two-thirds of exports. The rapid increase in exports to EEC states between 1977 and 1988 can be partly accounted for by the accession of Greece, Spain and Portugal in the 1980s which opened up new export markets for the FRG. As with imports, the main export markets for German products are the Netherlands, France, Italy, Belgium/Luxembourg and Denmark. Exports to CEECs have increased rapidly since 1988, while exports to ELDCs remain low (the main markets are the Middle Eastern states of Saudi Arabia, Egypt, Iran and Libya).

Table 5.3 highlights that Germany is a net importer of agricultural products. Germany carries a trade deficit with all export regions except CEECs (although a deficit was also recorded with these states in 1995). Germany has a trade deficit with all 15 EU member states except Britain, Sweden, Finland, Austria and Portugal. However, this trade deficit in agricultural products is more than offset by Germany's trade surplus in manufactured goods (in 1990 Germany had a trade surplus of over DM 78 billion) (Haase, 1991).

This brief overview of the development of agricultural trade in the EU and Germany provides the context in which to discuss the development

Table 5.2 German agricultural exports (billion DM[a])

	1967	*1977*	*1988*	*1991[b]*	*1993*	*1995*	*1997*
EU[c]	1.2	8.6	19.3	24.6	24.4	25.0	30.5
CEE	n/a	n/a	0.8	3.3	4.5	4.9	7.0
USA	n/a	n/a	n/a	n/a	0.9	1.0	1.2
ELDCs	0.2	1.4	2.2	2.9	2.4	3.0	3.0
Others	0.7	2.3	4.4	4.8	2.5	3.0	2.2
Total	2.2	12.7	26.7	35.8	34.7	36.9	43.9
EU% of total	56	67	72	69	70	68	69

Notes
[a]Not inflation adjusted.
[b]From 1991 onwards statistics refer to united Germany.
[c]1967 = EEC6; 1977 = EEC9; 1988–92 = EC12; from 1993 statistics are for EU15.
Source: *Agrarbericht* (1994, 1997, 1999).

Table 5.3 German agricultural trade balance (billion DM)[a]

	1967	1977	1988	1991[b]	1993	1995	1997
EU[c]	−5.9	−9.6	−14.3	−20.6	−14.5	−17.2	−17.3
CEE	n/a	n/a	−0.6	+0.8	+2.1	−11.3	+3.6
USA	n/a	n/a	n/a	n/a	−1.8	−1.6	−1.7
ELDCs	−4.1	−8.6	−8.1	−9	−8.2	−9.4	−14.5
Others	−3.8	−6.6	−1.9	−2.5	−2.2	−2.5	−1.0
Total	−14.7	−25.8	−25.4	−32.2	−24.6	−28.6	−30.9

Notes
[a]Not inflation adjusted.
[b]From 1991 onwards statistics refer to united Germany.
[c]1967 = EEC6; 1977 = EEC9; 1988–92 = EC12; from 1993 statistics are for EU15.
Source: *Agrarbericht* (1994, 1997, 1999).

of international trade policy in agricultural products under the GATT. It might be expected, given Germany's position as major exporter of manufactured goods and net importer of agricultural goods, that Germany would favour policies to liberalise world trade and lower food prices. However, as discussed in Chapters 2 and 3, Germany has a long tradition of agricultural protectionism to protect farmers' incomes (Fearne, 1997), and has been a staunch supporter of the principle of community preference in the CAP. Politicians have been prepared in the past to support a costly agricultural sector in return for farmer support, and have been able to fund this from the wealth generated from the manufacturing sector, and from consumers who have been prepared to pay high food prices. This apparent paradox is important for understanding Germany's position on the CAP and international trade policy.

5.3 Agricultural trade negotiations in the GATT

5.3.1 Early GATT rounds

The GATT Treaty was signed by 23 states (known as contracting parties or CPs) in 1947 in Geneva (Greenaway, 1991). The FRG was not a founder CP as it was still under Allied occupation, and it did not accede until 1951. The GDR and most other CEECs (except for Romania, Poland, Hungary and the Czech and Slovak Republics) never joined, having their own Soviet-controlled trading system. The aim of the GATT was to reduce trade barriers and promote free trade following the protectionism of the 1930s and the impacts of the Second World War (Josling *et al.*, 1996). The original intention was to establish an international trade organisation to oversee implementation of the GATT Treaty, but no international agreement was reached (Josling *et al.*, 1996). Instead, the GATT has convened eight rounds of multilateral trade negotiations since 1947. At each round, new areas of trade have been addressed and greater liberalisation has been achieved. The number of CPs in each round has increased, making the talks more complex. There were 103 CPs in the 1986 Uruguay Round, and the end of the cold war in the 1990s opened the way for yet more CPs. The USA and EU, however, as the world's two largest trading blocs, have had the greatest influence on GATT negotiations.

Although each EU member state is a separate CP to the GATT, they are represented at GATT talks by the European Commission, which negotiates on their behalf in consultation with the CAM and a special committee of foreign ministers (known as the '113 Committee' after the relevant article in the Treaty of Rome). Thus, Germany (since 1957) has not negotiated directly at GATT talks but has worked with other member states to reach a common position. This need to achieve unanimity has inevitably involved trade-offs between member states, especially as the EEC/EU expanded from 6 to 15 members and the range of trade interests has increased. On agricultural trade matters the member states can be divided broadly into two camps: countries favourable to trade liberalisation (the 'free marketeers') which include Britain, Denmark, the Netherlands and Sweden, and countries in favour of managed trade (the 'market manipulators') which include principally France and Germany but also Belgium and Austria, with other member states falling in between these positions. Interestingly, this division cuts across the importer/exporter divide noted above, and reflects the trade policies that member states pursued prior to EU membership. The European Commission has also tended to favour the market manipulator camp on agricultural matters (Hoggart *et al.*, 1995). The market manipulators, including the heavyweight Franco-German axis as well as the European Commission, have dominated EU agricultural trade policy in the past, although we do not wish to imply that all the market manipulators subscribe to a unified policy position for, as discussed in Chapter 3, the policy positions of France, Germany and the Commission have diverged on a number of occasions.

The GATT treaty laid down three principles: non-discrimination, reciprocity and transparency. The non-discrimination principle prohibits bilateral agreements between two countries, and states that each CP will treat all other CPs in the same fashion; the reciprocity principle states that any trade benefit negotiated for one country must be offset by a benefit to others; while the transparency principle states that border protection must be through 'transparent' tariffs rather than 'obscure' measures such as import and export quotas (Greenaway, 1991). Despite the non-discrimination clause, GATT allows for customs unions like the EU, provided that the external tariffs are not higher or more restrictive than those existing before in individual member countries.

The GATT has provided a framework for the development of world trade since 1947, but progress in implementation has been slow and uneven, particularly for agriculture. From the start, agricultural trade was treated as a special case and was granted concessions. For instance, the GATT Treaty prohibits quantitative import restrictions, but permits import quotas on agricultural products if domestic restrictions on production (supply control measures) are in force (Tracy, 1989). Even with concessions like this, CPs have continually flouted GATT principles over agricultural trade. For instance, the CAP's use of non-tariff measures, such as variable levies and export subsidies, are blatantly against GATT principles (Josling *et al.*, 1996). Although the Commission has come to be seen as the main obstructor in agricultural trade policy, Hoggart *et al.* (1995) note that in the 1950s and 1960s the USA was the main culprit. In 1955, for example, the USA used import quotas to protect its dairy farmers even though it had no supply control measures (Tracy, 1989). As will be discussed later in this section, it is only in recent decades that the USA has identified agricultural trade liberalisation as being in its interests.

The first four GATT rounds (Geneva 1947; Annecy 1949; Torquay 1950; Geneva 1956) did not even discuss agriculture (Greenaway, 1991). The first round of GATT talks at which agriculture was discussed was the Dillon Round which lasted from 1960 to 1962, and which coincided with discussions on the formation of the CAP (see Chapter 3). The USA feared that the CAP would be a highly protectionist policy and would negatively affect its trading interests (Ingersent *et al.*, 1994a; George, 1996). The Commission was reluctant to allow the GATT talks to intervene in negotiations over the CAP, although it supported further liberalisation of trade in manufactured goods (Josling *et al.*, 1996). The FRG, as Europe's leading manufacturing exporter, supported trade liberalisation, but also, as discussed in Chapter 3, was largely responsible for the high level of price support in the CAP. In the end a deal was reached between the USA and Europe whereby the USA accepted the CAP's variable levies and export subsidies in return for free access to the EEC6 market for oilseed, oilmeal, soya beans, soya meal, cotton and corn gluten feed exports (so-called 'cereal substitutes') (Josling, 1997). This agreement applied to third countries as well. At the time, imports of these commodities into the EEC6 were limited, but the volume of imports subsequently increased and soon came to represent a significant concession to the USA (as the largest exporter) on the part of the Commission (Tracy, 1989). The growth in EEC6 demand was largely due to livestock producers switching from expensive European feedgrains to cheaper, imported cereal substitutes. As noted in Section 5.2, demand was particularly high in the FRG where the high DM meant that cereal prices were higher than elsewhere in the EEC6 (Josling, 1997).

It was intended to include agriculture on the agenda in the Kennedy Round of 1963 to 1967, but this came to nothing because of basic differences of opinion between the Commission and the USA: the Commission argued for managed international markets under a World Commodity

Agreement whereby international commodity prices for key products (cereals, beef and veal, some dairy products, sugar and oilseeds) would be fixed by international agreement at 'reasonable' prices. The USA favoured greater liberalisation of trade and objected to the Commission's variable levy system. As a result, the USA refused to negotiate (Tracy, 1989). In the Tokyo Round of 1973–79, agriculture was again on the agenda but, once more, stalemate between the USA and the Commission halted negotiations. The USA still objected to the Commission's variable levies and export refunds, while the Commission still refused to negotiate on the CAP (Josling *et al.*, 1996).

The 1970s was a boom period for US and EEC agricultural trade, which could explain why the USA did not push harder for a GATT agreement on agriculture in the Tokyo Round. In 1970, the USA accounted for nearly 35 per cent of world wheat exports, 50 per cent of maize exports and 90 per cent of soya bean exports (Tubiana, 1989). Between 1972 and 1974, world prices for cereals and soya beans soared due to a poor harvest in the USSR and, consequently, an unexpected demand for grain imports from the USSR which caused a world grain shortage (Josling *et al.*, 1996). In response, US farmers intensified production (Potter, 1998). Between 1970 and 1980, US exports of wheat and feedgrains more than tripled in volume (Buttel, 1989) and, as shown in Section 5.2, the EEC also became a net exporter during the 1970s.

However, the 1970s export boom was followed by a bust in the early 1980s. World demand for feedgrains dropped due to the emerging Third World debt crisis and world recession stemming from the second oil crisis (Josling *et al.*, 1996). What has been termed the 'international farm crisis' (Goodman and Redclift, 1989) highlighted to the USA that the EEC9 had emerged as an unwanted competitor in world agricultural trade. For instance, the EEC9's share of the North African wheat market had increased from 2 per cent in 1977 to 42 per cent in 1980, while the USA's share decreased from 42 to 26 per cent (Gardner, 1996). In response, the USA introduced subsidies on exports of wheat to win back its share of the North African market. Despite this measure, the USA's share of world wheat sales declined from 48 per cent in 1981 to less than 30 per cent in 1985, while the EEC10's share rose to 15 per cent in 1987. The EEC's agricultural trade deficit with the USA steadily declined over the course of the 1980s, and in 1986 the value of EEC10 agricultural exports exceeded the value of US exports (Josling, 1997). The costs of agricultural support policies in both the USA and Europe soared due to the need to pay for storage of growing food surpluses and for export subsidies, as the gap between internal and world market prices widened (see Chapter 3).

It is, therefore, not surprising that tensions between the USA and EEC grew. In December 1985, the Commission introduced a ban on hormone-treated meat due to consumer concern, threatening US exports of beef by-products to the EEC10 (an embargo on imports of US beef by-products was imposed in January 1989). The USA objected that this was trade discrimination and imposed a punitive tariff on EEC agricultural exports to the USA. In 1988, the US government complained to the GATT that the EC12 was indirectly subsidising production of oilseeds by subsidising processing, and thereby discriminating against US soya bean producers (Tracy, 1989; Josling *et al.*, 1996). EC12 oilseed production had grown from 3.2 million tonnes in 1980 to 11.6 million tonnes in 1987, which represented half of Europe's oilseed consumption needs (Josling, 1997). There was also friction over the EC12 proposal to impose a tax on imported vegetable oils and fats to protect olive oil prices (following Spain's accession to the EC) and butter prices (by raising the cost of margarine relative to butter). The USA saw this as an attempt by the EC12 to impose restrictions on US exports. Following US objection, and with support from the FRG and Britain, the proposal was dropped. Accession of Spain and Portugal to the EC caused further tensions as the USA objected that its cereal exports to these markets would be disadvantaged by accession. A trade war was only avoided by an agreement that Spain would, until 1990, import a certain amount of feedgrain from the USA at a reduced levy (Tracy, 1989).

Given deteriorating relations between the USA and EC12, the urgency of including agriculture in GATT talks increased. The USA and the so-called 'Cairns Group' of agricultural exporting countries[1] pushed for its inclusion (Ingersent *et al.*, 1994b). There was general agreement that a freeing up of world markets, and an end to subsidised exports, would lead to a rise in world prices due to a better alignment between supply and demand. For instance, world prices for sugar, beef, dairy products and rice could rise by between 30 and 50 per cent (Reeves, 1987; Moyer and Josling, 1990), while grain prices could rise by 12 per cent (Gardner, 1996). This would benefit agricultural exporting countries, particularly those exporting temperate commodities (hence the pressure from the USA and Cairns Group), but might disadvantage agricultural importing countries, including some developing countries (Guyomard *et al.*, 1993).

In 1982, the OECD set up a committee to investigate how barriers to world trade in agriculture in OECD states could be reduced. For the first time, its 1987 report enabled direct comparisons to be made between levels of support given to agriculture by different OECD countries. This was done by calculating 'producer subsidy equivalents' (PSEs), based on the level of subsidy that would have to be paid to farmers to maintain their incomes if all agricultural support measures were withdrawn, expressed as a percentage of the domestic value of agricultural output (Buckwell, 1997). The report showed generally rising PSEs through the 1980s, but with large variations between countries. Japan had the highest level of protection with almost 80 per cent in 1986, followed by the EC12 with almost 50 per cent and the USA with about 35 per cent (Moyer and Josling, 1990). Some countries, such as Australia and New Zealand, which had already partly liberalised their agricultural sectors, had much lower PSEs (O.J. Wilson, 1994). The OECD called for its members to reform domestic farm policies and reduce levels of support (Moyer and Josling, 1990). This paved the way for negotiations on agriculture in the next GATT round.

5.3.2 The Uruguay Round

The Uruguay Round was formally launched in September 1986. It was the most complex round yet in terms of the number of CPs (123) and the number of issues on the agenda; for instance, trade in services and intellectual property rights were on the agenda for the first time (Greenaway, 1991). Agriculture was one of the main issues, however. The declaration on agriculture stated the round's intention to achieve greater liberalisation of agricultural trade by: (a) improving market access (reducing protection); (b) improving the competitive environment (phasing out all direct and indirect subsidies that affect world agricultural trade); (c) minimising barriers to trade placed by health standard regulations (Tracy, 1989). Two new concepts were introduced into the agriculture negotiations. Firstly, to achieve any reductions in domestic support, an overall measure of support was needed. This was termed 'aggregate measure of support' (AMS). Secondly, to make protectionist trade policies more transparent, all non-tariff measures (such as variable levies or import quotas) would have to be converted into tariff equivalents. This process was termed 'tariffication'.

For the first time it was explicitly recognised that domestic agricultural policies were also under scrutiny, and that reforms to domestic policies were needed to achieve any breakthrough in world trade (Reeves, 1987; Moyer and Josling, 1990; Redclift *et al.*, 1999). Also, for the first time, agricultural negotiations were linked to other areas of negotiation. In other words, agreement on industrial tariffs could not be reached without an agreement on agriculture. These linkages increased the pressure to achieve a successful outcome to the agriculture negotiations, and raised the public and political profile of farm lobbies (Greenaway, 1991). This point is important for understanding the FRG's position in the Uruguay Round talks. The FRG industrial lobby now saw the farm lobby as a direct threat to its interests, and FRG farmers were faced with the possibility of being directly blamed for obstructing trade liberalisation (see below).

CPs were given to the end of 1987 to submit their proposals as to how to implement the declaration (Moyer and Josling, 1990). The USA proposed a so-called 'zero option': elimination of all barriers to free trade over a ten-year period (1990–2000). The Commission, in contrast, proposed a phased reduction in levels of support to negotiated lower levels (Harvey, 1997). The Cairns Group proposed a compromise between the USA's and European Commission's positions: a freeze on current support levels followed by a phased reduction of support over a ten-year period and a tightening of GATT rules to ensure compliance (Tracy, 1989). The radical position taken by the USA was tactical to put pressure on the EC12 (Moyer and Josling, 1990). Although the USA had a more efficient agricultural sector than the EC12 and would gain more benefits from liberalisation, certain sectors would suffer. For instance, US producers of animal feed would suffer from falling demand from EC12 livestock producers because they would turn to cheaper cereals. The US dairy sector was also heavily protected and would suffer from removal of protection. The Commission recognised that reform of the CAP was necessary due to the need to curb its escalating costs, and limited reforms had already been introduced in the 1980s (see Chapter 3). However, the Commission was unwilling for third countries, especially the USA, to dictate further reforms of the CAP, and it recognised how politically sensitive this issue was with EU12 member states, particularly with the influential French and German agricultural lobbies (Hoggart *et al.*, 1995).

Little progress was achieved by the mid-term review in Montreal in December 1988, as the Commission was stalling until the 1988 US presidential elections had been held (no doubt in the hope that the new incumbent would be more sympathetic to Europe's position). Meanwhile, a drought in the USA in 1988 led to a poor harvest and a rise in world grain and soya bean prices, so that the immediate crisis was partly solved. This took away the urgency of finding short-term crisis management measures (Moyer and Josling, 1990). In October 1989, the USA softened its hardline position and issued more moderate proposals. It called for a 90 per cent reduction in export subsidies over ten years (starting from 1986, when the Uruguay Round commenced) and a 75 per cent reduction of the AMS over the same period. In November 1990, the Commission also softened its position, and offered to reduce the AMS by 30 per cent between 1986 and 1995, and to convert all non-tariff measures into tariffs; but it argued that there was no need to fix specific targets for reduction of export subsidies, as the need for them would decrease anyway with lower domestic support. However, it added that agreement on these measures was conditional upon other CPs accepting the principle of 'rebalancing', meaning that commodities subject to no tariffs should become subject to tariffs. This demand was directed at US oilseed and non-grain feed imports which, as stated earlier, had been exempted from tariffs in the Dillon Round (Guyomard *et al.*, 1993). The Uruguay Round was due to end with a meeting in Brussels in December 1990, but negotiators failed to reach agreement and the talks collapsed. Inability to reach agreement on agriculture was seen as the major cause of failure, and the Commission was seen as the main culprit (although, as George, 1996, pointed out, agreement on trade in services proved equally difficult to reach due to US intransigence).

What was Germany's position in the talks? Opinion within Germany was divided: the industrial lobby strongly supported further trade liberalisation and pushed for a successful outcome to the Uruguay Round talks, even if this meant making concessions on agriculture (Smyser, 1993), while the agricultural lobby, led by federal Agriculture Minister Kiechle, strongly opposed the proposals because of the negative impact they would have on farmers' incomes (*Agra-Europe Bonn*, 22.10.1990). As discussed in Chapters 2 and 3, support for farm incomes has been a key pillar of German agricultural policy in the post-war period, and any threat has been strongly resisted by the DBV. During the Uruguay Round talks in 1989/90, Kiechle was criticised by the German media for obstructing the progress of the talks. Kiechle countered by arguing that Germany was an important exporter of agricultural goods and, therefore, the agricultural lobby also wanted a successful outcome to the Uruguay Round talks (although this argument was hollow given that most German food exports went to other EU countries). This brief analysis reveals that the linkage of an agreement on industrial liberalisation with agreement on agriculture in the Uruguay Round talks highlighted the paradox between Germany's agricultural and national interests, by placing them in direct opposition to one another.

Despite pressure from the industrial lobby and the media for a successful outcome to the Uruguay Round, Kiechle received support for his intransigent position from across the whole political spectrum, including the FDP, the Greens, Bündnis 90[2] and the consumer lobby, as well as his own supporters from the CDU and CSU, and the DBV. Even the SPD gave their support (*Agra-Europe Bonn*, 12.11.1990; von Cramon-Taubadel, 1993). Chancellor Kohl stated that a successful outcome to the Uruguay Round talks must not be at the expense of farmers (*Agra-Europe Bonn*, 22.10.1990). To understand why politicians supported an obstructive position in the talks, when this was against Germany's national interests, it is necessary to consider the domestic political situation at the time. Electoral politics played a part in the pro-farming rhetoric of the CDU and other parties in the run-up to the federal elections of December 1990. Reunification could also have been a factor, as Kiechle and Kohl would have been anxious not to upset farmers in both the old and new *Länder* who were worried about the impact of agricultural restructuring on the domestic agricultural market. Kohl was also anxious not to antagonise France, which was strongly against any challenge to the CAP, in the run-up to reunification.

5.4.3 CAP reform

With the Uruguay Round abandoned, the Commission could return to the issue of CAP reform without appearing to be pressured by the USA (Potter and Ervin, 1999). In May 1991, therefore, the Commission published a set of proposals for the future development of the CAP (known as the MacSharry proposals after Ray MacSharry, the agriculture commissioner at the time). These contained many radical reform measures, including price cuts of 35 per cent for cereals and 15 per cent for butter, and stricter production control measures such as a 5 per cent cut in the milk quota, together with modulated (capped) compensation payments, that would enable the EC12 to meet the conditions for agricultural reform set out in the Uruguay Round negotiations (Manegold, 1991; Swinbank, 1997). This development encouraged Arthur Dunkel, director-general of GATT, to put forward a new compromise set of proposals in December 1991 known as the Draft Final Act (Guyomard *et al.*, 1993). The USA pressured the Commission to respond constructively by threatening to impose trade sanctions on EC12 agricultural exports to the USA, including white wine exports, which was a warning to the French. The Commission and the free-marketeer member states were now happy to use international pressure from the GATT as a lever on reluctant member states, including Germany, to agree to the MacSharry proposals, although the link between CAP reform and the Uruguay Round negotiations was never explicitly acknowledged in negotiations of the CAM (Josling *et al.*, 1996; Tangermann, 1997).

Predictably, Kiechle and the DBV opposed the MacSharry proposals as such radical price cuts threatened core German agricultural policy values. Gerd Sonnleiter, then president of the Bayerischer Bauernverband, called the proposals 'a declaration of war' (*Der Spiegel*, 1991b). Kiechle, as in the late 1980s, argued against price cuts and, instead, for a strengthening of the CAP's production control programmes, such as set-aside and milk quotas, and production neutral AEPs (see Chapter 6). However, the German government's position had shifted since the 1990 breakdown of the Uruguay Round talks. This time Kohl spoke out strongly in favour of a successful agreement to the Uruguay Round and argued that the EC12 must take a more flexible position on agriculture (Smyser, 1993). Kohl's change of heart can be explained by two main factors. First, Kohl could afford to anger the farm lobby as Germany was in an inter-electoral period (von Cramon-Taubadel, 1993). The negotiating position of Kiechle and the farm lobby was, therefore, weakened, although Hendriks (1994) noted that two upcoming *Länder* elections in Baden-Württemberg and Schleswig-Holstein (both *Länder* with important agricultural electorates) might have made Kohl more cautious. A second 'pro-change' factor, however, was that Germany was entering recession and so there were strong economic reasons for a successful outcome to the Uruguay Round talks. In 1991 Germany recorded its first trade deficit for ten years (Hoggart *et al.*, 1995), and pressure from the German industrial lobby and the German media was mounting (*Der Spiegel*, 1991b, 1992a).

It is debatable whether German reunification was a factor behind Kohl's change of position. Von Cramon-Taubadel (1993) and Hendriks (1994) argued that the economic costs of reunification made a costly agricultural policy less attractive to the government while, politically, reunification made Germany more anxious to be a partner in Europe and not an obstructor. On the other hand, Tangermann (1997) and Möhlers (1997) argued that reunification was not a key causal factor, as the CAP reform proposals were drawn up too soon after reunification for this event to have had a large impact.

Under pressure from Kohl, Kiechle was forced to play a more conciliatory role in negotiations on the MacSharry proposals. He accepted the principle of price cuts, but argued that any cuts must be accompanied by income compensation, set-aside and AEPs, which must be non-negotiable in the Uruguay Round talks (Hendriks, 1994). Following lengthy negotiations, the CAM finally reached agreement on CAP reform in May 1992. The reforms have been hailed as a turning point in the development of the CAP (*Agra-Europe London*, 12.1.1996), but closer inspection of the reform measures revealed that the final agreement was a watered-down version of the original MacSharry proposals (Manegold, 1992; Potter, 1998). There was nothing revolutionary about the proposed reforms for the dairy sector which was largely left untouched, as was the sugar regime. Many southern products, such as fruit, vegetables, wine and rice were not even included in the reforms.

The main elements of the reform were: new market measures, which consisted of phased reductions in price support offset by compensation payments, together with tighter production control measures; and so-called 'accompanying' measures (production-neutral policies such as early retirement and agri-environmental schemes). These latter measures were seen as allowable in the Uruguay Round talks because payments to farmers are not linked to production and, therefore, do not encourage increased production. They are thus termed 'decoupled' payments (Potter, 1998). For the arable sector (cereals, oilseeds and protein plants) a new arable area payments scheme was introduced. The target price for cereals was to be cut over a three-year period by 29 per cent from 155 ECU/tonne in 1992/93 to 110 ECU/tonne in 1995/96 (compared to the original MacSharry proposal of a 35 per cent cut). The intervention price was also to be lowered accordingly. However, to offset loss of income, producers were to be paid compensation, which would rise over the three-year implementation period as the target price was reduced. Compensation payments would be calculated according to regional average yields (over a reference period of three years for 1989–91 in specified regions). Each farmer would receive a compensation payment equal to their arable area multiplied by the regional average yield, in addition to payment for the sale of their crops. The suggestion of modulating payments in the MacSharry proposals was not implemented. This new price policy was combined with a production control policy to reduce output. To be eligible for compensation, farmers would have to enter 15 per cent of their arable area into set-aside. Set-aside, therefore, became more or less compulsory, although small farmers producing less than 92 tonnes of grains/oilseeds a year were exempted. Assuming that this exemption roughly equates to farms of up to 20 ha (Swinbank, 1997), this would include over half of Germany's arable farms but only 14 per cent of Germany's arable land area (*Agrarbericht*, 1994; see also Table 2.1). Only small changes were made to the dairy sector. Butter prices were to be reduced by 2.5 per cent per year in 1993/94 and 1994/95 (compared to a 15 per cent cut proposed by MacSharry). Milk quotas were to be cut by 1 per cent in 1993/94 and again in 1994/95, but this cut was less than half of the cut proposed by MacSharry. Production controls and price cuts were also introduced to the beef sector, together with cutbacks in the volume of beef which could be purchased into intervention (phased over a five-year period). Production control measures consisted of extensification measures (meaning beef farmers had to reduce livestock numbers per hectare to qualify for premiums), with additional extensification premiums payable to farmers who further reduced stocking densities to less than 1.4 LU/ha. The sheep sector was also subject to new supply controls, with premium payments for sheep limited to 500 sheep in non-LFAs and 1000 in LFAs.

The final MacSharry reforms incorporated Germany's demands for unmodulated compensation for price cuts, for a strengthening of the set-aside scheme (which had proved popular in Germany; see Chapter 3) and for accompanying measures, so Kiechle could not oppose them, but he was obviously unhappy about the reforms. He tried to justify his 'about-turn' from obstructor to supporter of the reforms by claiming credit for having watered down the original MacSharry proposals to protect the interests of German farmers (Willer, 1993). First, he assured farmers that compensation payments would be permanent (*dauerhaft*) and dependable (*verläßlich*) (Tangermann, 1997). This should be seen as a commitment by Kiechle rather than by the Commission, as no definite provision was made in the 1992 CAP reform for a continuation of compensation payments beyond the reform period of 1993–96, although it was implied that payments would continue until at least 1999. Second, Kiechle had successfully supported Britain and Denmark in their opposition to the proposal to modulate compensation payments according to farm size, because this would disadvantage large farms in the new *Länder*. Third, Kiechle claimed credit for negotiating the option for farmers to grow bio-resources on their set-aside land and still claim some set-aside premiums (see also Chapter 6). Fourth, he had argued for regional, as opposed to farm-level, base areas for calculating set-aside requirements, as this would be simpler to administer and would give farmers some flexibility. Fifth, he had argued strongly to protect dairy farmers from any cut in quota or intervention price, and claimed credit for the low cuts agreed (von Cramon-Taubadel, 1993; Willer, 1993; BML, 1994a). Finally, he had fully supported the accompanying measures which, as will be discussed in Chapter 6, were already an important part of German agricultural policy. It is clear, however, that personal opposition to the CAP reforms was a major factor behind the resignation of Kiechle in early 1993 (von Cramon-Taubadel, 1993).

5.3.4 The Uruguay Round agreement on agriculture

In November 1992 (in between the Bush and Clinton presidencies) an agreement was reached between the USA and the Commission on agricultural trade reform (the so-called Blair House Agreement), despite continuing protests from European farmers, and in particular French farmers who could exert pressure on the government because of uncertainty over the outcome of the French referendum on the Maastricht Treaty (*Der Spiegel*, 1992b). In return for the USA's acceptance of the CAP reform, the Commission agreed to settle the long-running oilseeds dispute by establishing a maximum area for oilseed production of 5.1 million ha, which would be subject to the same set-aside rules as cereals (Manegold, 1992; Goeman, 1996). In addition, a 'peace clause' was agreed which stated that, as long as domestic agricultural policy measures did not directly contravene GATT regulations, they could not be challenged by another country or by the GATT before the end of 2003. The Commission saw this clause as giving legitimacy to the CAP for the first time, as it meant that the CAP could not be challenged by the USA or any other CP before 2004 (*Agra-Europe London*, 13.1.1994).

With CAP reform in place and a deal agreed between the USA and the Commission, an agreement on agriculture could finally be reached, and the 'Final Act' was signed at Marrakesh, Morocco, in April 1994. The URA came into effect on 1 July 1995 and remains in force until June 2001. It is administered by a new World Trade Organisation (WTO) which replaces the GATT. The main measures agreed to are shown in Table 5.4. Significantly, the agreement on reduction of the AMS allowed so-called 'blue box' (production limitation) payments to be excluded from calculation of AMS, as well as 'green box' (production neutral) payments. This allowed the Commission to class compensation payments as blue-box payments (as demanded by Kiechle), even though payment levels are partially linked to production levels (regional yields). This was a substantial concession to the Commission, as compensation payments now form the main expenditure of the EAGGF (Gardner, 1996), and their exclusion from the calculation of the AMS has allowed the EAGGF budget to continue to increase (*Agra-Europe London*, 18.7.1997c).

5.4 Implementation of CAP reform and the URA

5.4.1 Implementation in the EU

The immediate impact of the URA on the reformed CAP was small, but commentators predicted that problems might emerge towards the start of the new millennium (Swinbank, 1996; Tangermann, 1996). The small initial impact of the URA is illustrated by the fact that the EU12 had already fulfilled the condition for a 20 per cent reduction in AMS in 1995.

Table 5.4 Main policy measures contained in the URA

Measure	Amount	Concessions
Reduction in domestic subsidies (AMS)	20% reduction in total domestic subsidies over 6 years (13.3% in developing countries) from a base period of 1986–88[a]	Allows for some flexibility (for instance, CPs can reduce level of support by more than 20% for some commodities and less for others). *Blue box* (production limitation) and *green box* (production neutral) payments are excluded from the calculation
Imports: reduction of import controls	Tariffication of all border protection measures, including import quotas and voluntary export restraint agreements and reduction by 36% over a six-year period from a 1986–88 base period (24% reduction over ten years for developing countries)	To protect domestic markets from a sudden increase in volume of imports or lower priced imports a country may impose additional duties if the price for a consignment of goods falls below a specified 'trigger' price. This is known as the special safeguard provision
Imports: minimum market access	Import opportunities for all agricultural commodities must not fall below levels existing in the 1986–88 base year. New import opportunities must be opened up for commodities where imports formed less than 5% of the market in 1986–88	

169

Table 5.4 Main policy measures contained in the URA (*continued*)

Measure	Amount	Concessions
Exports: reduction of export subsidies	36% reduction in expenditure on export subsidies over six years (24% for developing countries) and a 21% reduction in the volume of subsidised exports over six years (14% for developing countries over ten years). Base period is 1986–90	Genuine food aid exports and processed food products are exempted

Note
[a]1986 was used as the base year as this was when the Uruguay Round began.
Source: adapted from Swinbank (1996) and Tangermann (1996).

This was only achieved, however, because compensation payments were excluded from the calculation of AMS. European concerns about a decline in community preference (protection from food imports) also seem unfounded, as the process of tariffication has led to tariff levels for most commodities that are as high or higher than the previous import duties. This is because the base period for calculating tariffs, 1986–88, was a period when world prices were low, and there was, therefore, a large gap between world and CAP prices. This enabled the Commission to set tariffs at high levels (Tangermann, 1996). Even the minimum access requirement is unlikely to pose too many challenges. Many commodities for which access must be increased (based on the 1986–88 situation) already meet the access requirements, for instance, due to preferential access agreements between the EU and CEECs signed since this period. This, together with high tariffs, means that few new import opportunities will be presented by the URA.

It is the requirements on subsidised exports that are likely to pose the greatest challenge for the EU in the longer term, as the CAP reform has not tackled fundamental supply problems and the EU15 may soon face the threat of unwanted surpluses. The initial impact of the new arable regime was positive, partly due to a fall in production (helped by some poor harvests), and partly due to an increase in demand for EU cereals from EU livestock producers (CEC, 1995b). This illustrates that price cuts have increased internal demand for domestic cereals at the expense of US soya meal exports. Cereal stocks in intervention dropped from 32.7 million tonnes in 1994/95 to under 3 million tonnes in 1995/96 (Goeman, 1996). An increase in world cereal prices in 1995 also led to a narrowing between world prices and EU15 prices and meant that the EU could easily stay within its subsidised export limits (CEC, 1995b). Indeed, in 1997 export taxes were charged on EU cereal exports to bring them up to world market prices (Swinbank, 1997). Cereal farmers have gained financially from the CAP reforms, as they have received compensation payments despite higher market prices than anticipated (*Agra-Europe London*, 18.7.1997a).

However, there have been many criticisms of the set-aside policy as a production control measure, as cereal harvests have continued to rise despite set-aside. For instance, cereal production in Germany increased from 35.8 million tonnes in 1994/95 to 45.5 million tonnes in 1998/98 (*Agrarbericht*, 1997, 1999). This can be explained by several factors. First, the favourable situation in the cereals sector has enabled a continual reduction in the set-aside requirement since the reforms were introduced (12 per cent in 1994/95, 10 per cent in 1995/96, 5 per cent between 1996/97 and 1998/99 and 10 per cent in 1999/2000). Second, in the original reform agreement farmers were not allowed to count land in permanent set-aside (20 years) towards their set-aside requirements,[3] but a CAM decision in 1995 reversed this policy, which is likely to lead to more marginal land being put into set-aside (as generally only farmers with marginal lands choose to enter the 20-year set-aside option). Third, farmers are now allowed to 'export' their set-aside liability to other farmers within a 20 km radius, a decision which further undermines the effectiveness of set-aside in controlling cereals and oilseed production (*Agra-Europe London*, 29.9.1995). This opportunity for farmers to place only their most marginal arable land into set-aside has been termed the 'selectivity effect' (Ilbery, 1990). Fourth, although regions that overshoot their base area are meant to be penalised the following year, so far the Commission has failed to enforce penalties, a failure termed 'political slippage' (Swinbank, 1997). Of course, the increase in Germany can also be attributed to rising yields on cereal farms in the new *Länder*.

The inability to reform the dairy sector means that it is unlikely that the minor reductions in quota and prices agreed in the CAP reform will enable the EU15 to meet the URA requirements on a reduction in subsidised exports (*Agra-Europe London*, 15.6.1992). The beef sector has faced an unanticipated blow due to the BSE crisis (see Chapter 6). EU consumer demand for beef dropped by almost 20 per cent in 1996 causing beef prices to fall, as well as surpluses and the costs of intervention buying to increase (*Agra-Europe London*, 1.11.1996).

5.4.2   Implementation in Germany

Although implementation of CAP reform and the URA at EU level has been relatively smooth, Germany has experienced many implementation problems, especially in the new *Länder*. Establishing production baselines, such as regional base areas for the Arable Area Scheme or milk quota levels, have been difficult because of the complete transformation of conditions of production since 1990. A balance had to be struck between not disadvantaging new farm businesses in the new *Länder* by being too strict, and not upsetting other member states by being too lenient. For instance, the base areas for the Arable Area Scheme, on which set-aside area is calculated, were initially calculated at too low a level (3.6 million ha), and in 1993 the new *Länder* overshot the base area by 9 per cent. This was partly due to a decrease in the area cultivated under fodder crops and a consequent increase in cereals (Willer, 1993). Under CAP reform rules, this would have led to penalties being imposed on East German arable farmers the next year: they would have had to place additional land into set-aside and would have received 10 per cent less in compensation payments. Because of the financially disastrous impact this would have had on farmers, the CAM agreed to increase the arable base area for the new *Länder* by 9 per cent to 3.93 million ha (*Agra-Europe London*, 13.1.1994). In addition, the Commission allowed the federal government to use West German cereal yields (which at the time were higher than yields in the new *Länder*) as a basis for calculating reference yields and, therefore, compensation payments, in the new *Länder*. There was also a problem in establishing a base area for oilseeds under the EC12–US oilseeds agreement (see above) because, although oilseed production was low during the GDR period, it had increased after reunification. As a result, Germany was awarded a higher base area (at the expense of France, Italy and Denmark) (BML, 1994a). However, the new *Länder* were not given preferential treatment for all commodities. The Commission initially awarded the new *Länder* a sugar-beet quota of 870 000 tonnes, but following protest from other member states this was reduced to 847 000 tonnes (Schultz, 1994).

As well as these technical implementation problems, the 1992 reforms have been criticised by both academics and the farm lobby (often from different perspectives). Academics have argued that the CAP reform obstructed restructuring of production, especially in the new *Länder*. Both Weinschenck (1993) and Ahrens and Lippert (1995) argued that insufficiently differentiated compensation payments, set-aside and agri-environmental payments, have allowed production to continue on marginal arable land in both the old and new *Länder* that, without subsidies, would not be economic to farm for arable crops (in other words they have the effect of fossilising production patterns). This can be seen in the new *Länder* where, in 1996, 45 per cent of Germany's compulsory set-aside land and 65 per cent of the voluntary 20-year set-aside land was located (*Agrarbericht*, 1997). The regional base yields used to calculate compensation payments benefit inefficient farmers, but penalise efficient farmers. Compensation payments also artificially raise land values and obstruct the land market and farm structural change (Tangermann, 1992). A similar criticism has been made of the impact of milk quotas in the new *Länder* by Forstner and Isermeyer (1998), who argued that they have also obstructed structural change by being awarded to existing dairy farms, many of which are economically unviable in the new policy climate. In the short term, however, the CAP reforms have been popular among farmers and policy-makers for this very reason. In the new *Länder*, there is a reluctance to contemplate policies that would take land out of production permanently. This is a hang-over from the GDR ideology of self-sufficiency, but it is also due to the fear that, without farming, whole regions would become depopulated (Ahrens and Lippert, 1995).

The DBV was initially hostile to the CAP reforms, arguing that farmers' interests had been sacrificed for industry. Von Cramon-Taubadel (1993) noted that the DBV played on the word *Bauer*, which in German means both 'farmer' and 'pawn'. Von Heereman, the DBV president, voiced disappointment over the politics of Franz Fischler, the Austrian agricultural commissioner (MacSharry's successor), who had proved to be a free-marketeer rather than an advocate of family farming (*Agra-Europe Bonn*, 10.7.1995a). He also continued to voice criticisms of compensation payments for making farmers more dependent on the state and more vulnerable to future cuts in support (*Agra-Europe Bonn*, 13.1.1997). A proposal in 1997 by the Commission to reduce the level of compensation payments received strong criticism from German farmers, who reminded the government that it had promised that these payments would be permanent (*Agra-Europe Bonn*, 24.3.1997). A further criticism over implementation has concerned the level of bureaucracy and cost required in administering set-aside and other production control programmes. This is a particular problem for Germany because of its federal structure, which means that administration falls to the *Länder* governments (see Chapter 2), leading to duplication of effort and pressure on *Länder* resources (von Cramon-Taubadel, 1993). Von Heereman, the DBV president, called the CAP reform and URA a *bureaucratisation* rather than a *liberalisation* of agriculture (von Heereman, 1993).

Once the reforms were implemented, however, the DBV's attention focused on farm incomes, and there has been concern that incomes have continued to fall behind national average incomes. In 1995, the DBV reported that average farm incomes were only 50 per cent of the national average (*Agra-Europe Bonn*, 10.7.1995e), while dairy farmers experienced a 20 per cent decrease in incomes between 1989 and 1994 (*Agra-Europe Bonn*, 10.7.1995g). Closer analysis of income figures, however, reveals a varied picture. The 1992 CAP reforms, and subsequent market movements, have created winners and losers. Generally, cereal farmers have benefited most since 1992, due to buoyant world market prices together with compensation payments. Pig farmers also benefited from windfall price increases due to the BSE crisis, which increased consumer demand for pork, and to an export ban on pigmeat from the Netherlands and Belgium in 1997 due to an outbreak of swine fever. Dairy, beef and fodder crop farmers have experienced generally falling incomes (*Agrarbericht*, 1997), although prices for these commodities started to pick up in 1997/98 (*Agrarbericht*, 1999). In addition to variations by commodity sector, incomes vary according to farm size, with larger and more commercial family farms (especially in the new *Länder*) proving to be more profitable than smaller farms. For instance, in 1995/96 full-time family farms in Sachsen-Anhalt (mainly arable farms with an average size of 146 ha) made average profits of almost DM 100 000, while full-time family farms in Bayern (mainly dairy and livestock farms with an average size of 30 ha) made average profits of under DM 50 000. Incomes of farms in LFAs continue to lag behind non-LFA farms, even when LFA compensation payments are considered. Interestingly, part-time farms (which in 1995 made up 59 per cent of all farms in Germany) have higher household incomes than all but the largest full-time family farms, due to the contribution of alternative income sources to household income (*Agrarbericht*, 1997). These statistics serve to underline the declining viability of family farming in Germany, and highlight the greater economic potential of the large farms (both private, corporate and cooperative) in the new *Länder*.

As discussed in Chapter 3, a key concern of the DBV has been European agri-monetary policy, as it has a direct effect on farm incomes. During the

1970s and 1980s FRG farmers constantly argued that they needed the protection of positive MCAs to prevent farm prices falling due to the strong DM. While agri-monetary policy was not a concern of the 1992 CAP reforms, the reforms coincided with the completion of the Single European Market which led to the phasing out of MCAs (as these internal tariffs went against the principle of the single market). The two issues have, therefore, been closely related and the DBV and BML campaigned strongly for continuing income protection. As a result, a complex set of stop-gap measures were adopted to cover the period from 1992 until the introduction of the single currency in January 1999. First, the 'switchover mechanism', introduced in 1984 (see Chapter 3), was retained (Ritson and Swinbank, 1997). Second, the CAM agreed that Germany could offer its farmers compensation payments for a limited period (until 1995). These comprised adjustment aid to farmers in the new *Länder* (see Chapter 4) and socio-structural compensation (a per hectare payment with a maximum ceiling of DM 6650) to farmers in the old *Länder*. Third, in 1995 the switchover mechanism was abolished, but was replaced by what was termed a 'mini switchover' compromise, whereby it was agreed that all compensation payments and funding for agricultural structural measures would be effectively fixed at the 1995 exchange rate until 1999, to guard against any further currency revaluations (BML, 1996a; Ritson and Swinbank, 1997). Fourth, the Commission agreed to a three-year compensation package for Germany and other hard currency countries in case of further currency revaluations, to be part-funded by the EAGGF and part by national governments (BML, 1996a). German farmers also continued to receive the 3 per cent VAT rebate that was introduced in 1984 (see Chapter 3).

Germany's insistence on protecting its farmers from revaluations of the DM against the ECU after the completion of the single market in 1992 has been criticised by academics. Tangermann (1992) argued convincingly that MCAs and any replacement to them distorted competition and, therefore, went against the spirit of the single market. In addition, they exerted an inflationary pressure on farm prices. Ritson and Swinbank (1997) also argued that the 'green money system' should have been phased out with the completion of the single market, as it had become an anachronism and was used as a political tool by national governments for maintaining the support of national farm lobbies. The introduction of the single currency on 1 January 1999 has finally ended German concerns over agri-monetary policy, and this has been supported by the DBV (*Agra-Europe Bonn*, 23.12.1996b). As a participating state, the exchange rate between the DM and the Euro has been fixed until the DM is phased out in 2001 (CEC, 1998b), and 'green rates' have been abolished for all EU15 member states (including those not participating in the single currency).

Despite implementation problems and criticisms of the 1992 CAP reforms, there are signs that the German position on agricultural policy has gradually shifted towards acceptance. Borchert, Kiechle's successor as agriculture minister, was more accepting of the reforms. In contrast to Kiechle, Borchert came from north Germany, and was more sympathetic to the interests of large farmers (including those of the new *Länder*). He put a positive spin on the CAP reforms, arguing that the old CAP was leading agriculture into a cul-de-sac, and that the URA was positive for German agricultural trade (BML, 1994a). He used rhetoric that Kiechle would never have used (von Cramon-Taubadel, 1993; Möhlers, 1997); for instance, he openly stated that German agriculture must become more efficient and competitive. His vision for agriculture (*Der künftige Weg* – the way forward) was a 'variously structured, competitive agriculture that not only delivers high quality food products and bio-resources, but that also protects the natural environment, the landscape and the attractiveness of rural areas' (BML, 1994a, p. 1). It is significant that he did not include the word *bäuerlich* (see Chapter 4), and that he stressed the multifunctional role of modern agriculture. The statement shows that Borchert recognised that German farmers must seek varied market positions in the reformed CAP to build a competitive advantage, with more commercial farmers focusing on efficient production of staple commodities, and smaller farmers focusing on the production of high-quality, environmentally friendly products. He stressed that Germany was the second biggest recipient of EAGGF Guarantee funding after France (BML, 1994a), with German farmers receiving between DM7 and 8 billion /year from the EAGGF for compensation payments alone (BML, 1996a). However, this is a misleading statement as Germany contributes twice this amount to the EAGGF (BML, 1996b).

The DBV has also changed its rhetoric in light of the 1992 CAP reforms and the appointment of Borchert, although it still uses the rhetoric of the family farm. At a conference of the DBV in Friedrichshafen in July 1995, the union stated that its farmers were prepared to become more competitive but also to accept their multifunctional role: '[German farmers] stand for the production of high quality, healthy food products ... they guarantee protection of landscape and preservation of living villages' (*Agra-Europe Bonn*, 10.7.1995f, p. 22). However, the DBV cautioned that this could only be achieved if farmers were assured of continuing political support. It warned of a climate of great uncertainty over the future of agriculture, a sense of betrayal that farmers' interests had been sacrificed for the interests of manufacturing exporters in the URA, concern over farm incomes and a perceived lack of a level playing field for farmers within the EU15. For instance, German farmers faced stricter building and environmental regulations which increased production costs (a complaint also noted in Section 3.7.1). The DBV claimed that this uncertainty was contributing to a decline in the farming population (as noted in Chapter 4), especially among the younger generation, and could lead to the economic and social decline of peripheral rural areas (*Agra-Europe Bonn*, 10.7.1995f). This fear was supported by von Cramon-Taubadel (1993) who noted that the number of students enrolled in agricultural colleges in Germany fell rapidly from the mid-1980s onwards. Thus, the 1992 CAP reforms did nothing to increase farmers' confidence in the future of agriculture. Indeed, tensions between the government and the DBV continued throughout the 1990s (see also Chapter 8), especially over continuing cutbacks in the federal agricultural budget between 1992 and 1997 (*Agra-Europe Bonn*, 27.1.1997).

5.5 Conclusions

Both the 1992 CAP reforms and 1994 URA are landmarks in the development of European agricultural policy: the CAP reforms because of the partial shift from price support to direct payments to farmers, and the URA because of reductions in levels of domestic support, import tariffs and export subsidies. Josling *et al.* (1996) claimed that the CAP reform represented the end of the long held urban–rural political compact, whereby governments have protected agricultural prices in return for the political support of farmers. Tangermann (1996) argued that, despite all the shortcomings of the URA, for the first time world trade in agricultural commodities was governed by a binding set of rules and commitments. Moyer and Josling (1990) noted that up until the Uruguay Round talks, domestic agricultural policies had dictated the international trade system in that trade policies had to be acceptable to domestic agendas. One of the main achievements of the Uruguay Round was the establishment of the principle that international trade considerations must take precedence over domestic policies, even if this requires unpopular domestic policy reforms.

Both policies have been heavily criticised, however, for their failure to achieve fundamental change. Neither the CAP reform, nor the URA, were as revolutionary as the original proposals. Swinbank (1996) concluded that the Commission followed the *detail* of the URA rather than the *spirit* of it (meaning that it exploited all the possible loopholes!). Guyomard *et al.* (1993) called the URA a 'deal' between the USA and EU to solve the immediate problem of international competition in cash crops. It has similarly been described as a 'management conspiracy' between the EU and USA (*Agra-Europe London*, 13.1.1994). Although the CAP reform enabled the EU to meet the requirements of the URA relatively painlessly (despite a question mark over the ability of the EU to stick to subsidised export limits), it did not solve the fundamental problems of oversupply, market imbalance and financial dependence of farmers on subsidies. Payment of compensation to farmers means that the cost of the CAP has continued to increase, and the reforms have introduced a greater degree of bureaucracy to control farmer compliance with set-aside obligations and other production limitation measures. Both the CAP reform and the URA, therefore, should be seen as the start of a process of liberalisation rather than as revolutionary events in themselves.

The German position on both the CAP reform and URA has gradually shifted from obstructor to partner. The farm lobby, supported by the then minister, Kiechle, initially opposed both the CAP reform and the GATT proposals and, therefore, joined the obstructor camp along with France. Hendriks (1994) placed much of the blame for the CAP crisis of the 1980s and the problems in reaching agreement in the Uruguay Round on the Germans. The German industrial lobby, however, was a strong supporter of a successful Uruguay Round, and the linking of agriculture with industrial liberalisation in the talks meant that the industrial lobby was forced to openly criticise the intransigence of the agricultural lobby. It would seem that in light of the high economic interests at stake, eventual German acceptance of the CAP reforms and URA was inevitable, despite hostile rhetoric from the agricultural lobby. This view is borne out by the fact that France, and not Germany, was seen as the main EU obstructor in the Uruguay Round talks by other CPs (Möhlers, 1997). Germany can take the dubious credit, however, for negotiating several concessions which weakened CAP reform. In particular, Germany fought to protect the dairy regime from any significant reform. Thus, reunification had little effect on Germany's negotiating position, which was firmly influenced by the politics of the West German family farm lobby outlined in Chapters 2 and 3. However, Germany supported concessions to the large farm sector of the new *Länder*, and this sector has been one of the major beneficiaries of the CAP reforms. The 1992 CAP reforms are especially significant as, for the first time in the history of the CAP, the German farm lobby has agreed to price cuts, a decision which will weaken their position in future price negotiations.

The reforms also mark a small but significant change in the way farming is viewed by policy-makers and the general public, from performing a productivist role to a multifunctional (or post-productivist) role. The implications for farming in the EU of this shift were considered by the Economic and Social Committee of the European Parliament in a review of the 1992 CAP reform: 'one may therefore question the attractiveness of a profession which relies increasingly on being "allowed" to produce, and whose income depends on public support, the legitimacy of which is not clearly evident' (ESCEP, 1997, p. 7). To what extent can farmers in the EU, and especially in Germany, adapt to their new role, and how many farmers will choose to leave the industry? These questions will be explored in more detail in the final three chapters of this book. Evidence from Germany in the 1990s, however, suggests that fewer people are prepared to stay in farming or enter farming (see Section 4.4).

The German farm lobby appears to have accepted and accommodated the 1992 reforms despite initial implementation problems and protests. However, the CAP reforms seem to have increased uncertainty among farmers over the future of agricultural policy, and tensions are evident between the DBV and BML (see Chapter 8). Germany's economic difficulties in the 1990s have led to concern among German politicians about the size of Germany's contribution to the EAGGF, and to moves to reduce the cost of agricultural support. This climate of uncertainty has been heightened by further changes to the CAP. In March 1999, the CAM agreed to another round of CAP reforms as part of the Agenda 2000 reforms of the EU. These latest CAP reforms are due to two external pressures: a new round of GATT (now WTO) talks on agriculture started in November 1999, and talks are under way on EU enlargement to include CEECs – developments that will be examined in Chapter 8 when we consider future perspectives for German agriculture. The next five years are, therefore, likely to pose further challenges for Germany's farm lobby.

6

German Agriculture and the Environment

6.1 Introduction

The previous chapters have outlined the development of agricultural structures and policies in the FRG, GDR and reunified Germany, within the
context of European agricultural policy and international trade policy.
Throughout the previous discussion the potential environmental implications of agricultural structural change and intensification of production
have been mentioned. The aim of this chapter is to analyse the past and
present situation of German agriculture and the environment[1] and to
investigate in detail environmental implications of recent policy developments in pre- and post-reunification Germany.

Following from the conceptual theme of Germany as either a leader,
partner or obstructor in European agricultural policy-making that underlies
the argument of this book, we will focus on the role that Germany (and the
FRG before 1990) has played in the development and implementation of
European AEP. The conceptual framework for the argument in this chapter
is based around the notion that policy (and therefore inevitably also politics) is the key regulatory framework for countryside protection in the EU
(we adopt an approach based on the notion of 'strong' policy; cf. Winter,
1990, 1996), and a specific focus will be placed on the question whether
AEPs are *environmental* policies or *farm income support* in disguise. We also
acknowledge that actors such as farmers, consumers and the general public
are important decision-makers in the environmental management process
(Wilson and Bryant, 1997) and may, at times, also strongly influence countryside management decisions (cf. Morris and Potter, 1995; Wilson, 1997c).

First, it is important to outline the environmental impacts of agricultural
practices on the German countryside in order to contextualise the parame-
ters within which AEPs have been established. Section 6.2 will, therefore,
analyse agricultural impacts on the environment in the FRG, GDR and
reunified Germany. Section 6.3 will then explore the policy framework for
German countryside management by investigating both EU and national

AEPs, and by looking in detail at the German agri-environmental programme and the German role in EU agri-environmental policy-making. Section 6.4 will analyse the geography of German AEP in more detail, and will discuss possible factors that have led to highly uneven implementation of AEPs in different German *Länder*, including a brief discussion of whether German agriculture has shifted from a productivist to a post-productivist ethos. The question whether German AEP mechanisms could act as blueprints for other EU countries is further explored in Section 6.5, with a specific emphasis on comparing the policy effectiveness of regulatory versus voluntary AEP approaches, and by discussing the success of food safety policies. Section 6.6 will draw together these arguments by exploring why voluntary and regulatory policy mechanisms have differed in their environmental effectiveness.

6.2 Agricultural impacts on the environment

Chapter 4 has discussed how agricultural policies, structures and ideologies differed between the former FRG and GDR. As a result, the nature and causes of agricultural environmental impacts also differed between the two countries. It is, therefore, necessary first to analyse the environmental situation of the countryside in these two countries separately (Sections 6.2.1 and 6.2.2), before investigating developments in reunified Germany since 1990 (Section 6.2.3).

6.2.1 The FRG

Environmental impacts of agriculture in the FRG were closely associated with the rapid agricultural structural change that took place after the Second World War outlined in Chapter 2. The rapid reduction in the number of farms and consequent farm amalgamation into larger and more efficient holdings (from an average size of 8.1 ha in 1949 to 24.1 ha in 1998; see Table 2.1), the rapidly increasing mechanisation of farms, the increasing intensity of farming with regard to livestock densities per forage area and applications of external inputs (especially fertilisers and pesticides on arable land), the conversion of permanent grassland to arable land, and reductions in the number of crops in rotations all resulted in rapidly rising pressures on the environment and subsequent degradation of water, wildlife and landscape resources (Priebe, 1985; RSU, 1985; Heißenhuber *et al.*, 1994). Structural changes coincided with the rapid disappearance of traditional farming systems – a process further aided by agricultural support mechanisms aimed at both increasing productivity of farms and raising farm incomes (see Chapter 2).

A few figures may illustrate the rapid environmental changes that took place in the FRG between 1949 and 1990. As in most other EEC9 member states at the time, the over-application of fertilisers and pesticides emerged as one of the major concerns, particularly during the 1970s and 1980s, prompting Knickel (1990, p. 384) to argue that N-fertiliser application rates in the FRG in the late 1980s were among 'the highest in the industrial and more densely populated countries of central Europe'. As early as the 1960s, the FRG stood at third place in the EEC6 (after the Netherlands and Belgium) for fertiliser use per hectare UAA (Kluge, 1989a; Fischbeck, 1993), emphasising the rapid pace of modernisation and intensification that had taken place since the Second World War. The expansion of external input use was actively supported by the government through market support subsidies and price fixing (Kluge, 1989a).

Table 6.1 shows that both fertiliser and pesticide applications increased substantially between the 1950s and 1980s, although by the end of the 1980s they began to decline. While applications of N-fertilisers and pesticides peaked in the late 1980s, applications of phosphate- and potassium-based fertilisers began to decrease as early as the 1970s. Concern continued, nonetheless, to be raised about excessive applications of external inputs throughout the 1980s (Werschnitzky, 1987). Höll and von Meyer (1996) highlighted how in 1986, for example, the annual N-surplus (defined as all N added to the soil minus withdrawals in crops and livestock products) still

Table 6.1   Fertiliser and pesticide applications in the FRG for selected years, 1951–90

Input	1951	1961	1971[a]	1981	1989	1990
N-fertilisers (1000 t)	362	619	1131	1551	1540	1487
N/ha UAA (kg)	26	43	83	126	129	125
Phosphate-based fertilisers (1000 t)	418	662	913	837	644	594
Phosphate/ha UAA (kg)	30	46	67	68	54	50
Potassium-based fertilisers (1000 t)	659	1007	1185	1144	887	791
Potassium/ha UAA (kg)	47	71	87	93	75	67
Herbicides (1000 t)	No data	No data	No data	21	17	19
Insecticides (1000 t)	No data	No data	No data	2.3	1.3	1.3
Fungicides (1000 t)	No data	No data	No data	6.5	12	11

Note
[a]Reliable data on pesticide applications have only been available since the mid-1970s (Fischbeck, 1993).
Sources: *Grüner Bericht* (1963); *Agrarbericht* (1973, 1983, 1992); Knickel (1990).

amounted to 167 kg N/ha UAA (a total of 2 million tonnes), leading to substantial soil and water pollution (see below). This figure stands in sharp contrast to only 10 kg N/ha N-surplus at the beginning of the 1950s (Knickel, 1990). It should, however, be noted that there have been large regional disparities of fertiliser pollution, and in particular in the southern parts of the country, with more grassland-based agricultural systems, less fertiliser was applied than in the intensive arable areas in the north (Priebe, 1990).

The result of increases in external input applications (in conjunction with rising average farm sizes, mechanisation and improved cultivation methods) was a dramatic rise in productivity per agricultural unit area (Knickel, 1990; Fischbeck, 1993). Table 6.2 shows that while average yields hardly increased between 1938 and 1950 (some, such as rape, even decreased), increased fertiliser and pesticide applications helped to increase yields substantially between 1950 and 1993 (for the former territory of the FRG). Fischbeck (1993) has outlined how yield increases in the FRG between 1950 and 1990 were among the highest in Europe.

Water pollution problems in the FRG have been closely related to agricultural mismanagement, particularly through excessive fertiliser and pesticide applications during the 1970s and 1980s (UBA, 1994; see also Dassau, 1988, for a good local case study), and through slurry pollution emanating from increasingly intensive livestock production units (von Schilling, 1982; Isermann, 1990; see Table 6.3). Map 6.1 shows areas of high water pollution emanating from agricultural sources in the former FRG, and indicates that the worst affected areas were (and still are) closely associated with intensive arable regions, areas with high livestock densities and intensive horticultural areas (compare with Maps 2.3 and 2.6).

As in most other EEC9 countries at the time (see, for example, Robinson, 1991, or Adams *et al.*, 1992, for Britain; Buller *et al.*, 2000), agricultural

Table 6.2 Increasing average yields of selected crops (t/ha) in the FRG

Crop	1938	1950	1970	1993[a]	Changes 1938–93 (1938 = 100)
Wheat	2.23	2.58	3.79	6.58	295
Rye	1.83	2.22	3.08	4.51	246
Barley	2.12	2.40	3.22	5.00	236
Potatoes	16.82	24.49	27.23	39.25	233
Sugar beet	32.72	36.16	44.01	54.83	168
Rape	1.75	1.58	2.18	2.83	162
Grass	4.93	4.76	6.79	8.06	163

Note
[a]For the former territory of the FRG.
Sources: Grüner Bericht (1956); *Agrarbericht* (1972, 1997); Fischbeck (1993).

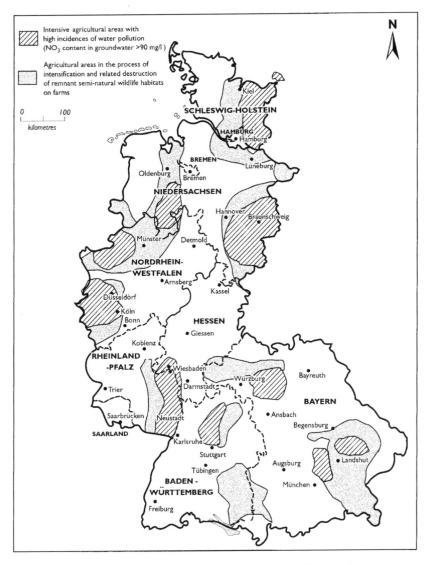

Map 6.1 Agricultural areas in the FRG (1989) with problems related to water pollution and wildlife habitat destruction (*Source*: adapted from Knickel, 1990)

intensification in the FRG also led to severe degradation of remnant wildlife habitats. The small family farm model adopted in the FRG (see Chapter 2), together with the fact that the FRG UAA had a large proportion of pasture[2] (37 per cent in 1988; high when compared with 8 per cent in Denmark and 28 per cent in Italy, but low when compared to 63 per cent pasture in Britain), led to the creation of a biodiversity-rich agricultural landscape (Priebe, 1990; Härle, 1992). About 50 per cent of endangered plants in the FRG depended on low-input land-use systems (RSU, 1985). Yet, amalgamation of farms into larger units, often encouraged through policies such as the Land Consolidation Act 1953 (see Chapter 2), led to the removal of shelterbelts, hedges and other landscape features (Hoisl, 1986; Werschnitzky, 1987). Possibly the most dramatic landscape changes induced by land consolidation measures occurred during the 1980s in the wine-growing areas around the Kaiserstuhl area in the Rhine valley (southwest FRG), where substantial reshaping of fertile loess-covered hills for the creation of high-efficiency large-scale vineyards led to a dramatic reduction of wildlife in previously species-rich small mosaic landscapes based on traditional terraced vineyards. Yet, as in other European countries, data on the destruction of landscape elements are hard to obtain (especially for the period between 1950 and 1980), but estimates suggest that more than half of the field boundaries that had been in existence in 1950 had been lost by 1990 (Knickel, 1990). Map 6.1 shows areas in the former FRG that were (and often still are) under highest pressure to intensify, leading to wildlife habitat losses (see also von Schilling, 1982). Wildlife habitat degradation was further exacerbated by fertiliser and pesticide pollution that led to dramatic decreases in the number of bird species (especially birds of prey at the top of the food chain), and by intensification on both arable and livestock farms that reduced biodiversity in fields and pastures (Härle, 1992).

Livestock farming became more and more intensive in the former FRG (especially during the 1970s), and in the brief period between 1971 and 1983, for example, the average LU per forage area increased from 14 to 21 (Kluge, 1989b). Table 6.3 shows that the trend of increasing livestock numbers (with the exception of poultry and sheep) continued until

Table 6.3   Livestock numbers in the FRG, 1950–90 (millions)

	Cattle	*Pigs*	*Sheep*	*Poultry*
1950	11.1	11.9	1.6	51.4
1960	12.9	15.8	1.0	63.4
1970	14.0	21.0	0.8	100.7
1980	15.1	22.6	1.2	85.6
1990	15.4	24.8	1.4	73.6

Sources: Kluge (1989b); *Agrarbericht* (1992).

reunification in 1990. The result was that, although the FRG was not the most intensive country with regard to livestock densities in the EC (compared to the Netherlands, for example) it nonetheless contained (and still contains) some of the most intensively farmed livestock districts in Europe (for instance, areas south of Oldenburg in the northwest of the FRG ranked tenth in terms of stock densities in EC12 regions in the late 1980s; Fleischhauer, 1987; Werschnitzky, 1987). Further, the high degree of mechanisation on FRG farms also led to increasing soil compaction and a reduction in traditional crop rotations that originally harboured higher biodiversity. Table 6.4 shows that in 1989 the FRG had substantially more machinery per hectare UAA than any of the other large EC member states, partly as a result of the small farm sizes and partly because many part-time farmers had sufficient off-farm earnings to purchase additional machines.

Of equal importance for biodiversity reduction and environmental degradation was the loss of agricultural land to urban, infrastructural and other non-agricultural uses (Tesdorpf, 1987). While in 1949 the total UAA in the FRG was 13.3 million ha, this had been whittled away to 12.75 million ha by 1970 and to 11.77 million ha by 1990 (*Agrarbericht*, 1994), a loss of 12 per cent since 1949, equivalent to a daily loss of 102 ha of agricultural land.[3] Again, the FRG has shared many of these problems with other European countries such as France, which lost 14 per cent of its agricultural land between 1950 and 1990, or Italy which lost 21 per cent in the same time period (Hoggart *et al.*, 1995). Agricultural intensification in the FRG thus occurred in the context of an ever-shrinking agricultural area on which production was intensified. It is important to note, however, that this trend has almost come to a standstill during the 1990s. Thus, by 1996 the UAA in the former FRG was virtually the same as in 1990 (11.67 million ha).

6.2.2   The GDR

While the environmental situation in the former FRG was well documented over time, data on environmental degradation in the countryside of the former GDR is more difficult to obtain. As Bruckmeier and Grund (1994, p. 182) argued, 'whether the scale of environmental damage through [agricultural] intensification was larger than in West Germany

Table 6.4   Degree of mechanisation of FRG farms in a European context, 1989

	D	DK	F	I	UK
Tractors/ 1000 ha UAA	123	60	47	70	27
Combine harvesters/ 1000 ha cereal area	28	21	15	8	14

Source: *Agrarbericht* (1991).

cannot be determined satisfactorily with the data available'. This lack of reliable data can be attributed to two reasons. First, the socialist agricultural ideology of production maximisation with little regard for environmental concerns meant that, even when environmental problems in the country-side became apparent (for instance, drinking water contamination with nitrates and livestock residuals), the GDR leadership was reluctant to admit that their socialist agricultural model could lead to environmental degradation (Huber, 1993). By the early 1980s, for example, the failure of the GDR state to control environmental degradation became obvious when the state refused to publish any data on the environmental situation in the country (after 1982 environmental information became a 'state secret'; Fulbrook, 1995). Second, smaller population densities in rural areas of the GDR meant that rural pollution problems may have been less apparent than in the FRG, and that pollution was largely branded as an urban and industrial problem (Dominick, 1998; Wilson and Wilson, in press).

There were, nonetheless, serious environmental problems in the GDR countryside (Würth, 1985), most of which were only uncovered after reunification when FRG and GDR scientists began to investigate the environmental situation in the new *Länder* (for instance, LUFT, 1993). GDR agriculture had been as intensive as that of many other Western European countries. Partly, this was because the GDR contained some of the most fertile soils in divided Germany (especially the loess soils around Magdeburg; see Map 2.3), and therefore it had a high arable to grassland ratio of 80 : 20 in 1990 (compared to 63 : 37 in the FRG; see Table 6.5), and partly because of policies that encouraged use of external inputs (see Section 4.2.2).

Many environmental problems in the GDR countryside related to water pollution from excessive fertiliser and pesticide applications. Table 4.4 has highlighted how the application of nitrates and phosphates increased about fourfold between 1950 and 1988, although yields in the GDR in the late 1980s still lagged behind those in the FRG (see also Table 4.5). Although most of the sources of water pollution came from industry (Würth, 1985), agricultural run-off also contributed to water contamination (LUFT, 1993). As a result, only 5 per cent of surface water in the GDR was suitable for drinking without treatment, and only a further 55 per cent was suitable with treatment (Wilson and Wilson, in press). The river Elbe, for example, was as polluted in 1989 as the Rhine in the former FRG during the early 1970s (the peak of pollution). As FRG scientists soon identified after reunification, groundwater was also heavily polluted, particularly by nitrates and phosphates from intensive and unregulated agricultural practices (BMBau, 1991). In 1988, for example, an average of 141 kg/ha N-fertilisers and 56 kg/ha phosphate fertilisers were applied to arable land in the GDR (see Table 4.4), compared to 129 and 54 kg/ha respectively in the former FRG[4] (see Table 6.1). Another source of localised nitrate pollution (especially for soil contamination) came from unregulated animal husbandry and the dumping of slurry waste from intensive livestock farms. However, as Map 6.2 indicates, in comparison to nitrate contamination of soils in the FRG, problems in the GDR were less pronounced, although local levels could exceed 150 kg N/ha.

The collectivisation of many small family farms into large LPGs (see Chapter 4) also led to the loss of biodiversity-rich field boundaries and other landscape elements important for wildlife. There are no precise data on the extent of loss of landscape elements since 1949, but about 50 per cent of the UAA, that had been farmed by family farms below 50 ha, were amalgamated into LPGs during the 1950s, where the use of large machinery (such as combine harvesters) led to the removal of traditional field boundaries and remnant wildlife habitats such as shelterbelts or small woodlands[5] (Bruckmeier and Grund, 1994; Vogeler, 1996). Despite this poor environmental record, the GDR countryside contained a high degree of biodiversity, and commentators such as Huber (1993) have argued that biodiversity was (and still is) higher in the GDR than in the FRG, particularly in the sparsely populated and largely rural northern parts.

6.2.3   Environmental impacts in reunified Germany

The reunification of the two Germanies not only had repercussions for agricultural structures and policies (see Chapter 4), but also for agriculture and the environment. The incorporation of the former GDR into Germany also meant having to tackle the environmental legacy left by decades of productivist socialist agriculture. Although the problems facing environmental policy-makers after reunification were worst for industrial pollution and contamination of land and water from industrial processes (Wilson and Wilson, in press), German policy-makers also had to quickly address some of the worst agricultural pollution problems in the former GDR countryside.

Shifts in land use ratios and increasing applications of external inputs

German reunification meant, first of all, that the balance of agricultural land uses changed. As GDR agriculture focused on arable production (see above), the ratio of arable to grassland changed from 63 : 37 in the former FRG to 70 : 30 in reunified Germany (Table 6.5). Applications of external inputs on arable land were high in the former GDR (see above) and have even increased since reunification, as farmers now have more capital and access to external inputs[6] (Bruckmeier and Grund, 1994; Vogeler, 1996). As a result, the general downward trend of applications of all types of external inputs that occurred until 1990 in the former FRG has been halted when considering Germany as a whole (Brouwer and Lowe, 1998). Although Table 6.6 highlights that average applications of nitrogen, phosphate and potassium per hectare UAA in Germany are now lower than they were in 1989 (some have halved between 1989 and 1995), the most recent data for

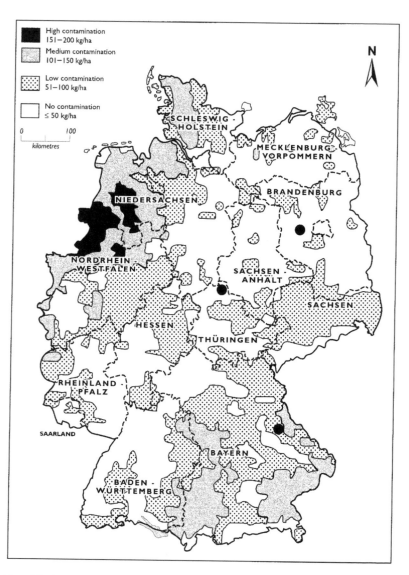

Map 6.2   Nitrate contamination of soils from livestock farming in the GDR and FRG
(*Source*: adapted from Bruckmeier and Grund, 1994)

Table 6.5 Arable to grassland area in reunified Germany, 1990 and 1995 (million ha)

	FRG			GDR			Germany		
	Arable	*Grassland*	*Ratio (%)*	*Arable*	*Grassland*	*Ratio (%)*	*Arable*	*Grassland*	*Ratio (%)*
1990	7.3	4.3	63 : 37	4.7	1.2	80 : 20	12.0	5.5	69 : 31
1995	7.4	4.2	64 : 36	4.4	1.1	80 : 20	11.8	5.3	70 : 30

Sources: Agrarbericht (1997); BML (1999a).

Table 6.6   Fertiliser and pesticide applications in the FRG and reunified Germany 1989–95 (1000 t unless indicated otherwise)

Type of external input	1989	1990	1991	1992	1993	1994[a]	1995
N-fertilisers	1540	1487	1368	1351	1280	1612	1787
N/ha UAA (kg)	129	125	115	114	108	94	105
Phosphate-based fertilisers	644	594	509	440	402	415	451
Phosphate/ha UAA (kg)	54	50	43	37	34	24	26
Potassium-based fertilisers	887	791	739	630	573	645	668
Potassium/ha UAA (kg)	75	67	62	53	48	38	39
Herbicides	17	19	17	19	16	13	15
Insecticides	1.3	1.3	1.5	4.0	4.1	4.3	4.0
Fungicides	12	11	11	10	9.4	7.7	7.7

Note
[a]From 1994 for reunified Germany.
Sources: Agrarbericht (1992, 1997); Brouwer and Lowe (1998); Kleinhanss (1998); BML (1999a).

the whole of Germany shows a rising tendency for these fertilisers between 1994 and 1995 (applications of N per hectare UAA have risen by 12 per cent in these two years) – thereby going against the current downward trend in external input applications in the EU as a whole (cf. *Agra-Europe Bonn*, 7.8.1995b). In environmental terms, the situation for pesticide applications is more promising, as quantities have stayed relatively stable despite the larger agricultural area in reunified Germany (suggesting a downward trend of applications per farm).

Although environmental pressures on the German countryside appear to have lessened since the 1980s, the trends indicate that there is no room for complacency (Wechselberger *et al.*, 1999). Höll and von Meyer (1996) have, for example, highlighted that despite reduced average applications of N-based fertilisers (see Table 6.6), nitrate concentrations in groundwater continue to pose severe problems due to long-term leaching processes with increases of about 1.0–1.5 mg N/litre a year (see also Poggemann *et al.*, 1999). As a result, EU limits (50 mg NO_3/litre drinking water; 0.0005 mg pesticide residues/litre drinking water) are currently exceeded in about 10 per cent of all German water supply units, with a rising tendency[7] (see also UBA, 1994), while the surplus of N/ha now amounts to over 60 kg/ha (the fifth highest surpluses of N in the EU after the Netherlands, Belgium, Denmark and Britain; Brouwer and Lowe, 1998; Kleinhanss, 1998).

The recent reduction in external input applications has not halted the continued decline of biodiversity, largely because of long time-lags between

pollution and the build-up of chemical residues in soil and water. It is estimated that at the end of the 1990s, about half of all animal and plant
species[8] are threatened with extinction (Bronner *et al.*, 1997; Tügel, 1998).
In more than two-thirds of the cases of endangered plant species, agriculture continues to be the main cause of decline, mainly through continued
destruction of semi-natural habitats through further amalgamation of field
units and farms, soil compaction due to use of heavy machinery and contamination of water and soils with pesticide and fertiliser residues (BMBau,
1993; *Agra-Europe Bonn*, 10.7.1995c).

Food quality issues and the environment

The 1990s also brought new environmental threats for German agriculture
with regard to food quality issues of a magnitude unknown in previous
decades (Nuhn, 1993; Tügel, 1998). Food quality problems have been major
environmental issues for a long time, highlighted by the fact that in the
FRG the first serious debates on pesticide residues in food emerged as early
as the 1970s (earlier than in many other European countries). Throughout
the 1980s, the FRG public particularly criticised mass livestock and poultry
installations, not only from a food quality perspective, but also from an
animal welfare perspective (*Der Spiegel*, 1997a). Outbreaks of severe epi-
demics, such as repeated incidences of swine fever (which result in the
mass slaughter of tens of thousands of pigs in affected districts), have
further sensitised the German public towards animal welfare and food
safety issues.

In the 1990s, however, the BSE crisis and concern over genetically
modified crops (thereafter GMCs) have created new levels of anxiety
among German consumers (von Braun and Virchow, 1998; *Agra-Europe
Bonn*, 21.6.1999a). With regard to agriculture and conservation issues since
1995, these problems have been at the forefront of media and consumer
debates (Götz and Himmighofen, 1998; Knauer, 1999). By August 1999,
only six cases of cattle with BSE had been reported in Germany (all
imported as live cattle from Britain), in contrast to over 175 000 BSE cases
in Britain (*Der Spiegel*, 1997b; *Agra-Europe Bonn*, 12.7.1999a). However, the
fact that 5200 breeding cattle imported from Britain and Switzerland (and
their 14 000 calves) were *suspected* of carrying BSE increased the unease of
German consumers about beef consumption (*Der Spiegel*, 1997).

As a result, the BSE crisis had a major impact on health-conscious German
consumers. Although meat consumption had already declined since the late
1980s, the BSE crisis accelerated a shift away from a meat-based diet. While
in 1988 (the peak of meat consumption in the former FRG) meat consumption stood at about 70 kg/person per year, by 1997 this had declined to a
little over 60 kg/person per year – a fall of over 14 per cent (*Pfaffenhofener
Kurier*, 1997) with immense economic repercussions for German (and other)
livestock farmers. From 1994 to 1995 alone, the average price of beef fell by

15 per cent, putting many German beef farmers on the verge of bankruptcy and leading to income losses in the order of DM3 billion/year (*Agra-Europe Bonn*, 7.8.1995c, 3.3.1997c). Arguably worst of all, the BSE crisis reduced the confidence of consumers in the German beef industry and in farmers more generally, thereby undermining the support that the German public have traditionally given to farmers (see Chapters 2 and 3).

Genetically modified crops

Equally disturbing for the German consumer has been the increasing importance of GMCs. In 1983, scientists in the USA for the first time implanted a bacterial gene into an agricultural crop (tobacco), and only 16 years later (1999) 40 million ha of genetically modified agricultural crops had been planted worldwide (maize, rape, potatoes, tomatoes and soya beans lead the international list of GMCs) (*Agra-Europe Bonn*, 19.7.1999d). This rapid increase was made possible because of a lack of regulatory mechanisms (for instance, no international regulation about the registration of GMCs). The main reasons for the introduction of GMCs have been to create plants resistant to specific herbicides, that may have inbuilt resistance to pests, and that may lead to longer shelf-life (Götz and Himmighofen, 1998). While it has been argued that the second type of resistance may be environmentally beneficial through reduced pesticide applications, the first type potentially has devastating effects as it allows the indiscriminate application of pesticides, killing any residual plant and animal life without affecting the crop itself (Tügel, 1998). Research evidence on the potential environmental impacts of GMCs is still patchy, but recent studies suggest that pollen from GMCs (such as genetically modified maize) may be toxic for wildlife feeding on pollen-coated plants, potentially leading to a drastic reduction in biodiversity.

Currently the debate rages on (as exemplified in recent discussions in Britain about a moratorium on any widespread planting of GMCs), and many environmental actors (especially the big multinationals Novartis, AgrEvo, Monsanto and Nestlé) continue to argue that environmental gains outweigh potential environmental losses (for instance, not only reduced pesticide need, but also reduced water use and higher yields; cf. *Agra-Europe Bonn*, 17.7.1995, 9.12.1996c, 19.7.1999b, 19.7.1999c; Götz and Himmighofen, 1998). However, recent experiments in various countries have shown that additional dangers also lie in unknown health effects through the consumption of GMCs (as the example of severe allergies resulting from the consumption of soy beans with implanted nut genes has shown), the emergence of resistant pests and, possibly most importantly, the genetic 'pollution' of other plant (and animal) species with unknown effects (also referred to as 'genetic smog'). The latter suggests that no GMCs should be grown near non-GMCs, although there is yet no scientific basis for establishing safe zones for different genetically modified plants.[9]

The commitment of a country towards GMCs is difficult to measure, particularly as many supermarket products are already classified as GMCs (for instance, virtually all products containing material from soybeans). However, the amount of GMC planting trials may be used as an indicator to gauge a country's commitment to GMCs (for instance, Tügel, 1998). Table 6.7 shows that of the 3706 known GMC planting experiments worldwide by June 1998, 96 had occurred in Germany (2.6 per cent of all planting trials). Although the German figure pales into insignificance compared with the USA or Canada, Germany nonetheless stands at sixth place in the international GMC table. Debate on GMCs intensified during 1999 as it was feared that German farmers would soon be given permission to plant GMCs commercially (*Agra-Europe Bonn*, 21.6.1999a, 19.7.1999b, 19.7.1999c).

The discussion highlights that modern German agriculture is faced with new environmental challenges that differ from the 'traditional' environmental preoccupations of the 1970s and 1980s. It is against this background of environmental degradation and increasing environmental uncertainty in the German countryside that Sections 6.3–6.5 will analyse the development and effectiveness of German policies aiming at addressing these problems.

Table 6.7 Global GMC planting experiments (June 1998)

Country	GMC planting experiments (No.)	GMC planting experiments (%)
USA	1952	52.7
Canada	461	12.4
France	280	7.6
Belgium	128	3.5
UK	111	3.0
Germany	96	2.6
The Netherlands	83	2.2
Argentina	79	2.1
Italy	79	2.1
China	60	1.6
Australia	47	1.3
Others[a]	330	8.9
Total	3706	100

Note
[a] Mexico (38 planting experiments), Chile, (37), South Africa (25), Japan (24), Denmark. (21), Puerto Rico (21), Sweden (21), Cuba (19), New Zealand (18), Hungary (17), Spain (17), Costa Rica (16), Russia (12), etc.
Source: Tügel (1998).

6.3 The German response to Regulations 797 and 2078: leader or partner?

AEP is now a widely accepted term in advanced economies that encompasses policy mechanisms put into place at EU, nation state and grassroots levels to address environmental problems in the countryside (Beaumond and Barnett, 1999). AEP can generally be divided into regulatory mechanisms legally enforced by state laws, and voluntary mechanisms that rely on the goodwill of farmers to participate. At the European level, the policy framework for implementation of AEP since 1985 (broadly speaking the time of the emergence of a post-productivist agri-environmental discourse) was provided by two key regulations:[10] Regulation 797/85 (also known as the ESA Regulation) and Regulation 2078/92 (usually referred to as the Agri-environment Regulation as part of the MacSharry reforms). In addition, member states such as Germany have also implemented their own agri-environmental schemes independent of, and parallel to, this EC/EU framework. As Whitby (1996) and Buller *et al.* (2000) have recently highlighted, Regulation 797/85 (hereafter Regulation 797) was an optional policy framework that was not adopted by all EC10 member states at the time (especially not by Mediterranean countries), while Regulation 2078/92 (hereafter Regulation 2078) made it obligatory for all EU member states to put into place agri-environmental programmes that would enable better environmental management of the countryside.

6.3.1 Regulation 797 and the FRG response: from reluctant policy partner to enthusiastic participant?

By the mid-1980s, many *Länder* in the FRG had already implemented their own agri-environmental schemes.[11] In most cases, schemes were initially implemented by the environmental administration of the *Länder*, and not by the BML (Fleischhauer, 1987; Grafen and Schramek, 2000). As a result, most of the early agri-environmental schemes in the FRG aimed at promoting environmentally friendly farming practices (usually for up to five years), with a specific focus on grassland extensification in areas threatened by intensification of livestock farming (see Map 6.1). Hardly any of these early schemes were aimed at reducing polluting external inputs in arable areas (Wilson, 1994; Heißenhuber *et al.*, 1994).

The introduction of Regulation 797 in 1985, and Regulation 1760 in 1987 that enabled EC co-financing of agri-environmental schemes (usually 50 per cent; 75 per cent in Objective 1 areas), changed the situation for AEP in the FRG. Responsibility for most of the existing schemes was transferred from the newly established federal Ministry of the Environment (the Bundesministerium für Umwelt, Naturschutz und Reaktorsicherheit which had been established in 1986 as a response to the impacts of the Chernobyl catastrophe) to the BML[12] – a move which stressed the increasing importance given to AEP as an agricultural market, social and structural policy mechanism (Plankl, 1997; Grafen and Schramek, 2000). The FRG's approach to AEP had, therefore, shifted from a policy framework initially focused almost entirely on environmental objectives to one dominated by socio-economic motivations.

This shift can easily be explained by the agro-political situation in the FRG during the late 1980s outlined in Chapter 3. Agriculture Minister Kiechle saw the emerging agri-environmental agenda (both at EC12 and national levels) as an ideal opportunity to tackle three of the most pressing issues facing FRG agriculture, namely farm incomes, environmental pollution from agriculture and food surpluses. First, agri-environmental payments could be used to bolster farm incomes at a time when farm incomes were stagnating or declining under market policies (Fleischhauer, 1987). Although the DBV was initially against the introduction of AEP, it quickly realised the financial benefits that could be gained from such policies and began to actively encourage farmers to participate in agri-environmental schemes – referred to by Heinze and Voelzkow (1993, p. 35) as the 'economisation of the ecological issue'. Second, these new types of payments could be used to address the emerging environmental problems in the countryside which were causing increasing debates among the wider FRG public (see Section 6.3.2). Third, at a wider European level AEP could also be used as an alternative to price cuts as a way to reduce food surpluses, and thereby protect farmers' incomes while also reducing the cost of the CAP. Thus, FRG support for AEP was a continuation of its support for milk quotas, set-aside and extensification in the 1980s (see Section 3.7.4).

As a result, the FRG was one of the few EU member states to implement Regulation 797 on a large scale. The *Länder* were in charge of defining objectives and targeting regions for schemes under Regulation 797, and decided the level of payments. It is important to stress that there was no federal framework for the implementation and financing of schemes under this regulation (Grafen and Schramek, 2000). Bayern, Schleswig-Holstein, Niedersachsen, Rheinland-Pfalz and Nordrhein-Westfalen (and the small region of Hamburg) implemented eight agri-environmental schemes, all co-financed by the *Länder* and the EC. The largest scheme, both in terms of UAA and participating farmers, was the Bavarian *Kulturlandschaftsprogramm* (KULAP), in existence since 1987 (with predecessor schemes since the 1970s initially funded entirely by Bayern), which aimed to extensify both livestock and arable farming. By 1988, the budget for the KULAP already amounted to 23 million ECU (MECU) – the largest budget devoted to any agri-environmental scheme in the EC12 at the time (CEC, 1997b). By contrast, the large British Environmentally Sensitive Areas (ESA) scheme only had a national budget of 18 MECU in 1988 (Hart and Wilson, 1998).

Much literature has highlighted the important role that Britain played in shaping Regulation 797 (for instance, Baldock *et al.*, 1990; Winter, 1996;

Hart and Wilson, 2000). Indeed, the original idea behind the establishment of zonal schemes with agri-environmental payments for income forgone is generally accepted to have emerged from Britain in 1984 and 1985 (O'Riordan, 1985; Baldock *et al.*, 1990). For the FRG, therefore, Regulation 797 initially did not seem to provide a suitable framework. However, Kiechle (and the farmers' unions in the various *Länder*) were quick to grasp the opportunities presented through the regulation. As a result, and only three years after implementation of Regulation 797, the FRG emerged as its most enthusiastic adopter in the EC12 and recognised the large potential that the emerging agri-environmental agenda could offer to small FRG family farms. FRG enthusiasm for AEP was further strengthened by the fact that FRG farmers responded well to schemes put in place under the regulation, resulting in some of the highest participation rates in Europe at the time (Buller, 2000). Knöbl (1989) highlighted that the schemes were particularly suited to farmers who had managed their land extensively before, and that for these farmers the schemes provided vital income support (see also Reimers, 1989). The income support orientation of FRG schemes under Regulation 797 (in contrast to environmental imperatives) was further stressed by the fact that early monitoring revealed little conclusive evidence of positive long-term environmental gains resulting from farmer participation.

By the early 1990s, just before implementation of Regulation 2078, agri-environmental schemes in the FRG had proved so successful as a farm survival mechanism that the FRG became interested in further broadening the scope of AEP at EC level. As a result, the German input into Regulation 2078 was much more substantial than during negotiations of Regulation 797.

6.3.2   Regulation 2078: how to make EU policy fit German needs?

The previous chapters have outlined how the FRG in the 1980s, and particularly reunified Germany after 1990, emerged as the most powerful member state in the EC12, and became increasingly assertive in European agricultural policy negotiations. While Chapter 5 outlined how the FRG was a reluctant partner in negotiations over market reforms to the CAP in 1992, it was much more enthusiastic about the accompanying measures, and particularly about the new AEP Regulation 2078 (Niendieker, 1998; Wilson *et al.*, 1999). Based on its positive experience with agri-environmental schemes implemented under Regulation 797 (see above), the set-aside policy (see also Chapters 3 and 5), and the Extensification Regulation (4115/88)[13], Germany increasingly saw AEP as a possible solution to appease both its outspoken farmers' lobby and the demands by other EC12 member states for Germany to further reduce market support subsidies. Germany was, therefore, willing to yield to long-standing pressure to further reduce these subsidies (and, for example, completely dismantle MCAs), as long as farmers' incomes could be maintained by putting in place comprehensive agri-environmental schemes that would, concurrently, also benefit the German countryside.

It comes as no surprise, therefore, that Germany became one of the most ardent supporters of Regulation 2078 (*Agra-Europe London*, 16.8.1996), and many commentators have argued that the structure of the regulation was best suited to the German situation (Keeler, 1996; Kleinhanss, 1998; Niendieker, 1998; Buller *et al.*, 2000). Wilson *et al.* (1999, p. 199) recently argued that

> the relative enthusiasm of Germany toward the Regulation may best be explained by both the conducive nature of its 'landscape stewardship ethos' which was also espoused by EU officials formulating Regulation 2078 and, possibly more importantly, Germany's relative weight in EU bargaining and its ability to have its agri-environmental goals adopted as EU goals.

While Regulation 797, with its emphasis on ESAs, was ideally suited to the British agri-environmental agenda (Clark *et al.*, 1997; Hart and Wilson, 1998), Regulation 2078 – with its broader remit, larger budget and clearer dual objective of income support and environmental protection[14] – was better suited to the German situation (Plankl, 1994). While Britain's role in EC/EU agri-environmental politics over time changed from that of a policy shaper to a policy receiver (Hart and Wilson, 2000), the reverse was true for Germany. As Chapter 8 will further argue, Germany has currently adopted a similar position on AEP components of the forthcoming Agenda 2000.

On the basis of the principle of subsidiarity enshrined in Regulation 2078, member state responses have varied considerably, with some countries enthusiastically embracing Regulation 2078 (at least in budgetary terms), while others have been more reluctant to put into place comprehensive agri-environmental programmes (Whitby, 1996; Clark *et al.*, 1997; Buller *et al.*, 2000). Table 6.8 shows differences in AEP budgets between the EU15 member states. Germany's expenditure on AEP/ha UAA for the period 1993–97 (including EU co-financing and national contributions) placed it among the high expenditure countries, while many Mediterranean countries and Britain were located towards the lower end of the scale (see also Deblitz *et al.*, 1998). However, it needs to be acknowledged that expenditure figures are a crude measurement of the possible commitment of a country towards AEP issues, and that they may often simply reflect different implementation strategies of 'broad and shallow' versus 'narrow and deep' schemes (see below). Nonetheless, expenditure figures still remain the best indicator of a country's commitment to the implementation of Regulation 2078.

Table 6.8   Total expenditure of agri-environmental programmes under Regulation 2078/92/EEC in EU member states, 1993–97 (MECU)

Member state	EU contribution	Member state contribution[a]	Total agri-environmental expenditure	ECU/ha UAA
High expenditure				
Austria	806	746	1553	450
Finland	399	399	798	306
Germany	918	376	1294	75
Sweden	126	126	252	73
Luxembourg	4	4	9	71
Medium expenditure				
Portugal	148	49	197	50
Ireland	163	54	217	49
Italy	432	282	714	41
France	509	509	1018	34
Netherlands	25	24	49	25
Low expenditure				
Denmark	19	19	38	14
UK	98	94	192	12
Spain	125	42	167	6.7
Belgium	3	3	6	4.4
Greece	11	4	15	2.6
EU15	*3787*	*2458*	*6244*	*46*

Note
[a] As member states contribute 25 per cent in Objective 1 regions and 50 per cent in other regions, member state contributions do not always match EU contributions.
Sources: CEC (1997b); Hart and Wilson (1998).

6.3.3   Regulatory versus voluntary agri-environmental policies?

As Grafen and Schramek (2000) have outlined in detail, an intense debate emerged in the FRG in the early 1980s over the best approach towards protection of the countryside against increasing environmental degradation caused by agricultural intensification and mismanagement. A heated debate ensued about the validity of two conservation principles: the polluter pays principle (PPP) and the payments for public goods principle (PPG) (Scheele and Isermeyer, 1989; Knickel, 1990). The PPP was advocated mainly by government advisors, scientists and ENGOs who argued that agriculture had contributed considerably to environmental degradation, although being almost completely exempt from environmental regulation through the special agricultural clause (*Landwirtschaftsklausel*[15]) in the

German environmental legislation (*Agra-Europe Bonn*, 2.12.1996). The PPP is essentially based on regulatory (non-voluntary) legally enforced levies or taxes on production inputs as the main way to prevent environmental pollution caused by agriculture.

The PPG, meanwhile, was the preferred option of the DBV and agriculture ministers Kiechle (1983–93) and Borchert (1993–98) (also advocated by some scientists and most state policy-makers), as it was based on the assumption that agriculture produces public goods, such as ecologically valuable landscapes or biodiversity, not paid for by agricultural markets (Priebe, 1985). Kiechle stressed that environmental protection could only be achieved with the help of farmers and criticised attacks on the agricultural clause (see above) – attacks which tended to brand farmers as bad land managers (reminiscent of debates in Britain in the 1970s and 1980s; cf. Newby, 1980; Shoard, 1980). The main argument behind the PPG centres around the assumption that society should pay farmers for the provision of public goods through voluntary agri-environmental schemes. Yet, and as already highlighted above, the PPG approach has been open to criticism for being a hidden income support mechanism, particularly as farmers may often receive payments for little change in environmental management practices. Mainly due to pressure exerted by the DBV during the 1980s, the PPG principle has become the guiding principle of German AEP, although Grafen and Schramek (2000) suggest that the recent economic recession and rising unemployment[16] have also led to a discernible shift in environmental policy away from costly legislation towards the voluntary approach of the PPG principle.[17] As a result, German agri-environmental schemes are voluntary (as in all other EU member states; cf. Buller *et al.*, 2000) and usually offer specific payments per ha for specific environmental management prescriptions.

However, the regulatory policy framework (administered by the Environment Ministry) has also been important in tackling some of the worst pollution problems in German agriculture. Policy mechanisms such as the Water Protection Act (*Wasserhaushaltsgesetz*), the 1977 Fertiliser Act (*Düngemittelgesetz*), the 1978 Pesticide Act (*Planzenschutzgesetz*), or the amendment to the Fertiliser Act in 1996 (*Düngeverordnung*)[18] have all been crucial in legally enforcing the reduction of use of nitrogen, pesticides and herbicides in ecologically sensitive areas and in regions important for drinking water (more than 10 per cent of the land area of the FRG was declared a water protection zone in the 1970s). These policies have been largely responsible for the gradual reduction in the application of external inputs in German agriculture outlined in Section 6.2.[19] Similarly, policies such as the Waste Disposal Act 1980 (for the regulation of slurry and manure storage) and nature protection laws (such as *Gesetz über Naturschutz und Landschaftspflege* 1972, *Landschaftspflegegesetz* 1975, *Bundesnaturschutzgesetz* 1976, and amendments) have been long-standing protection mechanisms aimed at preventing the degradation of ecologically valuable habitats in the countryside. By 1970, for example, 1000 nature protection areas covering about 3000 km^2 had been established (Kluge, 1989b) and by 1993 about 5000 areas were in existence (of which about 800 were in the former GDR) covering 6300 km^2 (BMBau, 1993).[20]

Further, Chapter 2 outlined in detail how the main emphasis of the Land Consolidation Act 1953 (and amendments) changed from a focus on field consolidation and land development in the 1950s and 1960s, towards soil protection and countryside conservation measures from the 1980s onwards. In general, little attention was paid to landscape changes, aesthetic qualities of newly consolidated land, or to effects on wildlife and habitats in earlier land consolidation legislation, but with the emergence of green thinking in the FRG during the 1980s the environmental impacts of *Flurbereinigung* were increasingly questioned (Hoisl, 1986; Woodruffe, 1989). As early as 1978, for example, about 300 ha of ecologically valuable habitats on farmland were set aside for protection in the 260 land consolidation programmes in operation at the time (Kluge, 1989b).

The regulatory policy framework had severe repercussions by restricting farming practices (see Section 6.5). Yet, the voluntary AEP framework has had the potential to have a more substantial impact, largely because many more farmers are potentially eligible for AEP payments compared to those affected by water and nature protection laws (Höll and von Meyer, 1996; Grafen and Schramek, 2000). As a result of the general adoption of the PPG principle, Germany now has one of the most comprehensive sets of agri-environmental schemes in the EU15, and 91 schemes were in place by 1994 with environmental protection as one of their main objectives (Wilson, 1994; see also Plankl, 1996a for a detailed description of available schemes). About 20 per cent of these schemes were in existence before co-funding became available from Brussels in 1987, emphasising that the FRG already had a vital head start for implementing countryside conservation mechanisms compared to many other European countries.

By the late 1990s, the number of schemes had been reduced, largely because of the amalgamation of some of the schemes into larger schemes. This has particularly occurred in Baden-Württemberg (through the *Marktentlastungs- und Kulturlandschaftsausgleich* programme [MEKA], Bayern (KULAP) and Hessen (*Hessisches Kulturlandschaftsprogramm* [HEKUL]) where, on the basis of Regulation 2078, several smaller agri-environmental schemes were combined into larger ones targeting the entire region. Agri-environmental schemes in Germany range from small schemes (for instance, the Scheme for the Protection of Marsh-marigold Wetlands in Schleswig-Holstein which comprises only a few farms) to large schemes such as the MEKA scheme in Baden-Württemberg or the KULAP scheme in Bayern that both target tens of thousands of farmers (see below). It is generally the larger schemes that have also received EU co-funding. The range of socio-economic and environmental scheme objectives varies accordingly. Both Wilson (1994) and Plankl (1996a) have highlighted that, apart from socio-economic objectives, many schemes also aim to encourage environmentally friendly farming near wetlands and water acquifers (and, therefore, often complement the regulatory mechanisms outlined above), or provide incentives for the conservation of remnant wildlife habitats on farms such as flower meadows, ponds, shelterbelts, wildlife strips or traditional orchards (Wilson, 1995). Payments to farmers also vary considerably, ranging from about 50 ECU/ha for some of the basic management tiers, to over 700 ECU/ha for measures that require substantial changes in farm management (Wilson, 1994; Grafen and Schramek, 2000). Compared to most other EU member states, agri-environmental payments in Germany are high (Buller *et al.*, 2000).

This discussion of the German agri-environmental programme has masked substantial regional differences in scheme implementation. It is, therefore, important to investigate in more detail why some *Länder* have been more enthusiastic about implementing AEP than others.

6.4 The geography of German agri-environmental policy

6.4.1 Agri-environmental policy powers between the *Bund* and the *Länder*

In Germany, as a federal state, responsibilities for AEP are shared between the federal (*Bund*) and the regional levels (*Länder*). Chapters 2–5 have outlined that market and social policy within agriculture are federal government responsibilities, while structural policy is a joint task, funded and implemented through the GAK. In Germany, Regulation 2078 has been delivered through the GAK (although individual *Länder* can supplement GAK policies with additional AEP funded by the *Land*). The GAK acts as an overarching policy framework with fixed payments for specific types of schemes, such as the management of extensive grassland systems, the conversion to (or maintenance of) extensive management on arable land and the conversion to (or maintenance of) organic farming (Dabbert and Braun, 1993; Mehl and Plankl, 1996). In theory, this should have enabled each of the *Länder* to implement a similar set of agri-environmental schemes. However, as the following discussion will highlight, there have been large differences between budgetary allocations for AEP between the *Länder*. Indeed, many *Länder* (such as Bayern) offer schemes (or parts of schemes) outside the GAK framework. It is, therefore, impossible to refer to 'the' German agri-environmental programme as it comprises many different regional approaches.

6.4.2 Regional differences in AEP implementation in Germany

Table 6.9 and Map 6.3 show that, despite the common GAK framework for all *Länder* (including the new *Länder*), the average annual spending per ha

Table 6.9   Annual spending of the *Länder* for agri-environmental schemes, 1993–96, under Regulation 2078[a]

Region	Total spending for agri-environmental schemes 1993–96 (MECU)	Average annual spending per ha UAA (ECU)
Baden-Württemberg	274	46.8
Sachsen	112	31.1
Bayern	401	29.8
Thüringen	83	26.0
Saarland	6.5	22.4
Hessen	58	18.6
Rheinland Pfalz	37	12.8
Brandenburg	63	11.8
Sachsen-Anhalt	45	9.7
Mecklenburg-Vorpommern	16	3.0
Schleswig-Holstein	7.4	1.8
Niedersachsen	17	1.6
Nordrhein-Westfalen	8.3	1.3
Germany	1130	16.3

Note
[a]Excludes the small *Länder* of Bremen, Hamburg and Berlin that have virtually no agricultural land.
Source: Grafen and Schramek (2000).

UAA for 1993–96 under the framework of Regulation 2078 has varied from less than 2 ECU/ha UAA in Nordrhein-Westfalen, Niedersachsen and Schleswig-Holstein to over 25 ECU/ha UAA in Baden-Württemberg, Sachsen, Bayern and Thüringen. This suggests a pronounced north–south divide for AEP spending in Germany. These figures partly reflect the different targeting approaches used by the different *Länder* for agri-environmental schemes. Many researchers argue that the southern *Länder* (especially Bayern and Baden-Württemberg) have used AEP mainly to stabilise agricultural structures and incomes (for instance, Plankl, 1996b, c; Mehl and Plankl, 1996). As Figures 2.3 and 2.4 have highlighted, these regions have been characterised by small family farms that are often economically marginal. It is not surprising that average payments per hectare are higher for these regions with small farm units, where the cumulative benefits per farm may not be substantially different from that of the larger northern German farms who receive lower payments per hectare. The MEKA scheme in Baden-Württemberg and the KULAP scheme in Bayern are cases in point and have been put in place mainly as income-support measures with additional environmental benefits as spin-off effects (cf. Bronner *et al.*, 1997; Grafen and Schramek, 2000). In contrast, the northern *Länder* (especially the three regions highlighted above with low AEP budgets) have politically

Map 6.3 Regional disparities in annual spending under Regulation 2078 for 1993–96 (*Source*: Authors)

been more oriented towards larger-scale and economically more competitive holdings (see Chapter 2), and have therefore tended to interpret AEP as an additional nature protection scheme for small and specific environmental pollution problems (Grafen and Schramek, 2000). Budget differences highlight, therefore, the different approaches by the *Länder* of broad and shallow schemes (such as MEKA or KULAP) with a clear income orientation, and deep and narrow schemes (akin to the British ESA scheme) with a greater emphasis on environmental protection. The latter are usually zonal schemes that target specific habitats and that, therefore, generally require smaller AEP budgets.

Map 6.3 also highlights that *Länder* with larger AEP budgets are not restricted to the old *Länder*, and that differences in AEP budgets cross the divide between East and West Germany. Indeed, both Sachsen and Thüringen stand out as regions with the second and fourth highest levels of expenditure for AEP/ha UAA (Kleinhanss, 1998). At first sight, this may seem surprising as the GDR until 1990 was characterised by productivist thinking based on the socialist agricultural model that gave little opportunity for environmental conservation policies (see above). Large levels of expenditure in Sachsen and Thüringen may, therefore, not necessarily be related to a sudden shift in attitudes, but can be largely explained by the fact that co-financing opportunities for Objective 1 regions (see Section 7.4.4) are more favourable under Regulation 2078 than in the old *Länder* (75 per cent co-funding from Brussels for AEP in the new *Länder* versus 50 per cent in the west). However, this does not explain why some of the new *Länder* have not implemented large-scale AEP programmes. Additional factors have to be considered to fully understand regional differences in AEP implementation within Germany.

6.4.3   Factors explaining differential AEP implementation

In a recent paper (Wilson *et al.*, 1999), we have attempted to identify the most important factors that may help explain differences between the *Länder* for AEP implementation and differences between German and other EU regions. First, the need for income support to small struggling family farms in areas with weak agricultural structures has provided a strong incentive for the implementation of large-scale agri-environmental schemes. Particularly in these regions (mainly south and south-west Germany; see Chapter 2), the regional farmers' unions have pushed for the implementation of AEP with income-support objectives. Regional farmers' unions were particularly in support of schemes such as MEKA (Baden-Württemberg) that did not require substantial management changes on farms, but nonetheless provided large financial benefits to scheme participants (see above). As Chapters 2 and 3 have highlighted, it is particularly in these regions that farmers' unions have held the largest political power, because of the large voter potential (in numerical terms) of the many small farmers. It is no coincidence, therefore, that high AEP expenditure regions shown in Map 6.3 more or less coincide with regions that generally have weaker agricultural structures (compare Map 6.3 with Maps 2.1, 2.4 and 2.5).

Second, of similar importance has been the relative wealth (per capita income) of the regions. Although we have so far portrayed Germany as a relatively wealthy country, there are nonetheless considerable differences between the different *Länder* (Smyser, 1993). Not only may this help explain the differences between the rich south and the 'poorer' north[21] of the former FRG for AEP budgets, but it may particularly help explain some of the east–west differences. Although wealthier new *Länder* such as Thüringen and Sachsen have put into place substantial agri-environmental programmes, the poorer regions of Mecklenburg-Vorpommern and Sachsen-Anhalt have had problems justifying high AEP expenditure in light of other more pressing economic problems such as high unemployment (over 40 per cent in some areas) and crumbling post-socialist industrial structures.

Third, previous experience with AEP also plays a key role in explaining differences between policy implementation within Germany (for instance, Höll and von Meyer, 1996; Grafen and Schramek, 2000) and across the EU15 (Wilson *et al.*, 1999; Buller *et al.*, 2000). It is no coincidence that two of the most enthusiastic supporters of AEP, Bayern and Baden-Württemberg, also have a long-standing record of AEP implementation (predecessors to the KULAP scheme, for example, started as early as the 1970s). Many *Länder* in the south of the former FRG already had substantial agri-environmental schemes in place long before co-funding became available from Brussels (Plankl, 1996b, c). Indeed, some of the *Länder* in the FRG were among the few to fully implement Regulation 797 (see above) and EC extensification programmes of the late 1980s (see Chapters 3 and 5). *Länder* with long AEP experience could benefit from a well-experienced administration used to problems of implementing AEP on the ground, familiar with selling the voluntary schemes to farmers, and with experience in monitoring scheme success and farmer satisfaction, all of which helped with implementation of new and more ambitious programmes – a factor that gave these regions a vital head start. The new *Länder* lacked any practical and administrative experience with AEP before 1990, and had to ascend a steep learning curve for successful implementation of complex policies. However, to help the former GDR with setting up agri-environmental schemes, each of the new *Länder* was chaperoned by one of the old *Länder*. Thüringen and Sachsen, for example, were looked after by Bayern with its long-standing AEP experience, and there is no doubt that this has played a role in both Thüringen and Sachsen being able to establish large and successful agri-environmental programmes (Plankl, 1997; Neander, 1999). Brandenburg, on the other hand, was chaperoned by Nordrhein-Westfalen, which started late with its own limited agri-environmental programme, and, therefore, had little practical and administrative experience with AEP (see Table 6.9) – a fact that may partly explain the sluggish implementation of AEP in Brandenburg.

Fourth, the nature and magnitude of agri-environmental problems has also influenced AEP implementation in different German regions. With regard to wildlife habitats, for example, there appears to be a correlation between high AEP expenditure and regions with grassland-oriented farming and greater biodiversity (especially in upland areas of the south and south-west). However, grassland and mixed farming systems in Germany are also usually associated with small-scale family farms in greater need of income support. The link between areas with substantial water pollution problems (see Map 6.1) and AEP implementation is less clear, as many *Länder* with severe agricultural pollution problems (especially intensive arable areas in the central and northern parts) have been reluctant to implement large-scale and costly agri-environmental schemes (see Map 6.3). As Buller *et al.* (2000) have highlighted, the existence of environmental problems is not necessarily a good indicator of AEP implementation.

6.4.4   Green thinking and the implementation of agri-environmental policies

Although the above-mentioned factors may help to explain most of the geography of AEP implementation in Germany, it is nonetheless important to consider the potential importance of green attitudes and thinking in Germany for agri-environmental schemes. Although we have already acknowledged that AEP in Germany has been used largely as an income-support measure, environmental objectives are also important. It can, therefore, be argued that implementation of AEP may be linked to the environmental attitudes of actors involved in the AEP implementation process. The notion of productivism versus post-productivism may provide a useful theoretical framework for this debate. In brief, productivism implies a focus of key decision-makers on maximising food production and viewing the countryside as a resource for the production of food and fibre. Post-productivism, on the other hand, is seen as a new period in agriculture in advanced economies where the emphasis has shifted away from food production to issues such as environmental conservation, animal welfare and the multifunctional use of the countryside (Whitby and Lowe, 1994; Ilbery and Bowler, 1998). Some German *Länder* may be more post-productivist than others, a factor which may influence the willingness to implement large-scale AEP, not only to support farmers' incomes but also to put into place policy mechanisms that help address environmental problems.

Little research has so far been undertaken on the extent of post-productivist thinking among different actors involved in AEP implementation in Germany (for instance, Wilson *et al.*, 1999). However, much evidence is available on public attitudes towards the environment (for instance,

Köstler, 1967; Leibundgut, 1985; Dieter, 1992; Schama, 1995), the predominant environmental discourses in the farming press (for instance, McHenry, 1996), attitudes of German farmers towards the environment (for instance, Pongratz, 1989; Bergmann, 1990; Rau, 1990; Bruckmeier and Teherani-Krönner, 1992; Wilson, 1995), and the environmental position of powerful policy actors such as the DBV (for instance, Heinze and Voelzkow, 1993; Ronningen, 1993) or ENGOs (Höll, 1994; Blühdorn, 1995). Historical literature stresses the strong attachment of the Germans to their landscape (*Landschaft*; although the German term is more holistic than the English term), and especially to German forests (Köstler, 1967). The heavily forested *Länder* in the south and south-west (including Thüringen in the former GDR) have been hailed as the birthplace of modern sustainable forestry practices in the eighteenth century, and many authors have highlighted how these regions look back at one of the longest traditions of landscape conservation in Europe (for instance, Schama, 1995). Is it possible that these historical roots of conservation-oriented thinking may also be related to a more holistic vision of countryside management that may be ingrained in post-productivist thinking of actors involved in AEP implementation? We are not suggesting an answer to this question, but this debate may usefully highlight that the explanation of differential implementation of AEP may partly lie in less tangible factors of public attitudes, differing perceptions of landscape and the countryside and the establishment of green thinking in the wider political debates.

The only geographic division between productivism and post-productivism that may be drawn relatively clearly in Germany relates to attitudinal differences between the new and old *Länder*. There is no doubt that over 40 years of socialist agricultural in the former GDR have instilled a strong productivist ideology. Since reunification, farmers and policy-makers may have been more anxious to catch up with productivity levels in the old *Länder* than to extensify production, a situation also observed in most Mediterranean countries (Buller *et al.*, 2000). The environmental data mentioned in Section 6.2, that have highlighted how agriculture in the new *Länder* has become more intensive, may be an indication that most actors – whether state policy-makers, street-level-bureaucrats or farmers – have not yet been willing to adopt post-productivist modes of thinking.

Another interesting dimension to this debate is the possible link between green politics and AEP implementation. As Chapter 1 stressed, environmental concerns have been well established on the political agenda in Germany since the emergence of Die Grünen as a fully fledged party in the early 1980s. Indeed, the FRG was one of the first countries with an outspoken and increasingly powerful environmental movement that rapidly became politicised thanks to the FRG electoral systems based on proportional representation (Wilson and Bryant, 1997). From the outset, Die Grünen became involved in political issues on agri-environmental concerns

(Werschnitzky, 1987). In the early 1980s, for example, they expressed increasing concern over the use of pesticides (see Table 6.1), and launched a campaign against potentially harmful herbicides used in agriculture (for instance, against paraquat, a powerful herbicide that was eventually taken off the market). However, there appears to be no direct link between the existence of a strong green political voice and the implementation of AEP in the German *Länder*. Although Hessen, for example, has had a SPD–Green coalition for a long time and has implemented a large-scale agri-environmental scheme (HEKUL), it is the conservative and right-wing *Länder* of Bayern (governed by the CSU Party) and Baden-Württemberg (mainly CDU governed) that have put in place the largest agri-environmental schemes. Bayern is a particularly interesting case as it established its own regional environment ministry as early as 1983, suggesting that despite the right-wing regional government (CSU) there was political willingness for the establishment of a separate environmental policy-making framework.[22]

Similarly, although in the new *Länder* Bündnis 90 (the counterpart to Die Grünen) have made substantial political inroads in regional parliaments, there are no clear links to the extent and nature of AEP implementation in the different regions of the former GDR. This also indicates that many politicians (including some from the green parties) do not perceive AEP as *environmental* policy, but as *agricultural* (income) policy, resulting in the fact that voluntary schemes may be perceived to be less important in environmental terms than the regulatory policy framework outlined above.

As a consequence, the role of local/regional actors may have been more important than green politics in explaining regional differences in both the nature and quality of AEP implementation in German *Länder*. In Baden-Württemberg, for example, the influence of regional representatives of BUND (an ENGO), in conjunction with the farmers' union of Baden-Württemberg, were instrumental in establishing the MEKA programme as one of the largest and most expensive AEPs in the EU (Wilson, 1995; Bronner *et al.*, 1997). This, combined with farmers' income needs, wealth of the region, previous AEP administrative experience, and high levels of biodiversity in upland ecosystems, explains why this region has been successful in implementing a substantial agri-environmental scheme that has been well received by farmers (see below).

Yet, even in the *Länder* most strongly committed to AEP implementation, such as Bayern and Baden-Württemberg, the enthusiasm for AEP has arguably faded in recent years (Plankl, 1997). Since reunification, individual *Länder* (as well as Germany as a whole) have had to deal with more substantive problems than to worry about the most appropriate policies for countryside conservation. Some have argued that there has been a withdrawal of general concern from the ecological primacy of the 1980s (for instance, Grafen and Schramek, 2000), and that there is a perception that more emphasis has to be placed on agricultural structures (especially due to the evident discrepancies between farm sizes in the former FRG and the former GDR; see Chapter 4). This situation has been further compounded by recent cuts in the GAK budget that have led to reductions in the funding for AEP. Concurrently, the environmental emphasis may have been reduced in some of the *Länder*.

6.5 German agri-environmental schemes: blueprints for Europe?

How successful have German agri-environmental schemes been in solving the environmental problems outlined in Section 6.2, and could some of the schemes act as blueprints for other EU countries? Based on the argument in the previous sections, the success of AEP cannot only be gauged in environmental terms, but must also consider the socio-economic effects of schemes. Indeed, in most cases the socio-economic and environmental effectiveness of schemes go hand-in-hand and are almost inseparable.

6.5.1 Environmental and socio-economic effectiveness of German agri-environmental schemes

Information about socio-economic effects of AEP is plentiful, but data on environmental effects are surprisingly limited. As we have highlighted for British AEP (Wilson, 1997c), the reasons for this lie mainly in the fact that long-term monitoring strategies are necessary to gauge the environmental success of policies. Socio-economic information can be easily obtained through published statistical sources (such as *Agrarbericht*) and interviews with farmers, while information on the environmental impacts of schemes usually requires long time-series often not available due to the recency of AEPs and the lack of systematic monitoring. The problems of assessing the effectiveness of AEP in Europe have been discussed by Buller *et al.* (2000), and recent studies also highlight the problems of 'policy-on' and 'policy-off' scenarios – in other words, how can we assess whether an observed change has been due to the participation of a farmer in a scheme or due to wider changes in market, attitudinal or farm structural factors?

There is little evidence about the success of early AEP in Germany. The KULAP scheme in Bayern is the best researched scheme due to its long existence (since 1983), and data on the effectiveness of the former grassland extensification scheme in Hessen (the precursor to HEKUL) is also available (for instance, Knöbl, 1989; HMILFN, 1998). For both schemes, studies revealed that the most likely scheme participants were farmers who managed their land extensively before the schemes were implemented, and who did not require substantial changes in farming practices after joining the schemes. This explains why few environmental benefits could be identified through these schemes, and evidence from the 1980s and early 1990s in Hessen indicated that only long-term extensification of grassland yielded positive effects on biodiversity. Grafen and Schramek (2000, p. 128), therefore, have argued that 'in general, there is little conclusive evidence of positive and long-term environmental gains resulting from these early schemes'.

Since implementation of more, and larger-scale, schemes under Regulation 2078 in the early 1990s, more information about scheme effectiveness has come to light as part of regular socio-economic and environmental monitoring exercises that are part of the AEP implementation process at EU level. One of the most successful agri-environmental schemes in Germany has been the scheme for the conversion to (or maintenance of) organic farming methods (Dabbert and Braun, 1993; Köpke and Haas, 1996). This scheme is co-funded by both Brussels and the GAK and is one of the schemes offered in all *Länder* (Köhne and Köhn, 1998). There is no doubt that this scheme has had the most tangible environmental effects of all German AEP (Freyer, 1994; Braun, 1995; Jungehülsing, 1996). Not only has it encouraged complete renunciation of the use of external inputs (according to specifications in the EU Organic Farming Regulation 2092/91), but it has also encouraged the planting of a greater variety of field crops and, perhaps most importantly, has further raised awareness of both farmers and consumers about food-quality issues (Köpke and Haas, 1996). Indeed, organic produce has a longer tradition in Germany than, for example, in Britain, and supermarkets (together with the four large associations for organic produce: Biopark, Bioland, Demeter and Naturland) have long-standing experience with the marketing of organic products (albeit at a higher price than conventional produce;[23] von Alvensleben *et al.*, 1994). Based on evidence from Austria, Groier and Loibl (2000) have argued that it is the more conservation-oriented post-productivist farmers that are more likely to participate in organic farming schemes, although this assertion has been challenged by Buller and Brives (2000) for France. Evidence from a recently concluded EU project on the effectiveness of EU AEP indicates that organic farmers in Germany are more likely to hold conservation-oriented attitudes compared to non-organic farmers (IFLS, 1999).

The GAK also provides support for the conversion to (or maintenance of) extensive farming on arable land. Participation in the scheme requires the renunciation of mineral fertilisers and pesticides and prevents the conversion of grassland to arable land. Implementation of this scheme has been less consistent across the *Länder*, and not all the regions have put in place schemes eligible for GAK payments. The first evaluations of this scheme suggest that farmers have been reluctant to participate, and only 7 per cent of all arable land is under any form of extensification agreements (Grafen and Schramek, 2000). As a result, the environmental effects of this scheme have, so far, been minimal.

The situation is different for schemes for extensification of grassland, which have generally been well received by farmers. These schemes are offered in all *Länder* and stipulate that livestock densities should not exceed 1.4 LU/ha forage area. This has meant only little change in farming practices for many already extensively farmed holdings, and explains the relative enthusiasm of farmers for the scheme. Overall, 25 per cent of the permanent grassland area in Germany now have management agreements for livestock extensification. Particularly in areas where scheme participants have been forced to substantially reduce livestock densities (usually in the more intensively farmed livestock areas), the scheme has had some environmental impacts on reduced pollution from slurry runoff and increased biodiversity on extensively used meadows (Grafen and Schramek, 2000).

Schemes aiming at the conservation of remnant wildlife habitats have also been implemented in all *Länder*. Many of these schemes have a long history and farmers are, therefore, familiar with the advantages and disadvantages of joining these schemes. As both Wilson (1994) and Plankl (1996a) have highlighted, many of these schemes target ecologically valuable grassland habitats (for instance, nutrient-poor grasslands or periodically flooded meadows), and extensive grassland measures have had significant uptake rates, especially in regions with large-scale agri-environmental schemes such as Bayern and Baden-Württemberg. Germany has also been one of the few EU member states to implement the scheme for the rearing of breeds in danger of extinction. In some *Länder*, certain farming practices (for instance, draining, conversion of grassland to arable, pesticide use) are prohibited in connection with this scheme. However, uptake by farmers has been poor, especially because the payments are low (110–160 ECU/LU) and because often substantial management changes are needed to accommodate the special needs of rare breeds.

As mentioned above, some German *Länder* have implemented schemes that only apply within their territories. One of these examples is the MEKA scheme in Baden-Württemberg which has been eligible for EU and GAK funding since 1994. It has been argued that MEKA is one of the most sophisticated schemes implemented under Regulation 2078 in the EU (for instance, Wilson, 1995; Pretty, 1995; Bronner *et al.*, 1997). MEKA provides compensation to farmers for market relief measures and the protection of the countryside, and is one of the largest and most expensive agri-environmental schemes in the EU to date. Sixty thousand farms with over 1.3 million ha agricultural land now participate in the scheme (about 70 per cent of all eligible farms in Baden-Württemberg!) at a yearly cost of 85 MECU (1996), and a total expenditure of over 300 MECU between 1993 and 1996 (Bronner *et al.*, 1997). MEKA, therefore, commands a larger budget than many national agri-environmental programmes in the EU. It is based on a unique system of eco-points which was developed by a variety of policy actors, including the farmers' union of Baden-Württemberg. This allows farmers to choose from a menu which gives them more flexibility than most other schemes in the EU, and is undoubtedly a major reason for high participation rates. However, MEKA has been criticised for being difficult to control and monitor because of the individual nature of each agreement (Wilson, 1995).

However, the environmental impact of MEKA has been limited. In an earlier study we highlighted that farmers were receiving large payments for few changes in environmental management practices (Wilson, 1995). Indeed, environmental restrictions emanating from the regulatory policy framework (see above) may have been more effective in halting environmental degradation than the MEKA scheme. For example, in districts in Baden-Württemberg falling under the jurisdiction of the Water Protection Act, farmers had already been forced throughout the 1980s to reduce external inputs and to farm in more environmentally friendly ways (Kleinhanss, 1998). Thus, as a result of MEKA only 14 per cent of the arable area is now managed less intensively, although Zeddies and Doluschitz (1996) have estimated that this has led to a reduction in nitrate leaching by about 10 per cent. In many ways, this reinforces the notion of MEKA as a broad and shallow income-support scheme rather than as an environmental scheme. Indeed, participants in MEKA have fared well with regard to incomes since the inception of MEKA. By 1994, for example, MEKA had already raised average farm incomes in Baden-Württemberg from about ECU 18 000/year to ECU 28 000/year, highlighting the important 'additionality effects' of AEP payments for small family farms (Wilson, 1995).

Although Germany has implemented one of the most ambitious agri-environmental programmes in the EU, the environmental effects of the agri-environmental schemes implemented in the different *Länder* have, thus far, been minimal. How successful have German agri-environmental schemes therefore been in tackling some of the environmental problems mentioned in Section 6.2? By 1996, more than 5 million ha of agricultural land in Germany were under some form of agri-environmental contract, representing about 30 per cent of the entire UAA. Although this figure seems high, especially when compared to other EU15 countries (cf. Potter, 1998; Buller *et al.*, 2000), almost 70 per cent of this area is managed under basic management tiers, which require little, if any, changes to existing practices. Grafen and Schramek (2000) have highlighted that among the remaining schemes, grassland extensification is the most important type of measure for area involved (1.4 million ha in 1996). In contrast, only 870 000 ha of arable land have management agreements, most of which are in Baden-Württemberg under the MEKA scheme.

Nonetheless, the organic farming scheme has been successful with regard to contracted area. In 1982, 700 farms were already classified as organic (12 500 ha; 0.1 per cent of UAA), and by 1985 this figure more than doubled to 1600 farms (27 000 ha), making the FRG one of the first countries to be able to provide a constant flow of organic produce to its consumers (Freyer, 1994; Nieberg, 1996). By the end of 1996, over 10 000 farms covering about 350 000 ha[24] were participating (*Agra-Europe Bonn*, 10.3.1997b; Grafen and Schramek, 2000), making Germany one of the most successful EU countries to have implemented this type of scheme (Jungehülsing, 1996; Lampkin, 1997). However, the percentage of UAA covered by organic farming is still small (about 2.2 per cent; Hessen and Baden-Württemberg have the highest participation rates), and organic farms are often spatially clustered in areas that had already been farmed extensively, which has led to few environmental benefits from a landscape ecology context.

Other schemes have been negligible for contracted area or livestock entered (for instance, only 11 000 LU have so far been entered in the scheme for rearing local breeds, and only 15 000 ha have been entered into schemes aiming at the preservation of specific biotopes). Participation in German agri-environmental schemes is highest where only small alterations of farming practices are needed – emphasising the pragmatic nature of farmers' responses to AEP highlighted in many other European studies (for instance, Brotherton, 1991; Morris and Potter, 1995; Wilson, 1996, 1997a, b; Potter, 1998). Only grassland extensification and organic farming schemes can, so far, be described as successful in environmental terms.

6.5.2   Bio-resources and environmental conservation

The planting of bio-resources is a sign of the greening of agriculture, as it is generally perceived to be more environmentally beneficial than harmful, and involves substantial changes in farm management practices not necessarily covered by government incentives (Kluge, 1989b; Höll, 1994; Haris *et al.*, 1996). Bio-resources enable energy production through fermentation processes of agricultural wastes (for instance, biogas), the production of bio-energy through the combustion of plant products, and the use of fibre crops for textiles and insulation materials (Narjes, 1987). Strongly supported by Agriculture Minister Ertl in the early 1980s, the FRG became an early leader in the EEC10 for bio-resource planting and processing (BML, 1993). Many research projects were established in the FRG aimed at identifying the most suitable crops and the best ways of transporting and processing these resources in the most environmentally friendly ways. The most promising plants include rape for the production of biofuels,[25] various cereals and herbaceous plants[26] (mainly for textile, padding, insulation and packaging uses[27]) and oil plants other than rape (such as linseed and sunflowers) (Höll, 1994).

The planting of bio-resources has been encouraged by a variety of government schemes that provide additional finance for the setting up of bio-resource processing facilities and marketing structures. These have, for example, included the establishment of a flax processing plant in Hessen in 1987, the establishment of a marketing programme for bio-resources (1995–98), and the subsidisation of a large biomass-fuelled heating plant in Bayern. However, no direct production subsidies have been provided for the planting of bio-resources, although farmers are allowed to plant bio-resources on set-aside land without any effect on set-aside premia (BML, 1993; Haris *et al.*, 1996). In addition to these national policies, the EC/EU also encouraged more research into the effectiveness of bio-resources (for instance, through the programme for European Collaborative Linkage of Agriculture and Industry through Research), and Germany made ample use of its EC presidency in 1988 to further encourage the planting of bio-resources across the EC. Yet, the enthusiasm of German farmers for the planting of bio-resources has remained limited, particularly as successful planting relies heavily on marketing possibilities (for instance, distance to markets), and insufficient thought was given to establishing a workable network of bio-resource processing plants. The issue of bio-resource planting has been further complicated by ongoing debates about whether bio-resources are necessarily greener than conventional crop production (Narjes, 1987; Höll, 1994; *Agra-Europe Bonn*, 9.12.1996d; Fennell, 1997).

By 1997, about 510 000 ha had been planted with bio-resources in Germany (4 per cent of UAA) – an area substantially larger than that under organic farming (see above). Rape accounts for almost two-thirds of all bio-crops planted in Germany (Table 6.10). By June 1999, the area planted in bio-resources had further increased to 760 000 ha, equivalent to about 6.5 per cent of the UAA (*Agra-Europe Bonn*, 21.6.1999b). Yet, as Haris *et al.* (1996) have argued, only a quarter of set-aside land in Germany is currently planted in bio-resources – an area that falls short of initial expectations. Interestingly, the ratio of planted set-aside land with bio-resources is higher in the new *Länder* (about 30 per cent), indicating that farmers in the former GDR have been more enthusiastic about grasping the new opportunities

Table 6.10 Bio-resources planted in Germany, 1997

Bio-resource	Area planted (ha)	Total bio-resource planting area (%)	Main uses
Rape	330 000	64.7	Biofuel, lubricants, chemicals
Cereals	120 000	23.5	Packaging, paper, textiles
Oil plants (linseed, sunflowers)	50 000	9.8	Paints, varnishes, linoleum
Flax	1 700	0.3	Textiles, packaging
Others (e.g. hemp, sugar beet)	8 300	1.6	Various
Total	510 000	100	

Sources: Haris *et al.* (1996); *Agrarbericht* (1998); BML (1999a).

offered through bio-resources. Lack of financial inducements was cited in Haris *et al.*'s (1996) extensive survey of farmers as the most common reason for farmers not to plant set-aside land in bio-resources.

6.5.3 Environmental issues insufficiently addressed by German agri-environmental policies

Recent research has highlighted that the preservation of landscape elements and wildlife habitats are becoming increasingly important in German AEP (Wilson, 1995; Grafen and Schramek, 2000), while the reduction of fertiliser and pesticide pollution is rarely mentioned as a specific scheme objective (Schulte and Steffen, 1984; Wilson, 1994; Plankl, 1996a). Tackling of agricultural pollution problems is, therefore, largely left to the regulatory nature protection framework outlined above.[28] It is not surprising, therefore, that most agri-environmental schemes in Germany have had little impact on the amount of fertilisers and pesticides used. The gradual reduction in applications of external inputs outlined in Tables 6.1 and 6.6 is, thus, more likely linked to strict regulatory policies, to the fact that excessive applications are branded as negative by the wider public, to the setting-aside of large areas of cereals during the 1990s, and to the fact that many German farmers may be beginning to adopt post-productivist attitudes towards the countryside (von Heereman, 1988; Hamm and Konrad, 1992; *Agra-Europe Bonn*, 3.3.1997b). The key question may, therefore, not be whether AEP have led to changes in farm management per se, but whether agri-environmental schemes have contributed towards changing attitudes of German farmers towards the environment.

So far there is little evidence that the schemes, perceived by many farmers as income subsidies rather than environmental policies, have led to substantial shifts in farmers' environmental thinking (Rau, 1990; Bruckmeier and Teherani-Krönner, 1992; Wilson, 1995; IFLS, 1999). Farmers have often expressed their concerns about criticisms of farming practices voiced by Die Grünen and ENGOs. As a result, many farmers have retrenched into traditional productivist action and thought (Hamm and Konrad, 1992). Interestingly, however, a coalition appears to have emerged recently between ENGOs and the Church (especially in Catholic parts of the country) that has begun to issue joint communiqués about social, humanitarian (for instance, food exports to the Third World) and environmental aspects related to agriculture (Tangermann, 1997). Some argue, therefore, that in the long term this may help shift farmers' attitudes towards post-productivism and may raise awareness about environmental issues in the countryside.

The federal structure of AEP implementation has been both an advantage and disadvantage for the effectiveness of German agri-environmental schemes. While the regional approach has enabled the implementation of policies that can be tailored to local and regional agri-environmental (and socio-economic) problems, it has also hindered coordination between the regions. In some ecologically homogeneous areas divided by regional boundaries (for instance, the Rhön mountains between Bayern, Hessen and Thüringen) completely different schemes with different payment structures and different agri-environmental aims have been implemented (Geier *et al.*, 1996; Wilson, 1998), impeding a holistic approach towards the management of vulnerable ecosystems.

Possibly the most important criticism of current agri-environmental schemes in Germany is that they tend to encourage *maintenance* rather than *change*. Extensive systems are maintained, while the most intensively farmed and most heavily polluting farm districts shown in Maps 6.1 and 6.2 have largely slipped through the AEP net. However, it is on these farms that changes in environmental management practices (and thinking) would yield the most beneficial environmental effects. Even ambitious schemes such as MEKA or KULAP have failed to enrol farmers from the most intensively farmed districts (Wilson, 1995), leading Grafen and Schramek (2000, p. 142) to conclude that German AEP has 'not been able to alter ... the increasing polarisation between intensive agricultural regions with good financial revenues on the one hand and ecologically sound but economically weak regions on the other'.

It is, therefore, premature to propose that German agri-environmental schemes may provide a blueprint for other EU countries, and that Germany has emerged as a leader for the implementation of *successful* AEP (especially in environmental terms). However, and as Section 6.3 stressed, Germany undoubtedly played a key role in EU negotiations on the implementation of Agri-environment Regulation 2078, with its influence seen in the framing of the regulation as a hidden income subsidy. Some have argued that the *income-support* element of most German agri-environmental schemes has also had positive *environmental* effects, in that it has helped to keep family farms on the land – especially in areas shaped by centuries of traditional extensive forms of farming (mainly upland grassland areas). The organic farming scheme has probably generated most environmental benefits, and recent studies suggest that biodiversity generally increases in organic farming systems, with concurrent reduction of soil, water and acquifer pollution (Köpke and Haas, 1996; Nieberg, 1996).

6.5.4 Food quality control and animal welfare: Germany as a leader in the EU?

Policies tackling food quality problems outlined in Section 6.2 have been more successful in environmental terms than agri-environmental schemes. Food quality control and animal welfare in Germany have been addressed by the regulatory framework and have, therefore, largely escaped socio-political pressures for raising farmers' incomes that have constrained the voluntary AEP framework. On the basis of a variety of factors already mentioned in previous sections (for instance, early established green thinking in German society; long-standing experience with food quality control and animal welfare mechanisms), Germany has been hailed as one of the most progressive countries for ensuring food quality (especially compared with countries such as Britain; cf. Ditt, 1996). Indeed, German consumers enjoy some of the strictest regulations regarding food quality issues in the EU15 (*Agra-Europe Bonn*, 17.3.1997a). For problems on food-quality issues (in particular the BSE crisis and the introduction of GMCs outlined above), this section will briefly discuss the effectiveness of existing policy mechanisms.

As early as the 1960s, the FRG voiced strong opposition against imports of hormone-treated beef from the USA (Kluge, 1989b). Increasing public concern resulted in innovative policies introduced through the Crop Protection Act 1968 (*Gesetz zum Schutz der Kulturpflanzen*), and further policies in 1969 that aimed to improve information to consumers through yearly food quality reports about treated or modified foods, and culminated in the ban on the use of toxic substances such as DDT in agriculture in 1971. By the late 1970s, these policies were further tightened regarding residual substances in food, particularly for the use of hormones in animal fattening processes and mass animal rearing. By that time, most local plant products were free from chemicals, and stricter controls were introduced for the use of chemicals still in use such as aldrin, endrin, lindane and mercury-containing compounds. 1983 saw a further tightening of the Crop Protection Act as a response to increasing criticisms about excessive pesticide use by farmers, and additional legislation for the compulsory labelling of food products. The FRG was one of the first EEC10 countries to adhere relatively strictly to Commission guidelines on food labelling (*Agra-Europe Bonn*, 31.7.1995b).

With strict FRG quality norms well in place by 1983, agriculture minister Kiechle attempted to impose similar norms at EEC level. This was partly a reflection of pressure from the FRG consumer lobby, but also shows that little change would have been needed in the FRG food industry to adjust to tighter EEC regulations. During debates with the Commission in the early 1980s, the German Beer Purity Law of 1516 (*Reinheitsgebot*), which prevented imports of beer not produced under specific norms specified in the law, was used as an example of a long-standing food quality control policy that had ensured high quality of German beer for many centuries (by specifying that no artificial additives were allowed in the brewing process). At the time, the FRG was under pressure from its EEC10 counterparts to open its market to foreign beer exports, particularly as member states accused the FRG of using environmental quality arguments as a disguise for protectionist beer import policies. Nonetheless, Kiechle's campaign in the 1980s for a continuation of the strict guidelines of the Beer Purity Law – at the same time guaranteeing protection for the national brewery industry – highlighted the fear that strict FRG food quality norms could be watered down at EEC level.[29]

These fears were also apparent in 1988, when FRG animal protection legislation was enacted that went beyond the suggested minimum standards in the EC12 (such as specific guidelines for indoor poultry and pig rearing), further tightened in 1997 through the new Animal Protection Act (*Tierschutzgesetz*). Similarly, Germany has also put into place one of the toughest legal frameworks for the control of animal transport in the EU through the Animal Transportation Act 1997 (*Tierschutztransport-Verordnung*), with stricter regulations applying in Germany than anywhere else in the EU15[30] (*Agra-Europe Bonn*, 3.3.1997d). This further exemplifies the leading role that the FRG was beginning to take on animal welfare issues. It should, however, be noted that implementation of these policies was, at times, strongly opposed by the DBV, because they were seen to increase the cost of production, and thereby damage the competitiveness of German farmers (see also Chapters 3 and 5). DBV pressure often led to the watering down of legislation. For controls on intensive poultry and pig installations, for example, DBV pressure resulted in the decision that only holdings with over 40 000 hens and over 2000 pigs would be scrutinised for animal welfare (*Agra-Europe Bonn*, 3.7.1995b). However, this did not deter Germany from urging the total abandonment of all battery farms in the EU (for instance, *Agra-Europe Bonn*, 17.3.1997b).

By the late 1980s, debates over imports of hormone-treated beef (especially from the USA) further intensified, resulting in an EC-wide ban on the use of growth hormones in animal husbandry. Commentators such as Kluge (1989b) and Hendriks (1991) have argued that this ban was put in place largely on the initiative of the FRG government, suggesting that there was a better basis for active scrutiny of food policy by the public than in most other EC member states at the time. By the mid-1990s, Germany had one of the tightest policy mechanisms in place in the EU15 for permissible hormone levels in meat (*Agra-Europe Bonn*, 10.7.1995b), and the emphasis on good-quality food (preferably from within the FRG under the slogan 'Aus deutschen Landen frisch auf den Tisch') increasingly gained ground among German consumers, while scepticism towards food imports of 'uncontrolled' quality grew (Plankl, 1997)

In 1990, the first policies were introduced to address potential problems associated with GMCs (see Section 6.2.3). The Gene Technology Act 1990 (*Gentechnikgesetz*) provided the basis for the regulation of GMCs and patenting rights for genetically modified plants (*Agra-Europe Bonn*, 9.12.1996c). In 1995, Germany was one of the first EU countries to insist on proper EU legislation for the labelling of GMCs (*Agra-Europe Bonn*, 3.7.1995a). Surveys conducted by *Agra-Europe Bonn* (7.8.1995a), and more recently by von Braun and Virchow (1998), have indicated that three-quarters of consumers are against GMCs on health grounds (half thought that the BML had not provided enough information), and the German public in general was strongly in favour of legislation on compulsory registration of GMCs (see also *Agra-Europe Bonn*, 21.6.1999a; Knauer, 1999). Yet, although Agriculture Minister Borchert had criticised the EU for permitting the planting of genetically modified maize by the end of 1996 (*Agra-Europe Bonn*, 23.12.1996a), the Kohl government had never been in favour of a complete ban on GMCs. Indeed, the government had permitted planting trials with GMCs (see Table 6.7),[31] and had been criticised by ENGOs and consumer organisations for taking the issue too lightly (for instance, *Agra-Europe Bonn*, 17.7.1995, 9.12.1996c). Nonetheless, partly due to pressure exerted by Germany, the EU implemented food regulations in 1997 that stipulated that food producers have to label products if they contain 'foreign' genes or proteins[32] (Knauer, 1999). By introducing a special label for non-GMCs ('ohne Gentechnik'), some German supermarkets (Familia-Märkte, Combi-Märkte, Tengelmann and Rewe) are now also providing additional information to consumers about food-production processes free from genetic manipulation (von Braun and Virchow, 1998; *Der Spiegel*, 1999b).

Policies addressing the BSE problem have been equally stringent. In contrast to Britain, for example, Germany put into place early legislation on the registration of cattle that enabled the family history of animals to be traced back to the late 1980s (*Agra-Europe Bonn*, 10.7.1995d). It is interesting to note that Bayern and Baden-Württemberg, who emerged as leaders on AEP implementation (see above), have also taken a leading role in the registration of beef cattle (*Agra-Europe Bonn*, 6.1.1997). Although these policies helped to provide a comprehensive framework for the identification of the origins of all German cattle, nonetheless they could not prevent some confusion when the first BSE cases emerged in Germany (see Section 6.2.3), especially as some infected imported cattle had also appeared on organic farms (*Der Spiegel*, 1997).

Largely due to pressure from consumers, Agriculture Minister Borchert felt compelled to lobby for the tightening of EU legislation regarding BSE. As a result, and partly due to German pressure, the Commission introduced Regulation 287/95 on the control of animal breeding in 1995, which provided the first comprehensive framework for tackling the BSE problem at EU level. However, following the British announcement of a suspected link between BSE and new variant Creutzfeld–Jakob disease, the Commission introduced a complete ban on British beef exports and on all products containing beef by-products in March 1996. Although Brussels lifted the export ban on British beef in August 1999, both Germany and France maintained their bans, with Germany not agreeing to lift its ban until March 2000.[33] Although Germany did not stand alone in the EU15 on enforcing the beef import ban (*Agra-Europe Bonn*, 3.2.1997), Germany nonetheless emerged as the most outspoken critic of the British government's (mis)handling of the BSE problem, and was one of the most fervent advocates for a continuation of an EU-wide ban (*Agra-Europe Bonn*, 19.7.1999e).

By 1997, *Agra-Europe Bonn* (17.3.1997a) described Germany as having been 'very sensible' about how it had handled the BSE problem. No cattle of German origin had contracted BSE, and although the killing of the 5200 cattle (and 14 000 calves) imported from Britain potentially carrying BSE (see Section 6.2.3) was strongly advocated by the BML, Germany was praised both nationally and at EU level for its meticulous monitoring of the few suspected BSE cases – as exemplified through the case of the infected Galloway calf 'Cindy' that featured prominently in the German media (see *Agra-Europe Bonn*, 3.2.1997, for a detailed discussion of this specific case). Germany's 'sensible' approach has also been apparent in the way it has treated its beef and dairy farmers affected by the crisis (at the height of the crisis German farmers lost about DM 300 per head of beef cattle). Agriculture Minister Borchert distributed DM 500 million (EU contribution 50 per cent) evenly to all beef farmers (16 million beef LU were eligible irrespective of whether milk or fattening cattle), and made DM 100 million available for further research on the possible health repercussions of BSE.

In the face of slumping meat consumption by German consumers (see Section 6.2.3), the BML bolstered the clean image of German meat through new control mechanisms re-emphasising the theme of superior nationally produced food. The 'programme for German quality meat from controlled raising' (*Deutsches Qualitätsfleisch aus kontrollierter Aufzucht*), for example, contains strict rules about the origin of meat and quality control. These efforts have been rewarded with increasing consumer confidence about the quality of German food. A recent survey has shown that while in 1970 only 35 per cent of German consumers thought that Germany provided the best-quality foods compared to other countries, this ratio had risen to 79 per cent by 1996 despite – or arguably because of – the BSE crisis (*Agra-Europe Bonn*, 16.12.1996a).

At the beginning of the twenty-first century, the successful handling of the BSE crisis by German policy-makers also has repercussions for how Germany's position on food-quality policies is perceived by other EU15 countries – again suggesting that Germany has been increasingly perceived as taking a leading role on European food quality standards.[34] This is best highlighted by recent debates over German standards on pesticide residues in babyfood. *Agra-Europe Bonn* (10.2.1997) recently argued that Germany strongly questioned EU criticism of German standards that were seen as too high. Germany took the position that the Commission had not learnt enough from the BSE scandal, and that 'with regard to human health, the regulations on pesticide residues [in human food] could not be strict enough' (*Agra-Europe Bonn*, 10.2.1997). The result has been that the Commission recently (1997) agreed to lower pesticide residue limits for babyfood to levels similar to the low levels set in Germany.[35] Germany's role as a leader in this respect is further exemplified by the fact that both the Food and Agriculture Organisation and the World Health Organisation have oriented their policies on German food-quality policies (*Agra-Europe Bonn*, 31.7.1995b).

6.6   Conclusions

The issue of German agriculture and the environment is complex, not only because of the long-standing productivist ethos of many of Germany's post-war agricultural policies (see Chapters. 2 and 3), but also because of environmental problems in the countryside in the GDR that only became apparent after reunification, new challenges for policy-makers concerning food quality control issues such as BSE and GMCs, and highly uneven implementation of AEP at the *Länder* level.

It is important to differentiate between the environmental impacts of regulatory and voluntary AEP mechanisms in the German countryside. The voluntary policy framework (essentially in the form of agri-environmental schemes) has only been partly successful in environmental terms, largely because Germany has cleverly influenced EU AEP to suit its own needs. Germany has been largely responsible for broadening the prescriptions enshrined in Regulation 2078 not only to address environmental issues in the countryside but also to provide vital income support to small German family farms. Thus, it has linked AEP to the family farm model that has underlain agricultural policy in the old *Länder* throughout the post-war period.

The issue of voluntary AEP in Germany, therefore, cannot be divorced from the issue of weak agricultural structures outlined in Chapter 2, and the gradual downscaling of market support subsidies to German farmers outlined in Chapters 3 and 5. Although there have been environmental successes (in particular, organic farming schemes), most AEPs implemented in Germany have required few changes in farm management and have, consequently, not led to substantial changes in either farmers' environmental attitudes or the environmental condition of the countryside. As in many other EU countries (cf. Buller *et al.*, 2000), German AEP has been more about the *maintenance* of existing farming practices than about *changing* the way farmers farm their land.

The regulatory AEP framework, on the other hand, has been more successful. Devoid of the socio-economic pressures that have marred successful implementation of environmental prescriptions in voluntary AEPs, the regulatory framework has achieved more tangible protection effects. This has been partly due to the long-standing tradition of landscape protection in Germany, but also because farmers have had no option but to adhere to the tight regulatory mechanisms applying on their land. Most importantly, however, most of the regulatory AEPs are implemented by the federal Environment Ministry (since 1986) and operated by the *Länder* ministries (both relatively independent of the BML) which has meant that the DBV has been less able to influence these policies to suit farmers' needs. Positive examples include water protection regulation and landscape protection, but also more recent issues of GMCs and food quality control. Indeed, for environmental legislation, Germany has been hailed as an increasingly important leader in the EU, best exemplified by the fact that the Commission has often agreed to implement stringent German environmental thresholds at EU level. As both Liefferink and Andersen (1998) and Lowe and Ward (1998) have recently highlighted, Germany also emerges as a forerunner for implementation of environmental policy as a whole.

Assessing the German role with regard to its influence in the EU15 is, however, complicated by the above-mentioned factors. When considering German lobbying in Brussels, budgetary allocations to its AEP programme, and the high rate of farmer participation in schemes, then Germany has undoubtedly been a leader for the implementation of AEP (Wilson *et al.*, 1999). However, it cannot be described as a leader in policies to protect the countryside. Countries such as Britain, that have implemented a financially and spatially less ambitious AEP programme than Germany through deep and narrow schemes, could be described as having a more honest set of AEPs whose objectives are more clearly aimed at addressing environmental issues (Hart and Wilson, 1998, 2000). Germany, meanwhile, has implemented an agri-environmental programme with a strong socio-economic component that has enabled it to provide income subsidies to farmers under the guise of environmental policy.

The recent change in government (1998) is unlikely to substantially change this complex and uneven policy situation. Early indications are that Die Grünen, as the new government coalition party with the SPD, will push for a further tightening of the regulatory mechanism, while the voluntary framework will continue to be largely in the hands of the DBV and the BML and is, therefore, unlikely to reduce the emphasis on income support aspects of AEP. However, as Chapter 8 will discuss in more detail, new options for agriculture and the environment in Germany may emerge through the recently implemented Agenda 2000.

7
Rural Planning, Policy and Development in Germany

7.1 Agricultural and rural change

So far in this book we have analysed structural changes in agriculture and changing agricultural policies in divided and reunified Germany in the context of national agricultural policies, the CAP and the GATT. In this chapter we argue that it is also important to view agricultural change in light of rural change more generally. As with agriculture, rural areas developed in contrasting ways in the FRG and GDR between 1945 and 1990, with the result that since reunification rural areas of the GDR have undergone profound social and economic changes to catch up with the old *Länder* and to integrate into the social market economy. One aim of this chapter is to examine the divergent paths of rural development in the FRG and GDR and to compare and contrast the problems facing rural areas in the two parts of Germany since reunification.

It is also our intention to highlight the interconnectedness of changes in agriculture and changes in the wider rural economy and society. On the one hand, changes in agriculture in the FRG since 1945 have had significant economic and social impacts on rural areas through loss of agricultural jobs, farm modernisation and amalgamation, and the specialisation and intensification of production (see Chapter 2). Today, few villages in the old *Länder* have more than 30 per cent of their workforce employed in agriculture (BMBau, 1990). The influence of agriculture on rural society in the FRG has, therefore, progressively declined. On the other hand, changes in rural areas have affected agricultural development. For instance, counterurbanisation has brought an influx of 'urbanites' into the countryside which has placed new demands on the countryside for amenity. As was discussed in Chapter 6, changing public attitudes towards the environment have also placed new demands on farmers (as well as creating opportunities). Further, farmers are inextricably linked to the wider economy and society. For instance, the continued importance of part-time farming in the FRG is an example of a direct link between the farm and non-farm economies, and many rural and urban jobs depend on the farm input and food-processing and distribution sectors. Moreover, in contrast to Britain, many farms in the FRG are located in villages, and therefore villages still have an agricultural character.

In the GDR, in contrast, agriculture retained its economic and social importance to a greater extent (see Chapter 4). The decimation of agricultural employment since reunification has, thus, had a sudden and dramatic effect on the rural economy and society. Moreover, lack of investment in rural areas of the GDR meant that a significant gap in living standards opened up between the FRG and GDR which has had to be addressed since reunification. Reunified Germany, thus, comprises two very contrasting types of rural economy and society.

A further aim is to analyse the development of rural policy in the FRG (and, subsequently, reunified Germany). As in Britain, the FRG never had a specific rural policy. Instead, responsibilities for planning and economic development in rural areas have been divided horizontally and vertically between the federal and *Länder* governments. At federal level, three ministries have been responsible for different aspects of rural planning and development: Planning and Urban Development (Bundesministerium für Raumordnung, Bauwesen und Städtebau or BMBau);[1] Economy and Technology (Bundesministerium für Wirtschaft und Technologie); and the BML (see previous chapters). Until the late 1980s, rural policy was largely subsumed within agricultural policy, both in Germany and the EEC, reflecting the post-war dominance of the productivist agricultural ideology (cf. Marsden *et al.*, 1993; Ilbery and Bowler, 1998). However, two political developments have raised the profile of rural policy since the late 1980s. First, at EU level policy-makers have identified the need to support the economic diversification of rural areas to reduce their economic and social dependence on agriculture. The 1992 CAP reforms have served to focus the minds of farmers and policy-makers on the diversification of the rural economy and the preservation of the rural environment (see Chapters 5 and 6). Second, reunification has generally raised the profile of rural development issues within Germany, due to the large gap in living standards between rural areas in the old and new *Länder*, and the additional problems caused by agricultural restructuring (Wirth, 1996). In response to these developments, policy-makers in Germany have had to rethink their approach to 'rural' and 'agricultural' policy issues. As discussed in Chapters 5 and 6, since the 1992 CAP reforms the agricultural productivist vision of the countryside has given way to a multifunctional or post-productivist vision.

This chapter is structured as follows: first, we examine the nature and extent of rural Germany to provide a geographical context for the discussion; second, we analyse key social and economic changes in rural areas (both FRG and GDR) since 1945; third, we consider the development of planning and economic development policies for rural areas in divided and reunified Germany at the regional, national and, more recently, the EU level.

This latter section will consider whether and to what extent a new rural policy agenda has emerged which is distinct from agricultural policy, and what role, if any, agricultural policy can play in wider rural development.

7.2 The nature and extent of rural Germany

Two factors that continue to differentiate rural from urban areas are population size and density, and given the ready availability of population statistics, these two factors are the most common indicators used by administrators, politicians and academics to differentiate rural from urban settlements. However, there are no universally accepted definitions, with different countries using different population thresholds to divide urban from rural (Robinson, 1990), although the OECD has suggested a threshold population density of 150 persons/km^2 as a cut-off point (DOE/MAFF, 1995). Even divided Germany used different definitions. The FRG defined all settlements of up to 10 000 population as rural, whereas in the GDR settlements of over 2000 population were classified as urban (Paas *et al.*, 1994). In reality, of course, these thresholds are arbitrary, and should be seen as administrative conveniences rather than meaningful social or economic divisions. However, the FRG has also developed a threefold regional typology for planning purposes, based on population density and level of urbanisation, which identifies three types of rural area in three types of regions (Table 7.1). Although still based on population density, the typology also includes a measure of peripherality, and thus provides a more relevant starting point for analysis of rural problems and policies. With reunification, the typology has been extended to the new *Länder*.

The geographical distribution of these regions and their component parts are shown in Map 7.1. Type 1 regions correspond to the main urban

Table 7.1   Regional planning typology

Regional type	Criteria
1. Agglomeration regions containing rural–urban fringe countryside	*Kreise* (districts) with a population density of over 300 persons/km^2 and/or a major urban centre of 300 000 plus population, and their hinterland rural *Kreise*
2. Urbanised regions containing accessible countryside influenced by urban proximity	*Kreise* with a population density of over 150 persons/km^2 and/or an urban centre of 100 000 plus population and hinterland rural *Kreise*
3. Rural regions which are peripheral, sparsely populated and with no large urban centres	*Kreise* with a population density of about 100 persons/km^2 and no urban centre above 100 000 population

Sources: Wild (1979); Henkel (1993).

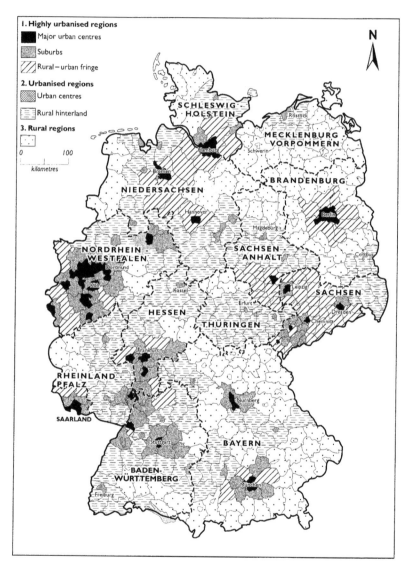

Map 7.1   Planning regions in Germany (*Source*: adapted from BMBau, 1991)

agglomerations in Germany, for instance, the Ruhr, the Rhein valley from Mannheim to Frankfurt, Hamburg, Hannover, Bremen, Stuttgart, München, Nürnberg, and in the new *Länder* Berlin, Chemnitz, Leipzig and Dresden. Countryside in this regional type is heavily influenced by urban proximity, and average population density exceeds the OECD's threshold (Table 7.2). Type 2 regions include areas with smaller urban centres and a decentralised industrial pattern (such as much of Baden-Württemberg), and densely settled fertile agricultural areas (such as the *Börde* lands from Hannover to Halle; see Map 2.3). It, thus, contains a mixture of rural–urban fringe and more open countryside, and contains almost a quarter of Germany's population. Finally, the most rural areas (Type 3) include the German Alps, eastern and northern Bayern, the Hünsruck (Rheinland-Pfalz), north-western and eastern Niedersachsen, northern Schleswig-Holstein, most of Mecklenburg-Vorpommern, Brandenburg and northern Sachsen-Anhalt. They tend to be (former) border areas, upland areas or areas of marginal soil quality. Overall, there is a high correspondence between these regions and LFAs. Bayern has the greatest number of Type 3 *Kreise* in Germany, although reunification has added considerably to this regional type, with the sparsely populated states of northern East Germany.

The implication of this typology is that the nature of rural problems vary geographically, and that different planning policies are required for different rural areas, with the key issues in Type 1 regions being development control and environmental protection, and the key issues in Type 3 regions being peripherality and economic and social development. Type 3 rural areas have, therefore, tended to be prioritised in rural development policies,

Table 7.2   Key characteristics of planning regions in reunified Germany

Regional type	Number of Kreise	Land area (%)	Population (%)	Population density (persons/km²)
Type 1:	185	26.13	53.43	453
Urban centres	47	2.56	25.42	2213
Suburbs	53	7.12	15.78	491
Surrounding rural areas	85	16.45	12.23	165
Type 2:	197	36.76	29.71	179
Urban centres	28	1.02	5.75	1244
Surrounding rural areas	169	35.74	23.96	149
Type 3: Rural areas	161	37.11	16.86	101
Total	543	100.00	100.00	222

Source: Henkel (1993).

but since reunification differences between these three categories have been overshadowed by the greater differences between rural areas in the old and new *Länder*. The following section outlines key social and economic changes that occurred in the FRG and GDR over the post-war period, and identifies the main problems facing rural areas in both parts of reunified Germany.

7.3 Social and economic change in rural areas

7.3.1 The FRG

Population is a key indicator of economic and social development, and rural areas throughout Western Europe have experienced both depopulation and repopulation in the post-war period. Following a period of rural population stagnation and even decline from the mid nineteenth century, rural Germany gained population during and after the Second World War, as people fled from the cities, and refugees flooded into Germany from lost German territories (Wild, 1979; Planck, 1983; Henkel, 1993; see also Chapter 2). Much of this migration was temporary, but many refugees settled down, and most villages retained new settlers.

Population growth has continued since, and the FRG population increased from 50.8 million in 1950 to 61.8 million in 1989 (Jones, 1994). While the 1950s was a period of rapid urbanisation, the rate of urban population growth began to slow down in the 1960s and was replaced by the onset of counter-urbanisation (Wild, 1983). For instance, between 1965 and 1970 the rural population grew by 11.3 per cent, while between 1970 and 1987 it increased by 14 per cent (BMBau, 1990). The FRG has not experienced any significant rural depopulation in the post-war period, despite a decline of almost 5 million in the agricultural workforce since 1949 (see Table 2.4). This stands in sharp contrast to the GDR (see below) and many Western European states such as France and Italy (Clout, 1984). This stability has been partly attributed by Wirth (1996) to the federal government's commitment to achieving equivalent and acceptable living standards in all regions, that was enshrined in the first Federal Planning Act 1965 (see Section 7.4.2). It also reflects the government's commitment to supporting the family farm, without which the loss of farm employment might have been much greater. The commitment to achieve equivalent and acceptable living standards has been pursued by the application of systematic planning principles, such as central place theory, to the planning of infrastructure, services, housing and employment (BMBau, 1993; Henkel, 1993), but also to agricultural and regional policy (see below). However, rates of population growth have varied geographically. In the more remote (Type 3) rural regions, and particularly the smaller villages (less than 500 population), population growth has been less rapid, and in some cases population has stagnated or declined (Table 7.3).

Table 7.3 Index of average population growth by size and location of rural settlement in the FRG, 1970–87 (1970 = 100)

Settlement size (population)	Average population growth index	Range
Up to 500	107.8	87.8–128.0
500–1000	109.2	97.9–120.5
1000–2000	119	100.9–127.4
2000–5000	111.2	105.4–116.5
5000–10 000	119.5	110.4–126.9
Location		
Type 1 regions	120	113.2–127.2
Type 2 regions	112	104.5–119.6
Type 3 regions	109.2	100.9–117.6
Average rural	114.2	109.7–118.6

Source: BMBau (1990, p. 62).

Counter-urbanisers have included mainly families with children and retirees (Johaentges, 1996). The main migration flow has been to accessible countryside, especially to rural–urban fringe countryside in Type 1 and 2 planning regions, as indicated by Table 7.3. This new migration has been a major factor in rural socio-economic change. Not only has it increased the percentage of the rural population employed in non-agricultural jobs, it has also led to a change in the balance of power with a decline in the power base of the farming interest in local politics (Henkel, 1993; *Der Spiegel*, 1996).

While many newcomers (and, increasingly, locals) commute to work in urban areas, many also work locally. Given the declining role of agriculture in the rural economy of Germany, a key factor underlying the vitality of rural communities has been their ability to diversify into new economic activities, especially in the more isolated Type 3 regions. Rural areas have a high percentage of population employed in manufacturing, and between 1960 and 1984 rural settlements were the only settlement category to experience a growth in manufacturing employment (Henkel, 1993). *Realteilung* areas (many of the Type 2 regions; see Map 2.1) have a tradition of small and medium sized enterprises linked to part-time farming, and therefore already have a well-established manufacturing tradition. However, even the remoter Type 3 rural areas have been successful in attracting small-scale manufacturing as a result of government policies (see below).

Important alternative sources of employment for many rural areas, particularly Type 3 areas, are tourism and recreation. However, while the importance of tourism to the rural economy has become increasingly recognised, it is not a panacea for all rural areas. Henkel (1993) identified four types of rural tourism attractions in the FRG: spas, the seaside, and upland areas for both summer and winter recreation and sports. The most successful tourist regions contain more than one of these attractions (for instance, the Alps, the Bayerischer Wald and the Schwarzwald offer spa tourism as well as summer and winter recreation and sports). The main market for rural tourism is domestic. Even in the internationally renowned Schwarzwald, 90 per cent of visitors are Germans (Mohr, 1992). However, the proportion of holidays spent in domestic resorts fell from over 60 per cent in 1962 to 40 per cent in 1982 (BMBau, 1986), and Germans now take proportionately more foreign holidays than any other nation (Ardagh, 1991). This does not necessarily mean that absolute numbers of domestic tourists have fallen, as the number of holidays has risen. Indeed, tourist numbers in the most popular resorts increased considerably between 1962 and 1980. However, the less popular resorts have suffered a downturn or stagnation in visitor numbers (BMBau, 1986). The latter include the upland areas of southern and middle Germany, such as the Harz mountains in Niedersachsen, which rely on summer and winter recreation, but have suffered from declining forest quality due to acid rain and increasingly unreliable winter snowfalls (BMBau, 1991; *Agra-Europe Bonn*, 3.3.1997a). One growth area of the domestic tourism sector has been farm tourism (*Urlaub auf dem Bauernhof*). The number of visitor nights spent in farmhouse accommodation rose from 2.5 million in 1972 to 19.4 million in 1995 (BMBau, 1986; *Agrarbericht*, 1997). However, following rapid growth in demand for farm holidays in the 1970s and 1980s, demand now seems to be levelling off, and Germany faces strong competition from neighbouring countries. For instance, in 1996 Germans took 230 000 farm holidays in the Alps, of which 69 per cent were spent in Austria and only 20 per cent in Bayern (*Agra-Europe Bonn*, 16.12.1996b).

Rural population growth has gone hand in hand with rural housing development (Wild, 1983). The appearance of many villages, especially in Type 1 areas, changed from the 1960s with the development of housing estates on village outskirts. This occurred along with road building and modernisation of basic infrastructure (such as piped water supplies, electricity and telephone links). In contrast to Britain, the demand for rural housing has mainly been for new housing with good insulation and modern amenities (Henkel, 1984). Many in-migrants buy a building plot and build their own house (Johaentges, 1996). Whereas in Britain old village housing has a premium for wealthy newcomers and has been a target for gentrification, in the FRG it still largely houses the local (ex)-agricultural population. This development trend has led to a spatial and social division developing between newcomers and locals in many villages (Johaentges, 1996), and tensions have arisen from the close proximity of farming and residential areas, for instance, over noise, smells and traffic from farms (Planck, 1987; *Der Spiegel*, 1996). However, local residents often gain financially from the presence of newcomers. The local government structure encourages house building, and although the *Gemeinden*[2] have to finance the costs of providing infrastructure to new building plots, they gain financially from the increase in population (through local taxes), and see this as a way to promote local economic development. They also take pride in the modernisation of their communities (Johaentges, 1996).

Despite generally rising population levels in rural areas, services have declined (as in other Western European countries), particularly in the remoter Type 3 areas, and loss of services is seen as a factor contributing to out-migration, especially of younger age groups (Planck, 1983). As well as contributing to living standards, rural services are an important part of village identity and their decline is seen as a decline of community. This is particularly the case with schools, as education services have been subject to centralisation in the post-war period. Henkel (1993) noted that until the early 1960s nearly every village had a kindergarten and a primary/junior school. But, with falling school rolls, *Gemeinde* reforms (see below), and the belief that one-class schools gave a lower standard of education, many schools were centralised. Rationalisation has also affected provision of post offices and shops. However, villages above 1500 population generally have a GP surgery, a dentist and a pharmacist (Henkel, 1993). This indicates better provision than in Britain, where a survey of rural service provision in England found that for villages with between 1000 and 3000 population only 37 per cent had a GP surgery, only 13 per cent had a dental surgery and only 46 per cent had a pharmacist (RDC, 1995). The FRG's more comprehensive provision of services may be attributed to the application of central place theory in settlement planning, which has enabled services to be maintained in central villages (Wild, 1983).

7.3.2 The GDR

Rural development in the former GDR was fundamentally different to that in former West Germany. During and after the Second World War villages in the SOZ received many refugees, and following the land reform of 1945 the population density of land reform areas increased through land settlement (Reichelt, 1992). However, since 1950 the rural population has declined due to outmigration and low fertility rates. Between 1972 and 1983, for example, the rural population declined from 4.3 million to 3.9 million, a decrease of 11 per cent (Krambach, 1985). Population decline was a characteristic of both rural and urban areas (with the exception of East Berlin), and the population of the country decreased from 18.4 million in 1950 to 16.6 million in 1988 (Schmidt and Scholz, 1991; Jones, 1994). In contrast to the FRG, no significant counter-urbanisation took place due to restricted housing and labour markets, cheap rents in urban areas, poor transport infrastructure and low car ownership rates (BMBau, 1991). Car ownership levels among rural households stood at about 68 per cent in

1988, but less than 7 per cent of rural households owned two or more cars (Feldmann, 1992).

Little rural housing development took place after the rural building boom engendered by the land reform, partly because of lack of building materials and lack of purchasing power among the population, but also because of population decline. Housing was built to standard designs, with no attention to local vernacular architecture. Blocks of flats were even built in small villages to house agricultural workers. Lack of building materials meant that it was difficult for owner-occupiers to maintain their homes, so the housing stock deteriorated and many houses lacked basic amenities. Since reunification, although some housing developments are occurring in rural–urban fringe areas, the emphasis has been on renovating existing housing and upgrading/modernising basic infrastructure (see Section 7.4.3).

As stated in Chapter 4, the rural economy of the GDR was dominated by collectives and state farms, with few alternative forms of employment. Manufacturing industry was state controlled and largely urban based (although the socialist principle of regional self-sufficiency meant that many industries were developed in small, previously non-industrialised towns so that every region had some industry). However, in contrast to the FRG, limited foreign travel opportunities meant high demand for domestic tourism, and tourist resorts developed along the North Sea coast, around the lakes of Mecklenburg-Vorpommern, in the Harz mountains of Sachsen-Anhalt and in the upland areas of southern and eastern Sachsen and south-west Thüringen (Oberlausitz; Thüringer Wald), with many of these resorts catering for mass tourism (Albrecht, 1992). For instance, in the late 1980s the Thüringer Wald received over 1 million tourists per annum (TMLNU, 1995).

The SED ruling party also expressed a commitment to achieve equivalent living conditions between urban and rural areas, but approached this goal in a different way to the FRG. A separate rural culture went against the socialist philosophy. It was argued that the capitalist system kept the farming population in a state of backwardness and exploitation (Seidel *et al.*, 1962). The aim of socialism was to free the agricultural population from this exploitative situation and to elevate them to the status of industrial workers. This was to be achieved, firstly, by expelling the 'capitalist landlords' through the land reform and, secondly, by 'urbanising' the countryside through the industrialisation of agriculture and the modernisation of villages (see Chapter. 4). However, by the 1980s this hard-line approach had begun to soften and the value of a rural way of life was officially acknowledged, partly because of concerns over continuing rural depopulation (Krambach, 1985).

In many ways, service provision was more comprehensive than in the FRG, and was not subject to the same rationalisation and centralisation trends. Nearly every village had its own kindergarten and primary school, and the larger villages also supported secondary schools (Seidel *et al.*, 1962). Primary health services were decentralised, and nearly every village also had a state-run shop. The collective and state farms were also important providers of community services (such as canteens, laundries, kindergartens and leisure facilities). While in terms of provision of basic utilities there was little difference between urban and rural areas in the FRG by the 1970s, in the GDR rural areas lagged behind, despite the state's commitment to equivalent living conditions in urban and rural areas. Overall, living standards stagnated in comparison to the FRG. Table 7.4 shows the gulf in living standards that had developed between the FRG and GDR by 1989 (rural and urban areas). Some of the indicators varied between urban and rural areas in the GDR. For instance, about 70 per cent of houses in rural areas were owner-occupied, which was well above the national rate, but for the other variables (except car ownership) provision in rural areas was worse than the national average. Driving speeds were so slow largely due to the poor state of roads, particularly in rural areas.

Since reunification, the rural economy of the new *Länder* has been decimated with a drop of 80 per cent in agricultural employment (see Section 4.3.3). The manufacturing and tourism sectors have also experienced widespread closures and employment losses. The official unemployment rate rose from practically zero before reunification to just under 12 per cent in 1991, and 18 per cent in 1994, before starting to decrease. However, unemployment rates in Type 3 rural regions were higher from the start, reaching almost 22 per cent in 1994 (Tissen, 1994). Unemployment rates for women have also been consistently higher than for men (Fink *et al.*, 1994). However, official unemployment rates underestimate the true extent of unemployment by up to 50 per cent due to short-term government employment and training schemes. As a consequence, the rate of out-migration in rural areas of the new *Länder* has accelerated, especially in Type 3 areas beyond easy commuting distance to urban areas or adjoining areas of the old *Länder* (MRLUSA, 1996). Further, in the years immediately

Table 7.4   Living standards in the FRG and GDR, 1988

Indicator	GDR	FRG
Housing stock owner-occupied (%)	40.4[a]	79.5
Dwellings with a telephone connection (%)	15.7[b]	93.2
Dwellings with indoor toilet (%)	75.6[b]	98.3
Dwellings with mains drainage (%)	58.0[b]	89.7
Dwellings with central heating (%)	47.2[b]	73.3
Number of cars per 1000 population	296[a]	485
Average car driving speeds (km/h)	39.4	70.8

Notes
[a]Percentage higher in rural than urban areas.
[b]Percentage lower in rural than urban areas.
Sources: Paas *et al.* (1994, p. 23); Statistisches Bundesamt (1996, p. 118).

following reunification, the birth rate collapsed. In Sachsen-Anhalt, for instance, the birth rate fell by over 50 per cent between 1988 and 1991 (MRSWSA, 1993) and in Mecklenburg-Vorpommern falling birth rates in rural areas threatened the survival of kindergartens and schools (MLNMV, 1995). As a result, many village schools have been downgraded to primary schools, as junior schools have been centralised. Many other rural services such as shops have also closed, but the population has also become more mobile with rapidly rising car ownership so that urban services are more easily accessible.

7.3.3 Key problems and opportunities for rural areas

The above discussion has highlighted the key social and economic trends in rural areas of the FRG and GDR. The contrasts in the order of problems facing rural areas in the two parts of Germany outweigh the similarities. Rural FRG has undergone a gradual process of adaptation since the 1950s, with a steady decline in agricultural employment and social recomposition of the rural population. Rural GDR has experienced a period of drastic restructuring since 1990, with agricultural employment collapsing and widespread unemployment. There is a wide gap in living standards between east and west due to a legacy of under-investment by the GDR state. Thus, the key focus for rural policy in the 1990s has been to tackle the problems of the new *Länder*, and six key challenges for rural policy in the new *Länder* have been identified (Grajewski *et al.*, 1994; Wirth, 1996): first, the restructuring of agriculture to become competitive within the CAP; second, creation of non-farm employment opportunities (diversification of the rural economy); third, provision of training opportunities to reskill the workforce; fourth, protection and improvement of rural services and utilities; fifth, protection/enhancement of the environment; sixth, maintenance of the rural population. Of these, the first has been considered in Chapter 4 and will not be discussed further here. The rest of this chapter will focus on the other five challenges in terms of options and policies. In particular, the issue of employment will be highlighted, as this has been identified as the key priority for rural development (Schrader, 1994; TMLNU, 1995). However, we will not solely concentrate on the new *Länder* for two reasons. First, the administrative and policy framework within which these challenges are tackled is one that has largely evolved in the FRG. Second, the government cannot ignore the continuing problems facing many rural areas in the old *Länder*, especially in Type 3 areas.

7.4 Policies for rural areas

7.4.1 The administrative framework

The administrative and policy framework of the FRG was transferred, largely unaltered, to the new *Länder* following reunification; thus, the following discussion refers to the FRG's, and now reunified Germany's, situation. Responsibility for planning and economic development is divided between many authorities, as set out in Table 7.5.

The powers and responsibilities of the federal government, *Länder* governments, district and local councils are set out in, and protected by, the constitution, but the regional councils date only from the 1960s, and are an optional layer of government that does not exist in all of the *Länder* (Hooper, 1988). Local councils (*Gemeinden*) play a key role in planning and economic development in the FRG, in contrast to Britain where parish councils hold few powers (Cloke, 1983). Each *Gemeinde* has a professional administration and an elected council headed by a mayor (Henkel, 1993). At local government level, therefore, there is still a division between urban and rural authorities, which enables the rural population to retain a degree of political independence and a separate identity to the urban population, in contrast to Britain where urban and rural districts were amalgamated in 1974 (Cloke, 1983).

The *Gemeinden* have been subject to administrative reforms, however. In 1961, 86 per cent of *Gemeinden* had a population of less than 2000 (Struff, 1992), but between 1965 and 1975 all the *Länder* carried out reforms to create larger *Gemeinden* to achieve efficiency gains, and to enable a more spatially coordinated approach to land use planning (Wild, 1983). This led to the disappearance of about 16 000 *Gemeinden* (two-thirds of the total number), and to an increase in their average population size (Henkel, 1993).

Table 7.5 The planning and economic development hierarchy

Administrative/policy level	*Responsibilities/powers*
Federal government (BMBau; BMWi;[a] BML)	• National planning principles and guidelines; planning law; regional economic development (joint task); agricultural structural policies (joint task)
Land government	• Strategic state planning; regional economic development (joint task); agricultural structural policies (joint task)
Regional council (*Regierungsbezirk*)	• Coordination of regional planning and economic development
District council (*Kreis*)	• Coordination of local planning and economic development
Local council (*Gemeinde*)	• Local land use and development planning; development control

Note
[a]Bundesministerium für Wirtschaft und Technologie.
Sources: Hooper (1988); Henkel (1993).

Where a village was subsumed into a larger *Gemeinde* it still retained an elected mayor and village council, but its role was downgraded to an advisory one. As a result of these reforms, many villages have lost their political autonomy and through that an important part of their identity, although it should be stressed that the reforms retained the separation of urban and rural administrations. Losers from these reforms were overwhelmingly the smaller settlements, while the villages designated as the centres of the new *Gemeinde* were often elevated to the status of low order central places (Henkel, 1993). However, in comparison to more centralised states such as Britain, rural areas in Germany still enjoy a high level of autonomy.

What administrative changes did the imposition of this structure on the new *Länder* require? The GDR had a more decentralised structure of government than the FRG, although, in practice, power was highly centralised. In 1952, the five *Länder* (excluding Berlin) were dissolved and replaced by 14 *Bezirke* (with East Berlin as a fifteenth), but the *Länder* were quickly reinstated after reunification in 1990. The GDR also had *Kreise* (see Table 7.5), and their number was increased from 132 to 227 during the 1950s (Schmidt and Scholz, 1991). The *Gemeinde* formed the lowest level of government, but, unlike the FRG, the *Gemeinden* were politically weak because of lack of finance, and they had less power than the collective farms to undertake village improvements (Grimm, 1992). *Gemeinde* reforms to rationalise local government were carried out (Krambach, 1985), but not to such a great extent as in the FRG. The result was that, with reunification, there was a significant discrepancy between the size of *Gemeinden* in the old and new *Länder*, with over half of the GDR *Gemeinden* having less than 500 residents (Paas *et al.*, 1994). *Gemeinde* reforms have, therefore, been carried out in all the new *Länder* since 1990, thereby also considerably reducing the number of *Gemeinden* and increasing their average population size. *Kreis* reforms have also been carried out to create larger, more viable administrative units. Many former *Bezirk* and *Kreis* centres have, thereby, lost their preferential status (Grimm, 1992).

7.4.2   Regional development policy

Until the 1960s regional policy in the FRG was largely a *Länder* concern, but since then the federal government has become more involved because of growing concern over regional disparities (Sturm, 1998). The two main disparities were the emerging north–south divide between declining old industrial regions of the north and emerging new industrial regions of the south, and the growing urban–rural divide as rural areas lagged behind in terms of income and standards of living (Jones, 1994). In 1969, regional development was incorporated into the FRG constitution as a joint responsibility of the federal and *Länder* governments, and this has been implemented since 1972 as the Common Task for Improving Regional Economic Structures (abbreviated to GRW in German) (Sturm, 1998). Regional policy is closely related to spatial planning policy, and the two operate under the guiding principle of equivalent and acceptable living standards in all regions. This principle was spelt out more clearly in the 1975 federal planning programme: 'equivalent living conditions are achieved when all regions of the federal republic have a quantitatively and qualitatively adequate provision of housing, jobs and public infrastructure and a clean environment' (Henkel, 1993, p. 199). The GRW contributes towards the achievement of equivalent living conditions by aiming to create and protect competitive long-term jobs, and to improve incomes in designated structurally weak areas (Struff, 1990).

More recently, the 1993 Federal Planning Act spelt out specific goals for planning policy in rural areas as seeking to

> maintain population in order to support the existing settlement structure and to maintain an acceptable provision of basic services, even where the population is declining. Economic viability should be promoted through training and jobs, both in and outside agriculture. The multiple functions of rural areas (agriculture and forestry, residential and employment as well as recreation and tourism) should be supported and improved. Ecological functions must also be taken into account. ... A prerequisite for the achievement of these objectives is the maintenance of agricultural and forestry land uses through economically competitive *bäuerliches* farming and a competitive forestry sector. At the same time, the environment and the cultural landscape should be protected and enhanced. *Bäuerliches* farming in particular is to be protected and has preference over other forms of agriculture. Suitable soils are to be protected for both agriculture and forestry. If new land uses are allowed, they must be ecologically sustainable (*Raumordnungsgesetz*, 1993, Articles 6 and 7, own emphases added).

These goals reflect both the government's commitment to the achievement of equivalent living conditions in all parts of Germany and the new discourse of agriculture's multifunctional role within the countryside that has been discussed in the preceding chapters. In the above quote the term *bäuerlich* appears again, but here with the broader meaning of environmentally sound agriculture rather than its more traditional association with family farming (see Section 4.3 for a discussion of the meaning of the term *bäuerlich*).

The GRW operates in a similar way to the GAK (see Chapters 2 and 4) in that the broad policy framework is agreed by the federal and *Länder* governments, funding is divided between the federal and *Länder* governments (50 : 50), and the *Länder* are responsible for implementation. The policy operates on the principle of spatial targeting of economically lagging regions. Map 7.2 shows GRW designated areas in 1996. These include

Map 7.2   Objective 1, 2 and 5b areas in Germany, 1994–99 (*Source*: Deutscher Bundestag, 1996b).

much of the FRG's former borders with the GDR and the border with the Czech Republic. These areas were cut off from traditional markets after 1949 and the whole border zone was designated as a development area (*Zonenrandgebiet*) in 1953 (Jones, 1994). This special status lasted until 1993 when reunification removed its justification. In addition to the former border, GRW designated areas include declining urban industrial and peripheral rural areas, and the whole of the new *Länder*. The two main policy approaches of the GRW are the improvement of manufacturing and tourist infrastructure, and the establishment or expansion of businesses (as long as this leads to new job creation or protects existing jobs). Grants are offered to local authorities and private entrepreneurs. For infrastructure projects grants are available for up to 50 per cent of the costs, and for establishing new businesses up to 23 per cent of the costs (BMBau, 1993). Since 1996, the *Länder* have also been able to fund training and research and development initiatives through the GRW, and funding levels have become more differentiated to target resources for the structurally weakest areas (Sturm, 1998; *Agrarbericht*, 1999).

In the new *Länder* the GRW has played an important role in restructuring the economy, and they have received the bulk of funding. In 1999, for instance, the new *Länder* received DM2.6 billion compared to DM 230 million for the old *Länder* (BMWi, 1999). Between 1990 and 1998, DM 70 billion of GRW funding was invested in the new *Länder*, helping to save or create 1.27 million permanent jobs (*Agrarbericht*, 1999). In addition, tax incentives have been offered to firms wishing to invest in the new *Länder* (BMBau, 1993). However, the GRW has been accused of urban bias. Grajewski *et al.* (1994), for example, noted that Type 2 and 3 rural districts in the new *Länder* received proportionately less funding per capita than urban districts and that the job creation rate was lower. They attributed this situation to the peripherality of many rural areas in the new *Länder*, and the lack of suitable infrastructure. This situation could also be linked to the lack of experienced and qualified planners, engineers and architects in rural *Kreise* and *Gemeinden*, especially in the early 1990s (Albrecht, 1992).

Funding for the GRW has been supplemented by additional policy measures and financial support for the new *Länder* in an attempt to close the large economic gap between old and new *Länder*. In 1990 a German Unity Fund (*Fond Deutsche Einheit*) was established to run until the end of 1994, with a budget of DM 115 billion, later increased to DM 177 billion (BMBau, 1993). It was jointly funded by the federal government (largely using borrowed money) and the old *Länder* governments. In 1991, a special two-year joint task force for rebuilding the economy of the new *Länder* (*Aufschwung Ost*) was established to supplement GRW funding, with a budget of DM 24 billion, largely funded by the federal government (BMBau, 1991). *Aufschwung Ost* was replaced in 1993 by a ten-year programme (*Aufbau Ost*) with funding of DM 6.6 billion per year (BMBau, 1993), now set to run until 2005. Altogether, it is estimated that between 1991 and 1998 the new *Länder* received a net subsidy of DM 595 billion from the federal government, and from the *Länder* and local governments in the old *Länder* (Gros and Glaab, 1999).

One economic sector which the GRW and other funds have focused on is tourism, which has been identified as a key economic development opportunity for rural areas in the new *Länder*, even though reunification has had mixed implications for tourism. The traditional tourist resorts have suffered from falling demand due to economic recession and growing demand for foreign holidays. Visitor numbers to the Thüringer Wald, for instance, plummeted in 1990, but have since recovered somewhat (TMLNU, 1995). The resorts suffer from outdated tourist infrastructure catering largely for mass tourism, and from pollution-related problems (Albrecht, 1992). Many state-run hotels were taken over by the THA following reunification, and unresolved property relations have delayed renovation work (Schmidt, 1994). To survive, infrastructure and accommodation standards have to be brought up to FRG standards.

Reunification has, however, created opportunities for green tourism in rural areas previously outside the main tourist destinations, and all of the new *Länder* governments have looked to tourism as a way of diversifying rural economies. The main markets for green tourism in the FRG are identified as short-break activity holidays (walking, cycling and horse-riding holidays) for mainly domestic tourists, and the day-tripper market (BMBau, 1986), and both these markets have much potential for expansion in the new *Länder*. In addition, heritage tourism is being developed (for instance, Sachsen-Anhalt is promoting a *Straße der Romanik*, a scenic route linking up villages, small towns and cities throughout the region with Romanesque churches; MRSWSA, 1993). Farm tourism, as noted above, is now an established sector of the rural tourism market in the old *Länder*, and has also been identified as a development opportunity in the new *Länder*. In 1991, the federal government set up an organisation to market farm tourism both in Germany and abroad, and since 1990 grants have been available through the GAK to farm families wishing to establish farm tourism enterprises (*Agrarbericht*, 1994). Many *Länder* governments also provide additional support for marketing and business development. However, as noted above, competition is growing in this sector and farms in the new *Länder* are at a competitive disadvantage in terms of tourist infrastructure and amenities.

7.4.3   Village renewal

While the GRW has focused on employment creation and infrastructure development at a district or regional scale, village renewal (*Dorferneuerung*) policy has focused on development at the local level. It is, thus, a truly rural policy. The concept of *Dorferneuerung* originated in the FRG in the

1970s in response to problems arising from changes in village form and function, but at *Länder* rather than federal level (see Chapter. 2). As discussed in Section 7.3.1, during the 1950s, 1960s and 1970s many villages expanded due to counter-urbanisation, and a social and spatial gap opened up between the mainly local population living in the village centre and the mainly newcomer population living on the village outskirts. At the same time, the reduction in farm population meant that the number of working farms located in villages declined (Wild, 1983). Those that remained faced constraints due to lack of space for expansion, and some farm families chose to relocate their farms outside the village, often in conjunction with a *Flurbereinigung* scheme (see Chapter 2).

In the 1950s and 1960s, the official planning response of the *Länder* to these trends was village redevelopment (*Dorfsanierung*). Whole village centres were demolished for redevelopment, especially in the crowded *Realteilung* villages of Baden-Württemberg and Hessen (Fastnacht, 1992; Henkel, 1993; see Map 2.1). At the same time, spontaneous restructuring of villages occurred as residents converted or redeveloped redundant farm buildings (Wild, 1983). This modernisation phase of village planning can also be seen as a reaction against the negative political associations of Germany's heritage, and part of post-war FRG's identity crisis (Henkel, 1984). Interestingly, parallels can be drawn between this approach and that taken in the GDR to modernise the countryside. From the 1970s onwards, however, social attitudes towards the countryside began to change with the emergence of a greater appreciation of the cultural and architectural value of villages, helped by the 1975 European Heritage Year which served to raise awareness of the FRG's rich rural heritage (Henkel, 1993). In 1969 a 'best kept village' competition was launched ('Unser Dorf soll schöner werden') which also raised the profile of village heritage. This new appreciation could also be linked to the realisation that traditional ways of rural life were fast disappearing with changes in farm structures, while the *Gemeinde* reforms of the 1960s and 1970s also contributed to a loss of tradition.

This change in social attitudes was mirrored by a shift in the focus of rural settlement planning from modernisation to conservation and renewal, embodied in the concept of *Dorferneuerung*. This new approach quickly gained the support of the federal government, with the result that *Dorferneuerung* has been financially supported by the federal government since 1977, and has been in the GAK since 1984.[3] It therefore comes under the umbrella of agricultural structural policy as a joint federal–*Länder* task. By the 1980s, *Dorferneuerung* was established as a mainstream policy and had been adopted by all FRG *Länder* and has become a key rural policy for the new *Länder* since 1990. The aims of *Dorferneuerung* and the implementation process will be discussed first, before its contribution to rural development is evaluated with particular reference to the new *Länder*.

The broad aim of *Dorferneuerung* is to improve rural living standards, not just for agricultural and forestry workers and their families but for the whole rural population, through improvements in living and working conditions, recreation opportunities and the environment (BML, 1995b). In contrast to earlier *Dorfsanierung* schemes, the emphasis of *Dorferneuerung* is on adapting village forms to serve modern functions rather than transforming them. From an Anglo-centric perspective, it may seem strange that a policy like this is funded from the agricultural structural improvement budget, but the still close association between villages and farming in Germany makes justification of this policy possible. The BML argues that *Dorferneuerung* indirectly benefits agriculture by revitalising villages and encouraging young people to stay on the land (BML, 1995b). It also helps to improve the viability of farm businesses, for instance, by improving access, or by providing funds for farm diversification (*Agrarbericht*, 1999). Only villages with an agricultural character are eligible for funding under the GAK, although this includes villages with former farms as well as working farms.

The measures that can be funded under *Dorferneuerung* and conditions for funding are set out in Tables 7.6 and 7.7. Funding is available for a wide range of public and private projects, although all subsidies must be

Table 7.6   Measures that can be supported under *Dorferneuerung* (1996–99)

- Preparatory work (surveys) (100% of costs covered)
- Planning costs (maximum DM 8000 per annum up to total of DM 40 000)
- Measures to improve village traffic conditions (such as resurfacing of roads, traffic calming)
- Flood-protection measures and water quality improvement (for example, clean up village streams/ponds)
- Small building/development projects to protect and enhance village character
- In the new *Länder*: larger building/development projects including the creation of squares and open spaces as well as greening of the village perimeter to protect and enhance village character
- Measures to protect and enhance agricultural and forestry buildings (in use or disused) that contribute to village character including farmyards, gardens and green spaces
- Renovation of agricultural and forestry buildings still in use or to bring these buildings back in to agricultural/forestry use to:
  – adapt them to the demands of modern living and working
  – integrate them into the village character or landscape
- Renovation, extension or conversion of shared agricultural and forestry buildings (such as machinery sheds, repair yards)
- The purchase of developed and undeveloped land parcels including, in certain circumstances, buildings to be demolished to achieve any of the above objectives
- In the new *Länder*: demolition of old, unusable agricultural buildings

Source: Deutscher Bundestag (1996a).

Table 7.7   Conditions on funding for *Dorferneuerung* (1996–99)

- Only villages with a farming character, small hamlets and isolated farmsteads are eligible for the scheme
- New village housing and industrial developments are not eligible for funding
- Village/local government groups can apply for up to 60% of the costs of building/development work (80% in the new *Länder*)
- Private individuals can apply for up to 30% of the costs (up to 50% in the new *Länder*) up to a maximum amount of DM 40 000 per project
- Up to 80% of the contribution of village groups/individuals to the costs of projects can be made in kind
- External building/renovation work only is eligible for funding. The only exception is for agricultural/forestry buildings where some internal work may be eligible for funding
- Projects funded must conform to statutory plans and policies, for example relating to spatial planning, environmental landscape protection and agricultural development

---

Source: Deutscher Bundestag (1996a).

matched by private or local government funds. Eligible measures largely consist of building renovation and village planning. Reflecting the fact that it is an agricultural policy, three measures are directed specifically to the renovation of used or disused farm/forestry buildings. Other buildings that contribute to village character can also be renovated. Village planning measures include road resurfacing, traffic control, flood protection and clean-up of village streams and ponds. Along with the general growth in environmental awareness, more emphasis is now placed on greening the villages: planting trees, creating new green spaces, and linking the village to the surrounding countryside with wildlife corridors (Grabski, 1989; Fastnacht, 1992). Key conditions are that new housing and industrial development are not eligible for funding; generally only external building work can be funded (such as renovation of façades, roofs, doors and windows); projects must conform with statutory planning policies.

The scheme is administered at *Land* level by the respective ministry of agriculture, and at the local level by district agricultural offices. The process of implementing the scheme is based on public participation and partnership. Once accepted into the scheme, the village council appoints a planner/architect to provide professional guidance. The first year is then spent drawing up a plan. A working group of 7–15 village residents is elected to work on developing a draft plan, with the guidance of the planner and district agricultural office and in consultation with other public authorities (such as water, electricity and drainage boards, heritage and conservation authorities). This involves carrying out a comprehensive survey and analysis of village character, problems and opportunities, and identifying and prioritising projects. The draft plan must be approved by the village community and the respective layers of government up to the *Land* level. Once the plan is agreed, applications can be submitted for project funding on a yearly basis (Urbisch, 1997).

The *Dorferneuerung* scheme was a success from the start, and funding for the scheme increased rapidly during the 1980s (Table 7.8). The key factors underlying this success are the local scale of the scheme and the requirement for public participation (BMBau, 1990). Within federal/*Länder* guidelines, villages have a high degree of freedom to develop their own village plan. That rural communities have a long tradition of partial autonomy over local development through the *Gemeinde*, means that communities have the experience and motivation to take control of village planning.

Although *Dorferneuerung* is aimed largely at physical improvement of villages (such as building renovation and greening measures), it aims to achieve more than this. Through village planning and renovation, an improvement of village living and working conditions can be achieved. Vacant or neglected public buildings and spaces can be restored and brought back into use, thereby strengthening village identity and revitalising the old village core, and through public participation a spirit of self-help can be engendered that provides momentum for further local, social and economic initiatives. This wider view of *Dorferneuerung* is illustrated by the following definitions by the BMBau (1990) as 'a policy to achieve a comprehensive improvement in living and working conditions in villages' (p. 13), and 'a process of winning back local identity and autonomy' (p. 42).

Table 7.8   Federal expenditure[a] on *Dorferneuerung* through the GAK (million DM)

Year	ex-FRG	ex-GDR	Total
1984	11.4	–	11.4
1985	30.0	–	30.0
1986	40.7	–	40.7
1987	43.4	–	43.4
1988	49.4	–	49.4
1989	49.2	–	49.2
1990	56.4	74.0	130.4
1991	84.5	130.0	214.5
1992	55.0	150.9	205.9
1993	54.9	175.7	230.6
1994	56.9	175.7	232.6
1995	54.7	115.1	169.8
1996	50.6	138.2	188.8
1997	–	–	136.0

Note
[a]Federal expenditure is supplemented by 40% by the *Länder*. Bayern and Baden-Württemberg operate *Dorferneuerung* programmes outside the GAK.
Source: Agrarbericht (1984–99).

Since 1990, the *Dorferneuerung* scheme has been operating in the new *Länder*. The problems facing villages in the new *Länder* are far greater than in the old *Länder*, however, and the expectations and demands of *Dorferneuerung* are more substantial (Wilson, 1999). The backlog of modernisation and renovation measures in the new *Länder* villages is enormous. While *Dorferneuerung* in the old *Länder* can be viewed in some ways as a gentrifying measure to protect and enhance village character, in the new *Länder* it is seen as a scheme of fundamental importance to help villages catch up from 40 years of neglect. In addition, it is seen as a way of stimulating rural development by helping to protect and create jobs and reinvigorating village social and cultural life, thereby reducing out-migration (Paas *et al.*, 1994). For instance, the agricultural ministry in Thüringen believes that *Dorferneuerung* can contribute to socio-cultural development by increasing residents' identification with the village and engendering a self-help ethos that will persist once the scheme itself has come to an end (TMLNU, 1995). The *Dorferneuerung* guidelines for Sachsen-Anhalt state that an aim of the scheme is to 'create a momentum for further local economic, cultural and social initiatives through intensive public participation' (MELFSA, 1991, para. 1.3). Grube and Rost (1995), in an analysis of *Dorferneuerung* in Sachsen-Anhalt, argued that it contributes to village identity and community spirit by creating new meeting places and amenity spaces for village residents, and by restoring valued village public places such as kindergartens, village halls and churchyards. The Agricultural Ministry in Brandenburg sees *Dorferneuerung* as part of an integrated rural development policy and believes that it should go hand in hand with socio-economic initiatives (MELFB, 1992). Similarly, the ministry in Mecklenburg-Vorpommern sees *Dorferneuerung* as an important component of economic and social regeneration (MLNMV, 1995).

In recognition of the scale of the task, the federal government has concentrated funding on the new *Länder* (see Table 7.8) and broadened the aims of the scheme to include the additional aims of creating jobs outside agriculture, improving infrastructure, restoring run-down historic buildings, and converting redundant farm buildings into alternative uses (BML, 1995b). However, the suitability of the scheme for the problems facing rural areas in the new *Länder* can be questioned, especially as it has been transferred largely unaltered from the old *Länder*.

Three main concerns about the *Dorferneuerung* scheme have been identified. First, there are differences in village structure and function between villages in the old and new *Länder*. Lack of significant modernisation and redevelopment during the GDR period (despite official rhetoric) means that most villages have been preserved almost unchanged since the 1930s (Habbe and Landzettel, 1994). This has left villages with a wealth of heritage but much dilapidation, and this is a particular concern for the *Dorferneuerung* scheme because of the many farm buildings that have lost their function but are important for village structure and heritage (Habbe and Landzettel, 1994). Most farm buildings fell into disuse in the 1960s and 1970s following collectivisation, as the collectives built new farm buildings on the village outskirts. Since reunification and the dissolution of the collectives, few families have decided to reinstate their farm businesses (see Chapter 4), and those who have find that the old village farmyards are too small or too dilapidated to be brought back into use, except for part-time farming (Grube and Rost, 1995). Thus, most villages only have one or two part-time farm businesses within the village and the majority of the village population are no longer involved in farming. A key objective of *Dorferneuerung* in the new *Länder* is to save the farm buildings that are not too dilapidated and convert them into alternative uses such as houses, flats, workshops or holiday accommodation (Grube and Rost, 1995). However, there are many problems. The layout of farmyards is often not conducive to conversion (lack of privacy, sunlight), and the cost of internal conversion work is not at present eligible for *Dorferneuerung* funding. Further, ownership of many village buildings is still not clarified, which is a further barrier to renovation/conversion (where ownership is not clarified *Dorferneuerung* funding cannot be given). Thus, conversion is only a solution for some disused farm buildings, and it is likely that many will eventually be demolished and replaced by green spaces or housing.

A second criticism is that, despite the larger budget allocated for *Dorferneuerung* in the new *Länder*, it is still not sufficient to meet the backlog of repairs and improvements in rural settlements. There are few villages that would not benefit from, or are not eligible for, *Dorferneuerung* (Paas *et al.*, 1994). *Länder* governments have had to decide whether to spread funding as widely as possible, in which case funding per village is less, or to concentrate funding on fewer villages. For political reasons, most *Länder* have chosen the former course. Sachsen-Anhalt, for instance, which has the largest commitment to the scheme, has set a goal of having all eligible villages (2100 or 80 per cent of total settlements) in the scheme by the year 2000 (Rakow, 1997). In the old *Länder*, *Dorferneuerung* schemes take an average of ten years to complete, but in the new *Länder* participation is limited to about five years because of resource constraints (Grube and Rost, 1995). A further financial constraint is the requirement for joint funding of all projects. Although funding levels are more generous in the new *Länder* (see Table 7.8), the *Gemeinden* only have limited budgets to co-fund public projects, and only residents in employment can obtain bank loans to co-fund private projects. The problem of lack of communal capital has been partly solved by introducing the concept of a temporary break in funding. The village can opt out of the scheme for one or two years until the *Gemeinde* has built up its funds again, when the village can once more opt in. The federal employment creation scheme has also enabled *Gemeinden* to carry out many public projects (such as road resurfacing and tree-planting/shrub clearance) that would otherwise have been unafford-able (Mühlnickel, 1997) (see Section 4.3.3).

Third, although *Dorferneuerung* has achieved significant improvements in living standards in villages of the new *Länder*, it has been criticised for con-centrating on physical rather than social and economic renewal (Paas *et al.*, 1994; Herrenknecht, 1995). This is partly because of the nature of the funding (subsidies are only available for building and environmental work), and partly because of the village level scale of the scheme which inevitably leads to a focus on parochial issues (Wild, 1983). *Dorferneuerung* represents a considerable workload for the village council, who do not have the time or expertise to maximise its potential by linking it to other social and econ-omic schemes, especially if the village has been subsumed within a larger *Gemeinde* and, therefore, has less administrative and professional support. It has been argued that to achieve social and economic improvements, village-level *Dorferneuerung* schemes must be coordinated at a higher level, and supplemented with regional level policies (Paas *et al.*, 1994; Grube and Rost, 1995). The success of the scheme at present depends on the initia-tive of the mayor or other key local actors. The challenge is to turn *Dorferneuerung* into 'village development' (*Dorfentwicklung*) and better still 'integrated rural development' (Paas *et al.*, 1994). Linked to this issue are tensions between different actors within the *Dorferneuerung* scheme over policy priorities, particularly between 'Wessis' (many holding key gate-keeper positions within the new *Länder* ministries) and 'Ossis' (local actors).

One innovative attempt to achieve additional socio-economic benefits from *Dorferneuerung* is an experimental project launched by a non-govern-mental organisation formed in 1992 in the new *Länder* (Förderwerk Land- und Forstwirtschaft e.V.) to support agricultural and forestry workers and to help unemployed agricultural and forestry workers into new employment. Its brief includes supporting social and environmental improvement in villages through *Dorferneuerung*. In 1994, it launched a pilot village advisor project in six villages. The role of the village advisors was to work alongside the village council with the specific task of increasing public awareness of, and partici-pation in, *Dorferneuerung*, and in addition to coordinate *Dorferneuerung* with other funding schemes to maximise potential social and economic benefits (Behrens, 1995). Village advisors were supported by regional advisors who have expert knowledge of funding schemes. The scheme has been supported by the *Länder* governments of Sachsen-Anhalt and Sachsen with more village advisors being appointed, but at present no state funding can be provided to pay the salaries of the village advisors so they are currently appointed as ABM workers on one-year contracts (Stert, 1997).

Despite these shortcomings, the *Dorferneuerung* scheme has achieved significant improvements in living conditions in villages in the new *Länder* in a short time. The impact of the scheme can be seen in new (or restored) village streets and street furniture, restored village squares and cemeteries, newly planted trees, restored building façades and new roofs (Wilson, 1999). *Dorferneuerung* meets the desire of villagers to improve their living environment and take pride in their rural heritage (Paas *et al.*, 1994). The scheme is now a well established part of rural settlement planning and rural development in Germany, and the concept has been adopted by the European Commission as part of its expanding rural policy agenda (see below). But its future importance depends on continued availability of funding. In the 1990s, an increasingly important funding source has been the European Structural Funds.

7.4.4   European policies for rural development

Rural (as distinct from agricultural) policy has been a recent development in the EU. Until the late 1980s, regional policy in EU member states was essentially a national concern (George, 1996), while EU policy for rural areas was defined in strongly productivist agricultural terms under the CAP. In the late 1980s, this situation changed for two main reasons. First, the 1986 Single European Act set out the goal to complete the single market by 1993. It was anticipated that this would generate wealth within the EU but in a spatially uneven way, with the main gains going to geographic and economic core regions at the expense of the periphery. This danger was increased by the accession of Greece, Spain and Portugal to the EEC in the 1980s, all of whom lagged well behind the EEC average in terms of GDP per capita and, therefore, threatened to significantly increase inequalities within EEC regions (George, 1996). To counteract this danger, and to spread the benefits of the single market, the Commission proposed an expansion of regional policy. Second, and related to this growing problem of inequality, but also to concern about the cost of the CAP, the Commission and the CAM belatedly recognised that the majority of the rural population were not dependent on agricultural employment, and that the percentage of the population still in farming would continue to decline (Winter, 1996). There were, therefore, political and economic incentives to broaden the scope of rural policy.

The publication of a report entitled *The Future of Rural Society* (CEC, 1987b) was a turning point in EEC rural policy away from a productivist agricultural focus towards a post-productivist rural vision, embracing a multifunctional agriculture within a diverse rural economy and society. The report provided a summary of the problems facing rural areas in the EEC and set out a strategy to tackle them. The main argument of the report was that rural areas could no longer be equated purely with agriculture, but served a variety of functions in modern society, as the following quote from the report illustrates:

> the concept of rural society ... refers to a complex economic and social fabric made up of a wide range of activities: farming, small trades and

businesses, small and medium-sized industries, commerce and services. Further, it acts as a buffer and provides a regenerative environment which is essential for ecological balance. Finally, it is assuming an increasingly important role as a place of relaxation and leisure (CEC, 1987b, p. 15).

The Commission's proposed strategy for rural development set out in the report was based on three aims: first, to promote economic and social cohesion within the EEC; second, to ease the 'unavoidable' adjustment of farming and consequent decline of agricultural employment; and third, to protect and conserve the natural environment (CEC, 1987b). In the same year, a reform of regional policy was agreed. The three Structural Funds – the European Regional Development Fund (ERDF), European Social Fund (ESF) and the Guidance section of EAGGF – which had until then been administered separately, were coordinated around a series of five objectives (see Table 7.9) and budgets were enlarged. The Structural Fund budget more than doubled between 1988 and 1993 from 7.2 to 15.5 billion ECU, and its share of the EC budget increased to about 25 per cent of the total (Williams, 1996).

Four of the objectives were targeted at designated geographical areas, of which three (Objectives 1, 5b and 6) include rural areas (with 5b specifically targeted at rural areas). Once designated, a policy framework had to be drawn up for each Objective area by the Commission, national government and respective regional authorities, to ensure that all policies were compliant with the aims of the Objective and with EU competition policy before funding was agreed. Funding was dependent on the three principles of: (a) additionality (EU funding must be matched by public or private funds, except in Objective 1 regions where the EU will contribute up to 80 per cent of funding); (b) partnership (the policy framework must be drawn up jointly between the local authorities, national government and the Commission); (c) accountability (all projects funded must be monitored and evaluated).

To what extent have the reformed Structural Funds, and particularly Objectives 1 and 5b, influenced rural policy in Germany? As the wealthiest member of the EU and a probable winner of the single market, the FRG was excluded from Objective 1 funding in 1988. Indeed, Germany was a reluctant partner in the expansion of the Structural Funds, as it was felt that Germany would lose out financially and, as a result, increase its net payments to Brussels (Geissendörfer *et al.*, 1998). It has been argued that Objectives 2, 5b and 6 were developed as a concession to the wealthier countries of the EU so that each member state would obtain some structural funding (Bachtler and Michie, 1994). No hard and fast criteria for Objective 5b were laid down, to allow member states and their constituent regions flexibility with which to argue their case for designation. Largely at

Table 7.9 The EU's regional development objectives (1989–99)

Objective	Criteria	Funding
1. Economic adjustment of regions whose development is lagging behind	• Regions (NUTS[a] level 2) with 75% or less of EU average GDP per capita	• 75% EU funding (80% for the cohesion states of Ireland, Greece, Portugal and Spain). 70% of total Structural Fund budget allocated (ERDF, ESF, EAGGF)
2. Economic conversion of declining industrial areas	• Regions (NUTS level 3) with unemployment rates above EU average; proportion of industrial employment not less than EU average; declining trend in industrial employment	• 50% EU funding (ERDF, ESF)
3. Combating long-term unemployment	• Focus on projects in Objectives 1, 2, 5b and 6 regions	• 75% funding in Objective 1 regions, 50% elsewhere (ESF)
4. Facilitating the adaptation of workers to industrial changes and to changes in production systems	• Focus on projects in Objectives 1, 2, 5b and 6 regions	• 75% funding in Objective 1 regions, 50% elsewhere (ESF)

Table 7.9 The EU's regional development objectives (1989–99) *(continued)*

Objective	Criteria	Funding
5. (a) Speeding up the adjustment of agricultural structures and fisheries	• All agricultural areas within the EU	• 75% funding in Objective 1 regions, 50% elsewhere (EAGGF)
(b) Economic diversification of rural areas	• Regions (NUTS level 3) with a high percentage of the working population in agriculture; low farm incomes; low GDP per capita	• 50% EU funding (ERDF, ESF, EAGGF)
6. Economic adjustment of regions with outstandingly low population density[b]	• Regions (NUTS level 2) with population density of less than 8 persons per km²	• 50% EU funding (ERDF, ESF, EAGGF)

Notes
[a] Nomenclature of territorial units for statistics (an EU-wide classification of administrative areas to achieve consistency between member states for statistical and planning purposes).
[b] This objective has existed only since 1995 in response to the accession of Sweden and Finland to the EU.
Sources: Schrader (1991); Williams (1996).

the insistence of the FRG, three even softer criteria were added to the list for Objective 5b eligibility shown in Table 7.9: low population density and/or out-migration; peripherality from large urban centres; and vulnerability to CAP reform in terms of income and employment, poor agricultural structures or age structure of the farm population, environmental problems, or location within an LFA (Schrader, 1991). As a result, the FRG succeeded in gaining Objective 5b status for 21.4 per cent of the land area and 7.4 per cent of the population. The political nature of the exercise is further indicated by the fact that all the old *Länder*, except for the city states, obtained some Objective 5b areas. Bayern emerged as the main winner, with almost half of the FRG's 5b areas and almost half the total budget of just over DM1 billion (*Agrarbericht*, 1992). Germany also influenced the selection of policy measures that could be funded by Objective 5b programmes, by lobbying to have existing GAK policies, including *Flurbereinigung* and *Dorferneuerung*, accepted.

The four priorities for rural development agreed for the FRG's Objective 5b areas were: (a) diversification and adjustment of agriculture, forestry and fisheries (including measures to support environmentally friendly production methods; production, processing and marketing of quality food products; agri-tourism; *Flurbereinigung* and *Dorferneuerung*) (28 per cent of total funding); (b) development and diversification of non-agricultural sectors and improvement of infrastructure (including support for small and medium-sized enterprises to create new jobs) (31 per cent); (c) development of human resources through training (16 per cent); (d) environmental and nature protection and landscape care (25 per cent) (Schrader, 1991). Most funding was, thus, earmarked for the second priority, in contrast to the EU as a whole where agricultural adjustment was awarded the highest priority, although funding priorities varied between the *Länder* (Plankl and Schrader, 1991). The first priority mirrored the aims of the GAK, and EAGGF funding was largely used to supplement funding for GAK policies, rather than develop new policies. Similarly, funding for the second priority was largely delivered through the GRW. Thus, the Objective 5b programme did not produce any significant change in the menu of rural policies, reflecting the success of the government in lobbying the Commission.

In the 1989–93 funding period, the FRG was the second largest recipient of Objective 5b funding in the EU after France, receiving over half a billion ECU, but one of the lowest recipients of structural funding overall, with most going to the Objective 1 countries (Hoggart *et al.*, 1995). The reunification of Germany in 1990, however, changed the political and economic map of the EU. Germany now had some of the poorest regions in the EU, which met the criteria for Objective 1. Although the Structural Fund budget for the period 1989–93 had already been committed, the EU put together a special package for the new *Länder* of 3 billion ECU (about DM6 billion) for the period 1991–93 (Schrader, 1994). Of this, 369 million

ECU were earmarked for agricultural structures, and 396 million for agricultural adjustment and rural development (*Agrarbericht*, 1994). The three priorities laid down for agriculture and rural development were: first, the development of agriculture, forestry and fishing and the restructuring of the food processing industry (to be funded as Objective 5a measures); second, the improvement of living and working conditions in rural areas; third, environmental improvement measures in agriculture and forestry (Schrader, 1991). As in the old *Länder*, funding largely went to supplement existing GAK and GRW policies, including *Dorferneuerung*.

In 1993, the Objectives were reviewed. It was decided to give even greater priority to regional development over the period 1994–99 in the run-up to the introduction of the single currency. The Structural Fund budget was, therefore, increased to 21.1 billion ECU in 1994, rising to 27.4 billion in 1999. This represented 37 per cent of the EU budget (Bachtler, 1998). The number of designated Objective 1, 2 and 5b regions was also increased. In Germany, the new *Länder* easily qualified for Objective 1 status and were allocated a budget of 3.1 billion ECU (about DM6 billion) for rural development for the 1994–99 period. Altogether, the new *Länder* were allocated structural funding of 13.6 billion ECU over the six years, which was the fifth largest allocation of Objective 1 funding in the EU and roughly 14 per cent of the total Objective 1 budget (Bachtler and Michie, 1994). The old *Länder*, not wishing to lose out, applied for a significantly increased number of Objective 5b areas (an increase in area of 45 per cent!) to cover 25 per cent of the area of reunified Germany (38.7 per cent of the old FRG area) and to include about 9.7 per cent of the population (CEC, 1996a). Map 7.2 shows a high, although not complete, correspondence between Objective 5b areas and the Type 3 rural regions (see Map 7.1), with an even greater concentration along the borders of the FRG, including the former *Zonenrandgebiete*. There is also a correspondence with LFAs. Funding for 5b areas also more than doubled to 1.2 billion ECU (*Agrarbericht*, 1996,), with 46 per cent allocated to Bayern. Germany was allocated 17.8 per cent of the total Objective 5b budget (CEC, 1996a), and was the second largest recipient after France (Bachtler and Michie, 1994).

As in the 1989–93 period, the Structural Funds were mainly used by the *Länder* to supplement existing policies in the GAK and GRW. The priorities for agriculture and rural development in the new *Länder* set out in 1991 continued for the 1994–99 period. In addition, ERDF and ESF funding targeted measures for the improvement of industrial and tourist infrastructure and human capital (*Agrarbericht*, 1996). In the old *Länder* 5b areas, three new key priorities were identified, although the emphasis on agricultural diversification and non-agricultural economic development continued: first, diversification of agriculture, development of biomass resources, renewable energy, agri-tourism, *Dorferneuerung*, leisure and recreation; second, development and diversification of the non-agricultural sector (and creation of long-term permanent jobs); third, development of indigenous human capital (*Agrarbericht*, 1996).

In addition to structural funding, both the old and new *Länder* have received additional funding through the LEADER community initiative (links between actions for the development of the rural economies). The LEADER programme was set up in 1991 to encourage innovative local level rural development initiatives for training, farm tourism, processing and marketing of local produce; for support of small businesses and environmental improvements; and to develop a rural development network throughout the EU to share information and ideas (*LEADER Magazine*, 1997). Local action groups (LAGs), covering areas of up to 100 000 population, can apply for funding, although the principle of additionality also applies. In the initial LEADER programme (1991–93), only 13 German LAGs received LEADER funding, all of them in Objective 5b areas in the old *Länder* (Geissendörfer *et al.*, 1998). Total EU funding amounted to 23.8 million ECU (*Agrarbericht*, 1994). However, in the second round of LEADER funding (1994–99), 146 German LAGs were funded, with a budget of 176.2 million ECU (*Agrarbericht*, 1999). The new *Länder* received 82 million ECU funding for the period 1994–99, while the old *Länder* received 94 million ECU (with Bayern again receiving the lion's share) (*Agrarbericht*, 1996).

The LEADER initiative differs from the Objective programmes in that it covers smaller areas, and is bottom-up in approach. Therefore, it encourages innovative and integrated approaches to rural development, and has been hailed by the Commission as a success throughout the EU and a blueprint for future rural policy (*LEADER Magazine*, 1997). An evaluation of LEADER 1 in Germany was cautiously optimistic about the initiative (Geissendörfer *et al.*, 1998). The evaluation noted, however, that while LEADER was viewed positively by the LAGs, it was viewed with some suspicion by the authorities, as the scheme does not fit well with existing policy-making structures, and the emphasis on partnerships and networking also fits uneasily with the German approach. As a result, the authorities were reluctant partners in the initial round of LEADER, and no federal or *Länder* funding was forthcoming (Geissendörfer *et al.*, 1998), but the expansion of participating LAGs subsequently suggests a more welcoming view of the initiative. The main strength of LEADER from the viewpoint of LAGs is that it has stimulated debate on innovative local approaches to rural development. It has also enabled the creation of new territorial decision-making units based on development needs rather than administrative boundaries (Ray, 1998). The LAGs provide an intermediate tier of decision-making between the *Gemeinden* and the *Regierungsbezirke*, which enables a balance to be achieved between local participation and regional strategic development. The evaluation of LEADER 1 found that the LAGs had achieved many positive outcomes, such as job creation, farm diversification, promotion of regional identity and infrastructural and environmental improvements. Often, LEADER funding had been used in conjunction with *Dorferneuerung* funding to increase the social and economic benefits of village renewal.

There is no doubt that EU funding has been crucial for rural development in the new *Länder*, and it has increased the budgets for rural development in the old *Länder*. For instance, Sachsen-Anhalt's budget for *Dorferneuerung* was increased by more than 50 per cent through the Structural Funds (MRLUSA, 1996). Early evaluations of the German Objective 5b areas indicate that economic convergence is occurring between Objective 5b areas and the federal average (Schrader, 1997). Between 1994 and 1996, about 20000 jobs were saved or created in Objective 5b areas (*Agrarbericht*, 1999). The new *Länder*, however, still lag far behind the EU average, let alone the federal average, in GDP per capita and unemployment, although rapid progress has been achieved. In 1996, nearly all of the old *Länder* had GDP per capita figures well above the EU average, while the new *Länder* figures were only about 65 per cent of the EU average (*Regional Trends*, 1999). Thus, the new *Länder* will continue to benefit from targeted financial support for some time to come, but as the gap in living standards between rural areas in the old and new *Länder* closes, so the new *Länder* will lose their special development status, and will increasingly identify with rural areas in the old *Länder*. New alliances and networks are likely to develop, therefore, between, for instance, Type 3 rural areas in both the old and new *Länder* with respect to rural policy and funding.

As well as boosting financial resources for rural development, the Europeanisation of rural policy has challenged Germany's top-down, sectoral policy-making framework in many ways. First, it has added another layer of government (the Commission) to Germany's already multilevel government structure. This was initially viewed negatively by the *Länder* as a threat to their autonomy, but they were prepared to cooperate to gain funding (Sturm, 1998). Second, the requirement for increased cooperation between different agencies and actors has encouraged a more integrated approach to rural development, which has been shown to be the most effective approach to achieve sustainable rural development (Pretty, 1998). Third, it has also introduced the processes of monitoring and evaluation to the policy process for the first time (Schrader, 1994), thereby encouraging a more reflexive approach to policy-making. There is evidence that policy-makers are beginning to think more innovatively and strategically. For instance, in 1997 the federal government launched a competition called 'Regions of the Future' to encourage *Länder*, regional and local authorities and other partners to set up innovative sustainable development projects (*Agrarbericht*, 1999). The emergence of a European dimension to rural policy is seen as a positive development in Germany by commentators, although not unproblematic (Bachtler, 1998; Geissendörfer *et al.*, 1998). In particular, different actors have different views as to how development policies should be monitored and evaluated and by whom (Schrader, 1994).

7.5　Conclusions

This chapter has examined key social and economic trends in the German countryside, comparing and contrasting trends in the FRG and GDR. We have also discussed key policies to tackle rural problems in reunified Germany, and shown how European funding is becoming more important for rural development in Germany. In this final section we will reflect on these trends and policies, and consider to what extent a new rural policy agenda is emerging within Germany.

The problems facing rural areas in the old *Länder* are arguably less severe than in most other EU member states. Although agricultural employment has declined significantly in the post-war era, and service closures have occurred, the rural population has remained relatively stable and has even grown in many areas. Rural areas in the old *Länder* have a diversified economy, and living standards are generally comparable with urban areas. There are only a few Type 3 rural areas where population is declining and living standards lag behind the national average. Counter-urbanisation has been a key process of socio-economic change in rural FRG, particularly in the more accessible Type 1 and 2 rural areas, and this has contributed to the 'urbanisation' of rural communities in terms of occupational and social structures. In contrast, agriculture retained its dominance in the economic and social fabric of the GDR countryside to a greater extent, although traditional social relations were forcibly transformed by the land reform and collectivisation of agriculture (see Section 4.2.1). The GDR period was characterised by lack of investment in rural infrastructure and out-migration, with the result that, by 1990, living standards lagged well behind those of the FRG (and most other EU rural areas). Despite the contrasting political conditions under which rural areas of the FRG and GDR developed between 1945 and 1990, however, some similarities are apparent. For instance, both states gave a commitment to bring rural living standards up to urban standards and, at the same time, to modernise rural society and economy.

Despite the declining importance of agriculture in the rural economy of the old *Länder* (and, more dramatically, in the new *Länder* since reunification), the agricultural sector still receives the majority of public subsidy for rural areas through the CAP, and the BML retains control of the main policy for rural development: *Dorferneuerung*. How can this continuing dominance be explained? First, the farm lobby has managed to retain public support for agricultural subsidies (see Chapters 3 and 5). Second, the social and cultural importance of farming outweighs its economic importance because of the prevalence of part-time farming, and the location of many farms within villages. Farms (and former farms) are an important part of Germany's rural architectural heritage and cultural landscape. Third, no other rural interest group has such an influential lobby group as the farmers through the DBV. For these reasons, a policy like *Dorferneuerung* can be funded as an agricultural structural policy. Nevertheless, the farm lobby has had to adapt to retain public support. This can be seen in the new rhetoric emerging from the BML and DBV emphasising the multifunctional role of agriculture in the modern countryside. More and more farm businesses must embrace post-productivist activities, such as farm tourism or direct farm sales, to survive. Arguably the task of maintaining public legitimacy is even greater in the new *Länder* where the social and cultural importance of farming is now weaker. The agricultural lobby's position is also being challenged by the Europeanisation of rural policy.

Given the scale of problems in rural areas of the new *Länder*, rural policy (as opposed to agricultural policy) has gained more prominence since reunification. The policy framework within which these problems have been tackled, however, has been transferred largely unaltered from the old *Länder*, albeit with greatly enlarged budgets. In addition, many key positions in new *Länder* government ministries have been taken by 'Wessis' with experience of the FRG policy-making framework. While substantial improvements in living standards in rural areas of the new *Länder* have been achieved through *Dorferneuerung*, critics have argued that the policy framework is not best suited to tackling the problems of the new *Länder*. For instance, the *Dorferneuerung* policy focuses on physical and environmental improvements rather than on job creation. There is also resentment among 'Ossis' that policies are formulated by outsiders who may not always be sensitive to local concerns.

The rural policy framework in reunified Germany is traditionally both top-down and sectoral, although rural communities have more autonomy and democratic representation than in Britain, for example. This framework is challenged by the Europeanisation of rural policy that has occurred since the late 1980s, despite the extra layer of government created by the Commission. This is due to the emphasis in the EU's Objective and LEADER programmes on partnerships and integrated rural development policies, and it is leading to more innovative and integrated approaches to rural development within Germany. For instance, the LEADER initiative can be tied in with *Dorferneuerung* schemes to achieve social and economic, as well as physical, improvements. LEADER areas do not necessarily coincide with administrative boundaries, helping to create new territorial identities and new networks of policy-making. However, it will take time for organisational attitudes and structures to change, and for a truly integrated rural policy framework to emerge. While Germany has shifted its position on the European Structural Funds from reluctant to supportive partner, and has been a leader for *Dorferneuerung*, this shift has largely occurred for pragmatic reasons to access the funding available (Sturm, 1998). So far, funding for rural development has been *in addition* to agricultural support. It is unlikely that the agricultural lobby would be prepared to see funding priorities shift from agricultural support to support for rural development. It is likely, therefore, that rural policy will become a more contentious topic in future, as pressure mounts to reform the CAP again. The latter issue will be the subject of Chapter 8 where, in conclusion to the book, we discuss future developments in the EU and the CAP and their implications for German agricultural and rural policy.

8
Conclusions – German Agriculture in Transition?

In this final chapter we have three main aims. First, we will analyse recent political and economic developments that have important implications for the CAP and have already led to a new package of reforms. Second, we will review the current situation of German agriculture and agricultural policy in the light of recent CAP reforms and the election of a new SPD–Green coalition government. Finally, we will reflect on developments in German agriculture and agricultural policy in the post-war period, and will highlight what we see as the main trends and distinctive features, before putting forward our analysis of how the current situation is likely to develop in the early twenty-first century.

8.1 Pressures for further CAP reform

The last years of the twentieth century, and the first years of the twenty-first, are again a key period for EU agricultural policy due to two external factors. First, the EU is likely to expand its membership to include CEECs. The inclusion of countries with much lower GDPs than existing member states, and with severe agricultural structural problems, will put further pressure on the CAP budget, and may create a momentum for further reform. Second, the URA is due to expire in 2001, and negotiations on the next round are already under way. The European Commission and member states are likely to have to make concessions on the CAP to comply with the next WTO agreement (Manegold, 1995; Swinbank, 1996). Already, the Commission and member states have taken a concrete step towards tackling both these issues, with agreement on Agenda 2000 for the future development of the EU that includes agreement on agricultural reforms (CEC, 1999a). However, at the time of writing there is considerable debate about the agreed agricultural measures, and whether these will be sufficient for the WTO or for eastern enlargement. The three related issues of eastward expansion, WTO talks, and Agenda 2000, will be considered in this section, with particular reference to Germany's position.

8.1.1 Eastward expansion

Discussion on a new round of EU expansion to admit CEECs began soon after the fall of Communist regimes in 1990 and 1991. The collapse of the Soviet Union left a power vacuum in Central and Eastern Europe which the EU was anxious to fill for strategic and economic reasons (Agra-Europe Special Study, 1997). However, the challenges posed by EU eastwards expansion are considerable. Since the EEC was established in 1957, expansion from 6 to 15 members has taken place gradually, with never more than three states joining at any one time. Ten CEECs (Poland, Hungary, Czech Republic, Slovak Republic, Slovenia, Romania, Bulgaria, Lithuania, Latvia and Estonia) were identified by the European Council in 1993 as potentially eligible for EU membership, however, providing that they met the necessary economic and political criteria (fully operating democracies, market economies and a good record on human rights). The addition of ten new members would increase the number of EU member states by two-thirds, which would place strains on the European Commission and the Council of Ministers, and EU decision-making and administrative structures would need to be reformed prior to expansion on this scale (Agra-Europe Special Study, 1997).

The economies of the ten CEECs (CEEC10) lag far behind those of the EU15, even behind the poorest member states (Table 8.1). Moreover, the economies of the CEEC10 are still adjusting to capitalist market conditions following almost 40 years of socialist government. To bridge this economic gap would place strains on the EU's budget and on the CAP and regional policy, and, most significantly, would place extra burdens on the budgets of the wealthiest member states. Although expansion will bring economic benefits to Germany's manufacturing sector and is strongly supported by exporters (Möhlers, 1997), expansion will further increase the size of Germany's net contribution to the EU budget. In 1996, Germany made 82 per cent of net contributions to the EU budget, while the wealthier countries of Luxembourg and Denmark were net beneficiaries. This became an election issue in the run-up to the 1998 federal elections, with German politicians of all parties calling for an urgent reform of budget arrangements (Traynor, 1997; Bachtler, 1998). Agriculture was singled out as the main source of Germany's net contributions, with Kinkel, the then finance minister, criticising the size of the CAP budget (*Agra-Europe London*, 2.5.1997).

Agriculture is a key factor in eastward expansion, because of the importance of agriculture in the CEEC10 economies and because of the problems expansion would pose for the CAP in its existing form. Membership by the CEEC10 would increase the EU15's population by 29 per cent, the land area by 33 per cent and the agricultural population by over 50 per cent (see Table 8.1). Although expansion would increase internal demand for food products, consumers in the CEEC10 have lower purchasing power than

Table 8.1 Indicative statistics for the CEEC10, 1993

Country	Population (millions)	UAA (million ha)[a]	Agricultural employment (% total)[a]	Contribution of agriculture to GDP (%)[a]	GDP per capita (ECU)
Poland	38.5	18.5	26.7	5.5	1 907
Hungary	10.3	6.2	8.2	5.8	3 150
Czech Republic	10.3	4.3	4.1	2.9	2 586
Slovak Republic	5.3	2.4	6.0	4.6	1 643
Slovenia	1.9	0.8	6.3	4.4	5 018
Romania	22.7	14.8	37.3	19.0	961
Bulgaria	8.5	6.2	23.4	12.8	1 110
Lithuania	3.8	3.2	24.0	10.2	627
Latvia	2.6	2.5	15.3	7.6	850
Estonia	1.6	1.5	9.2	8.0	938
CEEC10	105.5	60.2	22.5	6.8	1 786
EU15	369.7	138.1	5.7	2.5	15 972

Note
[a] 1996.
Source: CEC (1995c; 1998a).

those in the EU15 and supply would far outstrip demand. Market prices for agricultural produce are much lower in the CEEC10 than the EU, which would mean that CEEC10 farmers would gain financially from CAP membership through significantly higher prices, but this would put a tremendous burden on the CAP budget. It has been estimated that the CAP budget would have to rise by up to a third if it was extended to the CEEC10 (Agra-Europe Special Study, 1997). Higher prices would, in turn, boost production levels in the CEEC10, agricultural output would increase substantially, which would then place pressure on internal market prices and would add to the threat of surpluses. These developments would further increase the cost of the CAP, as well as increasing the EU's role as an agricultural exporter, which might in turn increase trade conflicts.

The agricultural sectors of the CEEC10 face similar, but even more severe, problems of restructuring than the former GDR (see Chapter 4). Without the benefit of EU and FRG financial backing that the former GDR enjoyed, the need for investment is enormous to bring farm productivity and food-processing standards of the CEEC10 to EU levels (Gregory, 1999). It is no wonder that agriculture is an important consideration in talks on expansion, and that member states are proceeding cautiously on this issue, with strong opposition to rapid eastward expansion from farmers' groups, including German farmers. While some economic benefits are expected, such as increased export opportunities for dairy products in which the CEECs are not yet self-sufficient (*Agra-Europe Bonn*, 5.7.1999c), disadvantages are seen to outweigh any advantages.

The announcement on 17 July 1997 by the European Commission that only five CEECs (Czech Republic, Poland, Hungary, Estonia and Slovenia; hereafter CEEC5), plus Cyprus met the eligibility criteria for EU membership, can be seen as an outcome of the concerns expressed over enlargement, although the official reason stated was that the other CEECs did not yet meet the eligibility criteria. Negotiations on accession of the CEEC5 began in March 1998 (*Agrarbericht*, 1999). Although no date for full membership has been agreed, it is unlikely to be before 2005 (Gregory, 1999). No decision on when the other CEECs will start the accession process has been made, although their eventual membership seems inevitable. As Table 8.1 shows, Hungary, the Czech Republic and Slovenia have the highest GDPs per capita of the CEEC10, and therefore will be absorbed most easily. Estonia and Poland have noticeably lower GDPs per capita, but Poland's location is geostrategically important, while Estonia's membership is important for the Scandinavian states, and will have little impact on the EU because of the small size of its economy.

8.1.2   The WTO round of negotiations

The current URA ends in 2001 and discussions on a new Millennium Round of negotiations started in Seattle, USA, in November 1999. The next round will focus on achieving further liberalisation of world trade, led by the USA and Cairns Group countries, which will put pressure on the EU to further increase market access and reduce export subsidies (Josling *et al.*, 1996; Smith, 1999). The EU's compensation payments (currently classified as 'blue box' payments) are likely to come under attack as being contrary to WTO principles, therefore increasing pressure for the EU to decouple these fully from production. The USA has laid down a challenge to the EU with its 1996 Federal Agricultural Improvement and Reform Act. This abolishes deficiency payments and replaces them and other subsidies with a single fixed per hectare payment decoupled from production and will, therefore, qualify as a 'green box' payment (Potter, 1998).

Changes in the world trading environment since the URA will also pose new problems and challenges for the WTO. For instance, the next round will contain more CPs than ever before (134), making it more difficult to reach common agreement. The European Commission has already set out its initial position by arguing that the next round should continue negotiations on reforms agreed in the URA. However, the Commission will seek to protect the multifunctional role of agriculture (now fully incorporated into official discourse as the 'European model of agriculture'), and will argue for the exemption of public good subsidies from negotiations which have little or no impact on trade (such as AEP and rural development); in other words it will argue for the continuation of green box payments but also, more controversially, for the continuation of blue box payments. It will also advocate the inclusion of social and environmental concerns on the agenda, such as food safety and quality, animal welfare and environmental standards, as the Commission believes that these are important trade concerns (CEC, 1999b). However, other CPs are likely to see these issues as an attempt by the Commission to find new excuses for the continuation of farm subsidies.

8.1.3   Agenda 2000

Negotiations over EU eastward expansion, together with the timetable and agenda for new WTO talks, provide the external political context within which the European Commission and member states drew up a package of reforms under Agenda 2000. These reforms, agreed by the European Council in May 1999, were the culmination of discussions and negotiations over more than three years. It is revealing to examine how the discussions relating to CAP reform progressed, to see what options were considered, and to observe Germany's position in the talks which started with Kohl's CDU-led government in power and ended under the SPD-led government of Schröder.

As in past reform discussions, the Commission and member states held widely diverging views on whether CAP reform was necessary, and if so, what form it should take and when it should occur. Three main policy positions were apparent between member states: the 'protectionists', the 'evolutionists' and the 'free marketeers'. The protectionist (or status quo) camp, headed by Germany, argued that no reform of the CAP was necessary. The evolutionists, headed by the Commission and France, favoured a continuation and adaptation of the 1992 reforms, while the free marketeers, headed by Britain, argued for radical liberalisation of the CAP (*Agra-Europe London*, 21.6.1996). Much of the debate centred on how agricultural markets would develop over the coming years, what negotiating stand the EU should adopt in the next WTO round and how best to absorb the agricultural sectors of the CEEC5 into the CAP. More fundamentally, the debate reflected differing national interests, and the relative powers of national farm lobbies.

In a 1995 strategy paper prepared for the Madrid summit, the Commission considered these three different policy positions, and argued strongly in favour of the evolutionary option (CEC, 1995b). It argued that, without CAP reform, surpluses would get out of hand and would make the CAP untenable in the long term. Moreover, there would be an intolerable strain on the CAP budget when enlargement took place, and the WTO would never accept a continuation of the current world trade agreement. The radical reform option, on the other hand, would be politically unfeasible and would threaten to undermine the whole basis of the CAP. Further evolutionary reform of the CAP, however, would make the CAP more competitive while preserving its integrity, and would be more acceptable to the WTO. The evolutionary approach would also support the multifunctional role of modern farmers who are not just agricultural producers but also 'stewards of the countryside, managers of natural resources, suppliers of services [and] rural entrepreneurs' (CEC, 1995b, p. 23). This statement reflects a significant change in the agricultural policy discourse away from a productivist ideology towards a new post-productivist vision, already noted in Chapters 5 and 6 in relation to Germany. That the German Agriculture Minister Borchert was using similar discourse, suggests an emerging consensus with the EU as to the future direction for agriculture.

A key issue in discussions was the question of compensation payments. As noted above, it was almost certain that the next WTO round of agriculture negotiations would target the EU's compensation payments as being contrary to WTO principles. To be acceptable to the WTO, they would have to be decoupled from production. As well as this consideration, compensation payments were a major source of CAP expenditure, and there was a debate over whether the CEEC5 would be entitled to compensation payments when they acceded to the EU. The Commission argued that the CEEC5 would be excluded from receiving compensation payments because they would experience higher prices from membership, and funding could instead be concentrated on improving agricultural structures and the wider rural economy, and on introducing environmental measures. The validity of this argument has, however, been questioned by Buckwell and Tangermann (1997).

The Commission's proposals prompted a negative response from the German farm lobby, who questioned the Commission's assumptions. For instance, Borchert spoke out against further reforms in a speech to the DBV in December 1995, arguing that the EU should not start to negotiate on CAP reform before the start of the next WTO talks, so as not to undermine the EU's negotiating position (*Agra-Europe London*, 8.12.1995). The deputy director of the BML, speaking in a personal capacity at a conference on CAP reform in October 1996, argued against reductions in price support because of an anticipated increase in world grain prices in the medium to long term (10–20 years). He also argued in favour of gradual expansion of the EU eastwards, with long transition periods before full membership to ease the financial burden on the CAP (Goeman, 1996).

Unofficially, however, the BML recognised the inevitability of further CAP reform. In June 1996 it produced a discussion paper as a basis for talks with the *Länder* governments (BML, 1996b; for an English summary see *Agra-Europe London*, 21.6.1996). In this paper the BML argued that the status quo option could not absorb the CEEC5 within acceptable budget limits. The BML, therefore, supported the Commission's evolutionary reform option. It recognised that the maintenance of compensation payments for farmers was politically and socially important, but that the present payments were barriers to structural change in agriculture. If compensation payments were decoupled from production, this would introduce a higher degree of market forces into the CAP and would be easier and cheaper to administer than the current compensation payments. The new payments could be linked to agri-environmental schemes, as opposed to the current system where the two were separate. The BML realised that any talk of reform would be politically unpopular with farmers as it would mean income losses. Therefore, the BML supported the concept of devolving responsibility for certain agri-environmental and social payments to the national level. In this way, Germany could continue using these national payments to partly offset income losses that farmers might experience (see Chapter 6).

The discrepancy between Germany's official and unofficial policy positions can be explained by political and economic factors. A key motivating factor in favour of reform was the need to contain Germany's EU budget contributions. The government also faced pressure from the industrial lobby to come to an agreement that would not jeopardise the EU's position in WTO talks (*Süddeutsche Zeitung*, 1998). It also reflected, perhaps, the growing influence of the new *Länder* in agricultural policy-making. In particular, the economic advantages of a liberalisation of the CAP for farmers in the new *Länder* were recognised (von Witzke, 1996; Wehrheim, 1998). The official obstructor position reflected the perception that most German farmers would lose out from the reforms, and showed a reluctance on the part of politicians to antagonise the farm lobby in the run-up to the 1998 federal elections.

A further source of discussion on CAP reform concerned rural policy and the Structural Funds (see Section 7.4.4). The Agricultural Commissioner Franz Fischler argued strongly for a broadening of agricultural policy to include rural development and environmental policies, in line with his post-productivist vision of farming. This approach would support a more diversified rural economy, and would enable further structural change in agriculture by creating alternative economic opportunities. While politicians in all member states favoured the principle of increasing the profile of rural development, tensions emerged over the budgetary implications of any increase in funding for rural development policy, particularly if this was to be at the expense of farmers.

An EU-sponsored conference in November 1996 entitled 'Rural Europe – Perspectives for the Future' in Cork, Ireland, put forward the Cork Declaration that set out a radical vision for the future of EU rural policy based on sustainable development (CEC, 1996b). The principles upon which this approach would be based were laid down in a ten-point rural development programme (Table 8.2).

While the Cork Declaration was welcomed by policy-makers and academics in the rural development field (for instance, Pretty, 1998), national governments were more cautious. German agriculture minister Borchert welcomed the Cork Declaration's goals, but did not want the declaration to pre-empt discussion on the future of the CAP in the CAM, and he feared that any increase in funding for rural development would be at the expense of farm subsidies (*Agra-Europe Bonn*, 23.12.1996d). He and the French Agriculture Minister refused to support the Cork Declaration, which meant that it could not be endorsed by EU member state leaders at the Dublin summit of December 1996. This obstructor position stresses the point made in Section 7.5 that any increase in rural development funding is likely to be seen as a threat by the farm lobby.

In July 1997 the Commission published the Agenda 2000 proposals, which largely reflected the Commission's evolutionary approach to CAP reform (CEC, 1997a). The key proposals were: to further reduce price support for the cereal, beef and dairy sectors; to partially compensate farmers for any income losses with a standard flat rate per hectare payment (for cereals) and per head premiums (for beef and dairy cattle) and to abolish set-aside, but to guarantee milk quotas until 2006. Some devolution of decision-making to the member state level was proposed (termed differentiation). For instance, member states could link compensation payments to environmental conditions (a policy principle known as cross-compliance). Further, member states would have some flexibility over setting payment rates and conditions. An increase in the budget for agri-environmental schemes was also proposed. The Commission claimed that these measures would make the

Table 8.2   The ten-point rural development programme for the European Union

Rural preference	The EU must give priority to sustainable rural development by reversing out-migration, combating poverty, stimulating employment and equality of opportunity and improving well-being, while at the same time preserving and improving the quality of the rural environment
Integrated approach	Policies that take a multidisciplinary and multisectoral approach, and apply to all rural areas in the Union, although giving greater financial support to areas most in need
Diversification	Policies that promote social and economic diversification of rural areas by providing a framework for self-sustaining private and community-based initiatives, and promoting the development of viable rural communities and renewal of villages
Sustainability	Policies that benefit today's generation without prejudicing the options for future generations
Subsidiarity	Policies that are as decentralised as possible and that are based on partnership and cooperation between local, regional, national and European levels
Simplification	Policies must be better co-ordinated to avoid overlap and reduce complexity
Programming	Each region must have a single rural development programme that is coherent and transparent
Finance	Greater attention must be paid to improving availability of private capital to finance local rural development initiatives
Management	Regional and local government and community groups must be given better support and back-up services
Evaluation and research	All policies must be monitored and evaluated to ensure their efficient and effective functioning

Source: CEC (1996b).

CAP simpler, more transparent, and more decentralised, with more emphasis on social and environmental considerations.

In addition, Agenda 2000 included proposals for the integration of the agricultural sectors of the CEEC5 into the EU. It was proposed that pre-accession aid be granted to support restructuring of the farm and food industries, and that a transitional phase would be implemented following accession before the agricultural markets were fully integrated into the CAP. CEEC5 farmers would not be eligible for compensation payments. The Commission's aim was to achieve as much convergence between the agricultural sectors of the CEEC5 and the EU15 as possible before accession, to minimise the impact of entry on the CAP. Agenda 2000 also included proposals for reform of the Structural Funds, with implications for agriculture and rural development. It was proposed to reduce the seven current objectives to three, thereby reducing the coverage of regional aid from 51 per cent of the EU's population to between 35 and 40 per cent. Objectives 2 and 5b would be merged into one objective, while Objective 5a funding would be transferred from the Structural Funds to the EAGGF Guarantee Fund to simplify funding arrangements. In addition, 45 billion ECU would be assigned to the CEEC5 as pre-accession regional aid.

Initial reactions to these proposals, as might be expected, were mixed. While the British government welcomed the proposals as a step in the right direction, the free-marketeer *Agra-Europe London* strongly criticised the reform package, arguing that the cost of the CAP would continue to rise, and querying whether the Commission could exclude the CEEC5 from compensation payments on EU entry (*Agra-Europe London*, 18.7.1997a). It also criticised the failure of the Commission to abolish milk quotas or to fully decouple compensation payments for cereals and livestock from production (*Agra-Europe London*, 18.7.1997b). The Germans and the Austrians were identified as the main culprits for inaction on milk quotas. Additionally, the proposals were criticised for the low profile given to the environment and to rural development, despite Fischler's personally stated commitment to these goals. The Agenda 2000 proposals were described as a stop-gap measure to postpone difficult decisions until the next WTO talks were under way and eastward expansion was imminent (*Agra-Europe London*, 18.7.1997a).

The proposals were also criticised, for different reasons, by farm lobbies. COPA warned that farmers' interests were to be sacrificed to pay for the costs of EU enlargement, and it opposed any further moves to switch from price support to direct payments. The French government and French farmers' unions criticised the proposals, arguing that they would undermine the EU's negotiating position in the next round of WTO talks (*Agra-Europe London*, 18.7.1997c), similar to Borchert's argument in 1995 (see above). The DBV published a detailed response to the proposals in April 1998, setting out its objections, and putting forward its own proposals (DBV, 1998). The main objections concerned the loss of jobs in Germany that Agenda 2000 would bring about (an estimated 300 000 jobs in agriculture and the food industry); loss of farm income due to only partial compensation for price cuts; a greater financial burden on Germany to fund the EAGGF; the danger of unfair competition developing within the EU because of partial renationalisation of the CAP; higher production costs due to stricter environmental standards; and a further increase in bureaucracy. There was also concern that the incorporation of Objective 5a funding into the Guarantee Fund, might threaten the budget for market measures. While the DBV welcomed continued Objective 1 funding for the new *Länder*, it was concerned that many areas in the old *Länder* would lose structural funding.

Further, the DBV was doubtful if the reform proposals would help strengthen the economies of rural areas. It feared, on the contrary, that they would weaken them through further job losses (*Agra-Europe Bonn*, 5.7.1999a).

The DBV concluded that the proposals would neither strengthen the EU's negotiating position in the next WTO round, nor help the entry of the CEEC5 into the EU. The DBV even questioned whether the reforms would support the Commission's vision of a multifunctional farm sector which was meant to be competitive, but also aimed at maintaining high environmental and social standards. The DBV argued strongly for a continuation of the current CAP, with only minor adjustments (mainly involving additional support, such as greater support for the production of bio-resources; see Chapter 6).

However, the DBV's negotiating position with the German government was considerably weakened following the federal elections in October 1998 and the replacement of the CDU/CSU coalition with a SPD/Green coalition government under Schröder. For the first time in the history of the FRG, the agriculture minister (Funke) came from the SPD (see Table 1.1), the party with the least allegiance to the farm lobby (see Chapter 2). Moreover, final agreement on the Agenda 2000 CAP reform measures was reached by agriculture ministers in March 1999 during the German presidency of the Council of Ministers, when the German government could not afford politically to be seen as an obstructor. The final reforms included some concessions to member states, but also some toughening of the original proposals (Table 8.3). For instance, the DBV's request for a continuation of set-aside was met, but other requests seem to have been ignored. Indeed, the agreed cut in the milk intervention price was greater than initially proposed (15 rather than 10 per cent). The reforms also allow for more subsidiarity of decision-making than before. For instance, many policies are optional (such as cross-compliance), and the national envelopes provide a measure of national discretion which will be welcomed by Germany.

8.2 German agriculture in transition?

Section 8.1 has focused on external factors influencing European agricultural policy. Equally important from Germany's perspective have been domestic political changes in the political complexion of the state. This final section of the book will discuss the likely implications for agricultural policy and for farmers of Germany's new SPD–Green coalition government (elected October 1998). First, we will outline the main agricultural policy changes introduced under the Schröder government, before reflecting on what prospects are in store for German agricultural policy and for German farmers in the early twenty-first century.

8.2.1 Agriculture in crisis?

One year into the new Schröder government, German agriculture is facing what some have termed its greatest crisis yet in the history of the FRG and reunified Germany (von Urff, 1999). The agricultural policy climate has changed for the worse from the DBV's viewpoint with the election of the

Table 8.3   Agenda 2000: policies for agriculture and rural development

---

Arable sector
- Reduction in cereals intervention price by 15% to 95.35 €/tonne over two years
- Set-aside to be retained at 10% (small farmers exempted)
- A flat rate compensation payment will be introduced of 63 €/ha. National governments can choose to link these payments to environmental services

Beef sector
- Reduction in intervention price by 30% to 1950 €/tonne over three years
- An increase in direct payments to beef farmers
- Each member state to be given a national envelope of funding to be spent on aiding beef farmers

Dairy sector
- Reduction in intervention price of 15% over three years starting in 2005
- An increase in direct payments to dairy farmers
- A 1.5% increase in quota for young farmers and farmers in mountain areas starting in 2005
- Each member state to be given a national envelope of funding to be spent on aiding dairy farmers

Accompanying measures
- Early retirement scheme
- Compensatory payments in LFAs
- Afforestation schemes
- Agri-environmental schemes
- Investments in farm businesses
- Aid for setting up young farmers
- Training for farmers and foresters
- Processing and marketing of agricultural products

Rural development measures
- Land improvement
- Land consolidation
- Introduction of agricultural management services
- Marketing of quality agricultural products
- Basic services for rural economies and populations
- Renovation and development of villages; preservation of rural heritage
- Diversification of agricultural activities and connected activities, aimed at creating multiple activities or alternative incomes
- Management of agricultural water resources
- Improvement of rural infrastructure linked to agricultural development
- Promotion of tourism and crafts
- Environmental protection linked to agriculture, forestry and nature management, and improving animal health
- Restoring the potential of agricultural production following damage by natural disasters and introducing appropriate preventative measures
- Financial engineering

Table 8.3   Agenda 2000: policies for agriculture and rural development *(continued)*

Reform of the Structural Funds

- Objective 1: underdeveloped regions, ultra-peripheral regions and the former Objective 6 regions. These regions to receive 70% of the Structural Fund budget, covering 22% of the EU population
- Objective 2: areas faced with particular reconversion difficulties: fragile rural areas (5% of EU population); areas undergoing socio-economic change in industry and services (10% of EU population); urban areas in crisis (2% per cent of EU population); areas dependent on fishing (1% of EU population). To receive 11.5% of the budget, with at least 5% for rural areas. Not to include more than 18% of the EU area
- Objective 3: adaptation and modernisation of policies and systems for education, training and employment in areas not covered by Objectives 1 or 2. To receive 23% of the budget
- Areas which lose Objective 1, 2, or 5b status after the year 2000 are eligible for transitional support until 2005
- LEADER+ community initiative for rural development, to promote the creation of integrated rural development schemes across the whole of the EU

Source: CEC (1999a,c).

SPD–Green coalition government and the appointment of the first ever SPD agriculture minister (Funke). SPD-led governments have historically tended to be less farmer-friendly than CDU-led governments, as the SPD's political base is firmly urban. Although SPD-led governments have only been in power in Germany for 14 years since 1949 (see Table 1.2), some general patterns are emerging. Chapter 3 highlighted how the Brandt and Schmidt governments (1969–82) adopted agricultural policies that often alienated farmers, such as the highly controversial Ertl Plan of selective subsidisation, and other drastic Ertl policies which left farmers worse off with regard to incomes than previous and subsequent CDU-led governments. Early indications are that the Schröder government is adopting a similar strategy that is likely to further alienate farmers, reinforcing the notion of a cycle of farmer-friendly CDU-led periods and relatively farmer-unfriendly SPD-led phases.

The most dramatic agricultural policy change since 1998 has been a radical package of public spending cuts amounting to DM 30 billion (Euro 15 billion) to be implemented in 2000 (rising to DM 50 billion in 2003), to reduce Germany's budget deficit and to reduce Germany's spiralling foreign debt (which increased dramatically during the 1990s due to the cost of reunification) (BML, 1999b). Proposed spending cuts and tax reforms are set out in a new government strategy entitled 'Plan for the Future 2000' (*Zukunftsprogramm 2000*), and will be enacted though a new budget reform law (*Haushaltssanierungsgesetz*).

The proposed cuts to the agricultural budget amount to DM 857 million for 2000, rising to DM 1.058 billion in 2001, DM 1.229 billion in 2002 and DM 1.429 billion in 2003 (*Agra-Europe Bonn*, 7.6.1999). For German farmers this will be equivalent to farm income losses of 5–10 per cent over the coming years (approximately DM 5 billion/year and equivalent to DM 5000–15 000/farm per year). Even the drastic budget cuts by Ertl in the late 1970s/early 1980s (see Chapter 2), and the dismantling of MCAs during the 1980s/1990s (see Chapter 3), pale into insignificance compared to such projected financial losses. The outlook for German farmers is all the bleaker as these budget cuts coincide with the implementation of Agenda 2000. Although the Agenda 2000 reforms do allow for some national discretion over agricultural subsidies (such as the national spending envelopes and AEP), it is doubtful whether these will be sufficient to offset predicted farm income losses arising from agricultural spending cuts and price cuts.

The main proposed spending cuts in the agricultural budget are to social security (particularly old age pensions and accident insurance). The GAK budget will also be frozen or cut, and diesel subsidies will be phased out by 2003 (at the same time petrol prices will rise due to higher taxes). Agriculture Minister Funke has stated, however, that he will protect the budgets for farm structural improvements and for farm diversification, and will increase spending on bio-resources (*Agra-Europe Bonn*, 7.6.1999, 28.6.1999). German farmers are, therefore, beginning to lose many of the hard-fought social payments gained during previous decades. The predicted outcome will be accelerated farm structural change (forced structural change according to the DBV; cf. *Agra-Europe Bonn*, 26.7.1999b), but in contrast to earlier phases of accelerated change (see Table 2.1) that were largely driven by pull factors (such as new employment opportunities in manufacturing industry), structural change in the early twenty-first century will be driven by push factors as farms become economically unviable. Yet, national unemployment levels are at their highest since the 1940s. Many German farmers are, therefore, caught in a double squeeze: they may be forced from their farms for economic reasons but there are few alternative employment opportunities available.

Although these spending cuts and their likely outcome for farmers may appear harsh, some argue that these measures are inevitable, and are a simple reflection of the fact that the German family farm model, advocated since the early 1950s (particularly by CDU-led governments), but recognised as unsustainable by Mansholt as early as 1968 (see Chapter 3), has finally been exposed as untenable (Höll, 1999; von Urff, 1999). We have shown in this book how successive governments have sought to support farm incomes by using backdoor subsidies such as MCAs, agri-environmental payments, tax rebates or social security payments to farmers. At the turn of the new millennium the federal government has neither strong economic nor political incentives to continue such backdoor subsidisation (Tangermann, 1997).

There are currently, therefore, a mix of circumstances, both domestic and European, that militate against the interests of German farmers.

It is no wonder that farmers are angered by the government's spending plans, and the DBV has openly criticised the government. Sonnleitner, the DBV chairperson (since 1997), has stated that 'the situation for German farmers is at its worst ever', and that, for the first time, the SPD is breaking the traditional party political consensus on the survival of German family farms (*Agra-Europe Bonn*, 28.6.1999). Arguments came to a head at a farmers' meeting in Cottbus (June 1999), where Chancellor Schröder openly antagonised farmers by arguing that more financial cuts had to be expected in the future (*Agra-Europe Bonn*, 12.7.1999b, 26.7.1999b). Schröder used the meeting to speak out openly against farmers' 'excessive' demands; a statement that was welcomed by the SPD electorate (von Urff, 1999), but that led to one of the largest and angriest demonstrations by farmers since 1949 (*Bayerisches landwirtschaftliches Wochenblatt*, 1999; *Agra-Europe Bonn*, 26.7.1999b).

8.2.2 From productivism to multifunctionalism

Despite the pessimistic forecasts for German farmers painted by the DBV, the picture is not all bleak, and there are both regionally and sectorally differentiated prospects for the farm sector. Key factors that will differentially affect the way farmers are affected by Agenda 2000 and by federal budget cuts are market trends for different commodities and *Land*-level agricultural policies. In the former case, it will be the larger, more efficient farmers who will gain the greatest potential benefits from Agenda 2000 through increased export opportunities. Large arable farms of the new *Länder*, as well as large family farms in Schleswig-Holstein and Niedersachsen are likely to be winners. For farmers in the new *Länder*, the early 1990s was a period of economic and social hardship, while the new millennium represents new opportunities. In fact, the farm sector in the new *Länder* is in a more competitive position than the farm sector in the old *Länder*, and the Agenda 2000 reforms have been welcomed by new *Länder* governments. Cuts in compensation payments will, however, disadvantage farmers in marginal farming areas throughout Germany with fewer opportunities to intensify or diversify production. Many newly established cooperative and corporate farms in the more marginal areas of the new *Länder* (much of Brandenburg and Mecklenburg-Vorpommern), many of which are indebted, will face further financial hardship, as will many farmers in hill and upland areas of the old *Länder*. The continuation of milk quotas until 2006 has postponed difficult decisions for dairy farmers, but it leaves dairy farming in a state of uncertainty and with a feeling that structural change is inevitable, especially among small family farms.

We have already highlighted how individual *Länder* have displayed differing commitments to AEP (see Chapter 6). This differentiated approach is likely to continue and become even more marked. For instance, the southern, wealthy *Länder* of Bayern and Baden-Württemberg, both with a large farm population and many marginal farming areas, are still highly committed to the family farm model and are strongly opposed to Agenda 2000. They are likely to seek to cushion the blow to small farmers through continued or increased use of backdoor subsidies paid from their own *Länder* budgets through agri-environmental schemes or other forms of farm support (under the umbrella of Agenda 2000). Other *Länder* are less likely to devote additional resources to farm support, either because they are too poor (for instance, Rheinland-Pfalz, Brandenburg, Mecklenburg-Vorpommern and Thüringen); because they have a competitive farm sector (for instance, Sachsen-Anhalt, Schleswig-Holstein and Niedersachsen); or because the farm lobby is too weak (for instance, Nordrhein-Westfalen, Hessen and possibly Sachsen).

The geography of agriculture and agricultural policy in Germany is, therefore, likely to become more differentiated, with Borchert's and the Commission's vision of a multifunctional agriculture becoming a geographical reality. Some regions will become more commercialised in their agricultural production, others will specialise in agri-environmental farming and the production of high-quality foods and 'amenity', and, most controversially, other regions will experience a retreat of agriculture. There will also be small pockets of specialised farming (for niche markets). Part-time farming is also likely to further increase its relative share of the farm sector as an alternative to exiting from farming altogether. A key challenge for the government, the DBV, farmers and rural policy-makers, therefore, will be to adapt to the new multifunctional agricultural policy framework, to smooth the transition of farmers and workers who leave the agricultural industry, and to support the adaptation and diversification of rural areas. Interestingly, the geographical division between the old and new *Länder*, which dominated Germany's agricultural policy agenda in the 1990s (and, arguably, dominated the agenda in the whole post-war period) will, gradually, be broken down and will be replaced by new geographical and sectoral divisions and alliances. Geographical differentiation will be increased by EU Structural Fund designations. The regions which obtain Objective 1 or 2 status will continue to receive European funding for agricultural adjustment and rural diversification, and, therefore, will have greater resources to smooth the transition.

As research in Britain has shown (for instance, Ward and Munton, 1992; Morris and Potter, 1995; Wilson, 1996, 1997a, 1997c), farmers who are forced to take on a set of policies that emphasise countryside protection over commodity production find it hard to adjust. The change in attitudes and behaviour that is required of farmers can only be achieved gradually and is likely to take several generations, as a change in the very identity of farmers is required (Burton, 1998). Yet, for many German farmers survival means having to take on new policy opportunities now, often without having been able to make the necessary attitudinal adjustments. It is likely, therefore, that many farmers will feel increasingly unhappy about their new roles as multifunctional farmers; a factor which may further influence farmers to seek opportunities outside farming or to become part-time farmers. Indeed, over 50 per cent of German farms are now farmed on a part-time basis, so that the response of these farmers to policy changes will be important. It is unlikely that the number of part-time farmers will decrease, given that they are generally in a financially more secure position than full-time farmers, and that farming is only part of their identity. However, the part-time farm sector contains a wide variety of farmers in terms of farm business size and attitudes towards farming, so that the future of part-time farming is likely to be as differentiated as it is for full-time farming.

8.2.3   The farm lobby

A central aim of this book has been to explore the apparent paradox that exists in Germany between agriculture's small economic contribution to, and increasing burden on, the national economy, and the powerful position that German farmers have held in national politics. This paradoxical position has enabled the farm lobby, represented by the DBV, to lobby the federal government to support farm incomes at national and European level. While farmers also wield considerable political power in other EU member states (notably France), in no other member state is the imbalance between economic and political power so marked.

We have explained this paradox by identifying the following reasons. First, Germany's federal structure and electoral system of proportional representation both favour the farm lobby. For instance, the farm lobby wields considerable power in the more rural *Länder* (notably Bayern), and, therefore, has influence in Germany's upper house (Bundesrat). Bayern has also played a pivotal role in many national coalition governments through its own political party, the CSU, which has been an important coalition partner for the CDU, and which draws much of its support from the farm population. Indeed, three agriculture ministers have come from the CSU (Niklas, Höcherl and Kiechle). The CDU has been the dominant political force in German politics in the post-war era, and has traditionally supported farmers' interests. The SPD and other parties, although relying less on the rural vote, have been reluctant to antagonise farmers, so that a consensus has reigned over agricultural policy, and it has rarely become a party political issue. This situation may be beginning to change, however, since the 1998 election of the SPD/Green coalition under Chancellor Schröder. The high level of autonomy enjoyed by the federal agricultural minister has also enabled successive ministers to follow their own policy agendas (which have often diverged from Germany's national interest).

A second reason is the success of the DBV in lobbying for farmers' interests. As discussed in Chapters 2 and 4, the DBV quickly re-established itself after the Second World War as the main farm lobby group, and managed to establish itself in the new *Länder* following reunification. It has been successful in maintaining a unified policy position based on the family farm model. As suggested in Chapters 2 and 4, this cohesiveness may be partly attributable to the ideological threat posed by the GDR which served to strengthen the FRG's political and ideological commitment to widespread property ownership. The DBV's power has been strengthened by close links with the BML, and even personal friendships between the DBV presidents and the agriculture ministers (such as between Kiechle and von Heereman). The longevity of DBV presidents has strengthened their authority and influence. The DBV has never been challenged by any other rural actor, as other rural interest groups such as the environmental lobby, the agri-business lobby or consumer groups, have failed to present a unified front. The DBV's power base, however, is threatened from within by its declining membership, and from without by changes to the CAP that threaten to open up divisions within the farm lobby. Reunification has also represented a challenge to the DBV's commitment to the family farm, as family farming has not become the dominant model in the new *Länder*.

A third reason is Germany's post-war economic prosperity, that has enabled the federal government to financially support an expensive agricultural policy in return for farmers' political support. Although the CAP has meant that Germany has been the main net contributor to the EU budget, this has been tolerated as a trade-off for Germany's gains from manufacturing exports to other EU member states. Consumers have also tolerated high food prices because of their high standards of living. There has been general public support for a high-cost agricultural policy that has delivered high-quality food products and has also socially supported farmers. This consensus is challenged, however, by internal economic strains arising from the cost of reunification, and external strains arising from the WTO, whereby agricultural policy is being linked to trade policy in other areas, notably manufacturing. Eastward expansion of the EU also threatens to increase the size of the CAP budget, and therefore increase Germany's net contributions.

Over the coming decade the political influence of the DBV is likely to continue to decline, however. Accelerated structural change in agriculture – leading to a decline in full-time farmers – will lead to a further decline in both DBV membership and influence over the farm vote. Further, it will be increasingly difficult for the DBV to present a united voice on farm policy issues, as the interests of German farmers after reunification have become more disparate. Finally, the size of the agricultural budget has become a political issue in Germany, and, given the declining political influence of the farm lobby, is now seen as a prime target for cuts. The era of generous backdoor subsidisation of farmers may be at an end, to be replaced with more targeted subsidies, although, as suggested in Section 8.2.2, agricultural policy may become more geographically differentiated.

Although German farmers are in arguably their weakest political position in the post-war period, they will not allow the SPD-led government to pursue farmer-unfriendly policies without any resistance, and the implementation of domestic budget cuts and Agenda 2000 reforms for the CAP and Structural Funds will be contested. For instance, Sonnleitner has argued that the government is breaking the spirit of the 1955 Agriculture Act (see Section 2.4.1), which laid down a commitment to equalise the living standards of farmers with those of other occupations (*Süddeutsche Zeitung*, 1999). Funke has already backed down on Agenda 2000 by agreeing to DBV demands that no cross-compliance or modulation of compensation payments will be introduced (*Agra-Europe Bonn*, 31.5.1999). The DBV remains the major farm and rural lobby group in Germany, with 550 000 members, and retains close links with the BML. Food scares such as the BSE crisis have served to stress to consumers (and politicians) the importance of ensuring high-quality food products. Future re-election of a CDU-led government (especially in coalition with the CSU) would also temporarily halt the decline in the farm lobby's fortunes, but it would be unlikely to reverse key farm policy decisions.

8.2.4 Germany's role in Europe

Another key question in this book has been whether Germany's role in European agricultural policy can be categorised as leader, partner or obstructor. Our analysis has suggested that Germany can be best categorised as partner, but a highly influential one, following its commitment to being a model European. Throughout most of the CAP's history, Germany has supported its development, even though the CAP has rarely been in Germany's national interest but has often been contrary to it, and has generally been opposed by the German farm lobby. For instance, in Chapter 3 we discussed how Germany only initially agreed to the establishment of the CAP as a trade-off for the establishment of the common market. However, although Germany has often compromised its interests on fundamental questions of European agricultural policy, its economic and political weight within the EU has enabled it to win important concessions over time which have tended to soften the impact of policy changes on German agriculture, and which have tended to have a negative influence on the CAP as a whole. For instance, initial agreement to the CAP was given in return for concessions on agricultural price levels, and much of the complex agri-monetary policy that subsequently developed was at Germany's insistence. The 1992 CAP reforms were also watered down at Germany's insistence. In fact, Germany has on many occasions successfully manipulated the CAP to pursue its own national interests and to protect farmers' incomes.

There have been few occasions when Germany has stepped out of its role as partner in European agricultural policy to become a leader or obstructor. In the latter case it could be argued that this has only been on occasions when Germany has faced extreme domestic pressure from its farm lobby, such as Kiechle's veto in 1985, or when Germany has been able to hide behind other, more vocal, obstructors, such as France (during the Uruguay Round GATT negotiations), or Britain (over the level of EU budget contributions). That Germany has always, to date, ended up compromising on agricultural policy issues has angered the German farm lobby, but has highlighted where Germany's political and economic priorities lie. Germany has tended to take an explicit leadership role only on (arguably) less important issues in European agricultural policy, such as AEP or food quality standards (see Chapter 6). On occasions leadership has been forced on Germany, however, such as when Germany has held the presidency of the CAM (see Section 8.2), but it is significant that Germany has never pushed for a German agricultural commissioner in Brussels (Möhlers, 1997).

It is also important to note that policy-making in Germany, not only on agricultural matters, has been influenced by EU membership. For instance, in Chapter 7 we commented on the Europeanisation of rural policy through the Structural Funds, which is challenging Germany's traditional top-down sectoral policy-making approach. While the European Commission represents an additional layer of government and bureaucracy, EU policies are enabling new alliances and territorial units of decision-making to emerge, which is changing the nature of rural governance at the local and regional level. It also further challenges the hegemonic position of the BML and the DBV over rural policy. As European integration proceeds, the policy-making powers of nation states will become ever more constrained, and instead governments will be increasingly forced to act within a European framework. Germany has been one of the leading advocates of European integration for this very reason, and, as illustrated in this book in relation to agricultural and rural policy, has so far successfully moulded European policies to suit its national interests (although not always its agricultural interests).

Germany's future role in European agricultural policy is likely to continue to remain as influential partner. Under the SPD-led government, however, it is likely to be more supportive of CAP reforms, as it will not allow the farm lobby to get in the way of any agreement on EU expansion or WTO trade policy, and is less likely to demand concessions for its farmers. This should pave the way for greater liberalisation of the CAP, although Germany (and other member states) are also likely to lobby for partial renationalisation of the CAP to enable some leeway for backdoor subsidisation. Yet again, Germany's agricultural interests do not coincide with Germany's manufacturing and wider strategic interests, and it seems inevitable that, once again, farmers' interests will be sacrificed for manufacturing interests.

Germany has played a key role in discussions on EU enlargement, as reunification has increased Germany's political weight within the EU, while the collapse of the Iron Curtain means that Germany now lies at the centre of Europe, occupying a pivotal position between Western and Eastern Europe. Reunified Germany is bordered by two CEECs (Poland and the Czech Republic), and is now a major country of transit for trade. Of all EU member states, Germany is set to benefit most from new export opportunities arising from the opening up of eastern economies (Agra-Europe Special Study, 1997). The decision to move Germany's capital from Bonn to Berlin is symbolic of Germany's new political and geostrategic position at the heart of Europe. These developments further increase Germany's political and economic weight within Europe, and increase the pressure for Germany to take a leadership role. However, it will always be difficult for Germany to adopt a strong leadership role, and, as Geiss (1996) noted, the Germans must face up to difficult questions regarding their place in Europe (see Chapter 1). Germany's role in Europe also depends on the roles adopted by other EU member states in relation to Germany, and the signs are that other EU member states are not yet ready to accept German leadership (Bertram, 1994).

8.2.5 Agriculture in reunified Germany

We stated in the introduction that German reunification in 1990 was an unforeseen event that added a new and potentially highly significant dimension to agricultural politics and policy-making in the new Germany. Our analysis has revealed that the most significant impact of reunification has been at the ideological level. First, the demise of the GDR has removed the Communist threat and, therefore, undermined some of the ideological justification for the family farm model. Second, the farm structure that has emerged in reunified Germany, comprising corporate and cooperative farms as well as large family farms, poses another threat to the family farm model by demonstrating the competitiveness of a more commercial farm model.

The dramatic restructuring of agriculture in the new *Länder* that has occurred since reunification has led to a competitive agricultural structure emerging, but this has been achieved at enormous social cost, with widespread unemployment. Reunification has served to raise the profile of rural development within Germany, and thereby shifted the rural debate somewhat away from analysis of farm incomes. This may further challenge the ability of the DBV and the BML to control the rural policy agenda in future.

Although it is still only ten years since reunification of Germany, and therefore still early to evaluate its full impact, it does appear as though the 1990s will be viewed in retrospect as a turning point in the history of Germany and Europe. The collapse of Communism has transformed the political and economic climate of Europe. It has removed the ideological and military threat to European democracy, and opened the door for a vastly expanded EU. These events have shattered the post-war prosperity and complacency of the FRG (Geiss, 1996) by precipitating Germany into its worst post-war recession, and challenging some long-held political and economic beliefs. In relation to agriculture, reunification has exposed the unsustainability of the family farm model, both ideologically and economically, although Germany is likely to remain a nation dominated by family farming for some time to come.

German agriculture has undergone many changes in the post-war period. It evolved along two contrasting political, economic and ideological development paths between 1945 and 1990 during the division of Germany, which, we have argued, influenced the agricultural policy trajectories of both the FRG and GDR. Reunification in 1990 has led to fundamental restructuring of the agricultural sector of the former GDR. In the FRG, the family farm model was the cornerstone of agricultural policy up until the 1990s, reinforced by the ever-present threat posed by the collective farm model of the GDR. Within the framework of the family farm model, farming in the FRG evolved to become one of the most mechanised and intensive farming systems in Western Europe, albeit with one of the most inefficient structures. Farmers were protected by their political influence and by Germany's economic prosperity, although they faced many challenges to their security, not least entry to the EEC in 1957, the formation of the CAP in the 1960s, the Mansholt Plan of 1968 followed by the Ertl Plan of the 1970s and the imposition of milk quotas in 1984. In the 1990s, however, the family farm model has been challenged from within by reunification and from without by the URA and by reform of the CAP.

The early years of the twenty-first century will see the development of a German agricultural policy founded on a vision of a multifunctional agriculture within a diversified and differentiated rural economy. The certainty and security that German farmers enjoyed in the post-war period are over, and farmers will have to adjust themselves to living in a climate of political and financial uncertainty for some time to come.

Notes

1 Introduction

1. Throughout this book we will use the term *Länder* for the German regions as there is no equivalent translation in English.
2. The singular of *Länder*.
3. One of the most influential foreign ministers in the history of the FRG, Hans-Dietrich Genscher, came from the ranks of the FDP.
4. Egon Krenz led the GDR Communist Party for a brief period in 1989.

2 FRG Agricultural Structures and Policies, 1945–90

1. We use the word 'deficiency' here with regard to the FRG's small and unproductive farm structures in the context of more efficient holdings in other parts of Western Europe.
2. Similar partible inheritance laws could also be found in Spain, northern France, the Benelux countries and Italy.
3. Until the early 1970s, the DBV possesed the monopoly of farm representation in the FRG. The part-time farmers' organisation (Deutscher Bundesverband der Landwirte im Nebenberuf) and the Arbeitsgemeinschaft bäuerliche Landwirtschaft, both established in the 1970s, have always been of minor importance (Hendriks, 1991; Höll and von Meyer, 1996).
4. The principle of the social market economy was particularly advocated by SPD-led governments between 1969 and 1982, and has formed the main economic philosophy since the establishment of the FRG in 1949. See Chapter 3 for a detailed discussion of the political background within which agricultural policies in the FRG have been formulated.
5. It needs to be noted, however, that available opportunities for off-farm employment also have to be seen as a cause for the small-scale nature of farms (i.e. farmers did not have sufficient time to manage large holdings).
6. This threefold classification was changed in 1995, and replaced by a twofold classification of full- and part-time farms (*Agrarbericht*, 1997).
7. It is important to note, however, that the discussion here focuses on *farm incomes* alone. As about 50 per cent of farms in the FRG have been part-time or side-line farms (see Table 2.3), these farmers supplement their meagre farm incomes with other, often relatively well-paid, earnings. For part-time farms the discussion should, therefore, only be seen in the context of *farm incomes* and not of the *total earnings* of farm households.
8. It is interesting to note that in retaliation to FRG criticism of collectivisation of holdings in Eastern Germany, the GDR described *Flurbereinigung* as 'fascist' – a clear indication of the political and ideological tensions that characterised FRG–GDR relationships between 1949 and 1990 (see Chapter 4).
9. This also included remote upland rural districts in Rheinland-Pfalz (Hunsrück mountains) portrayed in the TV series *Heimat*.

10. The problems of selective subsidisation were a main incentive for the formation of the farmers' union for part-time farmers (Deutscher Bauernverband der Landwirte im Nebenberuf), a new lobby group fighting for the rights of part-time farmers in the FRG and reunified Germany (never a real challenge to the DBV).

11. The new Agriculture Minister Funke (since 1998) comes from the SPD and has, like Ertl, a more confrontational position towards the DBV (see also Chapters 4 and 8).

12. Again, it needs to be stressed that these farm households often had additional incomes from non-farm employment which exceeded their meagre farm incomes.

13. By 1982, for example, farmers' net yearly average income (full-time farms) amounted to only DM 26 000, while an industrial worker was on average earning DM 33 000 (Pfeffer, 1989b).

14. By the early 1990s, agricultural social policy made up about half of the yearly budget of the BML (Henrichsmeyer and Witzke, 1994).

15. Despite the substantial budget needed for the farmers' pension scheme, FRG farming in the 1970s was less burdened by elderly farmers than many other EEC member states. In 1975, for example, only one-quarter of FRG farmers were aged 55 or over, while the EEC9 average was 45 per cent (Kluge, 1989b).

16. For political reasons, the FDP left the coalition with the SPD and realigned itself with the CDU (its former coalition partner before 1969).

17. The Greens entered the Bundestag in March 1983 for the first time, changing the FRG's three-party structure to a four-party model.

3   The FRG and the CAP 1957–90: Leader, Partner or Obstructor?

1. It is important to note that the FRG only received full sovereignty in 1955 (Paris Agreement). Before that date, the freedom to decide about its relative position vis-à-vis other European countries was severely curtailed. In 1955, the FRG was invited to join the NATO in a move by the Allies to strengthen the ties of the FRG with the Western military alliance.

2. A view also shared by Priebe (1985) in his book entitled 'The subsidised absurdity' (*Die subventionierte Unvernunft*) and by the FRG Council of Economic Experts (*Sachverständigenrat*) (cf. Schmitt, 1981).

3. The NPD only obtained 4.3 per cent of the national vote and therefore failed the 5 per cent threshold limit for party representation in the Bundestag.

4. Exchange rate turmoil was linked to the abolition of the 1944 Bretton Woods agreement in 1971 (following the devaluation of the US$), which meant that world currencies were now no longer fixed within agreed US$ exchange rate bands.

5. It should be stressed that the fixing of common market prices during currency revaluations led to a situation whereby the market prices of the revalued currency fell by the level of revaluation, while currency devaluation led market prices to rise by the devalued amount. Since the fixing of currencies through the Euro on 1.1.1999, countries in 'Euroland' (for the first time) do no longer face these problems (see also Chapter 5).

6. As will be discussed in Chapter 5, MCAs were in place until 1993 when they were eventually abolished through the establishment of the Single European Market (Folmer *et al.*, 1995).

7. The following levels of self-sufficiency were achieved in the FRG for selected products by 1989: cereals (106 per cent), sugar (132 per cent), beef (112 per cent), pork (85 per cent), butter (76 per cent).

8. It was originally envisaged that the end of the transition period for the three new member states in December 1977 would also mark the end of the MCA system, but this optimistic goal could never be implemented. The European Monetary System was, in the end, established in 1979 (the birth of the ECU).

9. Between 1985 and 1989, for example, FRG farmers were granted a turnover tax relief of up to 3 per cent of VAT.

10. In the 1980s, only one member of the Bundestag was also a member of the Consumers' Association.

11. After 1979, transactions within the CAP were expressed in European currency units (ECU) (Ritson and Swinbank, 1997). In this book we, therefore, 'switch' from expressing financial figures in DM before the late 1970s to ECU thereafter.

12. Ertl stayed on as agriculture minister for one year despite the change of government in 1982 (see Chapter 2).

13. In the late 1990s, COPA comprises more than 30 national farmers' unions with over 9 million members.

14. The first veto occurred in the early 1960s when Agriculture Minister Schwarz vetoed a proposal by Mansholt which suggested shortening the CAP transition period to six years (a veto also supported by other EEC member states at the time; see above).

15. Although extensification and set-aside policies have an environmental component and became to some extent linked to the accompanying measures of Agri-environment Regulation 2078 in 1992 (see Chapter 6), they were essentially mechanisms aimed at reducing agricultural surpluses in the EC, and are therefore best discussed in this chapter.

16. It is interesting to note that the Green Party accused Kiechle of 'stealing their ideas' about set-aside and production extensification, although they argued largely from an environmental point of view, while Kiechle argued that set-aside was mainly an income-support measure.

17. This became even more evident after reunification and through Germany's influence with regard to the shaping of EC/EU agri-environmental policy (see Chapter 6).

4 The Challenge of German Reunification

1. These were demonstration/research farms which had often been specialist farms owned by public institutions before the land reform. They specialised in seed and livestock breeding (Zierold, 1997).

2. It should be noted, however, that not all farmers' unions in the former GDR agreed to join the DBV. The Verband der Neuen Landwirte, for example, refused to merge with the DBV as they felt that the DBV would not wholeheartedly fight for the interests of the *Wiedereinrichter* (Krüger, 1997).

5 Germany, the CAP, the GATT and Agricultural Trade

1. Argentina, Australia, Brazil, Canada, Chile, Columbia, Hungary, Indonesia, Malaysia, New Zealand, Philippines, Thailand and Uruguay.
2. A coalition party including the centre-left party Neues Forum, formed to fight the 1990 elections in the GDR.
3. The 20-year set-aside option is a voluntary agri-environmental policy (see also Chapter 6).

6 German Agriculture and the Environment

1. 'Environment' in this context not only includes the landscape, resources and wildlife habitats, but also genetic manipulation and modification of food and fibre products, as well as health risks to humans emanating from environmentally unsustainable farming activities.
2. Recent transnational environmental studies have shown that the greatest biodiversity is usually found in extensively farmed grassland systems (e.g. Beaufoy *et al.*, 1994).
3. It should be noted that the forested area increased during the same time period.
4. It should be stressed, however, that average figures for applications of external inputs in the GDR may be inaccurate as they most likely were altered for political reasons to 'fit' the expectations of the socialist agricultural model (see Bruckmeier and Grund, 1994, and Dominick, 1998, for good discussions on the political constructions of environmental discourses in the former GDR).
5. In this respect, the environmental problems in the GDR countryside were not dissimilar to those created by early *Flurbereinigung* in the FRG (see above).
6. Although livestock numbers have dropped dramatically and extensification measures have been introduced (see Chapter. 4).
7. A consequence of this has been that the Commission sued Germany in June 1999 for non-compliance with the EU Nitrate Directive (*Agra-Europe Bonn*, 5.7.1999b).
8. These data refer mainly to the territory of the former FRG, as no complete inventory of biodiversity decline has yet been completed for the former GDR.
9. A recent study conducted in the UK (September 1999) highlighted that bees may carry genetically modified pollen for up to 5 km away from the GMC planting trials, suggesting that 'safety zones' need to be extended further than hitherto thought.
10. It is important to note here that EU 'regulations' are not *regulatory* mechanisms at the nation state level, but provide the framework for the introduction of *voluntary* AEP. The term 'regulation' in this context should, therefore, not be confused with the national regulatory policy framework discussed below.
11. Section 6.5 provides a detailed analysis of individual agri-environmental schemes implemented in Germany.
12. There are, however, some differences with regard to the administration of the schemes. Although in most *Länder* the BML is the responsible authority for both agricultural and agri-environmental policy, in some regions (e.g. Schleswig-Holstein and Rheinland-Pfalz) responsibilities are shared between the Environment Ministry and the BML (Wilson *et al.*, 1999).

13. Schemes under this regulation were implemented in Germany for all *Länder* by 1991 (including the new *Länder*), aiming largely at conversion to organic farming. Uptake was high compared with other EC member states, with over 400 000 ha supported through the organic scheme by 1992.

14. The following aid schemes are co-funded under Regulation 2078:
    (a) schemes aiming at the reduction of external inputs and supporting organic farming;
    (b) schemes encouraging the extensification of arable land or conversion of arable land to grassland;
    (c) schemes aiming at reductions in livestock densities per forage area;
    (d) schemes encouraging the use of alternative farming practices compatible with environmental protection and the rearing of local breeds in danger of extinction;
    (e) schemes ensuring the upkeep of abandoned farmland or woodland;
    (f) long-term set-aside (20 years); note that this form of set-aside has a clear environmental objective and is, therefore, classified as an *agri-environmental scheme* (contrary to the earlier set-aside scheme);
    (g) schemes encouraging the management of land for public access and leisure activities;
    (h) schemes may also include measures to improve the training of farmers in environmental management practices (this part of Regulation 2078 was optional for member states to implement).

15. As in other European countries (cf. Whitby, 1996; Potter, 1998), a heated debate has developed with regard to the definition of 'good agricultural practice' as a key component of the *Landwirtschaftsklausel*. Some argue that German farmers have always been good 'stewards of the land' (e.g. DBV), while others (especially ENGOs and academics) increasingly criticise the assumption that all German farmers follow good agricultural practice for environmental conservation (e.g. Hagemann and Jäger, 1990; Brunner *et al.*, 1995; *Agra-Europe Bonn*, 25.9.1995, 2.12.1996).

16. By June 1998, the number of unemployed in reunified Germany had reached 4.1 million, one of the highest figures since the Second World War (*Der Spiegel*, 1998).

17. For two main reasons it is generally assumed that the PPG approach is cheaper. First, it may involve fewer participants that require financial compensation than the PPP which often includes large areas and many farmers (e.g. water protection areas). Second, because of its voluntary nature the PPG may allow a more targeted policy approach, either through geographical targeting of schemes (zonal programmes) or socio-economic targeting (e.g. older or economically less successful farms). As Buller *et al.* (2000) have highlighted, it comes as no surprise that relatively wealthy countries such as Switzerland, Sweden or Denmark have placed relatively great emphasis on the PPP to control environmental pollution in the countryside.

18. The *Düngeverordnung* forces farmers (on holdings over 10 ha) to restrict applications of N-fertilisers within specified thresholds established for each holding.

19. It should be noted, however, that increasing costs of N-fertilisers have also led to a reduction in their use by farmers (von Urff, 1999).

20. In a European context, national parks have played a relatively minor role in German environmental policy. Most of the 14 existing national parks (in 1999) have been established relatively recently (covering less than 1 per cent of the

land area), and only few contain susbstantial areas of ecologically valuable agricultural land.

21. This, of course, is a relative term as in a EU comparison most of the northern *Länder* (and even many of the new *Länder*) still rank relatively favourably.

22. Additional factors in Bayern that have been conducive to early implementation of AEP include the high ratio of part-time farmers and the resultant importance of farm-based tourism that has relied on 'green and clean' farming (Plankl, 1997).

23. As Chapters 2 and 3 already highlighted, the relatively affluent German consumers have been willing to pay more for better food quality than consumers in many other European countries.

24. Not all of these farms were covered under Regulation 2078. In 1996, many farms were still part of the 'old' extensification scheme (Regulation 4115/88).

25. Public transport in some German towns is now based on biofuels (e.g. buses in the town of Bad Tölz in Bayern; taxis in Bremen), and farmers can fill up their tractors with biofuels at over 400 filling stations across Germany (same price as conventional diesel fuel). Research has shown that the burning of biofuels produces less pollution than conventional diesel fuel.

26. The German Ministry of Health is currently contemplating whether to allow the planting of cannabis as a bio-resource for the production of indusrial fibre, oils and textiles, as is already the case in France (6000 ha planted) and the UK (1000 ha) (Drescher and Brodersen, 1997).

27. German car manufacturers (e.g. Mercedes-Benz) are increasingly using bio-resources for insulation purposes in the passenger compartments of cars.

28. The same is true for other environmental issues in the German countryside, such as the rapid increase of wind farms. Although acknowledged as a source of green energy (Germany is among the leading nations with regard to electricity generation from wind farms), they are seen by some as spoiling the tradtional German countryside. Currently, there are about 4500 wind turbines in operation (producing 2 per cent of the national electricity production) with another 7000 planned soon. Arguments have been raised that the control over wind farm location and expansion should also come under the umbrella of AEP, rather than being regulated by the German planning legislation, as it has direct implications for agriculture and conservation (e.g. *Der Spiegel*, 1995).

29. By the 1990s, a policy compromise was reached with regard to beer quality issues and foreign imports that enabled German breweries to continue brewing beer according to the law of 1516, but that also opened the German market for imports from other countries.

30. Within Germany, animals are not allowed to be transported for more than eight hours in closed vehicles.

31. Early indications are that the new government under Schröder (since 1998) has not substantially altered its position to GMCs compared to the Kohl government. Recent reports in *Agra-Europe Bonn* (19.7.1999d) and *Der Spiegel* (Knauer, 1999) highlight that the government supports 'green' GMCs as long as they do not result in 'environmental damage'.

32. This does not, however, prevent GMCs from entering the food chain via animal feed that still does not have to comply with the relatively strict labelling regulations in place for human food (Knauer, 1999).

33. It should be noted, however, that, even before the ban, Germany only imported about 100 tonnes of British beef per year – a negligible amount compared to British beef exports to other EU countries.

34. Nonetheless, critics (especially the UK media) have also argued that the German handling of the BSE crisis was synonymous with 'backdoor protectionism' of German beef farmers and the German food industry.
35. Dieter (1992) provides a good discussion of how a similar leading role has been played by Germany with regard to EU drinking water regulations.

7 Rural Planning, Policy and Development in Germany

1. In 1998, this ministry was restructured to form the Ministry for Transport, Development and Housing (Bundesministerium für Verkehr, Bau- und Wohnungswesen).
2. See below for an explanation of the administrative role of *Gemeinden*.
3. For larger villages (2000–10 000 population), *Dorferneuerung* schemes are funded under the urban renewal programme (BMBau, 1990).

Bibliography

P. Ackermann, *Der Deutsche Bauernverband im politischen Kräftespiel der Bundesrepublik* (Tübingen: Mohr, 1970).

W.M. Adams, N.A.D. Bourn and I. Hodge, 'Conservation in the wider countryside: SSSIs and wildlife habitat in eastern England', *Land Use Policy*, 9 (1992) 235–48.

Agra-Europe Bonn, 'Ordnungspolitische Grundsätze für die Land- und Ernährungswirtschaft der DDR' (2.7.1990).

Agra-Europe Bonn, 'Probleme einer Integration in den EG-Agrarmarkt' (23.7.1990).

Agra-Europe Bonn, 'DDR-Landwirtschaft vor erneutem Umstrukturierungsprozess', (27.8.1990).

Agra-Europe Bonn, 'DBV-Stellungnahme zur deutschen Einigung' (8.10.1990).

Agra-Europe Bonn, 'Erfolg der GATT-Verhandlungen von grosser Bedeutung' (22.10.1990).

Agra-Europe Bonn, 'Kiechle: Maximalforderungen für GATT-Agrarverhandlungen abgelehnt' (12.11.1990).

Agra-Europe Bonn, 'Auswirkungen der deutschen Vereinigung' (26.11.1990).

Agra-Europe Bonn, 'Auswirkungen der Integration in den EG-Agrarmarkt' (18.2.1991).

Agra-Europe Bonn, 'Markt und Meinung: Situationsbericht' (2.3.1992).

Agra-Europe Bonn, 'Umgestaltung der Agrarwirtschaft in Ostdeutschland' (28.3.1994).

Agra-Europe Bonn, 'Europäisches Parlament hat letzte Chance: Kennzeichnung von gentechnisch veränderten Lebensmitteln' (3.7.1995a)

Agra-Europe Bonn, 'Genehmigungsgrenze für Betriebe mit Tierhaltung deutlich anheben' (3.7.1995b).

Agra-Europe Bonn, 'Anhaltender Strukturwandel in der deutschen Landwirtschaft' (3.7.1995c).

Agra-Europe Bonn, 'Deutscher Bauerntag 1995: starke Bauern – lebendiges Land' (3.7.1995d).

Agra-Europe Bonn, 'Bäuerlicher Familienbetrieb kein Auslaufmodell' (10.7.1995a).

Agra-Europe Bonn, 'Verwendung von Hormonen in der Tierhaltung abgelehnt *Agra-Europe Bonn*' (10.7.1995b)

Agra-Europe Bonn, 'Landwirtschaft gerät mehr und mehr ins umweltpolitische Blickfeld' (10.7.1995c).

Agra-Europe Bonn, 'Schärfere EU-Handelsbeschränkungen gegen britisches Rindfleisch' (10.7.1995d).

Agra-Europe Bonn, 'DBV fordert Erhöhung der Vorsteuerpauschale' (10.7.1995e).

Agra-Europe Bonn, 'Friedrichshafener Thesen 1995 des Deutschen Bauernverbandes' (10.7.1995f).

Agra-Europe Bonn, 'Berufstand fordert Verläßlichkeit und Ermutigung' (10.7.1995g).

Agra-Europe Bonn, 'Risiken bei gentechnisch veränderten Lebensmitteln möglich' (17.7.1995).

Agra-Europe Bonn, 'Rahmenplan der Gemeinschaftsaufgabe "Verbesserung der Agrarstruktur und des Küstenschutzes" für den Zeitraum 1995 bis 1998' (24.7.1995).

Agra-Europe Bonn, 'Leitbild des bäuerlichen Familienbetriebes hat sich bewährt' (31.7.1995a).

Agra-Europe Bonn, 'Wertvolle Impulse für eine Harmonisierung des Lebensmittelsrechts' (31.7.1995b).

Agra-Europe Bonn, 'Skepsis gegenüber gentechnisch veränderten Lebensmitteln überwiegt' (7.8.1995a).

Agra-Europe Bonn, 'Pflanzenschutz- und Düngemitteleinsatz je Hektar in der EU12' (7.8.1995b).

Agra-Europe Bonn, 'Rinderangebot in der EU stagniert' (7.8.1995c).

Agra-Europe Bonn, 'Die Agrarwirtschaft in den neuen Ländern' (4.9.1995).

Agra-Europe Bonn, 'DBV beharrt auf der Landwirtschaftsklausel' (25.9.1995).

Agra-Europe Bonn, 'Vergleichbare Definitionen der "guten fachlichen Praxis" nötig' (2.12.1996).

Agra-Europe Bonn, 'Der Strukturwandel in der Landwirtschaft geht weiter' (9.12.1996a).

Agra-Europe Bonn, 'Agrarstrukturen in der Europäischen Union: Deutschland im EU-Vergleich immer noch "mittelbäuerlich" geprägt' (9.12.1996b).

Agra-Europe Bonn, 'Gentechnik verantwortungsvoll weiterentwickeln' (9.12.1996c).

Agra-Europe Bonn, 'Verbrennung von Biorohmasse zur Wärme- und Stromgewinnung' (9.12.1996d).

Agra-Europe Bonn, 'Image deutscher Nahrungsmittel' (16.12.1996a).

Agra-Europe Bonn, 'Deutsche zeigen Interesse am Bauernhofurlaub in Österreich' (16.12.1996b).

Agra-Europe Bonn, 'EU-Zulassung für gentechnisch veränderten Mais' (23.12.1996a).

Agra-Europe Bonn, 'Deutsche Bauern für Europäische Währungsunion' (23.12.1996b).

Agra-Europe Bonn, 'Novelle des Landwirtschaftanpassungsgesetzes tritt in Kraft' (23.12.1996c)

Agra-Europe Bonn, 'Schelte für den Dubliner EU-Gipfel' (23.12.1996d).

Agra-Europe Bonn, 'Bayern bei kontrolliertem Rindfleisch Spitze' (6.1.1997).

Agra-Europe Bonn, 'Bauern nicht immer stärker vom Staat abhängig machen' (13.1.1997).

Agra-Europe Bonn, 'DBV gegen weitere Haushaltskürzungen' (27.1.1997).

Agra-Europe Bonn, 'Eilverordnung zum Schutz vor BSE in Kraft' (3.2.1997).

Agra-Europe Bonn, 'Kritik an Kommissionsklage wegen deutscher Pestizidwerte' (10.2.1997).

Agra-Europe Bonn, 'Stuttgarter Landesregierung steht zum bäuerlichen Familienbetrieb' (24.2.1997).

Agra-Europe Bonn, 'Niedersachsen sucht agrarpolitischen Mittelweg' (3.3.1997a).

Agra-Europe Bonn, 'Landwirte zur Mitarbeit im Umwelt- und Naturschutz bereit' (3.3.1997b).

Agra-Europe Bonn, 'Milliardenverlust durch BSE und Schweinepest' (3.3.1997c).

Agra-Europe Bonn, 'Tierschutz beim Transport verbessert' (3.3.1997d).

Agra-Europe Bonn, 'Sonnleitner sieht Einheit des Verbandes als wichtigste Aufgabe: Gemeinsamkeiten von Ost und West' (10.3.1997a).

Agra-Europe Bonn, 'Landwirtschaft wurde umweltverträglicher' (10.3.1997b).

Agra-Europe Bonn, 'Qualität hat ihren Preis: mit dem BSE Problem von Anfang an sehr verantwortungsbewußt umgegangen' (17.3.1997a).

Agra-Europe Bonn, 'Käfighaltung beherrscht die Bundestagsdebatte zum Tierschutz' (17.3.1997b).

Agra-Europe Bonn, 'Protest gegen Sparpläne aus Brussel und Bonn' (24.3.1997).

Agra-Europe Bonn, 'Funke hält nichts von Cross compliance und Modulation' (31.5.1999).

Agra-Europe Bonn, 'Bundeslandwirtschaftsminister will eine halbe Milliarde DM einsparen' (7.6.1999).

Agra-Europe Bonn, 'Einstellung gegenüber Genfood soll objektiviert werden' (21.6.1999a).

Agra-Europe Bonn, 'Nachwachsende Rohstoffe weiter im Aufwind' (21.6.1999b).

Agra-Europe Bonn, 'Bald grünes Licht für Änderung des Flächenerwerbsprogramms?' (21.6.1999c)

Agra-Europe Bonn, 'Sonnleitner: Sparpläne gefährden den Agrarstandort Deutschland' (28.6.1999).

Agra-Europe Bonn, 'DBV fordert Kurswechsel in der Agrarpolitik: Stärkung der Wettbewerbsfähigkeit wieder in den Vordergrund politischer Entscheidungen stellen' (5.7.1999a).

Agra-Europe Bonn, 'EU-Kommission bring Deutschland vor den EuGH' (5.7.1999b).

Agra-Europe Bonn, 'Osterweiterung stärkt Marktposition der Milchwirtschaft' (5.7.1999c).

Agra-Europe Bonn, 'Anzahl der Fälle von Boviner Spongiformer Enzephalopathie' (12.7.1999a).

Agra-Europe Bonn, 'Sparpläne der Bundesregierung werden nicht hingenommen' (12.7.1999b).

Agra-Europe Bonn, 'Sachsen: Neuaufbau der Landwirtschaft ist abgeschlossen' (19.7.1999a).

Agra-Europe Bonn, 'Landwirtschaft kann auf Gentechnik nicht verzichten' (19.7.1999b).

Agra-Europe Bonn, 'Beim Anbau von Bt-Mais mit dem Gesetz im Einklang' (19.7.1999c).

Agra-Europe Bonn, 'Bundesregierung bekennt sich zur grünen Gentechnik' (19.7.1999d).

Agra-Europe Bonn, 'Kritik an Exportfreigabe für britisches Rindfleisch' (19.7.1999e).

Agra-Europe Bonn, 'Legehennen-Richtlinie formell gebilligt' (26.7.1999a).

Agra-Europe Bonn, 'Das Sparpaket muß im Agrarsektor abgespeckt werden' (26.7.1999b).

Agra-Europe London, 'CAP Reform Agreement: groundwork for fundamental change' (15.6.1992).

Agra-Europe London, 'World GATT Agreement on Agriculture concluded' (13.1.1994).

Agra-Europe London, 'When farm set-aside is no longer set-aside' (29.9.1995).

Agra-Europe London, 'German farm minister resists further CAP reform' (8.12.1995).

Agra-Europe London, 'CAP: the unavoidable pressures for reform' (12.1.1996).

Agra-Europe London, 'Bonn faces up to need for CAP reform' (21.6.1996).

Agra-Europe London, 'Germany nets 20% of EU agri-environmental aids' (16.8.1996).

Agra-Europe London, 'Ministers blunder into beef disaster' (1.11.1996).

Agra-Europe London, 'Long debate ahead on Agenda 2000 financing' (2.5.1997).

Agra-Europe London, 'Commission unveils "Agenda 2000" plans' (18.7.1997a).

Agra-Europe London, 'Commission fails to convince on dairy reform' (18.7.1997b).

Agra-Europe London, 'Member states critical of CAP reform plans' (18.7.1997c).

Agra-Europe Special Study, *Central and East European Agriculture and the European Union* (London: Agra-Europe, 1997).

Agrarbericht, Agrarbericht der Bundesregierung (Bonn: BML, 1971–99).

H. Ahrens and C. Lippert, 'Agrarpolitik für die neuen Bundesländer', *Agrarwirtschaft*, 44 (1995) 213–15.

AID, 'Zur Betriebsstruktur in den neuen Bundesländern', *AID-Informationen für die Agrarberatung*, 40 (1991) 2–9.

W. Albrecht, 'Mecklenburg-Vorpommern: the Mezzogiorno of the Federal Republic of Germany?', in P. Huigen, L. Paul and K. Volkers (eds), *The changing function and position of rural areas in Europe* (Utrecht: Nederlandse Geografische Studie No. 153, 1992) 141–51.

E. Andrlik, 'The farmers and the state: agricultural interests in West German politics', *West European Politics*, 4 (1981) 104–19.

J. Ardagh, *Germany and the Germans: after reunification* (London: Penguin, 1991).

W.F. Averyt, *Agropolitics in the European Community: interest groups and the Common Agricultural Policy* (New York: Praeger, 1977).

F. Baade and F. Fendt, *Die deutsche Landwirtschaft im Ringen um den Agrarmarkt Europas* (Baden-Baden: Nomos, 1971).

J. Bachtler, 'Reforming the Structural Funds: challenges for EU regional policy', *European Planning Studies*, 6 (6) (1998) 645–64.

J. Bachtler and R. Michie, 'Strengthening economic and social cohesion? The revision of the Structural Funds', *Regional Studies*, 28 (1994) 789–96.

D. Baldock, C. Cox, P. Lowe and M. Winter, 'Environmentally Sensitive Areas: incrementalism or reform?', *Journal of Rural Studies*, 6 (2) (1990) 143–62.

D. Baldock and P. Lowe, 'The development of European agri-environmental policy', in M. Whitby (ed.), *The European environment and CAP reform: policies and prospects for conservation* (Wallingford: CAB International, 1996) 8–25.

A. Balmann, 'Ansätze zur Erklärung einer Dominanz und Persistenz "suboptimaler" Betriebsgrößenstrukturen in der Landwirtschaft', *Agrarwirtschaft*, 43 (1994) 227–35.

A. Baring (ed.), *Germany's new position in Europe: problems and perspectives* (Oxford: Berg, 1994).

M. Baumgartner, *Landwirtschaft und Lebensmittelqualität* (Kassel: Gesamthochschule, 1988).

Bayerisches landwirtschaftliches Wochenblatt, 'Die Konfrontation gesucht: Bundeskanzler Schröder stößt Bauern vor den Kopf', *BWL* , 2 (1999) 27.

G. Beaufoy, D. Baldock and J. Clark *The nature of farming: low intensity farming systems in nine European countries* (London: IEEP, 1994).

H.C. Beaumond and A. Barnett, 'Trade liberalisation and European agriculture: opportunities and risks for the rural environment', in M. Redclift, J.N. Lekakis and G.P. Zanias (eds), *Agriculture and world trade liberalisation: socio-environmental perspectives on the Common Agricultural Policy* (Wallingford: CAB International, 1999) 104–18.

H. Behrens, 'Intermediäre Akteure in der Dorf- und Regionalentwicklung', in H. Behrens (ed.), *Dorf- und Regionalentwicklung in den neuen Bundesländern: Beiträge aus der Praxis* (Göttingen: Agrarsoziale Gesellschaft e.V., Kleine Reihe No. 54, 1995) 107–34.

W.H. Berentsen, 'Regional change in the German Democratic Republic', *Annals of the Association of American Geographers*, 71 (1981) 50–66.

T. Bergmann, 'Socioeconomic situation and the perspectives of the individual peasant', *Sociologia Ruralis*, 30 (1) (1990) 48–61.

T. Bergmann, 'The re-privatisation of farming in Eastern Germany', *Sociologia Ruralis*, 32 (1992) 305–16.

F. Bernhardt, 'Überlegungen zur optimalen Größe von Produktionseinheiten in der Milchviehhaltung', *Berichte über Landwirtschaft*, 74 (1995) 481–93.

C. Bertram, 'The power and the past: Germany's new international loneliness', in A. Baring (ed.), *Germany's new position in Europe: problems and perspectives* (Oxford: Berg, 1994) 91–106.

I. Blühdorn, 'Environment NGOs and "new politics"', *Environmental Politics*, 4 (2) (1995) 328–32.

BMBau [Bundesministerium für Raumordnung, Bauwesen und Städtebau], *Entwicklung ländlicher Räume durch den Fremdenverkehr* (Bonn: BMBau, 1986).

BMBau [Bundesministerium für Raumordnung, Bauwesen und Städtebau], *Bericht der Bundesregierung zur Erneuerung von Dörfern und Ortsteilen (Dorferneuerungsbericht)* (Bonn: BMBau, 1990a).

BMBau [Bundesministerium für Raumordnung, Bauwesen und Städtebau], *Raumordnungsbericht* (Bonn: BMBau, 1990b).

BMBau [Bundesministerium für Raumordnung, Bauwesen und Städtebau], *Raumordnungsbericht* (Bonn: BMBau, 1991).

BMBau [Bundesministerium für Raumordnung, Bauwesen und Städtebau], *Raumordungsbericht* (Bonn: BMBau, 1993).

BMBau [Bundesministerium für Raumordnung, Bauwesen und Städtebau], *Raumordungsbericht* (Bonn: BMBau, 1994).

BMIB [Bundesministerium für innerdeutsche Beziehungen], *DDR Handbuch* (Bonn: BMIB, 1985).

BML [Bundesministerium für Ernährung, Landwirtschaft und Forsten], *Fragen und Antworten zur Agrarpolitik für die neuen Bundesländer* (Bonn: BML, 1991a).

BML [Bundesministerium für Ernährung, Landwirtschaft und Forsten], *Politik für unsere Bauern* (Bonn: BML, 1991b).

BML [Bundesministerium für Ernährung, Landwirtschaft und Forsten], 'Nachwachsende Rohstoffe', in BML (ed.), *Die Agrarreform der EG* (Bonn: BML, 1993) 28–31.

BML [Bundesministerium für Ernährung, Landwirtschaft und Forsten], *Aktuelle Fragen zur Agrarpolitik: Bundesminister Borchert antwortet* (Bonn: BML, 1994a).

BML [Bundesministerium für Ernährung, Landwirtschaft und Forsten], *Agricultural economy in the new federal Länder: topical survey* (Bonn: BML, 1994b).

BML [Bundesministerium für Ernährung, Landwirtschaft und Forsten], *Soziale Sicherheit für unsere Landwirtschaft* (Bonn: BML, 1994c).

BML [Bundesministerium für Ernährung, Landwirtschaft und Forsten], *Agrarwirtschaft in den neuen Ländern* (Bonn: BML, 1995a).

BML [Bundesministerium für Ernährung, Landwirtschaft und Forsten], *Für unsere landwirtschaftlichen Unternehmen* (Bonn: BML, 1995b).

BML [Bundesministerium für Ernährung, Landwirtschaft und Forsten], *Fragen zur Agrarpolitik: Bundesminister Jochen Borchert antwortet* (Bonn: BML, 1996a).

BML [Bundesministerium für Ernährung, Landwirtschaft und Forsten], *Perspektiven der Agrarpolitik im kommenden Jahrzehnt: konzeptionelle Überlegungen* (Bonn: BML, 1996b).

BML [Bundesministerium für Ernährung, Landwirtschaft und Forsten], *Statistisches Jahrbuch über Ernährung, Landwirtschaft und Forsten* (Münster-Hiltrup: Landwirtschaftsverlag, 1999a)

BML [Bundesministerium für Ernährung, Landwirtschaft und Forsten], *Der Agraretat 2000 (Regierungsentwurf)* (Bonn: BML-Informationen No. 26, 1999b).

BMWi [Bundesministerium für Wirtschaft und Technologie], 'Neufestlegung der Fördergebiete der Gemeinschaftsaufgabe "Verbesserung der regionalen Wirtschaftsstruktur" (GA) und Verabschiedung des 28. Rahmenplans', *Tagesnachrichten*, 10871 (26.3.1999), http:www.bmwi.de.

K. Borchardt, *Perspectives on modern German economic history and policy* (Cambridge: CUP, 1991).

H. Born, 'Ein überflüssiges Gesetz? Das Landwirtschaftsgesetz ist 40 Jahre alt geworden', *Deutsche Bauernkorrespondenz*, 9 (1995) 306–9.

M. Born, *Die Entwicklung der deutschen Agrarlandschaft* (Darmstadt: Union, 1974).

I.R. Bowler, *Agriculture under the Common Agricultural Policy* (Manchester: MUP, 1985).

F. Brandkamp, 'Entwicklung der landwirtschaftlichen Einkommen', *Berichte über Landwirtschaft*, 60 (1982) 494–510.

J. Braun, 'Auswirkungen einer flächendeckenden Umstellung der Landwirtschaft auf den ökologischen Landbau', *Agrarwirtschaft*, 44 (7) (1995) 247–56.

H. Brezinski, 'Private agriculture in the GDR: limitations of orthodox Socialist agricultural policy', *Soviet Studies*, 42 (1990) 535–53.

G. Bronner, R. Oppermann and S. Rösler, 'Umweltleistungen als Grundlage der landwirtschaftlichen Förderung: Vorschläge zur Fortentwicklung des MEKA-Programms in Baden-Württemberg', *Naturschutz und Landschaftsplanung*, 29 (12) (1997) 357–65.

I. Brotherton, 'What limits participation in ESAs?', *Journal of Environmental Management*, 32 (1991) 241–49.

F. Brouwer and P. Lowe, 'CAP reform and the environment', in F. Brouwer and P. Lowe (eds), *CAP and the rural environment in transition: a panorama of national perspectives* (Wageningen: Wageningen Pers, 1998) 13–36.

K. Bruckmeier and H. Grund, 'Perspectives for environmentally sound agriculture in East Germany', in D. Symes and A. Jansen (eds), *Agricultural restructuring and rural change in Europe* (Wageningen: Wageningen Sociologische Studies, 1994) 180–94.

K. Bruckmeier and P. Teheranni-Krönner, 'Farmers and environmental regulation experiences in the Federal Republic of Germany', *Sociologia Ruralis*, 30 (2) (1992) 66–81.

H. Brunner, F.-X. Maidl, M. Köbler and A. Heissenhuber, 'Untersuchungen zur Konkretisierung des Begriffs "ordnungsgemäße Landwirtschaft" im Sinne des Gewässerschutzes', *Berichte über Landwirtschaft*, 73 (1995) 242–57.

A. Buckwell, 'Some microeconomic analysis of CAP market regimes', in C. Ritson and D.R. Harvey (eds), *The Common Agricultural Policy*, 2nd edn (Wallingford: CAB International, 1997) 139–62.

A. Buckwell and S. Tangermann, 'The CAP and Central and Eastern Europe', in C. Ritson and D.R. Harvey (eds), *The Common Agricultural Policy*, 2nd edn (Wallingford: CAB International, 1997) 307–42.

H. Buller, 'Agricultural change and the environment in Western Europe', in K. Hoggart (ed.), *Agricultural change, environment and economy* (London: Mansell, 1992) 68–88.

H. Buller, 'Regulation 2078: patterns of implementation', in H. Buller, G.A. Wilson and A. Höll (eds), *Agri-environmental policy in the European Union* (Aldershot: Ashgate, 2000) 219–54.

H. Buller and H. Brives, 'France: farm production and rural product as key factors influencing agri-environmental policy', in H. Buller, G.A. Wilson and A. Höll (eds), *Agri-environmental policy in the European Union* (Aldershot: Ashgate, 2000) 9–30.

H. Buller, G.A. Wilson and A. Höll (eds), *Agri-environmental policy in the European Union* (Aldershot: Ashgate, 2000).

S. Bulmer and W. Paterson, *The Federal Republic of Germany and the European Community* (London: Allen and Unwin, 1987).

S. Bulmer and W. Paterson, 'West Germany's role in Europe: "man-mountain" or "semi-Gulliver"?', *Journal of Common Market Studies*, 28 (1989) 95–117.

R. Burton, 'The role of farmer self-identity in agricultural decision-making in the Marston Vale Community Forest' (Bedford: De Montfort University, 1998), Unpublished Ph.D. thesis.

F.H. Buttel, 'The US farm crisis and the restructuring of American agriculture: domestic and international dimensions', in D. Goodman and M. Redclift (eds), *The international farm crisis* (London: Macmillan, 1989) 46–83.

CEC [Commission of the European Communities], *Memorandum on the reform of agriculture in the European Community (Mansholt Plan)* (COM 68–1000) (Brussels: CEC, 1968).

CEC [Commission of the European Communities], *Reflections on the Common Agricultural Policy*, COM (80)800 (Luxembourg: Official Publications of the European Communities, 1980).

CEC [Commission of the European Communities], *Fact sheets on the European parliament and the activities of the European Community* (Luxembourg: Official Publications of the European Communities, 1987a).

CEC [Commission of the European Communities], *The future of rural society* (COM 88–371) (Luxembourg: Official Publications of the European Communities, 1987b).

CEC [Commission of the European Communities], *A Common Agricultural Policy for the 1990s* (Luxembourg: Official Publications of the European Communities, 1989).

CEC [Commission of the European Communities], *The agricultural situation in the European Community* (Luxembourg: Official Publications of the European Communities, 1991).

CEC [Commission of the European Communities], *The agricultural situation in the European Community* (Luxembourg: Official Publications of the European Communities, 1995a).

CEC [Commission of the European Communities], 'Study on alternative strategies for the development of relations in the field of agriculture between the EU and the associated countries with a view to future accession of these countries' (COM 95–607), Paper presented to the Madrid European Council (Brussels: DGVI, 1995b).

CEC [Commission of the European Communities], *Agricultural situation and prospects in the Central and Eastern European Countries: summary report* (Brussels: DGVI, 1995c).

CEC [Commission of the European Communities], *Germany: briefing material for the press for the European Conference on Rural Development* (Brussels: DGVI, 1996a).

CEC [Commission of the European Communities], *The Cork Declaration: a living countryside* (Brussels: DGVI, 1996b).

CEC [Commission of the European Communities], *Agenda 2000 – For a stronger and wider Union*, COM 97/6 (Luxembourg: Official Publications of the European Communities, 1997a).

CEC [Commission of the European Communities], *Report from the Commission to the Council and the European Parliament on the application of Council Regulation (EEC) no. 2078/92 on agricultural production methods compatible with the requirements of the protection of the environment and the maintenance of the countryside* (COM 97–620) (Brussels: DGVI, 1997b).

CEC [Commission of the European Communities], *Special accession programme for agriculture and rural development* (CH-87-98-007-EN-C) (Brussels: DGVI, 1998a).

CEC [Commission of the European Communities], *The Euro and the reform of the agrimonetary system* (CH-87-98-017-EN-C) (Brussels: DGVI, 1998b).

CEC [Commission of the European Communities], *Berlin European Council: Agenda 2000, conclusions of the presidency* (CH-AA-99-003-EN-C) (Brussels: DGVI, 1999a).

CEC [Commission of the European Communities], *The fifteen at the WTO: a stronger, more united voice* (CH-AA-99-010-EN-C) (Brussels: DGVI, 1999b).

CEC [Commission of the European Communities], *CAP reform: rural development* (CH-25-99-008-EN-C) (Brussels: CEC, 1999c).

R. Cecil, *The development of agriculture in Germany and the UK; I: German agriculture 1870–1970* (Ashford: Centre for European Agricultural Studies, 1979).

J.R. Clark, A. Jones, C. Potter and M. Lobley, 'Conceptualising the evolution of the European Union's agri-environment policy: a discourse approach', *Environment and Planning A*, 29 (1997) 1869–85.

P. Cloke, *An introduction to rural settlement planning* (London: Methuen, 1983).

P. Cloke and M. Goodwin, 'Conceptualising countryside change: from post-Fordism to structured coherence', *Transactions of the Institute of British Geographers*, 17 (1992) 321–36.

H. Clout, *A rural policy for the EEC?* (London: Methuen, 1984).

S. Dabbert and J. Braun, 'Auswirkungen des EG-Extensivierungsprogramms auf die Umstellung auf ökologischen Landbau in Baden-Württemberg', *Agrarwirtschaft*, 42 (2) (1993) 90–9.

P. Dassau, 'Die Dümmerregion: Perspektiven eines Konflikts zwischen Landwirtschaft und Landschaftsschutz', *Geographische Rundschau*, 40 (6) (1988) 26–30.

A. Dawson, 'Agrarian reform in Eastern Europe', in M. Pacione (ed.) *Progress in agricultural geography* (London: Croom Helm, 1986) 149–66.

DBV [Deutscher Bauernverband], 'Vermögensauseinandersetzung und Umstrukturierung der Landwirtschaft in den neuen Ländern', *Schriftenreihe des Deutschen Bauernverbandes*, 3 (1995) 2–32.

DBV [Deutscher Bauernverband], *Geschäftsbericht des Deutschen Bauernverbandes für das Jahr 1995* (Bonn: DBV, 1996).

DBV [Deutscher Bauernverband], *Argumente 1997: Trends und Fakten zur wirtschaftlichen Lage der deutschen Landwirtschaft* (Bonn: DBV, 1997).

DBV [Deutscher Bauernverband], *Stellungnahme des Präsidiums des Deutschen Bauernverbandes vom 21. April 1998 zu den Verordnungsvorschlägen der EU-Kommission vom 18. März 1998 über die Reform der Gemeinsamen Agrarpolitik im Rahmen der Agenda 2000* (Bonn: DBV website, 21.4.1998).

C. Deblitz, H. Buller, O. Röhm, J. Schramek and G.A. Wilson, 'Ausgestaltung und Inanspruchnahme der Agrarumweltprogramme in den EU-Mitgliedstaaten', *Berichte über Landwirtschaft*, 76 (1) (1998) 55–73.

M. Dennis, *German Democratic Republic: politics, economics and society* (London: Pinter, 1988).

G. Denton, 'Restructuring the EC budget: implications of the Fontainebleau Agreement', *Journal of Common Market Studies*, 23 (1984) 117–40.

Der Spiegel, 'Wir wollen keine Spekulanten', *Der Spiegel*, 20 (1990) 130–42.

Der Spiegel, 'Hier geschieht Unrecht', *Der Spiegel*, 19 (1991a) 70–81.

Der Spiegel, 'Wahnsinn ohne Ende', *Der Spiegel*, 29 (1991b) 21–2.

Der Spiegel, 'Der Welthandel wird leiden', *Der Spiegel*, 4 (1992a) 82–4.

Der Spiegel, 'Ungleich verteilt', *Der Spiegel*, 10 (1992b) 132–34.

Der Spiegel, 'Jauche vor die Haustür', *Der Spiegel*, 41 (1993) 146–9.

Der Spiegel, 'Alle zahlen drauf', *Der Spiegel*, 41 (1994) 125–7.

Der Spiegel, 'Parade der Tüddelmasten: Windkraftanlagen in Deutschland', *Der Spiegel*, 41 (1995) 194–200.

Der Spiegel, 'Der Bauer als Störenfried', *Der Spiegel*, 40 (1996) 164–6.

Der Spiegel, 'Wahnsinn aus deutschen Landen', *Der Spiegel*, 5 (1997b) 32–5.

Der Spiegel, 'Projekt Deutschland 2000', *Der Spiegel*, 31 (1998) 39–45.

Der Spiegel, 'BSE: Brüssel gibt Zeit', *Der Spiegel*, 32 (1999a) 21.

Der Spiegel, 'Lebensmittel: sicheres Label', *Der Spiegel*, 34 (1999b) 19.

Deutscher Bundestag, *Rahmenplan der Gemeinschaftsaufgabe 'Verbesserung der Agrarstruktur und des Küstenschutzes' für den Zeitraum 1996 bis 1999* (Document 13/4349) (Bonn: Deutscher Bundestag, 1996a).

Deutscher Bundestag, *Rahmenplan der Gemeinschaftsaufgabe 'Verbesserung der regionalen Wirtschaftsstruktur' für den Zeitraum 1996 bis 1999* (Document 13/4349) (Bonn: Deutscher Bundestag, 1996b).

K. Dexter, 'The impact of technology on the political economy of agriculture', *Journal of Agricultural Economics*, 28 (1977) 211–19.

H.H. Dieter, 'German drinking water regulations, pesticides and axiom of concern', *Environmental Management*, 16 (1) (1992) 21–32.

C. Dirscherl, 'Agrarsoziologische Beobachtungen zur landwirtschaftlichen Arbeitsorganisation in einer LPG', *Berichte über Landwirtschaft*, 69 (1991) 341–53.

K. Ditt, 'Nature conservation in England and Germany (1900–70): forerunner of environmental protection?', *Contemporary European History*, 5 (1996) 1–28.

DOE/MAFF [Department of Environment and Ministry of Agriculture, Fisheries and Food], *Rural England: a nation committed to a living countryside* (London: HMSO, 1995) Document CM-3016.

H. Doll and K. Klare, 'Einfluss der Privatisierung von Treuhandflächen auf die Pacht- und Grundstücksmärkte', in K. Klare (ed.), *Entwicklung der ländlichen Räume und der Agrarwirtschaft in den Neuen Bundesländern (Landbauforschung Völkenrode Sonderheft)* (Braunschweig: FAL, 1994) 121–35.

R. Dominick, 'Capitalism, Communism, and environmental protection: lessons from the German experience', *Environmental History*, 3 (3) (1998) 311–32.

K. Drescher and C.M. Brodersen, 'Bestimmung der Wettbewerbskraft von Hanf in Deutschland', *Agrarwirtschaft*, 46 (2) (1997) 100–8.

E. Ehlers, 'The agricultural landscape of the Federal Republic of Germany and its changes since 1949', *Geographische Rundschau*, Special Edition (1988) 57–67.

W. Ehrenforth, 'Bodenreform und Enteignungsentschädigung', *Berichte über Landwirtschaft*, 69 (1991) 489–516.

M. Eichenauer and D. Joeris, 'Das historische Verhältnis von Flurbereinigung und Naturschutz/Landschaftspflege', *Berichte über Landwirtschaft*, 72 (1994) 329–50.

G. Endruweit, 'The chances of agricultural interests in local decisions', *Sociologia Ruralis*, 30 (1990) 76–87.

J. Ertl, 'Agrarpolitik seit 1969: Rückblick und Ausblick', *Berichte über Landwirtschaft*, 58 (1980) 480–501.

J. Ertl, *Agrarpolitik ohne Illusionen* (Frankfurt: BML, 1985).

J. Ertl, 'Herrschaft der Verbände? Macht und Ohnmacht der Landwirte', in H. De Rudder and H. Sahner (eds), *Herrschaft der Verbände? Interessenverbände: Gegenregierungen oder Partner?* (Berlin: Berlin Verlag Arno Spitz, 1988) 93–107.

ESCEP [Economic and Social Committee of the European Parliament], *Stocktaking of the first three years of the CAP reform* (Brussels: ESCEP, 1997) CES108/97 F/CAT.

FAO [Food and Agricultural Organisation], *The dynamics of agrarian structures in Europe: case studies from the Federal Republic of Germany, Hungary, Italy, Norway and Poland* (Rome: FAO, 1988).

H. Fastnacht, 'Dorfentwicklung in Baden-Württemberg', in E. Frahm and W. Hoops (eds), *Dorfentwicklung: aktuelle Probleme und Weiterbildungsbedarf* (Tübingen: Tübingen Vereinigung für Volkskunde e.V., 1992) 21–42.

A. Fearne, 'The history and development of the CAP 1945–1990', in C. Ritson and D.R. Harvey (eds), *The Common Agricultural Policy,* 2nd edn (Wallingford: CAB International, 1997) 11–56.

W. Feld, *West Germany and the European Community* (New York: Springer, 1981).

S. Feldmann, 'Zu einigen Aspekten der Entwicklung der Sozialstruktur ostdeutscher Dörfer', in G. Henkel (ed.), *Der ländliche Raum in den neuen Bundesländern* (Paderborn: Essener Geographische Arbeiten Band 24, 1992), 21–42.

R. Fennell, *The Common Agricultural Policy of the European Community,* 2nd edn (Oxford: BSP Professional Books, 1987).

R. Fennell, *The new Common Agricultural Policy: continuity and change,* (Oxford: Clarendon Press, 1997).

M. Fink, R. Grajewski, R. Siebel and K. Zierold, 'Rural women in East Germany', in D. Symes and A. Jansen (eds), *Agricultural restructuring and rural change in Europe* (Wageningen: Wageningen Agricultural University, 1994) 282–95.

G. Fischbeck, 'Entwicklungsphasen in der Steigerung der Hektarerträge wichtiger Kulturpflanzen des Ackerlandes in der Bundesrepublik Deutschland 1955–1990', *Berichte über Landwirtschaft,* 71 (1993) 567–79.

K. Fischer, *Reorienting the cooperative structure in selected Eastern European countries: case study on the former German Democratic Republic* (Rome: FAO, 1994).

E. Fleischhauer, 'Suche nach einem ökologischen Weg aus der Agrarkrise: eine Herausforderung für die europäische Politik', in W. von Urff and H. von Meyer (eds), *Landwirtschaft, Umwelt und ländlicher Raum: Herausforderungen an Europa* (Baden-Baden: Nomos Verlag, 1987) 217–52.

C. Folmer, M. Keyzer, M. Herbis, H. Stolwijk and P. Veenendaal, *The Common Agricultural Policy beyond the MacSharry Reform* (Amsterdam: Elsevier, 1995).

Förderwerk Land- und Forstwirtschaft, *Dorf- und Regionalentwicklung* (Berlin: Förderwerk Land- und Forstwirtschaft e.V., 1995).

B. Forstner and F. Isermeyer, 'Zwischenergebnisse zur Umstrukturierung der Landwirtschaft in den neuen Ländern', *Berichte über Landwirtschaft,* 76 (1998) 161–90.

S.H. Franklin, *The European peasantry: the final phase* (London: Methuen, 1969).

V.D. Freeman, *Agricultural development and rural change in the German Democratic Republic* (Sheffield: Sheffield City Polytechnic [Department of Geography and Environmental Studies], 1979) Occasional Paper No. 1.

B. Freyer, 'Ausgewählte Prozesse in der Phase der Umstellung auf den ökologischen Landbau am Beispiel von sieben Fallstudien', *Berichte über Landwirtschaft,* 72 (1994) 366–90.

P. Friedrich, 'The SPD and the politics of Europe: from Willy Brandt to Helmut Schmidt', *Journal of Common Market Studies,* 13 (1975) 77–98.

M. Fulbrook, *A concise history of Germany* (Cambridge: CUP, 1990).

M. Fulbrook, *Anatomy of a dictatorship: inside the GDR 1949–1989* (Oxford: Oxford University Press, 1995).

H. Gaese, 'Die Agrarintegration im europäischen Intergrationsprozess', *Berichte über Landwirtschaft,* 53 (1975) 238–57.

B. Gardner, *European agriculture: policies, production and trade* (London: Routledge, 1996).

U. Geier, G. Urfei and J. Weis, *Stand der Umsetzung einer umweltfreundlichen Bodennutzung in der Landwirtschaft: Analyse der Empfehlungen des Schwäbisch-Haller Agrarkolloquiums der Robert-Bosch-Stiftung* (Berlin: SHA, 1996).

I. Geiss, 'The Federal Republic of Germany in international politics before and after unification', in K. Larres and P. Panayi (eds), *The Federal Republic of Germany since 1949: politics, society and economy before and after unification* (London: Longman, 1996) 137–68.

I. Geissendörfer, O. Siebert and H. von Meyer, 'Ex-post Evaluierung der Gemeinschaftsinitiative LEADER I in Deutschland', *Berichte über Landwirtschaft, 76* (1998) 540–79.

S. George, *Politics and policy in the European Union*, 3rd edn (Oxford: OUP, 1996).

F. Gerbaud, *La transition agricole dans les nouveaux Bundesländer: une transition sous tutelle? Une response géographique?* (Berlin: Centre Franco-Allemand de Recherche en Sciences Sociales de Berlin, 1994).

D. Goeman, 'The Member States: establishing factors determining policy reform and the future of the Common Agricultural Policy: the German perspective', Paper presented at the conference 'CAP Reform 1996–2000 and beyond', 1–2 October 1996, London.

D. Goodman and M. Redclift, 'Introduction', in D. Goodman, and M. Redclift (eds), *The international farm crisis* (London: Macmillan, 1989) 1–21.

R. Götz and W. Himmighofen, 'Biotechnologie für den Agrar- und Ernährungsbereich: zukünftige Schwerpunkte für Forschung und Entwicklung', *Berichte über Landwirtschaft, 76* (2) (1998) 210–22.

U. Grabski, 'Ökologie und Dorfentwicklung: Strukturprobleme der Dörfer aus ökologischer Sicht und Wege zu ihrer Lösung', *Geographische Rundschau, 41* (1989) 163–8.

A. Grafen and J. Schramek, 'Germany: complex agri-environmental policy in a federal system', in H. Buller, G.A. Wilson and A. Höll (eds), *Agri-environmental policy in the European Union* (Aldershot: Ashgate, 2000) 119–44.

R. Grajewski, H. Schrader and G. Tissen, 'Entwicklung und Förderung ländlicher Räume in den neuen Bundesländern', *Raumforschung und Raumordnung, 8* (1994) 270–8.

D. Greenaway, 'The Uruguay Round of multilateral trade negotiations: last chance for GATT?', *Journal of Agricultural Economics, 42* (1991) 365–79.

M. Gregory, 'Agricultural restructuring in Central and Eastern Europe', Unpublished paper presented at the Department of Geography, De Montfort University Bedford, Bedford, UK, May 1999.

F. Grimm, 'Ländlicher Raum und ländliche Siedlungen in der Siedlungs- und Raumordnungspolitik der ehemaligen DDR', in G. Henkel (ed.), *Der ländliche Raum in den neuen Bundesländern* (Paderdorn: Essener Geographische Arbeiten No. 24, 1992) 1–6.

M. Groier and E. Loibl, 'Austria: towards an environmentally sound agriculture', in H. Buller, G.A. Wilson and A. Höll (eds), *Agri-environmental policy in the European Union* (Aldershot: Ashgate, 2000) 169–84.

J. Gros and M. Glaab, *Faktenlexikon Deutschland* (München: Wilhelm Heyne Verlag, 1999).

J. Grube and D. Rost, *Dorferneuerung in Sachsen-Anhalt: Alternative Siedlungsentwicklung* (Magdeburg: Ministerium für Ernährung, Landwirtschaft und Forsten, 1995).

Grüner Bericht, *Grüner Bericht der Bundesregierung* (Bonn: BML, 1956–1970).

P. Guerrieri and P.C. Padoan (eds), *The political economy of European integration* (Hemel Hempstead: Harvester Wheatsheaf, 1989).

H. Guyomard, L.P. Mahé, K.J. Monk and T.L. Roe 'Agriculture in the Uruguay Round: ambitions and realities', *Journal of Agricultural Economics*, 44 (1993) 245–63.

F. Haase, 'Entwicklung des ernährungswirtschaftlichen Außenhandels der Bundesrepublik Deutschland', *Berichte über Landwirtschaft*, 69 (1991) 199–221.

K. Haase, 'Die politische Ökonomie der Agrarpolitik', *Agrarwirtschaft*, 98 (1983) 234–49.

C. Habbe and W. Landzettel, *Die Gestalt der Dörfer: Dorferneuerung in Sachsen-Anhalt.* (Magdeburg: MELFSA, 1994).

H. Hagedorn, 'Die Bauernfrage in Deutschland-Ost', *Berichte über Landwirtschaft*, 70 (1992) 396–409.

K. Hagedorn, 'Financing social security in agriculture: the case of the farmers' old age pension scheme in the Federal Republic of Germany', *European Review of Agricultural Economics*, 18 (1991) 209–29.

K. Hagedorn, V. Beckmann, B. Klages and M. Rudolph, 'Politische und ökonomische Rahmenbedingungen für die Entwicklung ländlicher Räume in den neuen Bundesländern', in A. Becker (ed.), *Regionale Strukturen im Wandel* (Opladen: Leske and Budrich, 1997) 355–500.

D. Hagemann and H.-J. Jäger, '"Umweltschonende" oder "umweltverträgliche" Landwirtschaft?', *Landbauforschung Völkenrode*, 40 (4) (1990) 284–92.

K.H. Halfacree, 'British rural geography: a perspective on the last decade', in A. Lopez Ontiveros and F. Molinero Hernando (eds), *From traditional countryside to post-productivism: recent trends in rural geography in Britain and Spain* (Murcia: Associaçion de Geografos Espanoles, 1997) 37–53.

U. Hamm and M. Konrad, 'Akzeptanzmindernde Faktoren beim EG-Extensivierungsprogramm', *Berichte über Landwirtschaft*, 70 (1992) 184–212.

J. Haris, M. Leininger and M. Lendle, 'Landwirte fordern bessere und stabile Rahmenbedingungen für den Anbau nachwachsender Rohstoffe', *Berichte über Landwirtschaft*, 74 (1996) 514–26.

J. Härle, 'Landwirtschaft und Umwelt in Baden-Württemberg', *Geographische Rundschau*, 44 (5) (1992) 303–10.

S. Harris and A. Swinbank, 'The CAP and the food industry', in C. Ritson and D.R. Harvey (eds), *The Common Agricultural Policy*, 2nd edn (Wallingford: CAB International, 1997) 265–84.

K. Hart and G.A. Wilson, 'UK implementation of Agri-environment Regulation 2078/92/EEC: enthusiastic supporter or reluctant participant?', *Landscape Research*, 23 (3) (1998) 255–72.

K. Hart and G.A. Wilson, 'United Kingdom: from agri-environmental policy shaper to policy receiver?', in H. Buller, G.A. Wilson and A. Höll (eds), *Agri-environmental policy in the European Union* (Aldershot: Ashgate, 2000) 95–118.

D.R. Harvey, 'The GATT, the WTO and the CAP', in C. Ritson and D.R. Harvey (eds), *The Common Agricultural Policy,* 2nd edn (Wallingford: CAB International, 1997) 377–408.

H. Haushofer, 'Die Schlüsseljahre 1968/69 in der Agrarpolitik', *Bayerisches landwirtschaftliches Jahrbuch*, 60 (1983) 5–21.

R.G. Heinze and H. Voelzkow, 'Organisational problems for the German farmers association and alternative policy options', *Sociologia Ruralis*, 33 (1993) 25–41.

W. Heisenberg (ed.), *German unification in European perspective* (London: Brassey's, 1991).

A. Heißenhuber, J. Katzek, F. Meusel and H. Ring, 'Landwirtschaft und Umwelt', in K. Buchwald and S. Engelhard (eds), *Umweltschutz: Grundlagen und Praxis* (Bonn: Paladin, 1994) 34–59.

G. Hendriks, 'The politics of food: the case of FR Germany', *Food Policy*, 12 (1987) 35–45.

G. Hendriks, 'Germany and the CAP: national interests and the European Community', *International Affairs*, 65 (1989) 75–87.

G. Hendriks, *Germany and European integration: the Common Agricultural Policy – an area of conflict* (Oxford: Berg, 1991).

G. Hendriks, 'The national politics of international trade reform: the case of Germany', in P.D. Lowe, T.K. Marsden and S.J. Whatmore (eds), *Regulating agriculture* (London: David Fulton, 1994) 149–62.

G. Henkel, 'Dorferneuerung in der Bundesrepublik Deutschland', *Geographische Rundschau*, 36 (1984) 170–6.

G. Henkel, *Der ländliche Raum* (Stuttgart: Teubner, 1993).

W. Henrichsmeyer, 'Konsequenzen veränderter Rahmenbedingungen für das System EG-Agrarpolitik', in E. Böckenhoff, H. Steinhauer and W. von Urff (eds), *Landwirtschaft unter veränderten Rahmenbedingungen* (Münster-Hiltrup: Schrödel, 1982) 123–47.

W. Henrichsmeyer, 'Auswirkungen der "neuen EG-Agrarpolitik" auf die deutsche Landwirtschaft', *Berichte über Landwirtschaft*, 64 (1986) 361–70.

W. Henrichsmeyer and H.P. Witzke, *Agrarpolitik II: Bewertung und Willensbildung* (Stuttgart: Ulmer, 1994).

A. Herrenknecht, 'Der Riss durch die Dörfer: innere Umbrüche in den Dörfern der neuen Bundesländer', in H. Behrens (ed.), *Dorf- und Regionalentwicklung in den neuen Bundesländern: Beiträge aus der Praxis* (Göttingen: Agrarsoziale Gesellschaft e.V. Kleine Reihe No. 54, 1995) 50–64.

HMLFN [Hessisches Ministerium für Landwirtschaft, Forsten und Naturschutz], *Ökologie-Forum Hessen: Flächenstillegungen in der Landwirtschaft* (Wiesbaden: HMLFN, 1990).

HMILFN [Hessisches Ministerium des Innern und für Landwirtschaft, Forsten und Naturschutz], *Veränderungen in der Kulturlandschaft, Lebensraum und Grünland* (Wiesbaden: HMILFN, 1998).

K. Hoggart, H. Buller and R. Black, *Rural Europe: identity and change* (London: Arnold, 1995).

K. Hohmann, 'Agrarpolitik und Landwirtschaft in der DDR', *Geographische Rundschau*, 36 (1984) 598–604.

R. Hoisl, 'Landschaftsveränderung durch Flurbereinigung', *Vermessungswesen und Raumordnung*, 48 (1986) 268–76.

A. Höll, *Bio-resources: requirements from the point-of-view of environmental conservation* (report for the Worldwide Fund for Nature Deutschland) (Frankfurt: Institut für ländliche Strukturforschung, 1994).

A. Höll, Personal communication, Danish Forest and Landscape Research Institute, Horsholm, Denmark, September 1999.

A. Höll and H. von Meyer, 'Germany', in M. Whitby (ed.), *The European environment and CAP reform: policies and prospects for conservation* (Wallingford: CAB International, 1996) 70–85.

A.J. Hooper, 'Planning and the control of development in the Federal Republic of Germany', *Town Planning Review*, 59 (1988) 183–205.

R. Hrbek and W. Wessels (eds), *EG-Mitgliedschaft: ein vitales Interesse der Bundesrepublik Deutschland?* (Bonn: Europa Union Verlag, 1984).

Y.-S. Hu, 'German agricultural power: the impact on France and Britain', *The World Today*, November (1979) 453–61.

L. Hubbard and C. Ritson, 'Reform of the CAP: from Mansholt to MacSharry', in C. Ritson and D.R. Harvey (eds), *The Common Agricultural Policy*, 2nd edn (Wallingford: CAB International, 1997) 81–94.

J. Huber, 'Ökologische Modernisierung: Bedingungen des Umwelthandelns in den neuen und alten Bundesländern', *Kölner Zeitschrift für Soziologie und Sozialpsychologie*, 45 (2) (1993) 288–304.

B. Ilbery, 'The challenge of land redundancy', in D. Pinder (ed.), *Western Europe: challenge and change* (London: Belhaven, 1990) 211–25.

B. Ilbery, 'The challenge of agricultural restructuring in the European Union', in D. Pinder (ed.), *The New Europe: economy, society and environment* (Chichester: Wiley, 1998) 341–59.

B. Ilbery and I. Bowler, 'From agricultural productivism to post-productivism', in B. Ilbery (ed.), *The geography of rural change* (Harlow: Longman, 1998) 57–84.

ILFS [Institut für ländliche Strukturforschung], *Implementation and effectiveness of agri-environmental schemes established under Regulation 2078/92* (Final Consolidated Report Project FAIR1 CT95–274) (Frankfurt am Main: IFLS, 1999).

K.A. Ingersent, A.J. Rayner and R.C. Hine (eds), *Agriculture in the Uruguay Round* (Basingstoke: Macmillan, 1994a).

K.A. Ingersent, A.J. Rayner and R.C. Hine, 'The EC perspective', in K.A. Ingersent, A.J. Rayner and R.C. Hine (eds), *Agriculture in the Uruguay Round* (Basingstoke: Macmillan, 1994b) 55–87.

K. Isermann, 'Forschungsbedarf sich ergebend aus der N-Bilanzierung/Verlustgefährdungsabschätzung der Landwirtschaft', in BMFT (ed.), *Statusseminar Bodenbelastung und Wasserhaushalt* (Bonn: BMFT, 1990) 23–9.

A. Johaentges, *Das Dorf als Wohnstandort: eine Analyse von Wanderungsbewegungen in ländliche Räume* (Bonn: Schriftenreihe der Forschungsgesellschaft für Agrarpolitik und Agrarsoziologie e.V. No. 306, 1996).

A. Jones, 'New directions for West German agricultural policy: Extensivierungsförderung in Schleswig-Holstein', *Journal of Rural Studies*, 6 (1990) 9–16.

A. Jones, 'The impact of EC set-aside policy: the response of farm businesses in Rendsburg-Eckernförde (Germany)', *Land Use Policy*, 8 (1991) 108–25.

A. Jones, *The new Germany: a human geography* (Chichester: Wiley, 1994).

A. Jones, F. Fasterding and R. Plankl, 'Farm household adjustments to the European Community's set-aside policy: evidence from Rheinland-Pfalz (Germany)', *Journal of Rural Studies*, 9 (1993) 65–80.

T. Josling, 'The CAP and North America', in C. Ritson and D.R. Harvey (eds), *The Common Agricultural Policy*, 2nd edn (Wallingford: CAB International, 1997) 359–76.

T. Josling, S. Tangermann and T.K. Warley, *Agriculture in the GATT* (Basingstoke: Macmillan, 1996).

J. Junghülsing, 'Entwicklung und Perspektiven des ökologischen Landbaus und dessen Rahmenbedingungen in Deutschland', in H. Nieberg (ed.), *Ökologischer Landbau: Entwicklung, Wirtschaftlichkeit, Marktchancen und Umweltrelevanz* (Braunschweig-Völkenrode: FAL, 1996) 3–12.

H.H. Kallfass, 'Der bäuerliche Familienbetrieb: das Leitbild für die Agrarpolitik im vereinten Deutschland?', *Agrarwirtschaft*, 40 (1991) 305–13.

J. Keeler, 'Agricultural power in the European Community: explaining the fate of CAP and GATT negotiations', *Comparative Politics*, 28 (1996) 127–49.

I. Kiechle, *... und grün bleibt unsere Zukunft* (Stuttgart: BML, 1985).

I. Kiechle, 'Agrarpolitik im Zwang zur Neuausrichtung', *Berichte über Landwirtschaft*, 64 (1986) 187–96.

B. Klages, Personal communication, Institut für Strukturforschung FAL, Braunschweig, Germany, March 1997.

B. Klages and K. Klare, 'So werden Alteigentümer jetzt entschädigt', *Top Agrar*, 5 (1995) 44–7.

K. Klare, Personal communication, Institut für Strukturforschung FAL, Braunschweig, Germany, February 1997.

W. Kleinhanss, 'Germany', in F. Brouwer and P. Lowe (eds), *CAP and the rural environment in transition: a panorama of national perspectives* (Wageningen, Wageningen Pers, 1998) 41–62.

U. Kluge, *Vierzig Jahre Agrarpolitik in der Bundesrepublik Deutschland*, Vol. I (Hamburg: Paul Parey, 1989a).

U. Kluge, *Vierzig Jahre Agrarpolitik in der Bundesrepublik Deutschland*, Vol. II (Hamburg: Paul Parey, 1989b).

S. Knauer, 'Genfood vom Mississippi', *Der Spiegel*, 50 (1999) 76.

K. Knickel, 'Agricultural structural change: impact on the rural environment', *Journal of Rural Studies*, 6 (1990) 383–93.

I. Knöbl, 'Das Bayerische Kulturlandschaftsprogramm', *Der Förderungsdienst*, 11 (1989) 336–40.

R. Koch, 'Counterurbanisation auch in Westeuropa?', *Informationen zur Raumentwicklung*, 2 (1980) 65–73.

M. Köhne and O. Köhn, 'Betriebsumstellung auf ökologischen Landbau: Auswirkungen der EU-Förderung in den neuen Bundesländern', *Berichte über Landwirtschaft*, 76 (3) (1998) 329–65.

W. König, 'Umstrukturierung und Neugründung landwirtschaftlicher Unternehmen', *Landbauforschung Sonderheft*, 152 (1994) 63–80.

W. König and F. Isermeyer, *The restructuring of East German agriculture in the course of the unification of Germany* (Braunschweig-Völkenrode: Institut für Betriebswirtschaft–FAL, 1993).

T. Kontuly and R. Vogelsang, 'Explanation for the intensification of counter-urbanisation in the Federal Republic of Germany', *Professional Geographer*, 40 (1988) 42–53.

U. Köpke and G. Haas, 'Umweltrelevanz des ökologischen Landbaus', in H. Nieberg (ed.), *Ökologischer Landbau: Entwicklung, Wirtschaftlichkeit, Marktchancen und Umweltrelevanz* (Braunschweig-Völkenrode: FAL, 1996) 119–46.

U. Köster, 'The chances for a thorough reform of the Common Agricultural Policy', *Intereconomics*, 15 (1981) 7–12.

U. Köster and S. Tangermann, 'Supplementing farm price policy by direct income payments: cost–benefit analysis of alternative farm policies with a special application to German agriculture', *European Review of Agricultural Economics*, 4 (1977) 7–31.

J.N. Köstler, *Wald, Mensch, Kultur* (Hamburg: Parey, 1967).

K. Krambach, *Wie lebt man auf dem Dorf? Soziologische Aspekte der Entwicklung des Dorfes in der DDR* (Berlin: Dietz Verlag, 1985).

P. Krause, 'Im Deutschen Bauernverband geht die Ära Heereman zu Ende', *Frankfurter Allgemeine Zeitung*, 7 April (1997) 12.

W. Krüger, Personal communication, DBV Aussenstelle Berlin, Berlin, Germany, April 1997.

S. Kruse, 'Entwicklung der Struktur der landwirtschaftlichen Betriebe in den neuen Ländern', *AID-Informationen für die Agrarberatung*, 3 (1995) 2–24.

N. Lampkin, 'Ökolandbau 1996 in Westeuropa', *Ökologie und Landbau*, 25 (1) (1997) 25–6.

Landwirtschaftliche Rentenbank, *DDR-Landwirtschaft* (Frankfurt am Main: Landwirtschaftliche Rentenbank, 1990).

K. Larres, 'Germany and the West: the 'Rapallo factor' in German foreign policy from the 1950s to the 1990s', in K. Larres and P. Panayi (eds), *The Federal Republic of Germany since 1949: politics, society and economy before and after unification* (London: Longman, 1996) 278–326.

K. Larres and P. Panayi (eds), *The Federal Republic of Germany since 1949: politics, society and economy before and after unification* (London: Longman, 1996).

LEADER Magazine, 'LEADER Symposium 1997', *LEADER Magazine*, 16 (Special Issue) (1997).

F. Lechi, *Agricultural policy formation in the European Community: the birth of milk quotas and CAP reform* (Amsterdam: Elsevier, 1987).

H. Leibundgut, *Der Wald in der Kulturlandschaft* (Bern: Haupt, 1985).

J.N. Lekakis, 'Environment and the CAP: a critical perspective', in M. Redclift, J.N. Lekakis and G.P. Zanias (eds), *Agriculture and world trade liberalisation: socioenvironmental perspectives on the Common Agricultural Policy* (Wallingford: CAB International, 1999) 73–87.

D. Liefferink and M.S. Andersen, 'Greening the EU: national positions in the run-up to the Amsterdam Treaty', *Environmental Politics*, 7 (3) (1998) 66–93.

J. Lingard and L. Hubbard, 'The CAP and the developing world', in C. Ritson and D.R. Harvey (eds), *The Common Agricultural Policy*, 2nd edn (Wallingford: CAB International, 1997) 343–58.

N. Long and J.D. van der Ploeg, 'Heterogeneity, actor and structure: towards a reconstitution of the concept of structure', in D. Booth (ed.), *Rethinking social development: theory, research and practice* (Harlow: Longman, 1994) 62–89.

P. Lowe and J. Goyder, *Environmental groups in politics* (London: Allen and Unwin, 1983).

P. Lowe and S. Ward, *British environmental policy and Europe* (London: Routledge, 1998).

F. Löwenthal, *News from Soviet Germany* (London: Victor Gollancz, 1950).

LUFT [Landwirtschaftliche Untersuchungs- und Forschungsanstalt Thüringen], *Möglichkeiten einer umweltverträglichen Umstrukturierung der Landwirtschaft in den neuen Bundesländern* (Jena: LUFT, 1993).

H. McHenry, 'Farming and environmental discourses: a study of the depiction of environmental issues in a German farming newspaper', *Journal of Rural Studies*, 12 (1996) 375–86.

E. McInnis, R. Hiscocks and R. Spencer, *The shaping of post-war Germany* (Toronto: JM Dent and Sons, 1960).

D. Manegold, 'Abbau des positiven Währungsausgleichs', *Agrarwirtschaft*, 33 (1984) 143–52.

D. Manegold, 'Aspekte gemeinsamer Agrarpolitik', *Agrarwirtschaft*, 40 (1991) 1–18.

D. Manegold, 'Aspekte gemeinsamer Agrarpolitik', *Agrarwirtschaft*, 41 (1992) 1–18.

D. Manegold, 'Aspekte gemeinsamer Agrarpolitik', *Agrarwirtschaft*, 42 (1993) 1–18.

D. Manegold, 'Aspekte gemeinsamer Agrarpolitik', *Agrarwirtschaft*, 44 (1995) 1–18.

A.S. Markovits (ed.), *The political economy of West Germany: modell Deutschland* (New York: Praeger, 1982).

T. Marsden, 'Exploring a rural sociology for the Fordist transition: incorporating social relations into economic restructuring', *Sociologia Ruralis*, 32 (1992) 209–30.

T. Marsden, R. Munton and N. Ward, 'Farm business in upland and lowland Britain: incorporating social trajectories into uneven agrarian development', *Sociologia Ruralis*, 32 (1992) 408–30.

T. Marsden, J. Murdoch, P.D. Lowe, R.J. Munton and A. Flynn, *Constructing the countryside* (London: UCL Press, 1993).

J. Marsh, 'The food industries and agricultural policy', in J. Marsh, B. Green, B. Kearney, L. Mahé, S. Tangermann and S. Tarditi (eds), *The changing role of the CAP: the future of farming in Europe* (London: Belhaven Press, 1991) 102–11.

A. Mayhew, *Rural settlement and farming in Germany* (London: Pion, 1973).

P. Mehl, Personal communication, Institut für ländliche Strukturforschung FAL, Braunschweig, Germany, March 1997.

P. Mehl and K. Hagedorn, 'Übertragung des agrarsozialen Sicherungssystems auf die neuen Bundesländer: Probleme und Perspektiven', *Landbauforschung Völkenrode*, 42 (1992) 276–92.

P. Mehl and R. Plankl, '"Doppelte Politikverflechtung" als Bestimmungsfaktor der Agrarstrukturpolitik untersucht am Beispiel der Förderung umweltgerechter landwirtschaftlicher Produktionsverfahren in der Bundesrepublik Deutschland', *Schriften der Gesellschaft für Wirtschafts- und Sozialwissenschaften des Landbaues e.V.*, 32 (1996) 57–68.

MELFB [Ministerium für Ernährung, Landwirtschaft und Forsten des Landes Brandenburg], *Der Brandenburger Weg* (Potsdam: MELFB, 1992).

MELFSA [Ministerium für Ernährung, Landwirtschaft und Forsten Sachsen-Anhalt] *Richtlinien über die Gewährung von Zuwendungen zur Dorferneuerung im Rahmen der Gemeinschaftsaufgabe 'Verbesserung der Agrarstruktur und des Küstenschutzes'* (Magdeburg: MELFSA, 1991).

MLNMV [Ministerium für Landwirtschaft und Naturschutz des Landes Mecklenburg-Vorpommern], *Erhaltung und Entwicklung der ländlichen Räume in Mecklenburg-Vorpommern: Interministerielle Arbeitsgruppe zur Entwicklung ländlicher Räume* (Schwerin: MLNMV, 1995).

R. Möhlers, Personal communication, Former Deputy Director DGVI, Brussels, Belgium, March 1997.

B. Mohr, 'Fremdenverkehr im Schwarzwald: neuere Entwicklungen in einem traditionellen Erholungsraum', *Geographische Rundschau*, 44 (1992) 296–302.

C. Morris and N. Evans, 'Research on the geography of agricultural change: redundant or revitalised?', *Area*, 31 (4) (1999) 349–58.

C. Morris and C. Potter, 'Recruiting the new conservationists: farmers' adoption of agri-environmental schemes in the UK', *Journal of Rural Studies*, 11 (1995) 51–63.

H. Moyer and T. Josling, *Agricultural policy reform: politics and process in the EC and USA* (Ames: Iowa State University Press, 1990).

MRLUSA [Ministerium für Raumordnung, Landwirtschaft und Umwelt des Landes Sachsen-Anhalt], *Landesentwicklungsbericht Sachsen-Anhalt* (Magdeburg: MRLUSA, 1996).

MRSWSA [Ministerium für Raumordnung, Städtebau und Wohnungswesen des Landes Sachsen-Anhalt], *Landesentwicklungsbericht Sachsen-Anhalt* (Magdeburg: MRSWSA, 1993).

R. Mühlnickel, 'Dorferneuerung und Dorfberatung gehören in Sachsen-Anhalt zusammen', *AID-Informationen für die Agrarberatung*, 3 (1997) 38–9.

H. Müller-Roschach, *Die deutsche Europapolitik 1949–1977* (Bonn: Harder, 1980).

K.H. Narjes, 'Nachwachsende Rohstoffe: ein Ausweg aus dem Dilemma der Agrarüberschüsse?', in W. von Urff and H. von Meyer (eds), *Landwirtschaft, Umwelt und ländlicher Raum: Herausforderung an Europa* (Baden-Baden: Nomos, 1987) 121–8.

E. Neander, 'Bisherige Entwicklung und aktuelle Situation der Neben-erwerbslandwirtschaft in der Bundesrepublik Deutschland', in BML (ed.), *Nebenerwerbslandwirtschaft in der Diskussion* (Münster-Hiltrup: BML, 1982) 5–53.

E. Neander, 'Agrarstrukturwandlungen in der Bundesrepublik Deutschland zwischen 1960 und 1980', *Zeitschrift für Agrargeographie*, 1 (1983) 201–38.

E. Neander, 'Nebenerwerbslandwirtschaft in den neuen Bundesländern: Informationen und Mutmassungen', *Landbauforschung Völkenrode*, 43 (1992), 169–75.

E. Neander, Personal communication, Institut für ländliche Strukturforschung FAL, Braunschweig, Germany, March 1997.

E. Neander, Personal communication, Institut für ländliche Strukturforschung FAL, Braunschweig, Germany, July 1999.

E. Neville-Rolfe, *The politics of agriculture in the European Community* (London: Policy Studies Institute, 1984).

H. Newby, *Green and pleasant land? Social change in rural England* (London: Hutchinson, 1980).

H. Nick, 'An unparalleled destruction and squandering of economic assets', in H. Behrend (ed.), *German unification: the destruction of an economy* (London: Pluto Press, 1995) 80–118.

H. Nieberg, 'Wirtschaftliche Folgen der Umstellung auf ökologischen Landbau: empirische Ergebnisse von 107 Betrieben aus den alten Bundesländern', in H. Nieberg (ed.), *Ökologischer Landbau: Entwicklung, Wirtschaftlichkeit, Marktchancen und Umweltrelevanz* (Braunschweig-Völkenrode: FAL, 1996) 57–74.

V. Niendieker, 'Die Ratsverordnung (EWG) 2078/92 als Instrument der europäischen und nationalen Agrarumwelt- und Agrarstrukturpolitik', *Berichte über Land-wirtschaft*, 74 (4) (1998) 520–39.

H. Nuhn, 'Strukturwandel in der Nahrungsmittelindustrie: Hintergründe und räum-liche Effekte', *Geographische Rundschau*, 45 (9) (1993) 510–15.

T. Opelland, 'Domestic political developments I: 1949–69', in K. Larres and P. Panayi (eds), *The Federal Republic of Germany since 1949: politics, society and economy before and after unification* (London: Longman, 1996) 74–99.

T. O'Riordan, 'Halvergate: the politics of policy change', *Countryside Planning Yearbook*, 6 (1985) 101–6

D. Paas, D. Timmermann, K. Hand, W. Riedel, H. Schenkel and E. Frahm, *Lösungswege einer Sinnvollen Dorferneuerung in den Neuen Bundesländern* (Bonn: BML, 1994).

C. Panzig, 'Changing the East German countryside', in H. Behrend (ed.), *German unification: the destruction of an economy* (London: Pluto Press, 1995) 119–38.

Pfaffenhofener Kurier, 'Weniger Lust auf Fleisch', *Pfaffenhofener Kurier*, 24 August (1997) 1.

M.J. Pfeffer, 'The feminisation of production on part-time farms in the Federal Republic of Germany', *Rural Sociology*, 54 (1989a) 60–73.

M.J. Pfeffer, 'Structural dimensions of farm crisis in the Federal Republic of Germany', in D.E. Goodman and M.R. Redclift (eds), *The international farm crisis* (London: Macmillan, 1989b) 183–204.

J. Pinder, *European Community: the building of a union* (Oxford: OUP, 1995).

U. Planck, 'Das Dorf: Idylle oder Illusion?', *Bild der Wissenschaft*, 20 (1983) 44–57.

U. Planck, 'Dorf ohne Bauern, Bauern ohne Dorf', in E. Frahm and W. Hoops (eds), *Dorfentwicklung: aktuelle Probleme und Weiterbildungsbedarf* (Tübingen: Tübingen Vereinigung für Volkskunde e.V., 1987) 44–57.

R. Plankl, 'Die Förderung umweltgerechter und den natürlichen Lebensraum schützender landwirtschaftlicher Produktionsverfahren', *AID-Informationen für die Agrarberatung*, 2 (2) (1994) 31–45.

R. Plankl, *Synopse zu den Argrarumweltprogrammen der Länder in der Bundesrepublik Deutschland: Maßnahmen zur Förderung umweltgerechter und den natürlichen Lebensraum schützender landwirtschaftlicher Produktionsverfahren gemäß VO (EWG) 2078/92* (Braunschweig-Völkenrode: Institut für Strukturforschung – FAL, 1996a).

R. Plankl, 'Analyse des Finanzmitteleinsatzes für die Förderung umweltgerechter landwirtschaftlicher Produktionsverfahren in den Ländern der Bundesrepublik Deutschland', *Landbauforschung Völkenrode*, 46 (1) (1996b) 33–47.

R. Plankl, 'Die Entwicklung des Finanzmitteleinsatzes für die Förderung umweltgerechter landwirtschaftlicher Produktionsverfahren in der Bundesrepublik Deutschland', *Agrarwirtschaft*, 45 (6) (1996c) 233–9.

R. Plankl, Personal communication, Institut für Strukturforschung FAL, Braunschweig-Völkenrode, Germany, March/April 1997.

R. Plankl and H. Schrader, *Politik zur Entwicklung ländlicher Gebiete in der Bundesrepublik Deutschland im Rahmen der Reform der EG-Strukturfonds und Grundprobleme der Bewertung* (Braunschweig-Völkenrode: Institut für Strukturforschung – FAL, 1991).

S. Poggemann, F. Weissbach and U. Küntzel, 'Reduktion der N-Überschüsse und Freisetzung von N_2O aus Grünland', *Berichte über Landwirtschaft*, 77 (1) (1999) 21–34.

H. Pongratz, 'Der Bauer als Buhmann: warum sich die Landwirte mit der Ökologiediskussion schwertun', *Öko-Mitteilungen*, 4 (1989) 34–6.

C. Potter, 'Conservation under a European farm survival policy', *Journal of Rural Studies*, 6 (1990) 1–7.

C. Potter, *Against the grain: agri-environmental reform in the United States and the European Union* (Wallingford: CAB International, 1998).

C. Potter and D.E. Ervin, 'Freedom to farm: agricultural policy liberalisation in the US and EU', in M. Redclift, J.N. Lekakis and G.P. Zanias (eds), *Agriculture and world trade liberalisation: socio-environmental perspectives on the Common Agricultural Policy* (Wallingford: CAB International, 1999) 53–72.

J.N. Pretty, *Regenerating agriculture: policies and practice for sustainability and self-reliance* (London: Earthscan, 1995).

J.N. Pretty, *The living land: agriculture, food and community regeneration in rural Europe* (London: Earthscan, 1998).

H. Priebe, *Die subventionierte Unvernunft: Landwirtschaft und Naturhaushalt* (Berlin: Siedler, 1985).

H. Priebe, *Die subventionierte Naturzerstörung: Plädoyer für eine neue Agrarkultur* (München: Goldmann, 1990).

N. Raabe, 'Gerd Sonnleitner: ein bürgerlicher Bauernpräsident', *Berliner Zeitung*, 7 April (1997) 6.

H. Rakow, Personal communication, Ministerium für Raumordnung, Landwirtschaft und Umwelt des Landes Sachsen-Anhalt, Magdeburg, Germany, March 1997.

T. Rau, 'Umwelteinstellungen und Umweltverhalten von Landwirten: eine Betrachtung ausgewählter Aspekte', *Berichte über Landwirtschaft*, 68 (1990) 125–38.

Raumordnungsgesetz, Raumordnungsgesetz in der Fassung der Bekanntmachung vom 28. April 1993 (Bonn: Bundesgesetzbuch 1.IS.630, 1993).

C. Ray, 'Territory, structures and interpretation: two case studies of the EU's LEADER I programme', *Journal of Rural Studies*, 14 (1998) 79–87.

RDC [Rural Development Commission], *Survey of rural services* (London: RDC, 1995).

M. Redclift, J.N. Lekakis and G.P. Zanias (eds), *Agriculture and world trade liberalisation: socio-environmental perspectives on the Common Agricultural Policy* (Wallingford: CAB International, 1999).

G. Reeves, 'World agricultural trade and the new GATT Round', *Journal of Agricultural Economics*, 38 (1987), 393–406.

Regional Trends, *Regional Trends* (London: HMSO, 1999).

H. Reichelt, 'Die Landwirtschaft in der ehemaligen DDR: Probleme, Erkenntnisse, Entwicklungen', *Berichte über Landwirtschaft*, 70 (1992) 117–36.

T. Reimers, 'Extensivierung in der Landwirtschaft', *Geographische Rundschau*, 41 (3) (1989) 156–62.

T. Rhenisch, 'The political and economic foundations of the Rome Treaties', in T.B. Olesen (ed.), *Interdependence versus integration: Denmark, Scandinavia and Western Europe 1945–1960* (Odense: Odense University Press, 1995) 147–66.

T. Rhenisch, *Europäische Integration und industrielles Interesse: die deutsche Industrie und die Gründung der Europäischen Wirtschaftsgemeinschaft* (Stuttgart: Franz Steiner Verlag, 1999).

C. Ritson and D.R. Harvey (eds), *The Common Agricultural Policy*, 2nd edn (Wallingford: CAB International, 1997).

C. Ritson and A. Swinbank, 'Europe's green money', in C. Ritson and D.R. Harvey (eds), *The Common Agricultural Policy*, 2nd edn (Wallingford: CAB International, 1997) 115–38.

C. Ritson and S. Tangermann, 'The economics and politics of Monetary Compensatory Amounts', *European Review of Agricultural Economics*, 6 (1979) 119–64.

G.M. Robinson, *Conflict and change in the countryside* (Chichester: Wiley, 1990).

G.M. Robinson, 'EC agricultural policy and the environment: land use implications in the UK', *Land Use Policy*, 8 (1991) 95–107.

H. Rodemer, *Die EG-Agrarpolitik: Ziele, Wirkungen, Alternativen* (Tübingen: Fleischauer, 1980).

H. Röhm, *Die westdeutsche Landwirtschaft: Agrarstruktur, Agrarwirtschaft und landwirtschaftliche Anpassung* (München: Parey, 1964).

K. Ronningen, 'Agricultural policies and landscape management: some examples from Norway, Great Britain and Germany', *Norsk Geografisk Tidsskrift*, 47 (2) (1993) 93–104.

RSU [Rat von Sachverständigen für Umweltfragen], *Umweltprobleme der Landwirtschaft* (BT-Drucksache 10/3613) (Bonn: RSU, 1985).

M. Sauer, 'Fordist modernisation of German agriculture and the future of family farms', *Sociologia Ruralis*, 30 (1990) 260–79.

S. Schama, *Landscape and memory* (London: HarperCollins, 1995).

M. Scheele and F. Isermeyer, 'Umweltschutz und Landschaftspflege im Bereich der Landwirtschaft: kostenwirksame Verpflichtung oder neue Einkommensquelle', *Berichte über Landwirtschaft*, 67 (1) (1989) 86–110.

H. Schmidt and D. Scholz, 'Die neuen deutschen Länder: Chancen und Probleme aus geographischer Sicht', *Berichte zur Deutschen Landeskunde*, 65 (1991) 65–82.

W. Schmidt, 'Tourismus in der Oberlausitz', *Geographische Rundschau*, 46 (1994) 525–31.

G. Schmitt, 'Zum agrarpolitischen Kapitel des jüngsten Gutachtens des Sachverständigenrates 1980–1981', *Agrarwirtschaft*, 30 (1981) 23–8.

G. Schmitt, 'Zum Problem der Mindest-Betriebsgröße in der Landwirtschaft', *Berichte über Landwirtschaft*, 68 (1990) 161–83.

G. Schmitt, 'Bedarf die "geschlossene Hofübergabe" noch des Schutzes durch das Anerbenrecht?', *Agrarwirtschaft*, 45 (1996) 129–31.

M. Schmitt, 'Women farmers and the influence of eco-feminism on the greening of German agriculture', in S. Whatmore, T.K. Marsden and P.D. Lowe (eds), *Gender and rurality* (London: David Fulton, 1994) 102–16.

H. Scholz, 'Lage der Landwirtschaft in den neuen Bundesländern', *Berichte über Landwirtschaft*, 70 (1992) 161–73.

R. Schöneweiß, *Die Agrarpolitik der Bundesrepublik Deutschland* (München: Schrödel, 1984).

H. Schrader, 'Reform der EG-Strukturfonds und Regionalförderung unter besonderer Berücksichtigung der Politik zur Entwicklung ländlicher Räume', *Schriftenreihe der Forschungsgesellschaft für Agrarpolitik und Agrarsoziologie e.V.*, 291 (1991) 29–64.

H. Schrader, 'Impact assessment of the EU Structural Funds to support regional economic development in rural areas of Germany', *Journal of Rural Studies*, 10 (1994) 357–65.

H. Schrader, Personal communication, Institut für Strukturforschung FAL, Braunschweig, Germany, March 1997.

W. Schubert, 'Development of agriculture in the German Democratic Republic in the eighties', in FAO (ed.), *Rural development in Europe: report of the special session of the FAO/ECE working party on agrarian structure and farm rationalisation* (Rome: FAO, 1990) 79–92.

J. Schulte and G. Steffen, 'Beurteilung von verschiedenen Umweltinstrumenten zur Reduzierung des Dünge- und Pflanzenschutzmitteleinsatzes in landwirtschaftlichen Unternehmen', *Zeitschrift für Umweltpolitik*, 2 (1984) 143–64.

O. Schultz, 'Entwicklungen im Vermarktungsbereich pflanzlicher Produkte', *Landbauforschung Völkenrode*, Sonderheft (1994) 51–62.

H-P. Schwarz, 'Germany's national and European interests', in A. Baring (ed.), *Germany's new position in Europe: problems and perspectives* (Oxford: Berg, 1994) 123–45.

Lord Justice Scott, *Report of the Committee on Land Utilisation in Rural Areas* (Cmd 6537) (London: HMSO, 1942).

G. Seidel, K. Meiner, B. Rauch and A. Thoms, *Agriculture in the German Democratic Republic* (Leipzig: VEB Edition, 1962).

M. Shoard, *The theft of the countryside* (London: Temple Smith, 1980).

H. Simonian, *The privileged partnership: Franco-German relations in the European Community 1969–84* (Oxford: OUP, 1985).

P.R. Sinclair, 'Bureaucratic agriculture: planned social change in the GDR', *Sociologia Ruralis*, 19 (1979) 211–26.

M. Smith, 'Agriculture: negotiators face a difficult task', *Financial Times*, 29 November (1999) 11.

W.R. Smyser, *The German economy: colossus at the crossroads*, 2nd edn (Harlow: Longman, 1993).

R. Sontowski, *Der Bauernverband in der Krise* (Frankfurt a.M.: Lang, 1990).

P. Stares (ed.), *The new Gemany and the new Europe* (Washington DC: The Brookings Institution, 1992).

Statistisches Bundesamt, *Statistik für Deutschland* (Wiesbaden: Statistisches Bundesamt, 1996).

H. Steinmetz and A. Höll, *Bedeutung der nebenberuflichen Landwirtschaft für die Neugestaltung ländlicher Räume in Thüringen* (Frankfurt am Main: Institut für ländliche Strukturforschung, 1993).

C. Stert, Personal communication, Gemeindeverwaltung Frose, Frose, Sachsen-Anhalt, Germany, March 1997.

R. Struff, *Von Notstandsprogrammen zu integrierten Entwicklungsmassnahmen? Entwicklung und System der deutschen Regionalpolitik* (Bonn: Schriftenreihe der Forschungsgesellschaft für Agrarpolitik und Agrarsoziologie No. 287, 1990).

R. Struff, *Regionale Lebensverhältnisse, Teil 1: Wohnen, Arbeiten und Sozialhilfe in Stadt und Land* (Bonn: Schriftenreihe der Forschungsgesellschaft für Agrarpolitik und Agrarsoziologie No. 293, 1992).

R. Sturm, 'Multi-level politics of regional development in Germany', *European Planning Studies*, 6 (1998) 525–36.

Süddeutsche Zeitung, 'Ost-Agrarbetriebe müssen Altschulden zahlen', 9 April (1997a) 1.

Süddeutsche Zeitung, 'Vorerst keine Altschulden-Pleiten', 10 April (1997b) 23.

Süddeutsche Zeitung, 'Die deutsche Industrie sieht sich durch die EU-Agrarpolitik behindert', 24 February (1998) 19.

Süddeutsche Zeitung, 'Es gibt eine sehr große Gerechtigkeitslücke', 3 August (1999) 13.

A. Swinbank, 'The Common Agricultural Policy and the politics of European decision making', *Journal of Common Market Studies*, 27 (1989) 45–58.

A. Swinbank, 'Capping the CAP? Implementation of the Uruguay Round Agreement by the European Union', *Food Policy*, 21 (1996) 393–407.

A. Swinbank, 'The new CAP', in C. Ritson and D.R. Harvey (eds), *The Common Agricultural Policy*, 2nd edn (Wallingford: CAB International, 1997) 95–114.

S. Tangermann, 'Germany's role within the CAP: domestic problems in international perspective', *Journal of Agricultural Economics*, 30 (1979a) 241–59.

S. Tangermann, 'Germany's position on the CAP: is it all the Germans' fault?', in M. Tracy and I. Hodac (eds), *Prospects for agriculture in the European Community* (Bruges: De Tempel, 1979b) 365–404.

S. Tangermann, *Agrarpolitische Positionen in den Mitgliedstaaten der EG und den Europäischen Institutionen* (Münster: Landwirtschaftsverlag, 1981).

S. Tangermann, *Agricultural and food policy in Germany* (Göttingen: Institut für Agrarökonomie, 1982).

S. Tangermann, 'European agricultural policy at the crossroads', *Intereconomics*, 18 (1984) 10–15.

S. Tangermann, 'European integration and the Common Agricultural Policy', in C.E. Barfield and M. Perlamn (eds), *Industry, services and agriculture: the United States faces a united Europe* (Washington: AEI Press, 1992) 407–51.

S. Tangermann, 'Implementation of the Uruguay Round Agreement on Agriculture: issues and prospects', *Journal of Agricultural Economics*, 47 (1996) 315–37.

S. Tangermann, Personal communication, Institut für Agrarökonomie, Universität Göttingen, Göttingen, Germany, February 1997.

J. Teller, 'Zum Außenhandel der DDR', *Agrarwirtschaft*, 39 (1990), 141–8.

E. Tenwinkel, 'Agrarsozialpolitik: Bestandsaufnahme und Entwicklung', *Schriftenreihe für ländliche Sozialfragen*, 99 (1987) 5–17.

J.C. Tesdorpf, 'Landschaftsverbrauch in der Bundesrepublik Deutschland: Hoffnung auf eine Trendwende', *Geographische Rundschau*, 39 (6) (1987) 336–42.

G. Thiede, 'Landwirtschaftliche Betriebe über 100 ha in der EG', *Agrarwirtschaft*, 40 (1991) 219–24.

G. Thieme, 'Agricultural change and its impact in rural areas', in M.T. Wild (ed.), *Urban and rural change in West Germany* (London: Croom Helm, 1983) 220–47.

K.F. Thöne, *Die Agrarstrukturelle Entwicklung in den neuen Bundesländern* (Köln: Verlag Kommunikationsforum GmbH, 1993).

G. Tissen, 'Sozioökonomische Entwicklung in ländlichen Räumen', *Landbauforschung Völkenrode*, Sonderheft 152 (1994) 3–10.

G. Tissen, Personal communication, Institut für ländliche Strukturforschung FAL, Braunschweig, Germany, March 1997.

TMLNU [Thüringer Ministerium für Landwirtschaft, Naturschutz und Umwelt], *Die Entwicklung ländlicher Räume im Freistaat Thüringen* (Erfurt: TMLNU, 1995).

M. Tracy, *Government and agriculture in Western Europe 1880–1988*, 3rd edn (Hemel Hempstead: Harvester Wheatsheaf, 1989).

I. Traynor, 'Bonn balks at its role as EU's grand paymaster', *The Guardian*, 26 July (1997) 15.

L. Tubiana, 'World trade in agricultural products: from global regulation to market fragmentation', in D. Goodman and M. Redclift (eds), *The international farm crisis* (London: Macmillan, 1989) 23–45.

H. Tügel, 'Revolution auf den Äckern', *GEO Magazin*, June (1998) 50–5.

UBA [Umweltbundesamt], *Stoffliche Belastung der Gewässer durch die Landwirtschaft und Massnahmen zu ihrer Verringerung* (Berlin: Erich Schmidt, 1994).

H. Urbisch, Personal communication, Möhlmann und Urbisch Associates, Braunschweig, Germany, March 1997.

I. Vogeler, 'State hegemony in transforming the rural landscapes of Eastern Germany: 1945–1994', *Annals of the Association of American Geographers*, 86 (1996) 432–58.

R. von Alvensleben, M. Plöger and A. Fricke, 'Die Nachfrage nach Bio-Produkten', *Agrarwirtschaft*, 43 (2) (1994) 99–105.

J. von Braun and D. Virchow, 'Pflanzengenetische Ressourcen zwischen Angebot und Nachfrage: Entwicklung institutioneller Rahmenbedingungen für Konservierung und Nutzung', *Berichte über Landwirtschaft*, 76 (1) (1998) 74–86.

S. von Cramon-Taubadel, 'The reform of the CAP from a German perspective', *Journal of Agricultural Economics*, 44 (1993) 394–409.

C.F. von Heereman, 'Ökologisierung der Agrarpolitik?', *Deutsche Bauern-Korrespondenz*, 11 (1988) 407.

C.F. von Heereman, Speech to the 13th Internationales Forum Agrarpolitik, 'EG-Agrarreform – noch Chancen für die Bauern?', *Schriftenreihe des Deutschen Bauernverbandes*, 1 (1993) 7–12.

H. von Schilling, 'Regionale Schwerpunkte intensiver Landbewirtschaftung', *Geographische Rundschau*, 34 (1982) 88–95.

W. von Urff, 'Die gemeinsame Agrarpolitik: Integrationsopfer der Deutschen?', in R. Hrbek and W. Wessels (eds), *EG-Mitgliedschaft: ein vitales Interesse der Bundesrepublik Deutschland?* (Bonn: Europa Union Verlag, 1984) 321–442.

W. von Urff, 'Die gemeinsame Agrarpolitik seit 1984: Konturen einer Neuorientierung', *Bayerisches Landwirtschaftliches Jahrbuch*, 65 (1987) 533–52.

W. von Urff, 'Agrar- und Fischereipolitik', *Jahrbuch der Europäischen Integration*, 1987/88 (1988) 109–20.

W. von Urff, 'The Common Agricultural Policy', in C. Schweitzer and D. Karsten (eds), *The Federal Republic of Germany and EC membership evaluated* (London: Pinter, 1990) 75–85.

W. von Urff, Personal communication, Lehrstuhl für Agrarpolitik der Technischen Universität München, Freising-Weihenstephan, Germany, August 1999.

W. von Urff and H. von Meyer (eds), *Landwirtschaft, Umwelt und ländlicher Raum: Herausforderung an Europa* (Baden-Baden: Nomos, 1987).

H. von Witzke, 'Das 1995er US-Farmgesetz: Ein Vorbild für die Reform der gemeinsamen Agrarpolitik', *Agrarwirtschaft*, 45 (1996) 221–2.

W. Wallace, 'Germany's unavoidable central role: beyond myths and traumas', in W. Wessels and E. Regelsberger (eds), *The Federal Republic of Germany and the European Community: the presidency and beyond* (Bonn: Europa Union, 1988) 297–304.

N. Ward and R. Munton, 'Conceptualising agriculture–environment relations: combining political economy and socio-cultural approaches to pesticide pollution', *Sociologia Ruralis*, 32 (1992) 127–45.

H. Watzek, 'Zu Problemen der Landwirtschaft in Ostdeutschland', *ICARUS*, 1 (1995) 9–13.

WBBELF [Wissenschaftlicher Beirat beim Bundesministerium für Ernährung, Landwirtschaft und Forsten], *Sammelband der Gutachten 1949–1974* (Münster-Hiltrup: Landwirtschaftsverlag Gmbh, 1975).

P. Wechselberger, M. Köbler and A. Heissenhuber, 'Ökonomische und ökologische Beurteilung von Bewirtschaftungsmaßnahmen bzw. unterschiedlichen Bewirtschaftungssystemen', *Berichte über Landwirtschaft*, 77 (2) (1999) 184–200.

P. Wehrheim, 'Agrarpolitische Lehren aus bisherigen EG (EU)-Erweiterungsrunden für die Integration der Länder Mittel- und Osteuropas (MOE) in die EU', *Berichte über Landwirtschaft*, 76 (1998) 366–81.

J. Weidner, 'Zur Weiterentwicklung der Alterssicherung für Landwirte', *Soziale Sicherheit in der Landwirtschaft*, 3 (1979) 239–53.

G. Weinschenck, 'Interdependenz der landwirtschaftlichen Entwicklung in Ost und Westdeutschland', *Agrarwirtschaft*, 41 (1992) 230–7.

G. Weinschenck, *GAP, GATT und die Folgen für die Agrarstruktur und die Agrarpolitik in Deutschland* (Göttingen: Schriftenreihe für ländliche Sozialfragen No. 116, 1993).

U. Weinstock, 'Der zu hoch festgesetzte Getreidepreis und die Folgen: Rückschau auf ein Vierteljahrhundert deutscher Politik in der Gemeinschaft', in W. von Urff and H. von Meyer (eds), *Landwirtschaft, Umwelt und ländlicher Raum: Herausforderung an Europa* (Baden-Baden: Nomos, 1987) 63–85.

U. Werschnitzky, 'Agrarwirtschaft und Umwelt', in W. von Urff and H. von Meyer (eds), *Landwirtschaft, Umwelt und ländlicher Raum: Herausforderung an Europa* (Baden-Baden: Nomos, 1987) 191–216.

M. Whitby (ed.), *The European environment and CAP reform: policies and prospects for conservation* (Wallingford: CAB International, 1996).

M. Whitby and P.D. Lowe, 'The political and economic roots of environmental policy in agriculture', in M. Whitby (ed.), *Incentives for countryside management: the case of Environmentally Sensitive Areas* (Wallingford: CAB International, 1994) 1–24.

T. Wild, *West Germany: a geography of its people* (Chatham: Dawson, 1979).

T. Wild, 'The residential dimension to rural change', in T. Wild (ed.), *Urban and rural change in West Germany* (London: Croom Helm, 1983) 161–99.

T. Wild and P. Jones, 'Spatial impacts of German unification', *The Geographical Journal*, 160 (1994) 1–16.

H. Willer, 'Neuausrichtung der EG-Markt- und Preispolitik: Bewertung aus der Sicht der politischen Administration', *Berichte über Landwirtschaft*, 71 (1993) 341–67.

H. Willgerodt, 'Die Agrarpolitik der Europäischen Gemeinschaft in der Krise', *Jahrbuch für die Ordnung von Wirtschaft und Gesellschaft*, 34 (1983) 97–139.

R.H. Williams, *European Union spatial policy and planning* (London: Paul Chapman, 1996).

G.A. Wilson, 'German agri-environmental schemes I: a preliminary review', *Journal of Rural Studies*, 10 (1994) 27–45.

G.A. Wilson, 'German agri-environmental schemes II: the MEKA programme in Baden-Württemberg', *Journal of Rural Studies*, 11 (2) (1995) 149–59.

G.A. Wilson, 'Farmer environmental attitudes and ESA participation', *Geoforum*, 27 (2) (1996) 115–31.

G.A. Wilson, 'Factors influencing farmer participation in the Environmentally Sensitive Areas scheme', *Journal of Environmental Management*, 50 (1997a) 67–93.

G.A. Wilson, 'Selective targeting in Environmentally Sensitive Areas: implications for farmers and the environment', *Journal of Environmental Planning and Management*, 40 (2) (1997b) 199–215.

G.A. Wilson, 'Assessing the environmental impact of the Environmentally Sensitive Areas scheme: a case for using farmers' environmental knowledge?', *Landscape Research*, 22 (3) (1997c) 303–26.

G.A. Wilson, 'Agri-environmental issues in Germany', in T. Unwin (ed.), *A European geography* (Harlow: Longman, 1998) 154–7.

G.A. Wilson and R.L. Bryant, *Environmental management: new directions for the 21st century* (London: UCL Press, 1997).

G.A. Wilson, J.E. Petersen and A. Höll, 'EU member state responses to Agri-environment Regulation 2078/92/EEC: toward a conceptual framework?', *Geoforum*, 30 (1999) 185–202.

O.J. Wilson, '"They changed the rules": farm family responses to agricultural deregulation in Southland, New Zealand', *New Zealand Geographer*, 50 (1) (1994) 3–13.

O.J. Wilson, 'Emerging patterns of restructured farm businesses in Eastern Germany', *Geojournal*, 38 (1996) 157–60.

O.J. Wilson, 'Village renewal and rural development in the former GDR', *Geojournal*, 46 (1999) 247–55.

O.J. Wilson and G.A. Wilson, 'Environmental problems and policies in former East Germany', in F.W. Carter and D. Turnock (eds), *Environmental problems of Eastern Europe*, 2nd edn (London: Routledge, in press).

M. Winter, *Rural politics: policies for agriculture, forestry and the environment* (London: Routledge, 1996).

S. Winter, 'Integrating implementation research', in D.J. Palumbo and D.J. Calista (eds), *Implementation and the policy process: opening up the black box* (Westport, Conn.: Greenwood Press, 1990) 19–38.

P. Wirth, 'Nachhaltige Erneuerung ländlicher Räume in den neuen Bundesländern', *Raumforschung und Raumordnung*, 10 (1996) 334–44.

B. Woodruffe, 'Rural land use planning in West Germany', in P. Cloke (ed.), *Rural land-use planning in developed nations* (London: Unwin Hyman, 1989) 104–29.

G. Würth, *Umweltschutz und Umweltzerstörung in der DDR* (Frankfurt a.M.: Peter Lang, 1985).

J. Zeddies and R. Doluschitz, *Marktentlastungs- und Kulturlandschaftsausgleich (MEKA)* (Stuttgart: Universität Hohenheim, 1996).

Zentralverwaltung für Statistik, *Statistisches Jahrbuch der DDR* (Berlin: Zentralverwaltung für Statistik, 1989).

G. Ziegler, 'Das Verbraucherinteresse und seine Durchsetzbarkeit', *Beiträge zur Politikwissenschaft*, 24 (1980) 34–45.

K. Zierold, 'Veränderungen von Lebenslagen in ländlichen Räumen der neuen Bundesländer', in A. Becker (ed.), *Regionale Strukturen im Wandel* (Opladen: Leske and Budrich, 1997) 501–69.

E.C. Zurek, 'Part-time farming in the Federal Republic of Germany', *Sociologia Ruralis*, 26 (1986) 377–84.

Index

(Information held in tables, maps or figures is indicated in bold)